Air Gunner

Air Gunner

The Men who Manned the Turrets

Alan W. Cooper

Pen & Sword
AVIATION

First published in
Great Britain in 2009
By Pen and Sword Aviation
An imprint of
Pen and Sword Books Ltd
47 Church Street,
Barnsley,
South Yorkshire
S70 2AS

Copyright © Alan W. Cooper 2009

ISBN 978-1-84415-825-6

Typeset in 10/12pt Palatino
by Mac Style, Beverley, E. Yorkshire

Printed and bound in Great Britain
by CPI UK

Pen and Sword Books Lieutenantd incorporates the imprints of Pen and Sword
Aviation, Pen and Sword Maritime, Pen and Sword Military, Wharncliffe Local
History, Pen and Sword Select, Pen and Sword Military Classics and Leo Cooper.

For a complete list of Pen & Sword titles please contact
PEN & SWORD BOOKS LIMITED
47 Church Street, Barnsley, South Yorkshire, S70 2AS, England
E-mail: enquiries@pen-and-sword.co.uk
Website: www.pen-and-sword.co.uk

CONTENTS

Dedication

This book is dedicated to all air gunners who so ably manned the turrets; their efforts, dedication and courage must never be forgotten. When it came to awards they were always at the back of the class or at the bottom of the heap but without them the aircraft could not have taken off, the lives of the rest of the crew lay in their hands and we shall never know how many aircraft returned because of the alertness and diligence of their air gunners.

The cost in loss of life was immense, in Bomber Command alone 7,000 air gunners perished. War Grave cemeteries all over Europe have many white War Graves headstones with the inscription Air Gunner. The majority were young men whose life ended when they were in the prime of youth.

We, today, owe so much to these young men who lived life to the full.

WE WILL REMEMBER THEM.

Acknowledgements

Norman Storey
Jack Catford DFC
Johnny Johnson Biggs DFC
Ian Blair DFM
Mike Henry DFC
Mike Smith
Peter Smith
Freddie Brown
W.T. Clark
J.Keating
K.R. Walker
Tony Burcher DFM
His Excellency Glafcos Clerides
    of Cyprus
R. Mayers
Pam Cruikshank
Mike King
Bob Baxter -Bomber Command
    website
R.W. Walker
E.E. Barnes
Art de Breyyne
D. Stallard
Robert Scott
Mrs J. Dodson
Jim Bigelow
B.R. Lillywhite
F/Lt G.G. Graham DFC, AE RAF Retd
F.G. Beauvoisin
G. Oakley
S.J. Willis
F. Allworth
Tammy Simpson DFC

E.L. Kightley
A.G. Peake
Len Moore
Bert Fitchett
Pete Skinner
R.E. Bowman
Art Sewel
Elizabeth Ellis
Percy Walder
E. Reynolds
P. Allen
S. Johnston

A. Robb CGM
Don Brinkhurst
Clare Hardy
Tony Winser

W. (Bill) Pingle
Majorie Little
A.E. Gregory
A. Medforth
Mrs A.M. Duffin
B. Freestone
Peter Twinn DFC
Len Manning
James Flowers
Eddie Edmonds
N. Didwell
Tom Maxwell DFC
Jimmy Flynn
Warren Radley
Albert Dickson

R. Downs
Russell Brown
J. Brown
Sdn Ldr K.R.Lusty Retd
Jimmy Wright DFC
J. Maddison
F. Stead
Ian Hunter
W. (Mo) Mowbray
George Cannon
Wg Cdr Joe Skinner DFC*
E. Phillips
Clive Bowles
Rick Pearson
James Savage JP
Wg Cdr B. Lewis AFC
P. Rivkin
P.H. Kilisker
G. Gillard DFM
S. Versey
E. Phillips
A.F.C. Smith
C.F. Scandrett
M. Smith
N.E. Richardson – TAGS Association
National Archives – Kew
Air Historical Branch – Graham Day
Air Gunners Association
Air Gunners Association (London Branch)

Tom Hale
Arthur Fowler
W.R. Hughes
Stan Reed
W. Wynn
J. Key
Ron Powers
L. Jealous
Roland Hammersley DFM
Len Bowman DFM
Ron Shargool
Ron Tyler
Mervyn Brown
Lynn Reed
T.R. Bennett
S. Johnston
A. More AFC
F. Flood
P.C. Price
P. Morrey
Mike Jackson
N.A. Davies MBE
J.A. Anderson

Sources
Last Flight for Tommy – Harry Bowman
Air Gunner – Mike Henry DFC
No Place to Hide – George (Ole) Olson
Great Mysteries of the Air – Ralph Barker
Footprints On The Sands Of Time – Oliver Clutton-Brock.

The Poems We Wrote – An Anthology of Air Force Poems – Compiled and edited by Eddy A. Coward.

My thanks go to Michael Maton for permission to use his unpublished book on his father, the late Wg Cdr C.A. Maton DSO.

Failing to Harmonize.

THE SEVEN DEADLY SINS OF A.G's. No. 2.

Failing to give Correct Patter.

Inability to Identify Aircraft.

THE SEVEN DEADLY SINS OF A.G.'s. No. 5.

Incorrect Timing of Combat Manœuvres.

Being Surprised.

THE SEVEN DEADLY SINS OF A.G.'s. No. 7.

Opening Up Too Soon.

C H A P T E R   O N E

The Men who Manned the Turrets

The Introduction of Air Gunners

What is an air gunner? A member of an aircrew who operates the guns. The idea of seeking volunteers from the ground crews to fly in the open rear-cockpit as air gunners was conceived in World War I as a means of providing protection from enemy aircraft while flying on scouting missions over enemy lines.

After 1921, with larger aircraft coming into service, wireless operators were trained in air gunnery and wore on their arms the winged-bullet badge, which became known as the Flying-Bullet badge, in addition to their wireless operator's badge and was known as the Sports Badge.

Discussions had taken place in 1923 to establish the trade of Air Gunner and to authorise the wearing of a trade badge of a winged bullet in brass and worn on the right sleeve. In 1939 the air gunner brevet was introduced but many of the 'old hands' preferred to keep their Flying-Bullet badge. The new design for an air gunner's brevet was submitted in 1938, it was designed by a Group Captain E H Hooper and had thirteen bird's feathers but as it was thought to be superstitious Hooper cut one off with nail scissors and the twelve feather air gunner brevet came into being under the Air Ministry Order 547/39 dated 21 December 1939. It was similar to the Observers brevet but with the inclusion of the letters 'AG' in the middle. The RCAF and RAAF brevet was similar although they had RCAF and RAAF below the letters AG.

On 18 December 1939, Air Vice Marshal Arthur Harris, the then AOC of No. 5 Group, sent a memo to Bomber Command HQ stating that operational aircrews should have a higher status than airmen of 'Non-Operational' duties and that aircrew pay should apply to all airmen who had qualified for flying duties. Consequently, on the 29 May 1940 a memo was sent from the Air Ministry to all commands and groups at home and abroad, including the BAFF:

With effect from the 27 May airmen mustered as whole time wireless operators (AG) and air gunners below the rank of sergeant will be promoted to sergeant at the following rates of pay. The daily rates:

W/Opt/AG   7s/9d
A/G   7s/0d

On the 27 June 1940, Air Ministry Order 416 stated that as a wartime measure to improve the status of W/Opt/AG and AGs and to introduce uniform scales of pay:

Promoted to Sgt (i) with effect from the 27 May all airmen below the rank of Sergeant would be promoted to the rank of Sergeant. (ii) Whilst under training for W/Opt/AG airmen will, hitherto, be remustered to Gp II and reclassify on completion of the W/Opt part of their training.

W/Opt and aircraft hands will be remustered to W/Opt/AG or air gunner and promoted to the rank of temporary sergeant on successfully completing the prescribed course of air gunner training.

In King's Regulations 1941 it stated that:

Commanding Officer's must asses that airmen employed as full-time air gunners had adequate opportunity to retain skill in the trade so that they may be competent to carry out their duties in those trades on reversion.

Commanding Officers would normally select airmen for duties as air gunners during the first twelve months of their service; the names of airmen selected, but not yet qualified, would be forwarded to the officer in charge (i/c) records in order that they be noted for a course of training when vacancies arose. The names of airmen who qualified at the Gunnery School as laid down in Air Policy 1112 would be notified to the officer i/c records and the commanding officer of their units, with a note that they were eligible for muster as AGs. Their records then would have the letter AG added to their trade qualifications. In the inter-war period training on gunnery and bombing (that developed their particular techniques as fighters, or bombers or on general reconnaissance, and in co-operating with the army.) for AGs and W/Opt/AGs was given on the squadrons.

Under the Air Ministry Order 271/21 volunteers were called for among tradesmen to act as 'aerial-gunners' in their squadrons. All tradesmen were eligible provided they were medically fit and recommended by the commanding officer; but in practice Group 1 tradesmen were preferred, especially W/Opts for obvious reasons. In addition to their trade pay they were offered crew pay at 2/-(two shillings) per day (reduced to 1/- from 1 February 1926) and 6d (sixpence) per day non-subsistence pay as air

War savings poster. *Alan Cooper*

gunners as long as they remained proficient in those duties. They accompanied the pilot on all flights to 'learn by doing' gunnery, map reading, and, where applicable, bombing.

During the summer period April to September inclusive, each squadron in the Home Command was attached for a month to one of the practice camps at North Coates Fitters, Catfoss or Sutton Bridge, where an intense course took place in air-to-air firing and in bombing practice on targets towed in the sea.

In 1934 an attempt was made to meet the problem of part-time air gunners by endeavouring to attract young men to enlist for training as straight air gunners for a period of service lasting four years. On a course lasting two months, extended to three in 1937, thirty recruits entered each month. At a school set up in North Coates they were taught the rudiments of gunnery and bombing, some pyrotechnics, the care of weapons, and also some practice in air-to-air firing. On passing out they were mustered in the new trade of 'air observers' promoted to corporal and employed as full-time air gunners. But somehow things went at too leisurely a pace and it was 1 January 1936 before the first course began. This scale of training had expected to produce 200 'air observers' per year. A number equal to that of the tradesmen/air gunners whom they were intended ultimately to replace.

At this time it was realised that the RAF was undermanned and various expansion schemes were adopted, each with different objectives aimed at enlarging the RAF. Each scheme was given a letter of the alphabet to identify it.

The number of air gunners being trained was quite inadequate to meet the objectives of expansion scheme 'F' by its estimated date, 1 April 1939; therefore the locally trained air gunners and the W/Opt/AGs were still needed to form crews for medium and heavy bombers during the next four years.

At an Air Ministry conference in February 1937 all the Command representatives emphasized a further cause of inefficiency among air gunners. They complained that there was not enough time to train these airmen to a good standard in squadrons before they were posted away as tradesmen by the air officer i/c records. The latter authority therefore undertook not to post tradesmen-borne establishments as air gunners until they had served at least eighteen months in the respective units. As a result of the conference the Chief of the Air Staff made the following decisions which considerably influenced other aircrew employment:

(a) All bomber crews must include at least one wireless operator/air gunner and one air gunner.
(b) Flying boats should carry two wireless operator/air gunners and two fitters trained in air gunnery.

This decision created a demand for 900 AGs, a number far beyond the capacity of the 'mutual and uneven local talent in each station with its inadequate training facilities'. Nothing was done immediately to provide schools for the extra aircrew members required, the Air Staff view being that deficiencies must be accepted. In fact the changes in establishment due to the new crewing policy had not been finally agreed until December 1937, ten months later. This was also discussed at the conference and in the 'Readiness for War Report' (July 1939), in which he emphasised the need for better air gunners and for the direction of development by means of a central gunnery school. The Chief of Air Staff said:

At present, apart from the need for elementary training for air gunners at gunnery schools, we have no instructors and no instruction to guide us in the service training of air gunners. Consequently, until we have a centre where the whole subject is studied our gunnery instructors remain in relation to the air gunners in the position of the blind leading the blind. Under these conditions we cannot possibly hope to reach a standard of efficiency which would permit our crews facing the enemy with any confidence.

At the time it was pilots who were needed and would take precedence over all other aircrew categories, and units engaged in gunnery training had to be content with such aircraft and equipment that could be made available after meeting operational demands e.g. Fairey Battles, Whitley Mk IIs and a small number of Demon aircraft. The first two however had no power-operated turrets and the last the prototype of all turrets: for air gunnery training it had to be accepted that operationally obsolete types had to suffice.

As a result the air gunnery portion of the wireless training did not produce sufficient numbers for aircrew employment, nor even those in quantity enough to meet immediate requirements.

Under the expansion scheme of April 1938 there was a deficiency of more than 2,000 W/Opt/AGs. The Air Member for Personnel therefore produced a plan to attract large numbers to aircrew trades. Employment as aircrew was to be regarded in the future as a full-time duty. The basis of recruitment for the aircrew trades other than pilot was to be restricted to boy entrants who enlisted for nine years as wireless operators, from whom by central selection at the end of their year's course the Air Ministry would choose men for training in air gunnery.

A start was made to provide some formal training for both classes of air gunner at two practice camps where instruction in ground subjects was given by armament instructors to an intake of thirty pupils at each school. Practical training in air firing followed after they were posted to squadrons, since armament instructors were not competent to teach the flying side of air gunnery. Practice camps were built on the west and south coasts. The armament training camps were:

No 4	West Freugh opened	January	1937
No 5	Penrhos	February	1937
No 6	Warmwell	June	1937
No 7	Acklington	April	1938 previously known as Novar Camp
No 8	Evanton	Aug	1937.

During the first half of 1939 the Air Ministry made a determined effort to increase the output of W/Opt/AGs and AGs who were much needed by Bomber Command. Four ATSs at North Coates, Acklington, Aldergrove, and West Freugh were converted into air observer schools and numbered 1, 2, 3 and 4 respectively. Under the war training organisation issued in April 1939 each school was staffed and equipped to give ground and air training to 120 pupils of whom thirty were AGs who took a short, four week course that included twelve hours flying time. On completion of the course they passed to units in operational commands or to group pools. But even this plan did not produce the numbers required. On 17 June 1939 the position in Bomber Command was typical of all the commands. Against an establishment of 1,576 air gunners the strength was 366 trained W/Opt/AGs with 491 under training, and 256 other trades W/Opt/AG qualified with 200 under training.

The Air Ministry hoped that this deficiency, in the order of 40 per cent, on gunnery and bombing would be made good in due time from the ranks of the Volunteer Reserve which had been calculated to provide under 'Scheme L' 6,750 W/Opt/AGs and 1,000 plain air gunners. For two years the AOC CinC Bomber Command had repeatedly warned the Air Ministry of the limited facilities for air armament training and that the serious shortage of air gunners would have grave consequences.

A conference was held on the 24 August 1939 to thrash out the problem. This was attended by the AOC CinC as well as the Assistant Chief of the Air Staff and commanders of the groups concerned directly with operations and training aircrew.

The AOC CinC again warned the Air Ministry that bombers were not fit to cross the line. He was willing to forgo for a time even the gunnery training of operational units at armament stations provided that through this renunciation production could be speeded to the point of furnishing for his command 500 W/Opt/AGs and plain air gunners in the shortest time.

Some of the difficulties were locations for airfields near enough to sites for bombing ranges and obtaining target-towing aircraft, cine camera guns, release hooks and other special gear that would be needed in large quantities from industry if air armament training was to be accelerated. However, protests about ranges were received by the Air Ministry. As one example, an entry in the Operation Records Book for Warmwell under the date July 1937 records the suspension of air firing owing to many objections by local inhabitants in the vicinity of Chesil Bank to low flying and to the dropping from aircraft of drogues having attached to them a ten pound weight that fell near buildings on the edge of the range. A dilemma existed. Though the complaints seemed not unreasonable, the trainees could only improve their accuracy by practice. After discussion, a proposal from No. 25 Group was accepted that could produce 5,000 trained air gunners in twelve months by forming, at existing stations administered by that group, a number of air gunnery schools without interfering too much with the attachments from service flying-training schools.

In 1939, twenty-four hours before the expiry of the ultimatum to Germany to pull-out of Poland, the Air Member for Supply and Organisation reporting to the Chief of Air Staff on the situation in the Metropolitan Force as regards aircraft and personnel should war commence in the immediate future, stated:

> The most serious limitations (to a sustained effort) is imposed by shortages of W/T operators (AG) or by Air Gunners and W/T Operators combined.

In September 1939, Air Gunnery courses at air observer schools were shortened to four weeks for air gunners and six weeks for observers. On the 13 September 1939, in a memorandum to the Air Member for Supply and Organisation, the Director of Training reviewed the effects of the deficiencies and wrote:

> As far as I can gather there will be a mixed bag of some 200 Wallaces, Battles, Demons, Hinds or Hart variants to meet this requirement. For a twin-engine attack trainer the Anson is not suitable but the Blenheims would do. Unless the Air Staff can be persuaded to give up some reserves the striking force will be reduced soon through lack of trained personnel.

On 7 October 1939, the Air Staff eventually agreed to hasten the provisioning of 400 Fairey Battles for use as target towers in aircrew training. On 6 November 1939 the Central Gunnery School was set up at

Warmwell. Its functions were to assist in the development of air gunnery tactics applicable to types of aircraft other than single-seater fighters and to train gunnery instructors who would be employed in group pools, bombing and gunnery schools. The syllabus was to train 'gunnery leaders' by inculcating sound ideas about drill, discipline, gun and turret manipulation, morale, leadership and physical fitness. Already in the war experiences had taught how much these attributes were needed by the air gunner in particular.

The first course began on the 13 November 1939 with an intake of fifteen pupils, this then rose to thirty.

By September 1939 the AOC CinC Bomber Command was convinced that a better type of man was needed in the tail turret of a heavy bomber. He wanted those accustomed to handling guns, such as experienced big-game hunters, who would supply leadership, example and influence which the air gunners at this command at present lacked. Appropriate action followed. For men of mature years (25–52) who possessed fighting spirit and the skills to shoot well, a course lasting four weeks in turret manipulation and fire control was deemed enough to fit them for duty.

By the 27 April 1940, 424 officer air gunners had been appointed, of whom 274 came direct from civilian life, eleven from the other two services, seventy-nine from the ranks and sixty from airmen recommended on completing their training. In addition, a further 133 from civilian life had been selected provisionally.

At a conference held by the Air Member for Personnel on 19 May 1940, it was decided to obtain Treasury approval for raising the maximum to 1,000 officers (which accorded with 14,000 aircraftmen air gunners in line with expansion scheme 'M') and to restrict in future the offer of commissions in that section of general duties trained and experienced air gunners. Two motives prompted the second decision: one was the duty to give an incentive to serving airmen; and the other recognised the increasing requirement in new types of aircraft for air gunners who had been trained also in wireless operating.

Gunnery leaders were supplied from the Central Gunnery School; and a ladder to promotion provided some prospect of improved status to men serving in this aircrew category.

The first step in December 1939 authorised the award of the air gunners brevet similar to that denoting the observer and worn above the left breast-pocket of the tunic taking over from the winged bullet worn since 1923. Murmurs of dissatisfaction continued to be heard despite this emblem of aircrew status and the Air Officer Commanding No. 3 Group voiced what he called 'a legitimate moan' from wireless operators/air gunner who found direct entry observers enjoying higher pay and better amenities as sergeants.

When consulted by letter all the Air Officers CinC agreed that, 'the air gunners in war carried, under very difficult conditions, a heavy responsibility that was scarcely less important than that of the pilots and observers with whom they flew' They also asserted that aircrew other than officers should be given equal status among themselves and men could mingle and mess together when off duty. The ideal of equality in comradeship thus quietly enunciated early in the war was later destined, during the big offensive, to reap great rewards.

However, there were many administrative difficulties to hinder the next step. The main problem was the financial system that fixed the pay of a sergeant pilot on the lowest rate at 12/6d per day while the rate for his colleague air gunner was 3/6d as an aircraftmen second class. It took some time to convince the Treasury that this disparity was unjust and that it precluded all possibility of members of a crew working as a team. The Air Ministry reiterated the theme that 'the safety of the aircraft in war depended on the efficiency and courage of the air gunners almost as much as on that of the pilots and observers.' Aircraftman who mustered as whole time W/Opts/ air gunners or as air gunner were promoted to the rank of temporary sergeant on consolidated daily rates of 7/9d for W/Opt AG or 7/- for an air gunner.

One gunnery school was due to be set up in France but owing to the German occupation of the area did not mature. But three schools in the UK were made ready for occupation:

No. 5 Bombing and Gunnery School, Isle of Man July 1940.
No. 7 Bombing and Gunnery School, coast of South Wales July 1940.
No. 2 Bombing and Gunnery School, Millom coast of Cumberland November 1940.

At the end of 1939 the multiplicity of turrets in aircraft tended to confuse armament instructors and their pupils. In 1940 the turrets in use were:

Armstrong Whitworth – three types of centrally placed in the aircraft.
Boulton and Paul – four types of either centre, mid-under, nose or tail of the aircraft.
Bristol – three types of centre nose or tail.
Fraser-Nash – thirteen kinds, depending on whether they were on the Manchester, Whitley, Wellington, Stirling, or Sunderland flying boat.
Vickers having Fraser Nash parts for Wellington Mk 1.

Starting in January 1940, in order to reduce within manageable limits the field of instruction on this brief course, bombing and gunnery schools (B&GS) prepared their pupils in handling turrets of certain aircraft. The cadets were posted to an operational training unit, which was equipped with similar types of turret, for example:

Hampden bombers in 1940. *Alan Cooper*

B & GS	Aircraft
No. 4 West Freugh	Hudson, Singapore, Wellington, Blenheim, Beaufighter, Defiant.
No. 5 Jurby	Blenheim, Beaufighter, Anson
No. 7 Porthcawl	Whitley
No. 8 Evanton	Hampden
No. 9 Penrhos	Hudson, Singapore
No. 10 Dumfries	Wellington
No. 2 Millom	Wellington

On 8 April 1940, the first batch of thirty aircraftmen under training as air gunners arrived at No. 4 Initial Training Wing Bexhill for a disciplinary course lasting four weeks. This was followed by up to sixty aircraftmen every two weeks throughout the year. The sequence of training during 1940 was:

Straight Air Gunner	Weeks
Reception and Initial Training Wing	6
Bombing and Gunnery School	6

Wireless Operator/Air Gunner	Weeks
Recruit Course	4
Electrical and Wireless School	24
Bombing and Gunnery School	6

In the middle of 1940 the training for air gunners was increased from 4 to 6 weeks.

The actual intakes of W/Opt/Ags and AGs was from September 1939 to January 1941; input 7,874 and output 6,626. In the period from January 1941 to January 1942 the input was 9,506 and the output 8,969.

By the end of 1941 Bombing and Gunnery Schools had been opened in Canada Australia and New Zealand under the Empire Training Scheme; they were:

Canada:
No. 1 Jarvis, Ontario
No. 2 Moss Bank, Saskatchewan
No. 3 Macdonald, Manitoba
No. 4 Fingal, Ontario
No. 5 Dafoe, Saskatchewen
No. 6 Mountain View, Ontario
No. 7 Paulson, Maintoba
No. 8 Mont Joli, Quebec

Australia:
No. 1 Evans Head, NSW
No. 2 Port Pirie, South Australia

New Zealand:
After initial training the W/Opt/AGs finished their training in Canada.

Also, under the Towers scheme a total of 900 W/Opt/AGs trained at Jacksonville and Pensacola, Florida, USA.

The year 1942 opened with a surplus of 5,000 straight air gunners awaiting vacancies in training. Despite the fact that in September 1939 the authority was delegated to group armament officers to issue the appropriate qualifications for tradesmen who had been trained in units as air gunners or as wireless operator air gunners, which meant that the flow of aircrew could be controlled; in January 1942 this authority was rescinded by the Air Ministry. This resulted in far too many aircraftmen waiting to be trained and who could only qualify after having been on organised courses in gunnery schools.

With the expansion of bomber forces and extra reconnaissance flights in Coastal Command the requirement for qualified air-gunners grew considerably. In Jan 1941, an output of ten W/Opt/AGs a month was sufficient, five months later the requirement grew to thirty-eight. But now the training was much longer:

Classroom Gunnery Training. *IWM*

To muster to W/Opt	9 months
To convert to W/Opt	6 months
Air Gunnery Course	6 weeks.

The Central Flying School, which started off in November 1939 with such high hopes was dogged by mischance during the years up to 1943. Four stations for one reason or another proved to be unsuitable. Warmwell was shared with No. 10 Bombing and Gunnery School until 15 July 1940, here there was a night-flying-practice ban because of the research and construction work on ASDIC well established by the Admiralty in Portland nearby. The repeated bombing attacks on the station drove all personnel under canvas in Knighton Wood from 29 April 1941 and on 28 June compelled the transfer of the school to a half prepared site at Castle Kennedy. At Wigtonshire flying was interrupted by bad weather and a waterlogged airfield. Out of 122 days available during the period sixty were lost, and pupils had to use West Freugh twelve miles down the road. On 4 December 1941, the school was moved to Chelveston near Higham Ferrers, Northants which was being built for 8 Group of Bomber Command while waiting for its permanent home at Sutton Bridge to be made available through the transfer of No. 56 Fighter OTU.

It was 4 April 1942 before the Central Flying School was able to use Tealing since early March. During a visit on 20 March 1942 the Inspector General suggested that morale was not very high owing to the poor

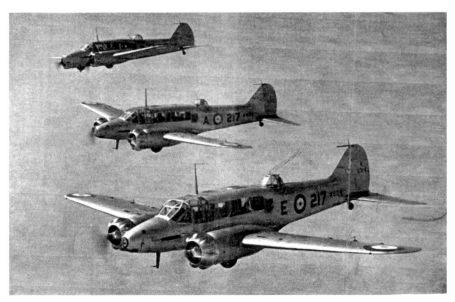

Two aircraft used for gunnery training, the Hudson and Anson. *Alan Cooper*

conditions. This, he said, did not help in raising the general level of air gunnery throughout the service to an expert level. The AOC CinC Bomber Command in general agreed with the points made and admitted that the present standard of performance in air gunnery at the time was deplorably low. Many times during 1943 Bomber Command had complained about the low standard of skill in air gunnery. The AOC CinC Flying Training Command confirmed the opinion and in April 1944 wrote:

> I have been concerned for a considerable time at the type of man selected to non-PNB aircrew, particularly for the air gunnery category. This is reflected in the number of failures at air gunnery schools and the poor material throughout the Service from which to select gunnery leaders and potential air gunnery instructors.

In June 1944 the Inspector General declared that there is no branch of training in which scientific investigation might be pursued with greater profit. His critical action brought prompt action. On 10 July the Air Member for Training set up a panel comprising officers and civilian specialist from the Air Ministry, HQ Flying Training Command and No. 25 Group who had experience in all stages of this kind of work. They were asked to investigate the whole field of air gunner selection and training up to the end of the operational unit stage.

A numbers of changes were recommended and the main proposals implemented as a matter of some urgency. No. 1 Air Gunnery School, Pembrey, was staffed and equipped with twenty-seven Wellingtons and nineteen Spitfires specially to carry out saturation tests in the methods of instruction, qualifying examinations and coordinate matters on a representative body of cadets with a view to devising suitable standards of teaching and of testing that could be uniformly applied in all air gunnery schools.

The first ninety cadets chosen in equal parts from the top and bottom of the initial training wing products arrived on 7 October 1944, followed by others on 7 November and 3 December. Their progress through each section of the syllabus was studied by a research team and members of the panel. By the end of October a start was made to re-equip all air gunnery schools with Wellingtons and Spitfires and the courses lengthened to ten weeks in the summer and twelve in the winter.

Ian Blair was recruited as an apprentice in 1935 into Group 11 Trades of Armourer, photographer and wireless operator. He underwent a year's training and he, along with other apprentices, were then posted to squadrons as 'boys' until they reached the age of 18 when they were considered to be airmen and could draw the appropriate pay as aircraftman 2nd class or higher.

Ian was posted to No. 101 Squadron stationed at Bicester. As he was only 17 he continued to work under supervision in the squadron armoury, until July 1936 when he became an AC2/Armourer. Among the armourers on

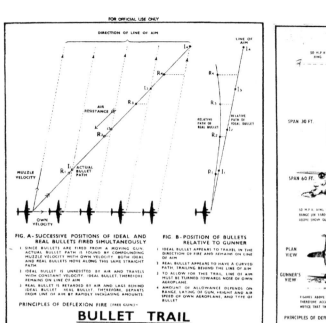

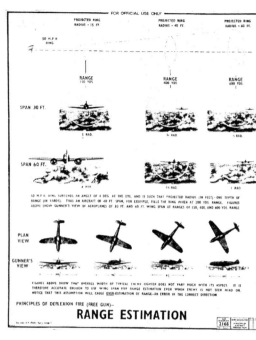

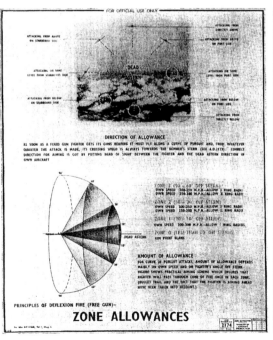

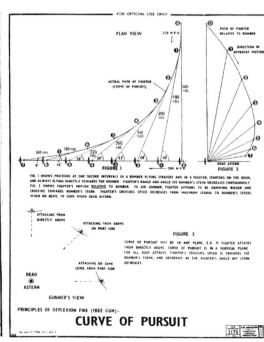

Gunnery training. *Alan Cooper*

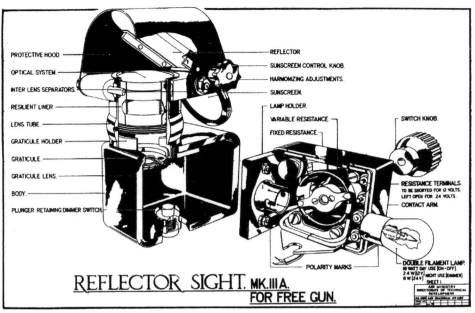

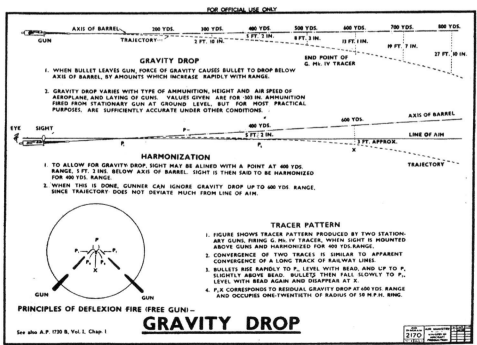

Gunnery training. *Alan Cooper*

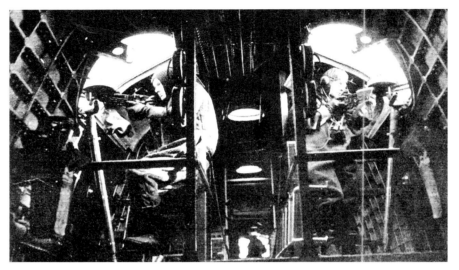

Gunnery training. *Alan Cooper*

101 were two corporals and two LACs, all of whom were qualified air gunners, and had carried out a tour of duty (five years) overseas. Not being old enough he was not allowed to fly, but just working with such experience was encouraging and he became interested in the additional flying skills.

When he reached the age of 18 he was recommended for an air gunners' course that led up to the award of the Flying Bullet award, and a four-week course at North Coates. He successfully completed the course and was awarded the Brass Bullet.

His only problem on the course was a lack of height, which meant he had difficulty in firing a Lewis Gun at the ground targets from the Hawker, Harts and Audax. The Westland Wallace aircraft was much better because there were 'firing steps' which permitted the gunner to stand about 6 to 8 inches higher thereby getting a better firing position behind the Lewis gun. Part of the course was to expose a number of films using a free mounted camera gun and Scarff ring against a target aircraft making diving attacks from above and alternate quarters. This was carried out at 15,000 ft and without oxygen.

Cpl. Arm/AG J.Blair DFM. *J Blair*

AC2 Blair Arm/AG 101 Sqn 1936.
J. Blair

It was then realised that swinging a gun from side to side under combat conditions was, to put it mildly, extremely tiring. He completed the course successfully and on return to the squadron duly qualified for the additional 10/6d increase in pay. From there he flew on a regular basis.

The type of aircraft on the squadron were Sidesstrands/Overstrands and the crew was two gunners and one observer (part-time) for each aircraft, and Ian was encouraged to 'learn on the job' under the watchful eye of one of the corporals in the armoury who was very experienced. He flew also during his time with 101 in the Rothermere bomber, which was the forerunner of the Blenheim bomber whose place it took on Boxing Day 1936.

On the formation of 144 Squadron at Hemswell he was posted as an AC2 Armourer/AG and flew on Audax and Anson aircraft. Later he was posted to No. 113 Squadron in Egypt in 1937. Many exercises were carried out between May 1937 and June 1940 and he was promoted to Corporal Armourer/AG.

John Keatings was trained on No. 45 Squadron, in Helwan, Egypt, a complete flight was posted from the UK in September 1945. Their aircraft were Hawker Harts. The Middle East Units were being reinforced because of Mussolini's Italian Air Force bombing of defenceless Eritrea. But when nothing came of this the complete flight was posted to No. 6 Squadron at Ismaliaon 6 January 1936. The commanding officer was Sqn Ldr H M Massey, a former first world war pilot. He was captured by the Germans during WWII and then as a Group Captain was in charge of Stalag III during the 'Great Escape' when fifty recaptured RAF and Allied officers were murdered on the orders of Hitler. On 30 April 1936, John qualified as an AC1. Armourer/AG and was posted to Palestine on Anti-Terrorist Operations.

The main trouble spots in the 1930s were Iraq, the Indian Northwest Frontier and Palestine. John now received 1/6d flying pay per day. On one occasion he was given a holster and Colt 45 prior to take off by his pilot Flt Lt Arthur Luxmore who was killed in May 1940 while commanding No. 144 Squadron. During the flight they had to land in the middle of nowhere and John realised the importance of the revolver. They were met by an English Colonel who got out of a British Armoured car. The Colonel's name was Dill, later to become Field Marshal Sir John Dill. John got out of his seat and Colonel Dill got in and the aircraft took off leaving John awaiting their return. A couple of hours later it returned, as did the armoured car, Dill got out and with John back in they flew back to Ramleh. When John asked Luxmore what he should put in his log book he was told, "Oh Operation Kolundia" and that was that. To this day John does not know what it was all about.

One morning they took off to answer a request for airforce backup against Palestinian terrorists, known as an XX Call. When they got to the area the code directed them to a cave in a hillside. They dived down to carry out their normal procedure which was to fire the front gun and then on the turn to use the Lewis gun. As soon as the front gun started firing John felt a shudder and instantly knew what had happened. The interpreter gear had not been synchronised. The aircraft had only been returned to them the day before after a major inspection and he assumed that the synchronisation had been done before the aircraft was returned to them. He now realised he should have checked; they had been shooting their own prop away. They headed for base and on landing found that the brass leading edges of the prop was badly gnarled and lots of holes in the wood. His pilot Luxmore said "My Office in ten minutes Keatings" Despite his pleadings John was given seven days confined to camp. Next day they were flying again and nothing was ever said. He returned to the UK on 25 November 1936. On arrival he was posted to No. 21 Sqn at Lympne in Kent.

In 1937 nearly all aircraft had fixed undercarriages and new pilots trained on such aircraft until the new aircraft such as the Anson and Blenheim came into service. There were incidents of pilots landing with

An Anson aircraft at Gunnery School, West Sale 1944. *Frank Alworth*

undercarriages up despite the fact that having remotely controlled warning systems of two green balls appearing on the pilot's console showing 'safe to land' As a further back-up to this system micro switches were linked to the undercarriage and the throttles so that a claxon horn sited adjacent to the pilot's head blared out when throttling back in readiness for landing and should it not be safe to do so.

This noise however was a distraction and irritating to crews to the extent that when a considerate pilot attempted to fly slow and steady in order to allow the air gunner to get a good score under his belt, when either firing at a drogue or at ground fixed targets, the noise from the klaxon was distracting. The problem was eradicated by the friendly pilot removing the fuse on the said circuit from its home nearby.

On one Fighter Affiliation Exercise Chas Scandrett of No. 233 Squadron based at RAF Leuchars took off with his Canadian pilot and when they got to 3,000 ft cruised around the Dundee and St Andrews area to await the 'enemy' aircraft of No. 41 Squadron based at Catterick. However when nothing showed up and no signals were received they flew back to Leuchars. At the time of year they were flying part of the airfield in one corner of the field became boggy and as they circled the airfield they saw one of the new Super Hawker Fury aircraft, with its up-rated engine and streamlining such as spats around the landing wheels, on the ground stray into this boggy area where the spats became choked with mud. As the pilot throttled up to get out the more he dug into the mud and ended up going up on his nose.

As Chas and his pilot came in across the River Eden to land the pilot realised he was too low and only just managed to get the stick back and

The Defiant Fighter/Bomber. *Alan Cooper*

make a landing. Sitting in the turret, however, Chas saw chunks of earth came all over them and both he and the pilot realised his error as he felt the fuse in his gloved hand. One small saving was that the Anson undercarriage wheels were designed to protrude a little lower than the line of the engine nacelles, which in this case were undamaged. This could not, however, be said for the props. Because of the level they were at it was not necessary to use the normal steps to disembark. The pilot was charged by the commanding officer with being careless, who himself was the next offender; Chas wondered if he fined himself.

In September 1938 and now at Montrose the order came to camouflage the then silver aircraft with green and dark earth paint. Also, there was a special treatment for the RAF roundels. This meant going into the local village and buying all the appropriate paint they had. Not long afterwards came the order to remove the camouflage: putting it on was hard enough but getting it off was a nightmare especially if the original fabric was not to be damaged in doing so. For a while there were Ansons in all manner of colours around the skies.

At RAF Leuchars the aerodrome was bounded on one side by a wooded area which was attended by the local gamekeeper. The ground targets that air gunners were to practise on were set up on a bit of scrubland nearby. One occasion the gamekeeper was not at all pleased when as he did his rounds he heard several rounds of .303 Lewis gun bullets splattering amongst the trees. It was put down to an air pocket!

In May 1939 Chas was posted to RAF Manston on a Fitter IIA course with advanced instruction on the new aircraft coming into service. With rumours of war they left the course in a hurry and in August 1939 he found himself as one of the early trainees in a partially built camp known as RAF Hednesford to continue the Fitter course. When war was declared the course was somewhat curtailed and November 1939 found Chas as a member of No. 37 Bomber Squadron at RAF Feltwell flying Wellington Mk IA and IC aircraft. After some while he expected to be issued with the new AG brevet and three stripes which were just coming out. When he got impatient with this and made noises in high places he was told that a lot of money and time had been spent training him up to the new aircraft and they then in turn were able to train new men to become AGs in six weeks. He was told to go off back to the hanger and help to get aircraft up the slope through the snow and ready on dispersals and that was that.

In 1940 Mike Henry was an AC2 and accepted for air gunner training; he had passed his medical as category A3-B which Mike described as the Plimsoll line for gunners and observers. He was posted to No. 5 Bombing and Gunnery School at RAF Jurby, Isle of Man, and just three days away from being in the RAF for a year he had a flight in a Fairey Battle. This aircraft had one Vickers gas-operated magazine-fed machine-gun which was easy to strip and reassemble and without there being with bits left over!

The clearance of stoppages at speed was of great importance: the safety of the aircraft and the rest of the crew may well have been the difference. Other subjects were the theory of sightings, deflection, shooting and aircraft recognition.

On 10 March 1940 he reported to the parachute section to be fitted with a harness and obtain a parachute. From there he went to the armoury to load up two ammunition magazines. Feeding the .303 rounds in the drums was simple enough, the hard part was putting the tension on the strong spring inside. One slip and you got a kick like the back leg of a horse. Then came the flying kit: Sidcot suit, thick woollen socks and flying boots, helmet and goggles, and out he went carrying his two magazines to report to the pilots for his first flight.

The Fairey Battle had two gunners, one standing and the other sitting on the fuselage floor with the gun mounted on a rocking pillar. It had a power mounted turret on a trolley equipped with two belt-fed .303 Browning machine guns. The turret had two padded chin rests, and an armour plate with slots to allow vision to the reflector sights.

In the event that the hydraulics failed and the turret became inoperative there was a small lever by the gunner's left foot which became known as the dead man's lever which, when depressed, allowed the turret to sink to its fully down position and the gunner was able to get out.

Stoppages were always a pain and often happened when gunners where firing at Drogues (which was a sleeve that resembled a wind sock). The reason in these cases for the stoppages was that the tips of the bullets were dipped in dope to distinguish whose bullets had hit the target but the dope would come off either inside the magazine or in the breech of the gun and so the gun would jam.

To the Target. *Alan Cooper*

Mike was awarded his Air Gunner brevet and became a W/Opt/AG but with the same rank of AC2 although he did get the magnificent sum of 6p per day making his weekly wage of £1 4s 6d. While at Squires Gate he flew eleven times in three days and fired a remarkable 2,200 rounds without a single stoppage.

On 7 October he flew on an operation to Boulogne. All went well until they arrived back at base. As they came into land Mike realised they were too low, as they raced across the runway he could have picked up a flare. The wing suddenly dropped, then he lost consciousness. He awoke to find himself still in his turret cupola but with flames around the fuselage. He was trapped there and there seemed no way out until he saw a hole in the fuselage which he put his head through and pushed; it gave way and out he fell. He was picked up and pushed into an ambulance but not before he saw that the pilot and navigator had also got out albeit with some injuries. They were lucky; having hit the ground at 100mph all that was left of Blenheim L9310 was a charred wreck.

The following are the musings of two Air Gunners:

IF I MUST BE A GUNNER

If I must be a gunner,
Then please Lord grant me grace,
That I may leave this station
With a smile upon my face.
I wished to be a pilot,
And you along with me,
But if we all were pilots
Where would the Air Force be?
It takes guts to be a gunner,
To sit out on the tail
When the Messerschmitts are coming
And the slugs begin to wail.
The pilot's just a chauffeur,
Its his job to fly the plane;
But its we who do the fighting,
Though we may not get the fame.
If we must all be gunners,
Then let us make this bet.
We'll be the best damn gunners
That left this station yet.

Cpl. George Harding (RCAF)

THE AIR GUNNER'S ROLE

The Air Gunner sits alone in his turret
Anxiously scanning the unfriendly skies
Looking for approaching enemy fighters
As on an operation his bomber flies.
Confined in the dismal, cramped quarters
In a circle his turret continually rotates.
Tensions mount as they near their target
Alert and on guard for any peril he waits.
For hours he must maintain constant vigil
On a Mitchell bomber, he's the only defence
The crew's survival depends on his alertness.
During an Op there's no break in suspense
An air gunner's life is barren of glamour
Recognition or medals are not in store
Overlooked when they hand out the glory
No fame for performing his dangerous chore.
To a bomber's crew the air gunner is vital
A thankless and dangerous task is his role
To protect his bomber from enemy fighters
Ensuring its safe return to base is his goal.
When a bomber is on an operational sortie
And comes under an enemy fighter attack
The crew will reply on their trusted air gunner
To provide the protection needed to get back.
From his crewmates he will gain recognition
Acknowledgement that on him they depend
They know that when their bomber is in peril
A capable air gunner will their aircraft defend.

George Olson 20 October, 1944.

Air Gunners Squad 1943. Norman Storey Third from the left back row. *Norman Storey*

CHAPTER TWO

Early Combats

One of the first operations of World War II was to search for the German Fleet in the Heligoland Bight area. Aircraft from No. 3 Group equipped with the latest and best armed bombers were given orders for day bombing which included the task of attacking the German Navy whenever they were found at sea.

The great majority of the Wellington bombers of 3 Group had Vickers turrets, which in the main were useless: the sights did not follow the guns and the ammunition belts stuck in the ducts. The Fraser Nash turrets fitted in the Wellington 1A bombers including the Fraser Nash retractable under-turret, described as a dustbin rotating through 365 degrees, and fitted aft could fire two degrees above the horizontal which was very useful in backing up the rear gunner in stern attacks. The turrets, front, rear and mid-under had two .303 Browning machine-guns which fired at 1,000 rounds per minute and had 1,000 round belts, one to each gun which were fed efficiently. The gunners were volunteer ground crew and not over trained. At this time there were no gunnery leaders and the only training given was when they were able to get on a training flight between their own ground duties.

At this time also there was no formation flying which was so vital in daylight operations. However, there was one squadron that had practised formation flying having flown on distance flights over France before the war began and now could fly in perfect formation.

On 17 December 1939, No. 9 Squadron received an operational order from HQ 3 Group to stand by for coastal duties. On the 18th a further order that nine aircraft were to stand by. The Commanding officers of Nos 9, 37 and 149 were summoned to Group HQ where they were briefed for an operation on the 19th: a sweep over the Heligoland Bight area searching for the German fleet. Wing Commander Kellet AFC, the Commanding Officer, of 149 was to lead. The force would be twenty-four aircraft in total with nine coming from his own squadron.

When approaching the harbour at Wilmshaven Flying Officer 'Cheese' Lemon of 37 Squadron had the bad luck to lower his flaps instead of opening the bomb doors and made a swift decent towards the sea.

Nevertheless, he was able to drop his bombs into the harbour and, while being attacked by German fighters, his rear gunner, Corporal Kidd, was able to shoot down an He 111.

Rear gunner AC1 Jimmy Mullineaux flying with Squadron Leader Harris, a flight commander with 149 Sqn, used up all his ammunition so Sandy Innes, the second pilot went down to him taking short belts containing 300 rounds of ammunition each which enabled Jimmy to keep firing while loading the other belts between engagements. He was not wounded in the attack but did have a bullet go through the sole of his boot. On his return he was awarded an immediate DFM. When AC1 Mullineaux was brought to see the CinC Bomber Command he promptly fainted. Later, as a regular air gunner, he joined No. 7 Squadron and flew on a number of operations with them but when posted to another squadron he was shot down and made a prisoner of war. Being nearly six foot tall he was really too tall for the position of air gunner.

Sgt John Ramshaw, also of 149, had to ditch on return and although all but one of crew were picked up, the body of LAC Walter Lilley, aged 21 from Yorkshire who had been killed in the fighter attack, went down with the aircraft. AC1 Charles Driver the front gunner with Ramshaw had remained at his post until both his guns were put out action and the

flooring set on fire which he put out with his bare hands. On ditching, it was Driver who launched the dinghy and assisted in saving the remainder of the crew. On the 21 December 1939 he was awarded the DFM which was gazetted on the 16 January 1940.

A number of the early air gunners in WWII served with Fighter Command in Defiant aircraft. One was Reginald Thomas Adams who joined the RAF (VR) at Southampton on 29 August 1939. Various courses followed until 10 August 1940 when he passed out as an air gunner, was promoted to Sergeant and posted to No. 5 OTU at Aston Down, Gloucestershire. On 7 September 1940, he was posted to 264 Squadron at Kirton-in-Lindsey and remained with them until posted to the newly formed 256 Squadron at Catterick, Yorkshire on 18 December 1940. On 7 April 1941, flying with Flt Lt D.R.

Sgt Adams with Defiant N3445 JT-F of 256 Squadron who with pilot F/Lt West shot down a JU88 and an HE111.
E.M.Marchant via R.Brown

West in a Defiant he scored 256 Squadron's first 'kill' of the war when he shot down a Ju 88 over the Ribble Estuary which crashed at Banks Marsh, near Stockport, Lancashire. On 7 May 1941, they claimed their last 'kill' when they shot down an He 111 that was taking part in a raid on Liverpool, this despite three of Sgt Adams four Browning machine-guns jamming. It was the most successful night of the war for 256, three He 111s destroyed, two damaged, and two Ju88s also claimed as damaged.

The report made by F/Lt Lt West:

On 7/8 April 1941, at 2345 I was ordered to patrol base at 10,000 ft. I decided to fly towards the anti-aircraft barrage, which I could clearly see over Liverpool. Suddenly, my gunner informed me of an aircraft below and to port. I looked in the direction indicated and immediately saw a black form moving in my direction some 1,000 ft below. I decided to carry out a Fighter Command attack. Sgt Adams identified the aircraft as a Ju88. When we were about 200 yards from the enemy I gave Sgt Adams the order to fire. The first burst was two seconds long, but extremely accurate registering a hit on the starboard engine which immediately burst into flames. It was then that the rear gunner of the enemy opened up with short bursts, which passed well over our heads. I then closed to 100 yards and Sgt Adams gave the target a further burst of one and half seconds causing the engine to catch even more alight. It was then that he started to lose speed and I took the opportunity to get ahead and below him to allow my gunner to fire directly into the cockpit. He again returned the fire but again it went over our heads. My gunner then silenced the enemy's guns with another burst of one and half seconds and hits were seen on the nose of the aircraft. With the enemy on my port side, he suddenly dived steeply and was enveloped in thick white cloud. I followed through the cloud and as I was breaking through noticed a vivid red flash from the shore, and turning observed a blazing wreckage.

The attack was carried out as described in the Fighter Command Training as the 'A' attack. This consisted of diving outwards, forwards, and downwards, finally skidding alongside the overtaking bomber. The German aircraft had crashed on Banks Marsh, near Southport and loud bomb explosions were immediately heard and the remains of one large bomb were afterwards found on the spot. Two of the crew landed by parachute, one being badly wounded in the right arm. Sgt Adams had fired 621 rounds, made up of 310 De Wilde, 272 armour piercing and 39 incendiary rounds. Oblt Klemm, who was wounded in the right wrist by a bullet, piloted the Ju 88. He and Lt Coster had baled out and landed on the mud flats of the River Ribble. The day after the crash Flt Lt West and Sgt Adams visited the crash site and made a cross from pieces of the wreckage as souvenirs which was nailed on the flight dispersal huts. The two Germans who were killed were buried in Southport Cemetery. On 15

May the third German who had been killed after baling out was found and buried at Lytham St Annes. Klem was later repatriated back to Germany because of his injuries and Coster was sent to Canada and arrived back from there to Germany in 1946. All three dead Germans were exhumed in 1962 and buried at the German Cemetery, Cannock Chase, Staffordshire. Coster died in 1971 and Klemm in 1972.

Flt Lt West records the report for the combat on 8th May:

> On the night of 7/8th May 1941, I took part in a fighter night over Liverpool at 1,600 ft. Soon after reaching our height my gunner sighted a bomber and tried to guide me to it, but without success. Having found the largest and most interesting fire I decided to sit over it and watch.
>
> Suddenly I sighted a Dornier about 800 yards ahead and immediately closed at 150 yards. After the enemy had opened fire I heard a dull thud and Sgt Adams telling me the guns would not fire. Eventually the Dornier was lost to sight. Although the guns were not working I decided to keep up the search and saw a Heinkel III, and Sgt Adams trying his best to get the guns working when suddenly he said that one gun was working. My order to open fire was followed by a short burst from our one gun and a perfect hit on the fuselage and starboard engine. But after further combat the one gun again jammed. Then again it worked and Sgt Adams fired short bursts into every vulnerable part of the Heinkel. One petrol tank was soon on fire then a furious fire occurred and it suddenly dived vertically into the cloud and the familiar vivid flash followed soon after.

Adams was then posted to 'A' Flight of 256 Squadron, which formed a new squadron, 153, at Ballyhalbert, in Northern Ireland. Then came on 23 April 1942 a transfer to Bomber Command, as he preferred to remain an air gunner he remustered as a radar/navigator on Beaufighters, which had by now replaced the Defiant. After a little while at 1484 Flight at Driffield he was posted to 405 (RCAF) Squadron based at Pocklington, Yorkshire flying on Halifax bombers. He was to die on 30 June 1942, on an operation to Bremen. Three 405 Aircraft were lost on this operation.

The Defiant had a single rear turret mounted with four Browning machine guns. It had been built in 1936 for the interception of bomber formations but in 1940 was being used as a fighter, the consequences were to follow.

The first squadron to equip with the Defiant was No. 264 in December 1939. Fred Barker flew with 'A' Flight of 264 Squadron throughout the Dunkirk period, and he described the Defiant as a wrongly maligned aircraft and thought it was a wonderful, beautiful aircraft and had a lot of positive characteristics. It had been designed to attack enemy bombers over the UK but this proved to be a disaster and it was as a night-fighter that it redeemed itself. There was a feeling that if the Defiant had been fitted with 40 mm cannons firing forward instead of the four Browning

Sgt Adams and Sgt E.R.Fremlin, both air gunners with 256 Squadron. Bill Fremlin was killed nine days later flying in Defiant T3955 which was recovered in 1982. *E.M. Marchant via R.Brown*

firing backwards and armed with two 250lb bombs it would have had a role as a ground-attack aircraft. It had an excellent front-gun platform and was solid in a dive.

Fred saw the beaches at Dunkirk crowded with troops, tankers burning and Stukas (Ju87) diving bombing the hospital ships. He and his pilot, Sgt Ted Thorn, were awarded the DFM after shooting down seven enemy aircraft and sharing one during the Dunkirk period. Both awards were Gazetted on 14 June 1940. On 31 May 1940 flying from Duxford over the beaches of Dunkirk they destroyed two He 111s. And on 24 August after taking off from Manston to patrol the coast they encountered twenty Ju88s escorted by Me 109s and He 113s, and managed to destroy one Ju88.

In combat with the enemy he had found the electrically powered turret to be excellent, and the Brownings never jammed. It could also rotate through 360 degrees

On 26 August 1940, after taking off from Hornchurch in Defiant L7005 to patrol over Dover they came into contact with a formation of twelve Do17s escorted by Me 109s in the area of Herne Bay and managed to shoot down two Do17s and one Me 109. They then found themselves being chased by other Me 109s by which time they were on fire and the pilot had dived the aircraft to put out the flames. As he came out of the dive he found an Me 109 on his tail so the pilot manoeuvred to engage the enemy and assist a Hurricane which came in to take on the German fighter in combat and it was not until the Me 109 had been shot down by the

A crew of 256 Squadron RAF Squires Gate in 1941. Left to right AG Sgt Walden RNAF. (Killed in 1942). Front row second from left AG Sgt Adams, (Killed in 1942) and third from left AG Sgt Clifford RNAF. (Killed in 1941) Second right AG Sgt Mulligan.

Hurricane that Ted Thorn was able to crash-land the aircraft and they got out with slight injuries. Both were awarded bars to the DFM. The recommendation was made on 16 December 1940 by AVM Keith Park AOC of 11 Group and countersigned by Air Marshal Sholto Douglas on the 18th and Gazetted on 11 February 1941, it is interesting to note that in both recommendations they are said to have baled out.

Two other Defiants from 264 were shot down. L7025 was shot down by an Me 109 and the pilot, Flying Officer Stephens, baled out into the sea having been wounded but the air gunner Sgt Maxwell was killed. The second was L6985 flown by Flt Lt Barham; he also was shot down by an Me 109 which scored hits near the cockpit and the aircraft caught fire. Barham told his air gunner Sgt Baker to jump and then turned the aircraft on its back and fell out. He was later picked up in the water but Baker was missing.

The 24 August 1940 was a very bad day for 264 Squadron. They had been deployed to 11 Group despite the decimation of 141 Squadron a month previously (on 19 July 1940 seven aircraft from 141 were shot down and lost). On 24 August six aircraft from 264 were shot down by Me 109s and Ju 88s east of Manston and seven crewmen killed including their Commanding Officer Sqn Ldr Philip A Hunter DSO, aged 27, who came from Chesham in Bucks. He has no known grave but is on the Runnymede

Memorial. Two of the six had been damaged in a scramble prior to take-off. The airfield at the time of the scramble was under attack by enemy bombers. One Ju 88 was shot down South of Manston by an aircraft of 264 Squadron.

Those air gunners killed from 264 and 141 Sqns during that period are:

24 August 1940:

141 Squadron

Pilot Officer Frederick Harry King DFM who was flying with Sqn Ldr Hunter.

Has no known grave but is on the Runnymede Memorial.

Sgt William Howard Machin Died of Wounds, now buried in Handsworth, Birmingham.

Pilot Officer William Alan Ponting age 30 from Whetstone, Middlesex on the Runnymede Memorial.

Sgt Alan Berry age 23 from Longsight, Manchester on the Runnymede Memorial.

264 Squadron

Sgt Robert Combie age 29 from Lightwater, Surrey on the Runnymede Memorial

Sgt Frederick Peter John Atkins from Edmont, Middx buried Boulogne, France

Pilot Officer J R G Gardner

Sgt John Francis Wise on the Runnymede Memorial

26th August 1940:

Sgt Walter Maxwell age 23 from Meols, Cheshire on the Runnymede Memorial.

Sgt Barrie Baker aged 27 from Kings Norton, Birmingham on the Runnymede Memorial.

The first Canadian to be awarded the DFM was Aircraftman Gordon Patterson from Saskachewen. Gordon had joined the RAF in 1938 and, amongst other trades, he was a qualified air gunner. At the time he was flying with No. 12 Squadron, who were operating on Fairey Battles. On 12 May 1940, came what seemed a suicide mission: the Maastricht Bridges over the River Meuse and the Albert Canal in Holland. They were promised a fighter escort as the area was alive with enemy fighters. The Fairey Battle had one fixed machine-gun used by the pilot and one free machine-gun operated by the air gunner. Each pan of ammunition carried 100 rounds. The problems with the Battle were a small bomb-load and single in-line liquid-cooled engine. The latter made it vulnerable to flak and fighters. Both pilot and air gunner were rather cramped; one standing and the other sitting on the fuselage floor.

After taking off on 12th the fighter escort from No. 1 Squadron somehow missed the rendezvous with the Battles. Gordon was flying with Pilot Officer Davey but when they reached the bridges and before they could dive to make an attack they were attacked by three Me109s when they suffered much damage and the order to bale out was given. Gordon was hit in the earpiece, right forearm and left leg. He landed in Liege, Belgium but he hit the ground rather badly and was knocked unconscious and immediately taken to hospital by some Belgians. As well as his injuries in the combat he had broken the arch bone in his left foot on landing. The area was soon under the control of the Germans and he was made a prisoner of war. Many PoW camps and force marches followed until he reached the village of Lubeck where he was librated by the British Army. He had gone out on the 12 May 1940 an aircraftman and when released in October 1945 he was a Warrant Officer.

His pilot, Pilot Officer Davey, dropped his bombs a mile west of Wilre, near one of the bridges. After Gordon and the other member of the crew, Sgt Mansell, had baled out he flew the aircraft home alone and made a forced landing. Sgt Mansell was also awarded the DFM and Davey the DFC although many thought it should have been the VC.

A second order to attack the bridges was received by 12 Squadron and, in particular, the Vroenhaven and Veldwezelt bridges over the Albert Canal in north-east France. At the time 12 Squadron was based at Amitontaine, France. Six crews were detailed but only five were able to take off, one aircraft having radio problems and when the crew changed to another aircraft there was a problem with the hydraulics on the bomb rack. Flying Officer Donald Garland led 'B' Flight and his crew were Sgt Thomas Gray and air gunner LAC Lawrence Royston Reynolds. They attacked the Veldwezelt Bridge from 1,000 ft and ran the gauntlet of 300 guns around the bridge. They were able to drop their bombs but were shot down and killed. It was later recorded that their bombs had done a certain amount of damage near the bridge. Both Garland and Gray were awarded posthumous VCs by the Commanding Officer of 12 Squadron, Wing Commander A G Thackeray, and this was approved on 6 June and gazetted on the 11th. For Reynolds there was not even a mention in despatches. Their bodies were all picked up by local French inhabitants and buried before the Germans could recover them. In 1945 they were exhumed and reburied at Heverlee War Cemetery.

Another air gunner who was in a very similar situation was AC1 WOpt/AG Clarke also in 12 Squadron and shot down two days after Gordon Patterson when attacking a bridge across the River Meuse at Donchery, near Sedan, where the Germans were making a breakthrough into France. On this day forty out of seventy-one aircraft operating were shot down. Of this total four out of five from 12 Squadron were lost and ten out of eleven from 218 Squadron. AC1 Clarke was promoted to Sergeant while a prisoner in Germany, then Flight Sergeant and finally Warrant Officer in 1943. He described it as promotion without trying.

Another squadron to lose its commanding officer at this time was No. 236. He was Wing Commander Weld-Smith. No. 236 were operating with Blenheim aircraft at the time and on 1 August 1940 were detailed to attack machine-gun and coastal gun-batteries along the French coast. As well as Weld-Smith, Squadron Leader Peter Drew flying in 3601-K was shot down attacking the target in a low attack at 50 to 70 ft. He and his air gunner Flying Officer Benjamin Nokes-Cooper aged 32 and from Salford, Lancashire were killed. Drew is now buried in Biville, Manche, France, and Cooper in Bayeux, Calavados, France.

LAC Clarence Evans was flying as an air gunner with No. 2 Squadron on 25 May. They were conducting a reconnaissance over France when attacked by fifteen Me109s. Despite bullets penetrating the rear cockpit from converging attacks Evans responded with his rear gun enabling the pilot to return to base safely. On 30 May 1940 he was recommended for the DFM, this was endorsed on 9 June and Gazetted on 6 August 1940.

Leslie Smith was born in Gravesend in 1917 and joined the RAFVR in August 1938 as an aircraftman general duties. During weekends at Biggin Hill he flew on Demons of No. 601 Squadron in the air gunner's seat. When called up on 1 September 1939 he began a WOpt/AG course at Blackpool. Having failed the Morse part of the course he remustered as an air gunner and after completing his course joined 219 Sqn at Catterick in July 1940 and crewed up with Sgt Gee. The aircraft then used by 219 was the Blenheim Mk 1 F with a dorsal turret and one Vickers K machine-gun.

On 18 August 1940, along with two other squadrons, 219 chased German Ju88s across the North Sea and back to their base in Denmark. In September he was posted to 'B' Flight of 141 Squadron operating with Boulton and Paul Defiants at Biggin Hill, Kent.

Here, because he only lived 20 miles from the station he was nicknamed 'Lucky Les', his luck got better when they were posted to Gatwick and then his home town Gravesend, only a mile from his home, where he stayed until April 1941.

Their task to patrol a protective 'patrol line' south of London from Canterbury, Kent to Guildford, Surrey. In spite of the warm weather flying kit was essential as it was freezing cold in the draughty turret at 10,000 to 15,000 ft. They also had balloons and trigger happy anti-aircraft gunners to contend with. While flying he could see fires raging below and thought of his mother and father being down there, but the frustrating part was never being able to locate the bombers who were the perpetrators. That is until 16 September 1940, the day after the day now known as 'Battle of Britain Day'. On this day they saw a Heinkel 111 and promptly shot it down. Also, on the 18th they handed out the same treatment to a Ju 88. These were the only two victories for 141 throughout the 24 weeks of the Battle of Britain.

In August 1941, Beaufighters replaced the Defiant and Les and the other gunners were no longer required. So in October 1941 he went off to Rhodesia to train as a navigator. His original squadron, 219, had by the end of 1941 destroyed forty-four enemy aircraft and by the end of September 1944 claimed 100 enemy aircraft destroyed.

John Keatings also served in 264 Squadron and remembers spending the summer of 1940 protecting convoys sailing down the east coast of the UK. Their biggest moment was when twelve aircraft were scrambled to intercept forty plus Ju88s at sea over Flamborough Head. Seven Ju88s were shot down and the only casualty to 264 was Sgt Arthur Dupee who was shot in the arm and although weak from loss of blood he directed Sgt 'Spike' Bannister, the air gunner, to belly land the Blenheim aircraft at Driffield despite the fact that, at the time, the airfield was being shot up by Ju88s. Both Dupee and Banister were awarded the DFM.

On 26 August Temporary Sergeant Fred Gash, also of 264 Squadron, was flying as air gunner to Flying Officer Frederick Hughes and shot down two Do17s. On 15 October he shot down a Heinkel III, another on 23 November 1940 and finally one on 12 March 1941. For his great efforts he was awarded the DFM and Flying Officer Hughes the DFC.

For Coastal Command and 10 Squadron, operating on Sunderland flying boats, came the first DFM awarded to a member of the squadron: Leading Aircraftman Milton Griffin who hailed from Sydney in Australia. On 30 June 1941, he was working inside the Sunderland's wing during the flight to repair an engine damaged in combat with a Kurier aircraft. The Sunderland had taken on the German aircraft in the Atlantic and the damaged Kurier finally fled into the clouds. However, the port engine of the Sunderland had been holed and oil was pouring out. It was only a matter of time before the engine seized. It was just possible for a small man to stretch out full length inside the wing, which Griffin volunteered to do. It could be dangerous if the engine seized and they had to land quickly; Griffin would not be able to get out in time. Further, the only light to help him see inside the wing was through the bullet hole and all the time oil was still pouring through the holes in the tank. He went back inside the aircraft and fetched plugs to put in the holes. At this time there was only a gallon of oil left in the tank which normally held twenty; after plugging the holes he poured in two gallons of oil using a peach tin. Having come out for a break he again went back in and poured a further two gallons into the tank and they made it home.

Bomber Command were also doing their bit at this time. Pilot Officer Frederick Chalk of 218 Squadron was detailed on 15/16 June 1941 to carry out a raid on Hanover. On the return trip his Wellington bomber was attacked by an Me110, which pressed home two attacks and came to within 200 yards range. In the face of accurate cannon and machine-gun fire from the enemy, which pierced the tailplane and set the port wing on fire, Pilot Officer Chalk fired two steady bursts which were seen to enter the enemy aircraft; it broke away after its second attack with flames coming from the starboard side. It was certainly damaged and probably destroyed. Since February he had taken part in twenty operations and on 16 June 1941 was recommended for the DFC, which was later approved.

Pilot Officer Reginald Taylor served with 26 Squadron and during a reconnaissance sortie in a Fairey Battle on 19 May 1940, in the Peronne area they spotted a section of tanks held up by a broken bridge. The enemy opened fire; the first burst wounding Taylor in the calf of his left leg. Despite this he kept his gun in action and when the pilot flew a low-level flying attack he replied to the enemies fire. On return at 6.30am it proved to be impracticable to evacuate him immediately and he was not admitted to hospital until 8pm. Despite this long wait and in obvious pain he remained cheerful and an example to all. On 29 May 1940 he was recommended for the DFC.

Aircraftman Chamberlain joined the RAFVR in April 1939 and was posted to No. 264 Squadron at Stradishall in October 1939. In January 1940 he went on a gunnery course at Hellsmouth in North Wales using, as he described it, the best quality 1918 Lewis guns. On return to the squadron now at Speke airfield near Liverpool he was posted to No. 500 (County of Kent) Auxiliary Squadron flying Ansons from RAF Manston, Kent. On 1 June 1940, Chamberlain was flying with Sgt Freestove in Anson MKH. He took off at 0834 on a patrol when they were attacked by Me109s over Dunkirk. At the time the Ansons were at 50 ft when eight Me109s dived from 1,000 to 1,500 ft to attack . In another Anson, MKV, P/O Peter and his gunner AC Smith were able to shoot down two of the Me109s. Sgt Freestove's aircraft was hit and Chamberlain wounded in the right forearm. When they landed at Manston he was taken to Ramsgate Hospital where his wounded arm was put in plaster. He was subsequently transferred to RAF Halton Hospital, Aylesbury, Bucks, where he was to spend 15 months. In September 1941 he was invalided out of the services and to a job with the Public Health Service until he retired in 1983.

Albert Gregory joined the RAFVR, in early 1939 and was mobilized at the outbreak of war in September 1939 as a partially trained air gunner and a then sent on a gunnery course to a gunnery school at RAF Aldergrove, Northern Ireland. After gaining his 'spurs' and flying bullet etc he was posted to No. 141 Squadron flying Blenheims at Grangemouth, Scotland. In March 1940 they began to convert to Defiant aircraft but Albert was a very tall man and although he did not have any trouble in getting in and out of the turret he was told that anyone over the height of 5 foot 10 inches was not suitable and he was told he was to be posted, and despite pleading with the Commanding Officer he was posted to No. 219 Squadron flying Blenheims at Catterick, Yorkshire. Their role was to provide air cover the East Coast of England. Later in 1940 141 squadron was sent down to Hawkinge in Kent and in July 1940 lost six out of nine aircraft on one patrol. Consequently, 219 were sent south and on one occasion Albert flew six sorties in one day and between 29 August and 31 August 1940 he was airborne fifteen times. And between May and October 1940 he was airborne 184 times. In December 1940 219 converted to Beaufighters but despite a lot of flying and much action achieved only one success: a Heinkel III destroyed over Sussex.

In July 1942 he went on a Gunnery Leaders Course at Sutton Bridge and then a posting to 605 Squadron, but after twelve operations he was told he was to be posted to an Operational Training Unit – which he said he did not want – and so was posted to Air Sea Rescue Squadrons 275 and 278 respectively flying Ansons, Lysanders, Walrus and Sea Otters. Altogether during WWII he flew on eight different aircraft, six squadrons, and flew 145 operational sorties. He was commissioned in 1942 and awarded the DFC in 1943. He left the RAF in 1945 but re-enlisted in 1947, and flew in Malaya in supply dropping to the troops in the Malayan jungle. He finally left the RAF in 1955 having flown over 200 operational flights.

On 20 December 1941, Sergeant Edward Ernest De Joux was flying with No. 7 Sqn on Stirling bombers. On this day he was flying to attack Brest when his aircraft was attacked by two Me109s, in the first attack the hydraulics were put out of action and only by the skilful use of his turret by hand rotation was he able to get a sight on one of the fighters and shoot it down which enabled them to get back to base. He was recommended for the DFM which was approved and gazetted on 9 January 1942. He had at the time flown on eighteen operations.

Memories of flying on Defiants are dim to Joe Wakefield DFC. In training he only flew 12 hours on the aircraft and on one occasion they climbed to 22,000 ft. During low practice one pilot flew under the Clifton Suspension Bridge. On the ground they took Browning machine-guns apart and then assembled them again. On one vertical dive he could see in the reflection

Air Gunners at RAF Burn in 1944.

in the Perspex dome that his facial skin was in folds near his ears and when the pilot pulled out he blacked out. The pilot called him up and asked if he was okay. Joe, having regained consciousness, replied "yes, but I blacked out". The reply was, "don't worry, so did I!"

William Walker qualified as an air gunner in March 1941 and joined No. 35 Squadron three weeks later. He was on the operation at La Pallice to sink the German Battleship *Scharnhorst* in July 1941 in which 35 Squadron lost three crews. He was flying with P/O Muller in Halifax L9491 and although his aircraft returned to base he was wounded in a fighter attack and detained in hospital. He did not fly on operations again until September 1944 this time with 578 Squadron at RAF Burn. His last operation was to Gelesenkirchen in February 1945. He was commissioned in October 1944 as F/O.

A crew of 578 Squadron in 1944. *W. Walker*

CHAPTER THREE

Turrets and Guns

The first effective gun for rapid fire was the Mitrailleuse, designed in Belgium in 1851. It had several barrels mounted round a common axis and was operated by a crank lever. At first the gun had thirty-seven barrels but was later reduced to twenty-five. The barrels were rifled and accurate up to 500 yards. The rounds were held in perforated plates which fitted into grooves at the rear of the gun and locked the breech so that each round lined up with its own barrel, and was fired by turning a handle. When all barrels had been fired, the breech was opened, the plate and empty cases removed and a fresh plate and cartridge inserted. With a good team twelve plates of cartridges could be fired per minute.

The next step in development was the Gatling gun, invented by Dr Richard J.Gatling, a Chicago engineer. It had from four to ten barrels which revolved around a central axis by turning a cranked handle. Each barrel had its own bolt or breechblock, the ammunition being fed by gravity by a stationary hopper on top of the breech. As the barrels turned the bolt moved in cam grooves, picked up a round from the hopper, and pushed it into the chamber; the round fired and the cases were ejected, thus providing a type of automatic feed. The rate of fire was about 350 rounds per minute, and much depended on how fast the operator turned the handle. If it was turned too fast, the gun was liable to suffer stoppages. Because each barrels was complete with its own breechblock the gun was very heavy and cumbersome. The first Gatling guns were used in British operations in 1879, but success was limited due to lack of mobility and the tendency to jam at critical moments. In common with the early machine guns, the Gatling suffered from the disadvantage that at the time of its introduction the solid drawn cartridge case had not been perfected. The British Boxer cartridge, which was then in general use, had a paper case with metal base and was unsuitable for machine guns.

About that time numerous inventors turned their attention to machine guns, but the most successful was a London banker named Thorsten Nordenfelt. His gun had two or five barrels in line fed by gravity from a hopper; the gun being operated by pushing a lever backwards or forwards. The mechanism was very assessable and one advantage was that if stoppages occurred in any one-barrel, that barrel could be put of action and fire continued on the remainder. It was designed so that all the barrels could fire together or in quick succession, rate of fire being approximately 350 round per minute. This gun adopted the solid drawn cartridge case, and although full advantage was not taken of this invention, one immediate outcome was that stoppages were less frequent.

The year 1883 brought the invention of a gun by Hiram K.Maxim which was to become the basis of all fully automatic machine guns. The principles laid down by Maxim were successfully used with practically no alteration by all machine-gun manufacturers except in mechanical details. The weapon introduced several new features, which it had not been possible to incorporate in other guns. In the first place, the gun was fully automatic; the operation of extraction and ejection of the empty cartridge case, feed and firing, being performed automatically by the gun itself. The barrel was 'free' in the casing and could move to the rear on recoil, and working through levers and springs, brought about the complete action of loading and firing the gun. The rate of fire was approximately 600 rounds per minute. Another feature was the replacement of a number of barrels by a single one and to keep the barrel cool it was encased in a jacket containing water. Gravity feed had been a source of trouble in all previous machine guns so Maxim introduced the well-known belt feed in which the belt containing ammunition was moved across by the action of recoil in time with the other movements. The Maxim gun was introduced into the British Army in 1891 and soon replaced other machine guns.

At the outbreak of the First World War military aircraft had very little spare lifting capacity for weapons, and those weapons consisted entirely of revolvers, service rifles or sporting guns firing chamin shot. The need for improved armament was immediately apparent. Experiments were made in two-seater pusher aircraft, in which a Lewis infantry machine-gun was mounted for use by the observer who sat in front of the pilot. These were standard infantry guns with an aluminium alloy radiator surrounding the barrel, and they utilised the forty-seven round magazine. As the war progressed, these guns were gradually stripped of their radiators and other non-essential parts in the aircraft version of the gun, and they were also modified to give a higher rate of fire. A ninety-seven-round magazine was also developed to reduce the 'dead' time due to magazine changing during combat. Tractor aeroplanes soon began to supersede the pusher types, as the former gave a better performance. There was one serious disadvantage from the armament point of view: the gun had to be mounted outside the aircraft.

The Browning .303 machine gun designed by John Browning was used by the RAF from the mid 1930s onwards. It was, in the main, reliable and in the event of stoppages it could be cleared by the air gunner using a special tool. At the end of the war the .303 was exchanged for the .05; a much larger gun being 5 ft long compared with the .303 which was 3 ft 6 ins.

In 1932 the design for a modern gun turret was submitted to the British Government; they, however, considered there was no serious necessity for anything better than the old wartime ring-mounting carrying a single gun.

The speeds of aircraft had increased over the years and it was becoming impossible to operate guns by hand without some kind of cover. This had become apparent in 1931 when the Hawker Hart type of aircraft was already showing that something better was wanted than the hand-mounted unprotected gunner.

It was Mr Frazer-Nash who began the development of power-operated gun turrets. It was necessary for the control to be accurate and sensitive and a use a minimum of effort to operate. It also had to have instantaneous, smooth, and continuous speed and have variation from full speed in one direction to full speed in the other. A number of ideas for this were considered and a hydraulic system was found to be the best and the one that Frazer-Nash chose. The turret had to have a free gun-mounting giving full rotation to the turret, coupled with full elevation and with depression on the beam down to vertical (or thereabouts). Since the sights available were mounted on the gun itself, it was necessary to provide the gunner with a seat, which would move in relation to the gun in such a manner that he could keep his eye always on the sight.

In addition to the gun, stowage for the gunner's parachute, telephones, clothing heating and oxygen had to be found within the turret which could not exceed 27 ins because this was the width of the Hawker Demon aircraft in which it had to be fitted. In 1932 the drawings for a turret that would accommodate all these things was submitted to the Air Ministry. They looked at it rather sceptically; but a model was made and Frazer-Nash took it to Eastchurch for testing and appraisal. This was received with some encouragement so a full-sized working mock-up of the turret was produced. In 1933 the Air Ministry wanted a power-operated turret suitable for the Hawker Demon fighter and gave the order to the newly formed company Nash & Thompson. It was not fully enclosed but had a metal cowl to protect the gunner from the aircraft's slipstream and had a single 0.303inch Lewis gun. When it proved to be a success more were ordered for Bomber Command.

The first power-operated turrets were fitted in the Handley Page Harrow bomber, the first heavy bomber to be fitted with such turrets. The Harrow had a single Lewis .303 machine gun in the nose and two in the tail. The Wellington and the Whitley followed soon installed these turrets. In the case of the Whitley its hand-operated turrets were replaced with power operated ones. With the realisation that WWII coming, guns and turrets production went into overdrive. But after the war had started it was soon realised that the bombers were no match for the German fighters, particularly in daytime. However, operations were, of course, much colder at night particularly in the winter of 1939/40 and the crews were having to wear very bulky flying kit, the gunner sitting all the time felt the cold more than the other members of the crew.

Rear turret guns elevated. *Alan Cooper*

Rear turret guns lowered. *Alan Cooper*

Mid upper gunner. *IWM*

The FN5 turret was designed for the Wellington but was also fitted to the Stirling and Manchester and later the Lancaster. The tail turret was the FN20 and soon became the turret fitted in the Lancaster. The mid upper turret was the FN50. The Bolton Paul turret also being developed in the 1930s was fitted in the Boulton Paul Overstrand medium bomber and used by 101 Squadron between 1935 and 1938. The use of Perspex for turret cupola panels made night gunnery difficult because the panels soon became scratched or useless because of moisture, frost, the reflection from turret lights or searchlight glare. In October 1940 Bomber Command suggested that a part of the turret cupola should be cut away to provide a direct vision panel for use at night.

Ian Blair remembers in August 1939 being re-equipped with the Blenheim bomber of which one of features was the turret and Vickers gas-operated (VGO) gun, 'the answer to all gunners prayers': rapid rate of fire and no stoppages. But being an armourer he was sceptical and always carried his tools with him for clearing stoppages and on many occasions he had to use them. On occasions having to crawl from the front to the back of the aircraft to clear a stoppage.

On 12 May 1943, a mark IIC Gyro sight was delivered to RAF Wittering, along with a F.N.120 turret, series II. They were installed in Lancaster II DS719 of 408 Squadron on 22 August, 1943 by workers of Messrs Frazer-Nash. On 24 August trials began and were completed on 21 September 1943. A total of 31 hours flying was carried out, including 6 hours 30 minutes by night. The object of the trial was:

1. To form an opinion on the tactical value of the Mark IIC Gyro Sight which was installed in the FN 120 turret by day and night.
2. To consider the amount and method of training necessary to obtain satisfactory results from the average air gunner.

The three air gunners who took part inn the trial were all experienced in normal turret manipulation, but they had not used the FN 120 or the Gyro Sight before.

A total of 770 ft of film was taken during the trials. Lancaster DS719 was later lost in April 1944 on a raid to Essen.

Turret
The FN 120 Series II turret differed from the FN120 in three main features:

An electric motor to assist the serve-feed.

The control characteristic was altered to give less course control for small turret movements at the cost of a small reduction in maximum speed.

The turret was modified to take the various components which fed an allowance for bullet trail into the Mark II Sight.

The gunner in his turret called up the Captain or 'Skipper' for the I.A.S and height that he was flying. Having obtained the information the gunner set the information on the height and airspeed controls. He switched on the sight, turned the selector switch to fixed and gyro with the 'Dimmer'

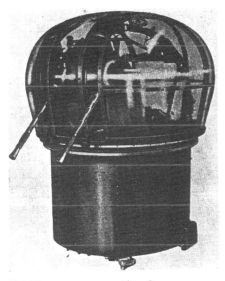

FN 50 upper turret. *Alan Cooper*

B.P. Type 'A' Mark III turret. *Alan Cooper*

turned to bright and checked that the graticules were illuminated. In day time he selected 'Gyro Day', raised the sun screen and/or adjusted the 'Dimmer' as necessary, and after adjusting the span setting to the most likely enemy aircraft type to be expected in daytime (probably an Fw.190), the gunner, if it was still early to expect enemy fighters, switched off the sight to prevent necessary wear and tear. Having reached the point where enemy fighters could be expected, the gunner switched on his sight. As he manipulated the turret during a search for the enemy he kept his right ranging pedal fully depressed; if he neglected to do this and if his turret was moved at speed, the moving graticule could blur for he knew that with his left pedal down the maximum range setting was made and consequently the greatest gyro deflection would take place.

Let us assume the gunner identified an Me 109 at about 1,200 yards, coming in from the port-quarter down. He quickly readjusted the span setting and with the right pedal still hard down he swung the turret on to the enemy and followed him with the graticule, momentarily he led the target and eased his left foot down and the graticule floated back onto the

Vickers G.O Gun. *Alan Cooper*

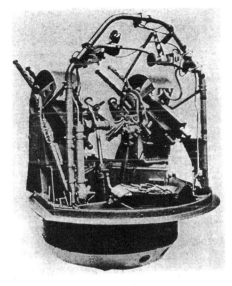

FN. 4 TAIL TURRET
(WITH CUPOLA REMOVED)

FN. 5 TAIL TURRET
(WITH CUPOLA REMOVED)

FN 4 tail turret. *Alan Cooper*   FN 5 tail turret. *Alan Cooper*

Lewis Gun on scarff ring. *Alan Cooper*

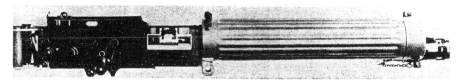

Vickers .303-inch Mark 1 ground gun. *Alan Cooper*

target. With the left pedal hard down and with the correct span setting on
the sight, the gunner knew that the enemy would just fill the graticule at
800 yards; as yet the 109 was still just outside the range. At 800 yards the
Me 109 was in range and the gunner pressed the trigger.

In May 1941 Mike Henry was posted to the Central Gunnery School at
Warmwell. Here there was a wonderful gadget which gave them practice
maximum-deflection shooting.

Each gunner took his turn to fire from a turret equipped with one gun
and fifty rounds of ammunition. A wooden model of an aircraft ran around
the track on rails in front of the gunner. It moved from starboard and astern
and went at speeds of up to 30mph. If the gunner was lucky enough to hit
it the holes were patched before it was sent around again for the next
gunner to fire at. It seems strange and ironic that the gunners who had
been in combat and shot down enemy aircraft had the lowest scores and
the inexperienced 'sprog' gunner the highest.

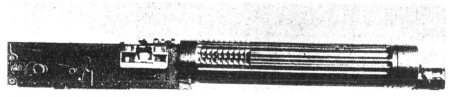

Vickers .303-inch Mark I. *Alan Cooper*

CHAPTER FOUR

Never Too Old, or Too Young

The average age of aircrew in WWII was 21, but there were a few who were much older and much younger but somehow managed to fly.

Sydney Carlin served in WWI in the 18th Hussars and was awarded the DCM and Military Cross but then lost a leg in action and was fitted with a wooden one. Having been discharged he somehow got back into the Royal Flying Corps/RAF and after a number of successful combats with the enemy he was awarded the DFC. When WWII began he tried to get back into the RAF as a pilot but, this having been refused, he was accepted as an air gunner. He flew on Defiants and then with Wg Cdr Percy Pickard DSO DFC, then commanding No. 311 (Czech) Squadron, on several operations over Germany. He was killed on 9 May 1941 while serving with 151 Squadron when the airfield he was on was attacked and he was cut down by enemy bullets. He was cremated at Hull Crematorium.

Squadron Leader William Fielding-Johnson had also served in the Royal Flying Corps in WWI and was awarded more than one Military Cross. In WWII he again served but this time as an air gunner and gunnery leader with 241 Squadron and later as officer commanding 1483 TT. and Gunnery Flight. He inspired others not only by taking part in operations himself since June 1940 but also by his spirit. He was 52 years of age at the time, more than twice the age of the men who he was not only commanding but flying with as an operational air gunner.

Sgt Alfred Bolton also served in WWI and in 1940 served as an air gunner with 220 Squadron. In August 1940 he was awarded an immediate DFM when his Hudson aircraft was attacked by a number of enemy fighters of which more than one was severely damaged by his fire power. It was his continuous fire that prevented the enemy fighters from pressing home their repeated attacks. He was 48 years of age at the time .

Wing Commander Lionel Cohen, or 'SOS' as he was known, was born in 1874. In 1893 he joined the South African forces as a trooper and served in the Matabele war. On discharge he did various jobs until the Boer War came along when he again enlisted. After that he had various jobs in South Africa. In the First World War he enlisted in the 1st South African Horse in 1915 and then transferred to the Royal Naval Air Service and became a pilot. By the end of the war he had been awarded the DSO and MC and no less than three mention in dispatches.

On leaving the services he had a number of jobs and in September 1939 at the age of 64, and still having a commission in the RAFVR as it became, he more or less insisted on rejoining the RAF. But having succeeded he had no intention of sitting behind a desk. And so for the next four years wearing, the flying badge of an observer, he flew a great number and variety of operations as a spare air gunner. He flew in most types of aircraft with Coastal Command and on one occasion was wounded by flak. In 1941 he was again awarded a mention in dispatches.

On his last operation as a rear gunner in a Halifax the aircraft was shot-up by flak and badly damaged. With an engine on fire they made a crash landing from which he escaped unhurt. He had flown sixty-nine operations, one for each year of his very full life. In the recommendation for his DFC, in February 1944, it mentioned that he was over 60. And in 1946 he was awarded the Air Medal from the United States, conferred upon him by the President for his services with the Fleet Air Wing Seven of the United States Navy between October 1943 and May 1944. He died in 1960 aged 86.

William Wedgewood Benn, The father of politician Tony Benn, joined-up in 1915 and served with the Royal Flying Corps and later the RAF as a pilot and observer and was awarded the DSO and DFC. In 1940 he rejoined at the age of 63 with the rank of pilot officer but soon rose to the rank of Air Commodore. When his son Michael was killed while flying, he had been awarded the DFC before he was killed, William felt the need to get into action again. Consequently, he went to Air Gunnery Schools and used his rank to 'persuade' Station Commanders to allow him to be trained as an air gunner and later he flew on operations (at the age of 67). Not surprisingly. when this came to light later he was grounded. However, he had by that time been mentioned twice in dispatches.

A few weeks after leaving the RAF he was given the Cabinet Post of Secretary of State for Air in the new Attlee government and later he became Viscount Stansgate.

Pilot Officer Sir Arnold Talbot Wilson was killed in action on 31 May 1940. He was born in 1884, went to Sandhurst in 1902 and was commissioned into the 32 Sikh Pioneers. In 1913/14 he was British Commissioner of the Turo-Persian Frontier and he was awarded the CMG. He served in WWI in Mesopotamia and was awarded the DSO in 1916 when a Captain. In 1918 he had reached the rank of Lt/Col and in 1919 was awarded the Order of St John and in 1920 knighted. Between the wars he went into politics and became the MP for Hitchin.

When WWII started he was 55 and having failed to get into the Army or the Navy he succeeded in getting into the RAF and was given the honorary title of Observer. After gunnery training at No. 1 Air Armaments School, Manby and the Central Gunnery School at Warmwell. He then became the gunnery officer with No. 37 Squadron flying on Wellington bombers. He described Warmwell as a great place and he flew every day, often at great heights when it was cold enough to make a man cry but having had cold baths all his life he was probably able to stand it better than most. In the crew list he was listed as P/O Sir Arnold Wilson and flew with a F/Sgt Gray. He flew on a number of missions until going missing in the Dunkirk area on 31 May 1940. At the time plans were afoot to transfer him to a Blenheim Squadron and then pull him out into a training as Group Gunnery Officer at No. 3 Group. When at No. 37 Squadron he said that he had marked his favourite rear turret and also a front turret which he liked second best. However, the mid-upper or 'Dustbin' was a disappointment. On the 19/20 May he went on an operation with the target being Given, south of Namur. During the flight he opened fire on a nest of machine guns which elicited a response on the inter-com, "Good, Sir Gunner, a very pretty pattern around them." However, his aircraft was hit by flak and with one engine on fire Gray was unable to maintain height. The navigator Sgt Axford baled out and in so doing broke his leg. When the Wellington crashed the second pilot Sgt Brown was killed as was Wilson. Gray was thrown out and died eight days later in hospital. Two of the crew: Axford and LAC Orland the W/Operator, or transmitter as it was known then, were taken prisoner. Both Wilson and the second pilot are buried today in Eringhem, ten miles south-west of Dunkirk. It is ironic that at the time there was a move in the Government to take him off active duty and give him a job at the Air Ministry.

P/O Dunstan joined the Australian Imperial Forces as an engineer, he was only 17 but had 'advanced' his age to be able to enlist. In 1941 he was hit in the right knee by a shell fragment which meant his leg had to be amputated and after five operations he was sent back to Australia. After seven months in hospital he was discharged with an artificial leg. He was now 19 and returned to school to study law at University but suddenly began thinking about flying and urged the RAAF to let him join. He was successful and in June 1942 he was accepted. He then went to the UK as a Sergeant and at the end of his air gunner training he joined No. 460 Squadron. His first operation was to Dusseldorf and to finish his tour he went again to Düsseldorf in November. He used to take his crutches on the aircraft with him and when he had to move down the aircraft he would crawl on one leg. In August 1943 he was given a commission. In October, during an attack on Kassel, a fighter attacked his aircraft and a shell smashed through Dunstan's turret and tore his sleeve. The turret was so badly damaged that on his return he had to be cut out. At the end of his tour he was awarded the DSO, the only Australian air gunner to gain this award and he ended the war as a gunnery instructor.

Roy Dotrice, who after WWII became a famous actor and whose daughter married another famous actor Edward Woodward, was born in the Channel Islands and when the Germans arrived he, with others, escaped to England in a small boat. He was only 14 and somehow managed to get into the RAF. After training he was posted to No. 106 Squadron as a rear gunner: at the time, the average life of a rear gunner was eight flying hours. No. 106 Squadron were operating with the infamous Manchester aircraft, the forerunner of the Lancaster. He suffered greatly with air sickness and actually hoped he would be shot down a by a German fighter to put him out of his agony. The commander of 106 was the later famous Wg Cdr Guy Gibson who would lead 617 on the Dambuster raid and be awarded the VC. One afternoon, as they were about to take off for a night flying test, a normal thing if one was flying on ops that night, Gibson came out and said, "Would you take my brother with you. He's never been up in a plane?" His brother Alick, an army officer in the Warwickshire Regiment, stood in the cockpit behind the pilot Len Hurd and Wilf Faxter the second pilot. He had no flying helmet and so was not plugged into the inter-com system. They went out over the Wash and tested the various equipment on the aircraft including Roy's guns. It was a the normal custom to beat up the WAAFERY on return, an old manor house a couple of miles from RAF Coninsgby, Lincoln, the home of 106. The crew were courting some of the WAAFS housed there. The aircraft was put into a dive and pulled out just over the old manor which informed the occupants that they were flying that night, a normal practice for aircrew but not for someone flying for the very first time. Len said, "Stand by lads, Waafery coming up". But, not being on the inter-com, Alick did not hear this and the aircraft went into a dive and came out with tremendous G force upon which Alick collapsed on the floor. After they had landed Gibson came up to Len and his crew and said, "What the hell did you do to my brother? I have had to lend him a pair of my trousers to go home in."

Roy soon got his wish to be shot down on the 2/3 May 1942 when, on his third operation in Manchester R5840 flown by F/Sgt Hurd, they came down into the North Sea. The operation was supposed to be what was known as a nursery trip, officially called Gardening 'Forget Me Nots'. (Dropping Mines). They were in a dinghy for three days until they came ashore in enemy territory and were captured on his 16th birthday. For the next three and half years he spent behind a wire in Germany, Poland and Lithuania. It was in Stalag III that he had his first acting part when he was asked to play the fairy godmother in Cinderella.

In 1943 Air Commodore Alfred Sharp was the Chairman of the Operational Planning Committee and charged with co-ordinating the bombing efforts of the 8th Air Force with those of the Royal Air Force, Fighter, and Coastal Commands. Realising the necessity for personally observing the operations of high altitude bombing missions he voluntarily served as a crew member on raids against important enemy installations and where intense enemy opposition might be expected. On 14 July 1943, while flying as observer and waist gunner on a B-17 aircraft they were attacked, viciously and persistently, by numerous enemy fighter planes. Alfred displayed great courage and gallantry in manning his guns and seeing off the enemy fighters. On this mission he also made many valuable observations and obtained combat information and data vital to successful operational planning. In his citation for the US Silver Star it said that his display in a dangerous position displayed the greatest honour upon himself and the armed forces of His Majesty's Government. This was presented to Sharp by Lt General Eaker the Commanding General of the United States Army Air Forces in the United Kingdom on 19 November 1943. His post at the time was Deputy Chief of Staff HQ USAA FUK.

OPERATIONS RECORD BOOK.

DETAIL OF WORK CARRIED OUT.

on 2305 hrs. 31 / 3 /40 to 0515 hrs.1 / 4 /40   By No. 37 Squadron.

Aircraft pe and No.	Crew.	Duty.	Time Up.	Time Down.	Details of Sortie
llington LA 305	P/Sgt. Gray.	Captain,	2305	0505	Four Aircraft, two "A" Fligh
	Sgt. Brown.	Navigator.			stood by for nickelling and
	Sgt. Axford.	Air Obs.			aircraft took off between th
	LAC. Orland.	W/T Op.			2315 to carry out reconnaiss
	P/O Sir. Arnold Wilson. A.G.				Form B105.
	AC. Henderson.	A.G.			Raid DCB 140 F/Sgt. Gray
					" DCB 141 S/Ldr. Bradf
18	S/Ldr. Bradford.	Captain.	2305	0540	

Operational Record Book for 37 Squadron.

CHAPTER FIVE

Outstanding Operations

I n WWII there were a number of operations in which air gunners were involved that have become famous. Perhaps the Dambuster raid of May 1943 has achieved more fame than most others and numerous books and a film in 1955 have made it one of the most famous operations of WWII. On this operation to attack the Ruhr Dams: Mohne, Eder, Sorpe and Ennepe dams on 17/18 May 1943, and carried out by the newly formed No. 617 squadron was a great success with both the Eder and Mohne being breached. But the cost was high: out of nineteen Lancasters that took off from RAF Scampton eight aircraft and fifty-six men failed to return. Of this total of, sixteen were air gunners and two of them survived to become prisoners of war.

Flying Officer Tony Burcher came from Sydney in Australia and joined 617 Squadron from No. 106 Squadron for the Dams raid. He had already been awarded the DFM and was on his 28th Operation. His pilot, F/Lt John 'Hoppy' Hopgood, DFC and Bar. Their target was the Mohne Dam and they in formation with Wg Cdr Guy Gibson DSO DFC and Bar as they did the Lancaster was raked from nose to tail with ground fire and Tony was hit in the stomach and groin. Despite this he was able to extinguish the

F/Lt Tony Burcher DFM. *Tony Burcher*

searchlight that was full in his face. Then a shell burst near the aircraft
and he a heard the flight engineer say the port outer engine was hit and
on fire. Because of the port outer engine controlled the hydraulics for his
turret Tony was unable to rotate the rear turret. The wireless operator
had been hit in the leg and was unable to move and there was no response
from the front gunner. 'Hoppy' carried on but it was obvious from what
Tony heard on the inter-com that he had been badly hurt and in fact
bleeding badly from a head wound. But in the best of Bomber Command
captains he carried on to the target. At the Mohne Dam Tony heard the
navigator tell 'Hoppy' to go lower and then from the bomb aimer 'Bombs
Gone' Then came a shout 'port inner engine on fire' with both engines
out 'Hoppy' gave the order to bale out. Unfortunately the bomb had been
dropped seconds too late and went over the dam wall and blew up the
power house on the other side. Tony in the meantime had to crank his
turret around with the dead man's handle so as to get into the fuselage
and pick up and clip on his chute, before he went he called 'Hoppy' on
the inter-com only to be told 'Get out you bloody fool, and if only I had
another 300 ft.' they had been hit by fire from the gunners on the dam
wall. As Tony looked down the fuselage he saw the wireless operator
who had been hit in the leg dragging himself towards him and the escape
hatch. His leg was nearly severed. All Tony could do for him was clip on
his parachute and push him out into the darkness. As he did he pulled
the D ring release, by this time with the height he had to bale out Tony
deployed his parachute in the aircraft and bundling up in his arms he
gave his last message to the pilot 'Rear Gunner abandoning aircraft'
Hoppy yelled back 'Get out.'

As Tony went out he hit the tailplane of the Lancaster, always a problem
if you pulled your ripcord to quickly but in the circumstances he had no
option. He landed with a thud. As he hit the ground his parachute took
him back up and according to the German Medical Officer who later
attended to him saved his life. From where he lay on the ground he saw
the Mohne Dam breach and the water burst out. Tony was picked up and
taken to a police station, here he asked for a drink of water but was told
because of him there was no water.

The front gunner P/O Officer George Gregory DFM was killed he had
enlisted in 1939 flown a full tour with No. 44 Squadron and been awarded
the DFM in 1941.

He had shot down an Me 110 night-fighter on one occasion and on
another directed his pilot in evading attacks by three enemy fighters. He
along with 'Hoppy' and the rest of the crew apart from Tony and Jim Fraser
the bomb aimer who also survived are now buried in the Rheinberg War
Cemetery. In 1993, the 50th Anniversary of the Dams raid 'Hoppy's' sister
Marna visited his grave and the place where he crashed for the first time.
She was given at the time a piece of her brothers aircraft. The author was
also given a piece at the same time.

Tony left the RAAF in 1946 but in 1952, and having married an English girl who had served in the WAAFs joined the RAF and served in Korea, Borneo and Malaya.

In 1955, and the premier of the now famous film 'The Dambusters' Tony had to be airlifted out of the Malayan jungle to attend. He was on an expedition to see how aircrew would fair if shot down in the jungle. During this expedition he carried a 50lb pack on his back.

His back having been broken when he baled out and because of a lack of plaster Paris being set in cement it troubled him for the rest of his life and eventually received from the Australian Government a 100% war pension.

Many years after the war he went back to Tasmania to live and has now passed up into that big airfield in the sky.

The other air gunner to survive was Flt/Sgt Freddie Tees. He was flying with P/O Warner Ottley DFC when shot down north of Hamm by anti-aircraft fire.

Somehow in the crash his rear turret broke away and although badly burned he survived to become a prisoner of war. He returned to the scene of the crash in the 80s where a memorial had been put to the memory of the members of his crew who had lost their lives. Somehow this played on his mind, how could he have survived and they not and it was not long after this that he died.

It is interesting to note that in the letter Guy Gibson sent to Freddie's mother he said he was the front gunner.

One of the fourteen gunners that perished on the Dams raid was Sgt Jack Liddell from Weston-Super-Mare. He joined the RAF in 1941 having been born in 1925 so at the time of joining the RAF he was 16. He flew a full tour of 30 operations with 61 Squadron, the Dams raid was his 31st. He was flying as rear gunner with F/Lt Barlow DFC of the RAAF, they had come as a crew from 61 Squadron. He was the first man to take off for the dams raid but their aircraft hit a high voltage cable en route and they crashed at Emmerich, all were killed instantly.

The bouncing bomb however was captured intact by the Germans and taken away to find out what it was it was and how it worked and although they did work on a similar type of bomb they never used it in anger.

The whole crew including Jack Liddell are now buried in the Reichswald War Cemetery, Germany.

A number of air gunners were decorated for the dams raid; one in particular was F/Lt Trevor-Roper who flew in the rear turret with Wing Commander Guy Gibson the commanding officer of 617. He began his flying with the RAF in 1940 with No. 50 Squadron. His pilot on Hampdens was Wing Commander Gus Walker later Air Chief Marshal Sir Augustus Walker. He flew well over fifty operations and was awarded the DFC for the dams operation having been awarded the DFM in 1942. He had fired upon the gun towers at the Mohne Dam taking the heat off the other incoming aircraft.

The grave of F/O Brian Jagger DFM in Cambridge. *Alan Cooper*

He was later killed on the infamous Nuremberg raid on 30/31st March 1944 flying with 97 Pathfinder Squadron. This operation was the greatest losses suffered by Bomber Command in WWII.

Gibson's front gunner George Deering was also awarded the DFC having used his guns on the outwards trip as well as on the Mohne Dam.

F/Lt Micky Martin's gunner F/Sgt Tammy Simpson was awarded the DFM having again attacked the defences at the Mohne Dam. Mick Martin went to become Air Marshal Sir Harold Martin.

F/Lt David Shannon's rear gunner P/O Jack Buckley was also awarded the DFC.

F/Sgt Bill Townsend's front gunner Dougie Webb and rear gunner Sgt Ray Wilkinson were awarded the DFM.

F/S George Powell. *George Powell*

F/Sgt John Hanaha VC. *Chas Bowyer*

Another operation that has over the year been made famous with books and films is the airborne operation to Arnhem in September 1944.

F/Lt William Dawson of No. 620 Squadron took part in three sorties on Arnhem. The first towing gliders and then two resupply missions, both of which were carried out under the most intense anti-aircraft fire. It was 26th operation of his second tour having completed one with Bomber Command. His sixty-two operations had been carried out in North West Europe, France, the Mediterranean and North Africa. He was in 1944 awarded the DFC. F/Sgt Jack Welton was awarded the DFM in 1944 flying with No. 190 Squadron on operations to Arnhem. On a supply drop to the troops on the ground at Arnhem and from a height of 1,500 ft the aircraft was attacked by a fighter. He gave a running commentary throughout the attack and with his skilful and accurate fire the fighter was seen to go into a dive with smoke pouring from it. A second fighter made an attack but soon broke off the engagement. It was his 20th operation.

F/Lt Sutton was awarded the Order of the Bronze Lion from the Dutch Government for his actions at Arnhem. He flew on three sorties to Arnhem with F/Lt Reg Turner DFC of No. 299 Squadron and on 21st September the third sortie his aircraft was hit by anti-aircraft fire and he was injured in both legs. The hydraulic pipe line leading to his turret was severed causing a severe fire in front and beneath his turret. Despite this he continued to operate his turret manually and kept up a continues and accurate fire on enemy ground positions. With the flames increasing and ammunition beginning to explode in the feed chutes leading to the turret he still kept on firing until the supplies had been dropped and the aircraft had turned away from the Arnhem perimeter. When he finally baled out his clothing was seen to be on fire.

Tammy Simpson in July 1943. *Tammy Simpson*

On the ground because of his wounds he had to crawl most of the time in an attempt to evade capture but was seen by the enemy and taken prisoner.

F/Lt W R Chalk was awarded the Order of the Bronze Cross by the Dutch. He was also in No. 299 Squadron flying with Commanding Officer Wg/Cdr Davis who sadly when the aircraft was shot down killed. F/Lt Chalk continued to fire until ordered to abandon the aircraft by his captain. He also was taken prisoner.

F/Sgt Ronald Bedford was 19 at the time of Arnhem. As they spotted the drop zone and at the time towing a Horsa glider the enemy fire was intense and accurate and when he spotted an anti-aircraft battery mounted on a truck at the edge of a field he tried desperately to turn his guns on it.

His fire seemed to do the trick as the battery stopped firing.

He described the scene in front of his eyes as chaotic with gilders everywhere going down in steep dives, and then levelling out and coasting down. He thought to himself I wonder how many will make it.

CHAPTER SIX

Telegraphist Air Gunners

Telegraphist Air Gunners, or TAGS as they were known, operated in the Fleet Air Arm from 1922 to 1950, providing communications by Morse Code and manning the rear gun. Three thousand TAGS were trained in the 28 year life span of the branch; 507 were lost through enemy action or flying accidents and sixty-nine became prisoners of war. Most TAGS served only for the period of WWII; returning to their civilian occupations in 1945/46. In 2003 their oldest member Teddy Wicks died at the age of nearly 98, now Clarry Train 95 is the oldest living member. He had to turn his hands to many things. Signals of every sort, wireless maintenance and operation, guns and armament generally, all were within his remit. On flying boats and seaplanes and when the machine was on the water, he became a sort of 'deck hand'. The TAGS were awarded two Conspicuous Gallantry Medals(Sea), 115 Distinguished Service Medals, twenty British Empire Medals and 134 men were mentioned in dispatches. They also served in seventy-seven different aircraft carriers, eleven Battleships/Battle Cruisers, thirty-six Cruisers, and a number of other ships.

TAGS training took 11 months and consisted of Seamanship, Radio Theory, and Morse Code (on the ground and in the air), Air Gunnery and some basic navigation. They were also expected to service and maintain their own radios and guns. Fifty per cent of TAGS were trained in the UK and fifty per cent in Canada. The aircraft they flew in consisted of Skuas, Swordfish, Albacores, Walrus, Fulmars, Barracudas and Avengers and in every theatre of the war. One of their roles was protecting Atlantic, Arctic and Indian Ocean convoys, as well as those searching for and attacking enemy shipping.

Their first kill was on 26 September 1939 when a Dornier 18 was shot down by CPO Bryan Seymour flying in a Skua of 803 Squadron. He had joined the Royal Navy aged 15 and after the war served in the RAF as a fire officer but died in 1976 aged 60.

Back in 1912, when the Royal Flying Corps was formed the Army airships and twelve aircraft to be used in conjunction with ships were given to the Royal Navy. In WWI the Royal Naval Air Service had 67,000 officers and men, 103 airships, 126 coastal stations and 2,949 aircraft. In WWII, and now called the Fleet Air Arm, it had 3,700 aircraft and 72, 000 officers and men.

In April 1940, Germany invaded Norway. Their landing forces were supported by two cruisers one of which was the *Konigsberg*. Various forces such as shore batteries and Bomber Command attacked the ship but with little effect. It was Lt Cdr Geoffrey Hare of 800 Squadron Fleet Air Arm who spotted the cruisers in Bergen harbour and with 803 Squadron it was decided to make a dawn attack on the harbour. But, as it was on the limit of the Skua aircraft's range when flying from Lossiemouth, it demanded spot-on navigation and formation flying. Sixteen aircraft and sixteen crewmen took off on 10 April 1940, and arrived over Bergen at 7.20 GMT. The first bomb dropped on the *Konisgsberg* knocked out its electrical power, which then in turn put out the 88mm guns and made the only other guns available have to operate on manual power. By the time the attack was over the ship was on fire and sinking by the bows. Two hours after the attack the ship sank with a portion of her stern protruding from the water. One aircraft was lost: Red 1 L2923 A8P flown by Lt. Bryan John Smeeton. On the return trip to base it went into a spin and crashed; he and his crewman (TAG) Midshipman Fred Watkinson, aged 18, were killed. Fred is now on the Lee-On-Solent Memorial.

On 26 April 1940, H.M.S. *Ark Royal* was operating in Norwegian waters. Six Skua aircraft of 801 Squadron took off from her deck at 1000 hours. At the same time three Heinkel IIIPs took off from Oslo to provide aerial support for German troops, but not finding targets to attack they started to look for secondary targets in the same area. To do this the formation split up and at 10,000 ft one Heinkel was confronted with 801 Squadron. The Skuas attacked from out of the sun and the Heinkel's ventral gunner was killed and both engines badly damaged. The pilot, however, was able to make a perfect wheels-up landing on a snow-covered mountain side. Two Skua pilots, Lt Cdr Bramwell and Lt Martyn, claimed the kill. Three of the Heinkel crew survived and, leaving the dead gunner, made their way for three days through deep snow to where they thought German troops would be camped. However, they fell into the hands of Norwegian troops who handed them over to the British and they spent the rest of the war as PoWs in Britain and Canada. When the aircraft was found in 1943 by a small Norwegian boy the body of the gunner, Willi Stock, was still in his turret having been well preserved in the conditions. On reaching his teens the boy returned and buried Stock by the side of his aircraft. Stock's body was exhumed after the war and is now buried in Oslo.

After the war a search was made for the crews of the two Skuas. Unfortunately, both pilots had died but Martyn's TAG Reg Davies was soon traced and also the observer Lt Collett who after the war became a

Captain. The German crew had also been traced. On 13 August 1979 they all met up and were taken to the crash site by helicopter. On the spot where the Heinkel had crash landed was a solitary, wooden cross that had been erected by Norwegians to the memory of Willi Stock. The Heinkel was recovered in 1976 and by the time the men met the aircraft had been fully restored to its original glory. The Germans were keen to show their British counterparts inside and while inside the aircraft John Collett informed the pilot of the Heinkel, Richard Gumbrect, that the Skua would not have caught them if they had been another 1,000 ft higher; the reply was, "Now you tell me."

In May 1941, it was Nos 10 and 818 Squadrons from HMS *Ark Royal* which led the attack on the German Battleship *Bismarck* which had earlier sunk HMS *Hood* with the loss of 1,416 crew. On 25 May the *Bismarck* was located 550 miles west of Land's End by a Catalina of 209 Squadron flown by P/O D. A. Briggs. HMS *Victorious* launched seven Swordfish armed with torpedoes and one torpedo hit the starboard beam of *Bismarck* but did not do very much damage and from the tremendous fire put by the ship two Swordfish were lost and two of the supporting Fulmar aircraft. A striking force from *Ark Royal* was despatched, but it was the second attack by fifteen Swordfish from HMS *Victorious* that did the damage. One torpedo hit the starboard quarter and wrecked the steering gear which caused the ship to steer in circles. This enabled HMS *Dorsetshire* to catch-up with the *Bismarck* and finish her off with further torpedoes.

One Swordfish of 852 Squadron was flown by Sub Lt Pat Jackson and in May 1941 he was engaged in the search for the *Bismarck* when he found he was running out of petrol and had to ditch in the sea. As he came down low he saw ahead in the water a lone lifeboat and having got down safely Jackson and his crew found the lifeboat was half full of water so he and his crew, including Leading Airmen Sparkes his TAG, started to bale out with their flying boots. At first they set sail for the coast of Scotland and then later, having survived a 12 hour gale, for the convoy routes. After a few days Sparkes, still wearing his flying boots found that his feet were turning black and Jackson started to massage his feet to keep the life in them. They then came in contact with another lifeboat full of Norwegians. For a few moment they discussed with the Norwegians the best route to take and then they went on their way. On the tenth day they saw a ship but although they fired cartridges from their Very pistol the ship failed to see them but when Jackson soaked a rag in oil and stuffed it into the barrel of the pistol which set the rag alight and within minutes the ship, the *Lagerfoss* from Iceland saw them and turned around and they were rescued.

In February 1942 came the infamous Channel Dash under the code name Operation Cerberus when the German ships the *Scharnhorst* and *Gneisenau* broke out from their French port in poor weather into the English Channel. At the time six Swordfish aircraft of 825 Squadron commanded by Lt Cmdr Eugene Esmonde DSO were based at Manston in Kent. (He had got his DSO for an attack on the *Bismarck* from HMS *Victorious*. His TAG on that occasion was PO Stanley Parker and it was he who signalled back 'Have attacked with torpedoes, only one observed.' Three TAGs were awarded the DSM including Parker). When Esmonde took off in W5984-H at 12.25 to attack the ships he was told he would have an escort of five Fighter Squadrons, but only one arrived and so he set off. Two of the escort squadrons were late and although they set off out to sea failed to locate Esmond's small force. It was Esmonde who went into attack first but his slow lumbering Swordfish was soon hit and with the port main wing shattered he crashed into the sea. Of the force of five not one returned although five men were picked-up out of the sea.

Some time later, Lt Cmdr Esmond's body was picked up in the River Medway and he is now buried in Gillingham Cemetery in Kent. He was 32 and came from Ireland. He had been a survivor from the first Royal Navy ship sunk in WWII, the carrier HMS *Courageous* sunk on 17 September 1939. His crew was TAG Petty Officer William Clinton now buried in Ruislip Churchyard, Middlesex, and observer Lt W H Williams now buried in Aylesham, Kent. Bill Clinton was last seen by a Spitfire pilot on the back of the fuselage trying to beat out the flames in the tailplane. The second Swordfish was piloted by Sub Lt Brian Rose and his TAG was Petty Officer Ambrose Johnson DSM, aged 22. Johnson was killed early on in the action and Rose was wounded in the back. The petrol tank had been fractured. The observer Lt Edgar Lee tried to take over the gun but could not move Johnson's body. They crashed into the sea and Lee was able to get Rose out of the cockpit and into a dinghy. Johnson's body was, unfortunately, jammed in the aircraft and went down with it. The third Swordfish was flown by Sub Lt (Pat) Kingsmill and his aircraft was hit in the engine and the upper port-wing was set on fire. In spite of this TAG Leading Airman Don Bunce was still firing and shot down an enemy fighter. After dropping their torpedo at a range of about 3,000 yards they were also shot down but survived and were picked up by an MTB within ten minutes. The last three Swordfish flew into an inferno of anti-aircraft fire and were not seen again. Johnson is now remembered on the Lee-On-Solent Memorial in Hampshire. Esmonde was later awarded a posthumous Victoria Cross, the four surviving officers a DSO and Don Bunce the Conspicuous Gallantry Medal. For this action 1 VC, 3 DSOs, 1 CGM and 12 MiDs were awarded. Admiral Ramsey, Flag Officer Commanding Dover said later "In my opinion the gallant sortie of these six Swordfish constitutes one of the finest exhibitions of self sacrifice and devotion to duty that the war has yet witnessed."

Leading Airmen TAG William G. Smith, age 22 and now buried in Gillingham Cemetery, Leading Airman TAG Ernest Tapping, age 26 and on the Lee-On-Solent Memorial and Leading Airman TAG Henry T.A. Wheeler age 30 also on the Lee-On-Solent Memorial were also awarded posthumous Mention in Dispatches.

In 1994 on the discovery of Will Clinton's grave the Kent Fleet Air Arm Association refurbished the grave and made it more fitting for a worthy hero. It was then that the story came out about him getting out of his cockpit, crawling along the fuselage and beating out the flames with his hands and then edged his way back into the cockpit and continued firing at attacking aircraft. Ken Phillips undertook his gunnery training at RNAS St Merryn, North Cornwall. The training was carried out on Fairey Albacore and Swordfish aircraft, equipped with a single .303 Vickers machine-gun on a Scarffe ring. Although they did not have an Avenger aircraft to train on they did have a turret mounted on a Queen Mary trailer parked at the cliff edge with the target, a large rock a few yards off shore. The turret was quite cramped and more suited to shorter men than the taller ones like Ken. But, in fairness to the Admiralty, most Avenger TAGs were short rather than tall. He later flew in Barracudas which had much more room but were scary in their own way.

Frank Grainger left school at the age of 14 and worked for a wrought-iron manufacturer. In 1939 he saw an advert in a National Newspaper showing a sailor walking along the deck of an aircraft carrier and an aircraft in the background. It went on to say, 'Pilots, Observers and Telegraphist Air gunners wanted to man naval aircraft. Defend your country now before it is too late, join the Navy and start training at once, enjoy sea and air? Frank posted his application that same day. A few weeks later he was asked to take an educational exam in a Manchester School. Two weeks after that there came a knock at Frank's door and a naval Petty Officer was standing there. He asked Frank if he would allow him to interview him for about 30 minutes, he was from the Birmingham Recruitment Office and he wanted to talk to him about the examination he had taken in Manchester. He had a sheet with fifty questions on it. The examination at Manchester had not been a success and he was trying out a new method of attracting recruits and establishing the educational standard. Less than a week after answering the questions he was summoned to go to the Birmingham Recruitment Office for a medical. Having passed this he was then asked to attend the next day when he would be enrolled in the Fleet Air Arm and transported to Portsmouth Barracks. Although his parents were not happy at him going to sea they wished him well. He was now a prospective TAG.

At Portsmouth Barracks, named HMS *Victory*, Frank and the other recruits were each allocated a room, and then they went to the stores to draw up a blanket and hammock. This was followed by kitting out and learning how to march. From there he went to HMS *St Vincent* a few miles away from Portsmouth. This was to be his home for the next six weeks. Here he learnt the basics of being a good sailor. Frank had a problem as he could not swim and when he left Portsmouth he still could not swim. He now says that if he had been able to look into a crystal ball he would have practised much more.

In 1940 he got the news he wanted, a posting to HMS *Kestrel* a Royal Naval Station at Worthy Down. But when they arrived there were no runways, just a large field and a few hangers and one or two training aircraft around. They turned out to be Blackburn Sharks, the mainstay training aircraft. The accommodation was wooden huts while the staff lived in brick accommodation. All acting TAGS were called by a senior officer as 'Cochranes Young Ladies' because, he said, they liked to prance around showing off in their flying kit. Here again he tried to learn to swim but after 3 months he still could not swim. Much of the training was on Morse Code which they had to work up to a rate of twenty-one words a minute. Later when serving in the Western Desert he received a return message that his Morse transmitting was excellent and he had been awarded top marks by the inspectors who monitored all transmissions. While at HMS *Kestrel* he contracted German Measles and was taken to the Royal Naval Hospital at Haslar. His training also consisted of stripping the Lewis gun and then reassembling it blindfolded. The Shark aeroplane was a three seater for pilot, observer and TAG with a metal body and no cover over the cockpit.

His first squadron was 823 at HMS *Sparrowhawk* on Orkney Island. They were equipped with Swordfish aircraft and the main duties were anti-submarine patrols and attacking shipping which was in support of the Norwegian campaign. For the first three months Frank carried out these duties in atrocious weather: heavy rain and then snow with high winds which made the open cockpit of the Swordfish most uncomfortable. On 22 October 1940, they took off for the usual rather boring anti-submarine patrol but after an hour the engine started to play up, cutting out and then picking up again. As the problem grew worse an SOS was put out by Frank and the depth charges jettisoned into the sea. As he looked over the side he saw the discarded depth charges were below them and following the same course as the Swordfish. The pilot was told and at that moment the engine broke into life and the aircraft climbed away. When the depth charges hit the water they exploded. On return to base it was found that there was water in the petrol tank, from then on all petrol was filled using a chamois leather as a filter. At the end of November 1940 they were posted to HMS *Argus*, an ancient aircraft carrier (nicknamed the coffin carrier). The carrier would then sail to Gibraltar where they would join up with HMS *Ark Royal* and on to Malta. However, the sea was too rough to land on *Argus* so they had to land at Prestwick and then travel into the town to be billeted in hotels.

They next day they managed to land on the flight deck of *Argus* but it was a very bad landing and all that stopped them going over the side was the arrester hook. The Swordfish was a write-off and later used for spares. Frank found it was much rougher on the carrier than he imagined and he was seasick all the way and consequently spent the entire journey to Gibraltar in the cockpit of the wrecked aircraft. He was now without an aircraft and rather on a limb. He then transferred to a ship on convoy duty to Malta. Here he joined HMS *Illustrious* but it had been badly damaged when a large bomb had penetrated its armoured flight deck and exploded in the hangar below killing a great number of the crew. He then boarded a destroyer bound for Alexandria and from there he went on to Hal Far airfield.

The first flight was on 2 February 1941, once again searching for enemy submarines but this time in the Mediterranean. On another occasion it looked as though Frank was about to use his guns and the black spot they could see in the distance got bigger and bigger until they recognised it as a Short Sunderland flying boat so all was well. It was then on to Crete where orders came to fly all their aircraft back to Dekheila, Egypt. All ground crew and most of the aircrew were taken to Suda Bay where they boarded SS *Destro* an old cargo ship and their escort to Alexandria was a submarine and a Dutch motor torpedo boat. The *Destro* was as primitive as one can get, no toilets, the food hard biscuits and tea and accommodation on the deck. Every day they were bombed and the ship next to them received a direct hit: it tipped up on its stern and sank within minutes. Frank was terrified that should a bomb strike his ship with him lying on a steel deck he would be wrapped in steel plating and trapped as the ship went down.

The German invasion of Crete occurred the day after they left that island. But they were soon off again this time on HMS *Flamingo* to Cyprus, with the airstrip at Lakatania. Here Frank became bored with not doing anything so he volunteered to fly in a Walrus amphibian plane flown by a Royal Marine officer. The role was searching for missing aircraft and anti-submarine patrols. He then went on a special trip to Port Said, Egypt and then on to Dekheila where they stayed for two days before flying to Palestine and then back to Cyprus.

As the Swordfish were showing signs of wear and tear they were sent to Dekheila for a major overhaul and they were replaced by Albacore biplanes. They had a metal fuselage with a Perspex cover over the cockpit. This was in contrast to the Swordfish whose fuselage was just metal tubes covered with a linen cloth and then painted with dope. However Cyprus was not the best place for the Albacore as it had a tendency to overheat but Frank wished they had them in the Orkney Islands. From Cyprus they sailed back to Dekheila to replenish stores and pick up more transports: one being a self contained radio lorry. Frank was detailed to drive this in a convoy and meet up with planes at a landing strip near the front line. The airfields were just cleared strips and each was given a number such as LG 002 etc. The accommodation was four TAGS to a tent. Here they were often attacked by German Ju 88s, some having the noisy siren attached to each bomb. Once the radios and guns had been checked it was back to business and flying at 2,000 to 3,000 ft attacking troops, tanks and enemy transport on the ground. The fire from the ground was at times fierce and accurate and on 7 December 1941(The Day Japan attacked Pearl Harbor) they were hit in the rudder but were able to carry out the task assigned and return to base. On one occasion they had to land behind enemy lines with an engine overheating. As they were not near any enemy installations they decided to stay there and let the engine cool down and then try to take off again. This they did and were able to get airborne and to land at the nearest Allied landing ground where the engine was examined but pronounced unfit for flying. They were able to get a lift on an American transport aircraft but as there were no seats they had to sit on the floor. Back at base they borrowed another aircraft and attacked a group of tanks and enemy transports and made a direct hit on a tank which exploded into hundreds of coloured lights. Frank was able to machine gun some of the transports.

When their replacement aircraft arrived they were told they had to go on a special mission but as an extra petrol tank was being fitted into the observer's cockpit it meant he could not go with them. The aircraft, each armed with a torpedo, left without Frank to go to Malta but were never seen again.

On Christmas Day 1941, the squadron was moved deep into the desert in the area of Tobruk. A new squadron, 821, was formed to take over the desert operations and Frank volunteered and was accepted to join it. As Frank waited for transport to take him to his new squadron a Royal Marine captain came and asked Frank who he was and where he was a going. When Frank told him 821 Sqn the officer said, "So am I as the new commanding officer" He went on to ask Frank about desert operations and other questions as it was his first experience of these conditions. No. 821 Sqn was based at Fsyid on the banks of the Nile.

On 4 April 1942, a flight of three Albacores was detailed to drop flares on a range of mountains to the west of the Red Sea. This would indicate a target to ships at sea, the main one being a rock on a small clearance in the mountain. After dropping their flares they waited for the first shell from the ship to arrive but just then the engine on the Albacore stopped and the observer told Frank to radio the ship and tell them not to shoot as they were about to crash on the target. Frank sent a message 'Do not fire, crashing on target'. They hit the mountain and then the rock and their ammunition was torn away from its mountings and hit Frank on the legs and chest. Despite this horrendous crash they all got out okay with only bruises and shock. A boat was launched from the ship and they were taken out to it.

On 13 June 1942, the day after Frank's 21st birthday, they landed on a strip operated by the RAF. There was going to be a big raid on Derna and they were detailed to drop flares over the target area. As they taxied in the pitch dark two Wellington bombers collided and were both set on fire. They went on to do a lot of mine laying in Derna and Tobruck harbours.

On 6 June 1942, they set off to drop bombs on Derna and as they arrived over the target Frank saw a flight of Me 109s but then they were lit-up by a searchlight. Frank pointed his gun towards it to try and knock it out but they had recently been fitted with electric reflector sights and as he swung the gun around the plug came out and he was left in the darkness with no reflector sight. Nevertheless, they were able to drop their bombs and make for home. As they crossed the bay on the way home Frank saw a motor torpedo boat but as he went to open fire the observer said, "Hold your fire, it may be one of ours" and with an Aldis lamp asked for a recognition reply. The MTB's reply was in the form of gun fire so Frank immediately opened fire and he saw his armour piecing bullets bouncing off the boat. As they circled he was able to fire four pans of ammunition but as the MTB was firing a heavy gun and the fire getting closer they decided to make for home.

It was certainly a busy period in the desert. Attacks on El Alamein, Mersa Matruh and supporting Wellington bomber attacks was only a fraction of the work done during this period. He then left 815 Squadron and volunteered for 821 Squadron but he was ordered back to the UK for a rest period.

In March 1943 Frank was promoted to Petty Officer Airman and posted to an instructing position at Lee-on-Solent. At the end of 1943 it was again time for operations and he joined 826 Squadron flying Barracudas but Frank did not take to the high tailplane which restricted the firing area for the rear gun.

In June 1944 he joined the new aircraft carrier HMS *Indefatigable*. The TAGS were allocated a large mess right up in the bows of the carrier. The one snag was that in heavy seas the bows would come right up and then go down with a thud. It was thought that they were heading for the Far East but they were hastily rerouted because of the serious threat from the German battleship *Tirpitz* now in a fiord in Northern Norway. Their job was to sink it; they were to carry a 1,600 lb armour piercing bomb and would be given a fighter escort. The other carriers with them were the *Formidable*, and *Furious* plus a few destroyers for anti-submarine protection.

They took off on 17 July 1944 on Operation Mascot. Ninety-five aircraft with *Indefatigable* force 820 and 826 being led by Lt Cdr Temple-West. As each aircraft took off it went out of sight below the deck as it initially lost height but slowly they all gained height. When all was in formation they headed northwards keeping low over the sea to avoid the German radar. When the coastline came they started to climb to avoid the mountains of Norway. By now the Germans knew they were coming and started to prepare. Consequently, when they arrived over the *Tirpitz* at about 10,000 ft they were met with gun fire and German fighters. The fighters were not much of a problem as the fighter escort was dealing with them. Their escorts were eighteen Corsairs from *Formidable*, eighteen Hellcats from *Furious* and twelve Fireflies from *Indefatigable*.

Because of a smoke screen from the ship and also shore generators only the tops of the masts of *Tirpitz* were visible so they decided to attack a tanker on the premise that the *Tirpitz* would need oil. Although they did not see the tanker hit, it was later reported that a tanker had been sunk.

In February 1941 a squadron of aircraft was transferred to the naval air station at Maleme in Crete. They were followed by Fulmars and Brewster Buffaloes from Egypt who would provide fighter cover for the Swordfish, the naval base at Suda Bay, convoys, and in general to combat the increasing force of enemy air attacks. When they took off to intercept large formations of Italian S.79s escorted by C.R 42s only one flown by Sub-Lt R.C. Kay with Leading Airmen Stockman as air gunner was able to intercept the enemy bombers. They shot down one, damaged two and two collided before they met their end. It was their first combat.

On Easter Sunday, 1942, an Albacore from HMS *Indomitable* was searching for the Japanese fleet in the Indian Ocean when attacked by a Mitsubishi 96. the air gunner from Yorkshire was hit in the arm but continued to fire his gun, he then made a signal and got out his sighting reports. Having driven off the enemy he extracted the bullet from his arm with a screw driver, put it back in his pocket and said, "Must keep this as a souvenir," then promptly fainted from loss of blood while the observer was applying first aid.

After a bombing raid on the seaplane base at Trondheim, a Skua pilot Lt A.B.Fraser-Harris with air gunner Leading Airmen G.Russell force-landed in a small fiord. They were compelled to swim ashore in very cold water. They met a group of Norwegians who, thinking they were Germans, were most unfriendly but as soon as they realised who they were they were given warm clothing and food. Dressed as Norwegians they walked to the head of the valley, where they then got a sleigh from a farm and travelled five miles up to a lake in the mountains. When they left the sleigh and walked for some miles ultimately arriving at another fiord and there travelled by boat to Folafo where the Norwegian police found them a taxi and in this they arrived at the British Brigade HQ having covered 69 miles in 24 hours, and eventually rejoined HMS *Glorious*.

Gordon Lambert a rear gunner from 820 Sqn recalled that one of the fighter-bomber squadrons carried parcels of aluminium strips or 'Window' as it was known to drop in the hope of confusing the German radar system. The losses were light: only one Barracuda and one Corsair failed to return. It was later revealed that although a near miss was felt no damage was done to the *Tirpitz*.

On 22 August 1944, another attempt to sink the *Tirpitz* was made, codenamed operation Goodwood, but this time from HMS *Formidable*. However, they obtained the same result because of the smokescreen. Yet again on 29 August, twenty-one Barracudas and seventeen Corsairs attacked the *Tirpitz*. This time the ship was hit when a 500 lb bomb fell on the top of 'B' turret and then a 1,600 lb bomb penetrated the main armoured deck and travelled through eight decks before lodging deep in the bowels of the ship but failed to explode. It was found by German experts to have only half the explosives it should have, the other half being sand. However, the ship never went to open sea again and was towed south to shallow waters near Tromso until 12 November when Lancasters of 9 and 617 Squadrons using 12,000 lb Tallboy bombs finally turned the ship over.

On returning to *Formidable* from their attack on the *Tirpitz* Frank and his crew found a strong swell and the carrier rising and falling. As they reached the stern of the ship and tried to land the ship suddenly rose striking the aircraft, the arrestor hook did not catch on the cables and they crashed into the safety barriers smashing the propellers and causing other minor damage.

From here they went to Lee-on-Solent where they were supplied with the American Avenger aircraft before flying back to HMS *Indefatigable* at Portsmouth and then they sailed for the Far East and the war against the Japanese.

In January 1945, the target was the large oil installations at Palembang in Sumatra. It would be the largest attack by aircraft executed by the Fleet Air Arm in WWII. The carrier would carry them as far as possible to the western coast but as the oil fields were on the eastern side of Sumatra they would have to climb over jungle-covered mountains and then fly a long distance over a stretch of jungle to reach Palembang. As the barrage balloons near the target came into sight so did the flak, the target for Frank's aircraft was the power house or the adjacent chemical plant. They dived and hit the power house at the same time as someone else scored a hit on it. The chemical plant was also destroyed.

During the return flight Frank looked through the inspection hole into the bomb bay and found one bomb had failed to detach itself. After two attempts the bomb finally left the aircraft. Their losses were not severe but nine of the crews lost were taken to Singapore and beheaded.

The fleet then proceeded to Australia; the aircraft took off and landed at Nowra field and the fleet went on to Sydney. While here Frank and the rest of the crews were given a week's leave in Sydney where they were treated very well by the residents.

On 1 April 1945, the captain told the crew that they were in for a busy day and were going to drop a load of Easter eggs on the Japanese. But as he was finishing his talk the actions stations sounded: the fleet was being attacked from the air. A kamikaze aircraft crashed on the flight deck and island (the bridge area on a carrier). Fourteen men, including the carrier's surgeon, a Canadian, were killed. The sick bay was a complete wreck and bodies were lying everywhere. Smoke was pouring from the funnel and Frank helped to carry the dead down to the weather deck to be prepared for burial.

Frank's last bombing operation was on 24 May 1945, part of operation Iceberg at Miyako Jima airfield. The Americans then captured Okinawa and Frank left for Australia on 26 May 1945.

One of the first TAGs was George Kent who joined the Royal Navy in 1909. Later he transferred to the Royal Naval Air Service and began flying as a gun-layer which was the early name for an Air Gunner in the RNAS. During WWI his aircraft, a Handley Page, was brought down and he became a PoW but owing to the ill treatment, including malnutrition, he never fully recovered and died in 1933 aged 40. After WWI he joined the

RAF, and served with the rank of Warrant Officer with No. 111 Fighter Squadron. In 1933, when he died, his widow with two small children was refused a pension because he had died of influenza/pneumonia.

Bob Vargerson became a TAG in 1944 having joined the Royal Navy at the age of 17. He had been trained in Nova Scotia and when he arrived back in the UK he joined 820 Squadron flying Avengers on HMS *Indefatigable* and was soon on his way to the Far East. The operation on the Palembang refineries 150 miles from the entry point on the Western Coast of Sumatra turned out to be not only one of the most dangerous operations but also the most successful in the Far East during WWII. The task was assigned to four carriers: the *Indomitable, Illustrious, Victorious* and *Indefatigable*. They sailed from Trincomalee on 16 January 1945 and the operation against the refineries was on the 24th. The *Indefatigable* had one Squadron of Avengers, two of Seafires and one of Fireflys.

The strike was to consist of twelve Avengers from each of the four carriers, the top and middle cover was provided by the Corsairs and Hellcats, the bow close cover by the Fireflys and the stern close cover by the Corsairs. Some Corsairs were also to provide 'Ramrod' strikes. There were two Walrus aircraft standing by for air Sea Rescue duties and some Seafires were to provide cover for the fleet.

All crews were briefed on strike and escape procedure including removing all rank insignia because the behaviour by the Japanese towards prisoners was well known . The oil fields were surrounded by airfields, anti-aircraft guns and balloons and heavy losses were expected. All the crews were issued with two bars of black chocolate, a box of matches, sea biscuits, compass, maps of Sumatra, a condom (to keep the matches dry) and twenty gold sovereigns. A .45 revolver was strapped to one leg, a knife strapped to the other and they also had an Indonesian/English phrase book.

On approaching the coast at 10,000 ft they were attacked by Zekes and Zero fighters from all directions and Bob remembers that firing his guns from this modern aircraft after the free mounted Lewis gun was like driving a Rolls Royce car compared to a VW Beetle. On arrival the target was well alight and they dived through heavy Ack Ack and the barrage balloons pulling out at one thousand feet and dropping four x 500 lb bombs into the refinery.

It was reported that the Avengers had done a great job at Palembang, and with the Browning .5, power-operated turret they were able to do a lot of damage: sixty-eight Japanese aircraft were shot down with seven probables. The damage to the oilfields meant the output was reduced to 35 per cent of normal. The downside was that the Fleet lost forty-one aircraft in the encounter. Bob's force lost a quarter of its aircraft. Nine of the aircrew shot down were captured by the Japanese but were executed after the surrender in the Far East had been declared. One was TAG Jim McRae and a memorial has now been set into the floor of the Fleet Air Arm Church, St Barthomolews, Yeovilton to the memory of the Palembang Nine. There is also a memorial in Changi Prison Museum in Singapore.

Bob's tour of duty in the Far East consisted of twenty-six dive-bombing strikes on islands and ships in the Pacific area with his ship ending up in Tokyo harbour for the signing of the armistice. All the aircraft were thrown over the side and the hangers turned into hospitals for returning PoWs, British, Australians and Americans. But when they arrived in Southampton on his 20th birthday in November 1945, they were greeted by a handful of dockers and kept on board for 24 hours before being allowed to go home, even the PoWs had to go through customs. From there on they became known as 'The Forgotten Fleet.'

George Dodwell served with 815 Squadron in 1941 on anti-submarine patrols. In the back of the Swordfish the rear cockpit was full of Very cartridges and two pistols. These were fired all over the sky at night to provide some sort of illumination for the pilot to carry out his attack. On one moonless night the pilot spotted a submarine on the surface. The observer tapped George on the back and he started to fire the Very pistol but it misfired. The misfired cartridge later exploded in his face but as he was wearing a flying helmet and goggles it saved his face but then the blazing cartridges fell into the open box of unused cartridges on the floor of the cockpit. This started a firework display with Very lights shooting out all over the place into the night sky, down the tail and into the observers cockpit. Therefore George started to throw cartridges, ammo pans and log books out of the aircraft and if the observer had not been attached he would have gone as well. Somehow they got back with most of the fabric burned off the rear of the fuselage and his cockpit a glowing mass. Having taken off his flying Irvine trousers he got out of the aircraft wearing only a short shirt and flying boots. Both his hands were badly burned and he was taken to the sick bay, to be seen by the MO and what he described as a gorgeous nursing sister. When they had finished and bandaged his hands he looked like a boxer.

'Murgy' Brown had been in the Royal Navy but began his training as a TAG in 1930. He started flying on a Bristol Fighter and although his pilot had only one leg he was an excellent pilot. Murgy soon learned that the slipstream in an open cockpit played havoc with component parts of a Lewis gun. The cocking handles and ammunition pans would fly about and drop over the side if you did not hang on to them. In six weeks of training three guns and four pans of ammo were lost. When the war started in September 1939 he was serving on the carrier HMS *Courageous* and on 17 September they set off from Plymouth to start operations in the Western Approaches.

At 8pm on 17th two torpedoes hit them on the port side and the carrier heeled over. Murgy was able to get out and on to a carley float when suddenly there was a huge wall of water looming up and over them and when he surfaced the carrier had gone taking 500 men with her. They were picked up by a tramp steamer and later transferred to the destroyer *Inglefield*. It was a miracle that only one TAG was lost.

Murgy became a Warrant Air Gunner and joined the carrier HMS *Slinger*. While off Harwich there was a huge bang and the lights went out. They

The Fleet Air Arm Memorial on the Embankment in London. *Alan Cooper*

were later towed up to dry dock where it was discovered that they were cracked from port to starboard. The next six months was spent in dry dock with an air raid every night.

The highest decoration apart from the Victoria Cross to ratings of the Royal Navy is the Conspicuous Gallantry Medal. Chief Petty Officer (Airmen) Leonard Francis Barrick was awarded the CGM for Operation Pedestal (the bid to get supplies to Malta). He was at the time operating as a TAG with 884 Squadron flying Fulmars on HMS *Victorious*.

During the operation he was badly wounded by an explosive bullet but still kept up fire with his gun and continued to give warning to his pilot of enemy fighters until he lost consciousness. Later, having regained consciousness he was able to help the pilot, who had been blinded, to control the aircraft. Opening the hood and standing on his seat Len conveyed the batman's signals on the deck to the pilot enabling the aircraft and its crew to land safely. His medal was presented to him in 1943. Further, in 1945 while taking part in Operation Iceberg in the Pacific and flying with 820 Squadron on HMS *Indefatigable* he was awarded the Distinguished Service Medal.

Naval Airmen 1st Class Donald Arthur Bunce was awarded his CGM for attacks on the German ships *Scharnhorst* and *Gneisenau* in 1942. He was a TAG on a Swordfish of 825 Squadron and with the aircraft on fire, and the engine failing, he stayed at his guns and engaged enemy fighters and he is believed to have shot one down. Donald Bunce was presented with the medal on 28 April 1942.

In 1947 the Telegraphist Air Gunners Association was open to anybody who qualified as a TAG in the Fleet Air Arm. The members today range from 75 to 96 in age. The youngest qualified TAG member is Bob Lea who falsified his age and was flying in the Atlantic when he should have been in school, and the oldest reached the age of 95 in August 2005. Each year the Association presents the TAGA Trophy and medal to the outstanding Air Engineering Mechanic of the Year by the Air Engineering staff of HMS *Sultan*. A total of 3,000 TAGS were trained during WWII. Their feats were shooting down the first German aircraft, and the sinking of the first U-Boat by CPO Ben Rice, Leading Airmen Maurice Pacey and Les Sayer MBE, DSM who is now the President of the TAGA.

CHAPTER SEVEN

Bomber Command

The largest contingent of air gunners were in Bomber Command, with the long flights to Germany, Norway, and Italy they could find themselves in many difficult situations. To publish all the stories concerning Bomber Command air gunners would mean going into volumes instead of one chapter; here it is only possible to publish a variety.

Bert Fitchett was trained at 10 AGS Walney Island and completed forty-seven operations with Nos 149, 199 and 171 Squadron but what happened to him was during his training and before he was posted to a squadron. On 13/14 July 1943, he was at No. 12 Operation Training Unit based at Chipping Warden and flying with the Commanding Officer Wg Cdr Norman Bray DFC; it was his first operational flight with Bomber Command. Their role was to drop 'nickel' (propaganda leaflets) in the area of Rennes. Four aircraft were detailed for this operation and three were successful and two were able to obtain photographs; all good practice for the real thing of dropping bombs. The fourth aircraft flown by Wg Cdr Bray was a mile or so off track when crossing the French Coast but when about 50 miles north-east of Rennes they encountered heavy flak which damaged the port engine and the port mainplane of the Wellington. The pilot decided to carry on but soon found this was impossible as the damage was causing the aircraft to lose height at over 1,800 ft per minute. The pilot instructed Bert, who was the Wireless/operator air gunner, to inform base that they were returning and a course was set for the French coast. The nickel was jettisoned but in so doing the trailing aerial was dislodged and lost. However, and, amazing as it sounds, the pilot found that maintaining height was easiest just above stalling speed at 85 to 90mph. Originally, the crew was ordered to put on their parachutes and prepare to bale out but this order was later rescinded as the pilot was sure he could make the French coast so they should prepare to ditch. They were now down to 2,000 ft and losing height to avoid the German coastal flak.

The crew carried out the full drill without a hitch and in such a cheerful and prompt manner that Wg Cdr Bray felt very proud of his crew and was confident that they would carry out a successful ditching. They hit the water tail down and Bray told the crew to put their trust in God. The first

Aircrew recruiting poster. *Alan Cooper*

bump was okay but the second one seemed as if the aircraft was diving to the bottom of the sea. Bray was thrown right forward and felt his face break the windscreen outward. At the same time his right ankle and thigh were gripped tightly and when he opened his eyes his head was just above the water. He managed with some trouble to get out of his flying boots and on top of the fuselage. The aircraft was sitting quite high in the water and the dinghy was floating astern on the starboard side of the aircraft. The bomb aimer, navigator and Bert were all aboard but the mid-upper gunner Sgt Perkins was absent so Bray went to back to the Astrodome and found he was still inside with his boots caught by the geodetics of the Wellington. With Bray's help he was able to get out and on to the wing which stood as firm as a rock. The rear gunner P/O Stokes had cut himself out and was swimming towards the dinghy. Finally they were all in the dinghy. The aircraft stayed afloat for about 15 minutes. Next came the sea sickness and cold and all the crew were full of salt water. Bray was bleeding from the nose and it did not stop until the first aid box was opened and gauze was cut and his nose plugged. The seasick capsules soon settled them down and stopped the retching on an empty stomach. The rations were worked out and with twelve cans of water they decided they could last for six days. When the French coast came into sight they started the long haul of paddling to keep away from it.

W/C Bray in the centre and his crew. Left: F/O Wilde, Right: F/O Parkinson. Left: Sgt Perkins, Right: F/Sgt Bert Fitchett A/G, P/O Stokes A/G at the top of the photograph. *Bert Fitchett*

On the morning of 15 July twelve Typhoon aircraft of 486 New Zealand Squadron came into sight and when Bray fired their second Very cartridge the squadron leader's wing went down. Four hours later a huge mass of fighters and Hudson aircraft came into sight. One Hudson pilot, F/O Hender also from New Zealand, dropped an airborne lifeboat to within 30 yards and from a height of 700 ft. They all got in and found the engines, tiller, keel and compass. Both the bomb aimer, F/O Parkinson and Bert had experience of two-stroke engines and they set off on a heading due north. The Typhoons having refuelled at Tangmere returned and spotted twenty enemy fighters above them. Led by S/L Scott DFC and Bar they went up after them and two enemy fighters were seen shot down. A little later thirty Fw190s turned up but in the meantime Fighter Command had sent out four squadrons of Spitfires and the Germans made a hasty retreat.

After three and half hours Wg Cdr Bray and crew were picked up by an Air Sea Rescue launch HSL 177 skippered by F/Lt Allan MacDonald. The circling Spitfires having led him to the lifeboat. The crew of the launch could not do enough for them. A second launch HSL 190 towed the lifeboat back. They landed at Newhaven and were taken to the Royal Naval hospital at Swanborough. Wg Cdr Bray had a broken nose and F/O Parkinson broken ribs.

The Channel battle, as it became known, was spoken of by Lord Haw-Haw on German radio on 15 July. The centre board of the lifeboat is now on display at Tangmere Air Museum with a list of 486 Sqn's victories and a yellow skull cap worn by Wg Cdr Bray.

Wg Cdr Bray wrote to S/L Scott on 16 July and said he would never forget No. 486 Sqn and its CO S/L Scott. The letter was signed by all members of the crew. They had been in the dinghy for 34 hours. Sadly, in August 2004 Bert made his last flight to the big airfield in the air. Unfortunately, not all such incidents ended so happily.

On 26 July 1943, F/O John Austin and his crew who had arrived from No. 1658 Conversion Unit to No. 78 Squadron were on their second operation; the target the German capital, Berlin. Before reaching the target they were attacked by enemy fighters and one engine was damaged and put out of action. The attacks continued and although another engine was hit they were able to shoot down two attackers and damaged a third. Over the North Sea the second engine that had been hit failed and they crashed landed in the sea. On this occasion the aircraft sank straight away. The bomb aimer drowned but the navigator and w/operator were located by an aircraft and a dinghy dropped near them. Sgt Russell, the rear gunner was the only one who could swim and considered that the other two needed help and went to their assistance. They were hanging on to wreckage for 16 hours in the water before they were picked up by a launch, but sadly the navigator and w/operator died as they were pulled aboard. The other four, including Austin, were lost with the aircraft and their names are on the Runneymede Memorial. Sgt Russell survived and was awarded the DFM.

On Sunday 26 July 1942, No. 115 Squadron was preparing for an operation to attack Hamburg. The CO, Wg Cdr Frank Wright, was leading in a Wellington BJ615-G, his crew were all second tour men and normally flew with flight commander S/L Cousens. Sgt Jim Howells from New Zealand had only flown five operations as a second pilot (known as second 'dickie') with another crew. On this night he was captain and had his own crew in Wellington X3412-L. Over the skies of Germany that night was *Hauptmann* Lent, a fighter ace who, when he was killed in 1944, had 102 night victories and eight day victories. His first victim was Wg Cdr Wright and his crew who crashed into the sea and the only member of the crew found was the wireless/operator air gunner P/O J Whittaker DFM. The flak over Hamburg was intense and very accurate so flying straight and level was not a good policy and many of the experienced pilots would stick their nose down into a shallow dive, building up speed and corkscrew like hell away from the target. But Sgt Howells, being a novice, kept to the straight and level rule and paid the price because he was soon found by the flak gunners and his port engine was hit, damaging the propeller as well as the engine itself. He soon began to loose height and when over the North Sea gave the order to prepare for a ditch; not the orders you want to be giving on your first operation as Captain. The Wellington hit the water and water tore through the fuselage. The crew was able to get into the dinghy but had lost all the marine signals stowed in the aircraft and had no means of attracting passing ships or aircraft. It was on the third day that they were spotted by a German seaplane who rescued them and took them back to captivity and a PoW camp.

Sgt Jim Smith was flying in BJ 723 on the trip to Hamburg, the crew's 9th operation. He arrived in the target area about the same time as Howells and his crew were able to drop their bombs but on the way back, between Bremerhaven and Wilhemshaven, they were hit by flak in the port engine. They also prepared to ditch and after a safe ditching they climbed into the dinghy. They were only in the dinghy for six hours before being picked up once again by a German seaplane.

Sgt Baden Fereday had fifteen operations in his log book. Sgt Kelvin Shoesmith RAAF was his rear gunner and his wireless operator was Sgt Glaafkos Clerides who was a Greek Cypriot but had been educated at an English Public School. In 1939 Clerides volunteered to join the RAF. His father had been a Major in the Cyprus Regiment. On his first pay and Church Parade in the RAF, being of the Greek Orthodox persuasion he was offered the choice of peeling a pile of potatoes or joining the Other Denominations; he chose the latter. Although he started his training as a pilot he later became a wireless/operator air gunner and with No. 115 Squadron took part in a number of operations including Hamburg, Cologne, and targets in the Ruhr.

The man who was his bomb aimer, and also manned the front turret, was Sgt Frank Skelley aged 19 who had transferred from the Merchant Navy which he had joined as a boy. Their aircraft was Wellington BJ670-K. They were carrying a 4,000 lb bomb which the Wellington was not designed to carry and therefore the bomb bay had to be modified to carry this bomb. Most of flotation bags which gave the aircraft buoyancy in the event of having to ditch had been removed. The target was Hamburg where Frank knew the red light district from his days in the Merchant Navy. The bomb was dropped and they set off towards the German coastline and home. Once again they were caught by heavy flak and a huge burst by the nose of the aircraft blew out the hydraulics rendering the gun turrets useless and causing and the undercarriage to drop down. Sgt Clerides was wounded in the leg and when he fainted on the floor of the aircraft his intercom plug was wrenched from its socket. From the rear turret Sgt Shoesmith also said he had been wounded. When Sgt Clerides came to and found the aircraft in a dive he called up on the intercom not realising he was no longer connected and receiving no reply he baled out of the emergency hatch at the rear of the aircraft. At 8,000 ft Sgt Fereday regained control of the aircraft and levelled it out. In the meantime Sgt Clerides landed near a town and the Germans, because of his Greek features, thought he was a Jew and attacked him. A detachment of the *Luftwaffe* turned up and obviously saved his life. He was taken to a hospital at Bremen and an immediate operation was carried out on his wounded leg. While there he was given civilian clothes and allowed to walk about the garden with his leg in plaster. But by 1 September his leg was now much improved so he hid in the garden and made for the rabbit hutch where he hid until dark. He then cut the wire surrounding the garden, found an empty shed where he changed his clothes and began walking south west. Near Verdun, having crossed the Wessen, his leg began to play up and he hid for three days in a park. He then jumped on a goods train and got to within 30 kilometres of the Dutch border but as he got off the train he was spotted by German soldiers and spent the next 14 days in a civil jail before being taken to Frankfurt.

While at a PoW camp at Lamsdorf he made another escape attempt, this time changing identity with a Cypriot soldier who was serving in the RASC and got out of the camp with a working party. They made out they were Greek workers and got civilian clothes and money from a Polish lady married to a German. Unfortunately, his escape had to be postponed owing to sabotage carried out by ten Cypriots working in the food distribution centre. He then became ill and had to return to the PoW camp, he spent three weeks in the hospital but his true identity not being discovered he was

Glafcos Clerides. *President Clerides of Cyprus*

Sgt Clerides. *President Clerides*

again allowed out on the same working party. The same lady got them tickets for a train to Vienna, and then a train to Graz. Then came various local trains and a four day walk to Yugoslavia. Here he was helped by another lady but the man she had arranged to take them across a river bridge failed to turn up and they set off themselves. Having got across the bridge they were seen by a man on a motorcycle and were then arrested by four German policemen. Another 14 days in a cell followed and then back to Lamsdorf and another 10 days in the cells. He had been out for 3 months and covered 700 kilometres and still his true identity was not discovered. When his camp was liberated he was flown back to the UK on 10 May 1945.

The Wellington without Glaafkos Clerides was now in trouble and a ditching was imminent. They were near Norderney, a *Luftwaffe* air sea rescue base, and now down to 1,500 ft. On hitting the water the undercarriage caught in the waves pitching them violently nose downwards. The pilot Baden Fereday went through the windscreen. Kelvin Shoesmith crawled out of his rear turret and fell into the sea. He became entangled in the trailing wire and was being dragged down by the sinking bomber.

Frank Skelly and Sgt Harry Linfley, the observer, swam over to him and released him. They all tried to inflate the dinghy which was riddled with shrapnel holes but failed.

In the Wellington there was a loose wooden box-like structure on the floor below the Astrodome. It was used for a crew member to stand on in the Astrodome. This had floated out of the open hatch just before the bomber sunk so they all swam towards it, each grabbing a corner with one hand and the other on to each other. Their skipper was dead and with two other crewmen also in dinghies the box was a luxury.

Kelvin Shoesmith had a piece of shrapnel in his side which had also pierced his Mae West. Harry Lindley constantly blew it up in an attempt to keep his head above the water. He then began to show signs of distress and his grip loosened and he became unconscious. The others tried to hold on to him but he slipped from their grasp and drifted away. They had now been in the water for several hours and their resistance to the cold water was waning. Frank Skelley began to pray out loud to God asking him not to let them die as he wanted to live but his grip began to loosen and he also drifted away. Within ten minutes of this a German *Luftwaffe* air sea rescue seaplane turned up by which time Harry had also become unconscious and remembered nothing of his rescue. They picked them out of the water and into the floor of the aircraft; they also picked up two bodies but finding they were dead put them back into the sea.

Nearly a month after ditching Kelvin Shoesmith's body was recovered from the sea at Ho Bay Denmark and he is now buried at Esbjerg (Fourfelt) Denmark and Frank Skelley's body was recovered off the Dutch coast and he is buried at Texel (Den Burg) The Netherlands.

After the war Glaafkos Clerides qualified as a barrister in Cyprus and became involved in politics but the opposition to his being elected set up a campaign accusing him of collaboration with the Germans when a prisoner. Both Baden Fereday and Harry Lindley were contacted and invited to Cyprus to refute the allegations against Glaafkos. They did and the story of the ditching and captivity was translated into Greek and published in the newspapers for all to read. Despite this he lost the election, but in 1996 he became the President of the Greek Cypriots. He has also been made an Honorary Life Vice President of the Aircrew Association.

The motto of No. 115 Squadron is 'Despite the Elements,' this was put to the test in July 1942. With war imminent Jack Catford wrote to the Air Ministry in August 1938, and volunteered to train as a fighter pilot. The reply was that at that time they had more volunteers than they needed. At the time the RAF had only 800 fighter planes, including biplanes. On the rebound Jack joined the Auxiliary Fire Service (AFS) at Wandsworth in south-west London. On the outbreak of war this became the National Fire Service so members of the AFS were automatically conscripted.

By the time war began Jack had a year's training as a fireman and was now a leading fireman, (later Sub Officer). It was September 1940 when the work started after the German bombing of the London docks. Their first fire was at Surrey Docks at Deptford where they found two acres of warehouses ablaze, and worked for 13 hours bringing it under control with bombs still raining down. After a few hours sleep they again went back to the same docks for another 12 hour stint. He attended all the City of London fires including the roof of the Guildhall and Cannon Street railway Station. He also went to Birmingham and Portsmouth. But by the time 1942 came, and with the bombing ceasing, Jack became bored but as a conscripted fireman he had no chance of getting into the RAF. That was until early in 1943 when a message came to all fire stations that release would be granted to any fireman who volunteered for aircrew duties in the RAF. Jack set off at great haste to the recruiting centre at Acton. And after passing all the required tests and exams he was considered to have an aptitude for wireless telegraphy and that he should consider this, but Jack said he wanted to be a straight air gunner and not a wireless operator air gunner. He was asked why and replied that he could be an air gunner within six months whereas a WOpt/AG would take 18 months. After a short break his wishes were granted he was sworn in, given the 'Kings Shilling' and the all important service number.

Within three months he had three stripes and was on operations. He found that he was the second oldest air gunner on 635 Squadron, the oldest was another later stalwart of the Air Gunners Association, the late Bobby Hurrell. After fifteen operations they became a centre of attention by new crews, both were double the age of the average air gunner. On one occasion over Mannheim with an inferno below Jack looked down and said,

"I know what you bastards are going through" meaning the German firemen. Jack felt that morale was a question of one's mental make up and imagination. He found operations exciting and with no sense of fear. But if they had experienced a difficult trip and enemy attacks particularly over well lit targets he felt very much afraid and asked himself 'Why the hell did I volunteer for this bloody job.' On those occasion he broke into a sweat and had to turn off his electrically heated suit. Even if at the time the temperature outside was 50° below. As soon the dangerous moment was over he began to freeze again and turned his heated suit back on.

Mentally and often physically he kissed the ground when getting out of his aircraft.

On one operation after being attacked by an Me110 and a Ju88 at 22,000 ft and somehow getting away without being hit Jack saw the mother of all explosions: a bomber nearby had exploded with a full bomb load; why was not evident as there was no flak, but a lone fighter may have crept in or it had been bombed by another bomber from above, all that was left was a small red and orange blast which got faster and faster and resembled a furnace. Then came green, red and orange flames, probably the flares of a Pathfinder aircraft. All that was left in the sky was a patch of black, oily smoke drifting along where a moment before an aircraft and seven men had been.

On 11 June 1944, Jack found that ops were on that night. At 1900 hours the crews assembled and the briefing commenced. They were told the operation would be like a 'piece of cake' and the weather man had little to say which was unusual. The target was the marshalling yards at Nantes and was of great importance as it served the Germans on the invasion front and the 'U' Pens at Brest and Lorient. Take-off was at 2341 but when they reached the target area the weather forecast proved to be 'dud', cloud 10/10 with no cloud breaks. They decided to go down lower below the cloud and hopefully bomb in the clear. They broke cloud at under 2,000 ft. The greeting was described by Jack as breathtaking. Every weapon from rifles to light flak was directed towards them plus hordes of searchlights. Fortunately the heavy 88 heavy flak guns could not operate because the angle was too low for them. Despite all this attention they were able to drop their markers and bombs but having done so they were still peppered with shrapnel shells and bullets, and one large hit on the aircraft which blew into the aircraft, damaging the vital Elsan toilet and overall the aircraft looked like a colander. Because of the low height Jack was able to give a good riposte and fire straight down a searchlight beam until it went out.

They soon climbed into the safety of the cloud and broke above the cloud into brilliant moonlight. Jack saw twinkling lights on the port side of the aircraft and to his horror it turned out to be another Lancaster firing at them. Jack shouted on the intercom to the skipper, "Dive, Dive. Another Lanc is firing at us" They dived back into the cloud where they stayed for some 15 minutes and when they came back out the rogue Lanc was not to be seen. He probably went back and reported he had fired at an enemy aircraft.

They made it back to base but as they landed the aircraft swerved wildly to port, off the runway and onto the grass finishing up near the control tower at Downham Market. They all climbed out to find that the port wheel tyre had burst.

The next day after inspection two .303 British bullets were found in the burst tyre and twenty-two bullet holes in the fuselage and cowling, a few from the rogue Lancaster. In January 1945, Jack, having completed forty-six operations and attacking targets such as Cologne, Stuttgart, and Essen, was recommended for the DFC. At the end of his thirty trips and a tour he and his crew immediately volunteered for a second tour and after that again for a third, all declining the normal six months 'screening': a rest from operational flying.

On 5 May 1945 they were engaged in bringing back prisoners from Lubeck. They stayed overnight at what had been the officers' Mess of a German night-fighter base. They decided to go for a walk in the countryside around the Mess and took with them their Weston .38 revolvers which they rarely took on operations. After about 3 to 4 miles they came across a German lorry lying on its side and climbing on board they found it was still loaded with German 'stick' grenades They each armed themselves with grenades and walked 10 miles down a lane and in turn pulled the cords attached to the grenades and threw them over a hedge into a field 30 ft below the hedge. Much time was spent looking for souvenirs but nothing was found. The prisoners they brought back were all Lascar ship crews captured in the Indian Ocean, from cargo and small war ships.

Jack lived into his 90s and rode a motor bike up to the age of 85. Why did he stop? His motor bike was stolen!

What was the life and routine of an air gunner like in the Winter of 1943/44? Sgt Norman Storey was with No. 103 Squadron at Elsham Wolds and he awoke one morning in a freezing cold Nissen hut. After dressing he walked across the snow-bound ground to the ablutions or wash rooms for a cold water shave and wash. Then by bike to the Sergeants mess for breakfast. Afterwards either report sick or with the rest of the crew to the flight commanders office for confirmation that all were fit for operations that day if required. If he was sick he had to try and find a spare gunner. They sat around in the crew room until 11am when the NAAFI wagon turned up for tea and a wad (bun). If the order came through that they were on ops Norman would go to the armoury to pick up his own set of four .303 Browning machine guns and take them out to the aircraft. With the aid of an armourer they set them to concentrate at 400 yards with a maximum of 600 yards. Back to the mess for lunch and the allotted time for briefing. After this the aircrew meal of egg and bacon then to the locker room to put on the flying kit. After all the checks prepare to taxi for take-off.

On return back to the dispersal, remove the guns from the turret and return them to the armoury. Into the crew room for hot tea and rum before debriefing and then to the mess for another egg and bacon meal. Then cycle back to the cold Nissen hut for a sleep and then the next day starts

Norman Storey. *Norman Storey*

it all again. This was a typical day in the life of a Bomber Command air gunner.

During this period Norman remembers that the rear gunner had three enemies: the three 'F's – Flak, Fighters and Frostbite. On the way back from Leipzig in December 1943 it was the third one that got Norman. The condensation in his oxygen tube froze and he was being starved of oxygen. This caused the effect of being drunk. He began thrashing about in his turret and after a while the turret light came on but how it came on he is not sure. The mid-upper gunner seeing this reported it to the pilot and having an idea what was wrong sent the wireless operator back using a portable oxygen bottle to the rear turret with a replacement helmet and oxygen mask. He removed the old one from Norman's head and replaced it with the one he had brought. But Norman's ears had already suffered frostbite and on return to base he was taken to the sick quarters where his ears were treated and bandaged. He remained there for three days and when released he was allowed to wear a silk stocking,

Norman Storey leans against the tail turret of a Lancaster. *Norman Storey*

courtesy of the wireless operator's wife, around his head but much to the frustration of the station warrant officer who could not charge him with being improperly dressed. He wore this at all times for the rest of the winter. Even after the war, in cold weather, he still has to wear a scarf around his ears. As time went by the problem became less and less painful but on a very cold day he still suffers pain down the back of each ear: a constant reminder of Leipzig.

Walter Johnson-Biggs (always known as 'Johnny' Johnson-Biggs) joined the RAF in 1935 and worked as a medical orderly in the station sick quarters. When war broke out he was in Palestine and he promptly volunteered for aircrew and was posted to No. 97 Squadron at Woodhall Spa but when he arrived he was still assigned to the sick quarters awaiting aircrew training. While there he had a run-in with a Squadron Leader, a flight commander with 97 Squadron, but as it turned out it was not all bad. While Johnny was walking around the station he saw the same squadron leader clay pigeon shooting and asked if he could have a try, whereupon he was handed the gun and the squadron leader's assistant was told to put up a couple of clay pigeons, he did and Johnny hit one but missed the other. Two more were fired and this time Johnny hit both. He was then asked what he was doing on the station. Johnny told him but said he wanted to be an air gunner. The squadron leader said, "Come with me" the next thing he knew he was an air gunner with 97 Squadron, no training no gunnery school, he bypassed them all. He was kitted out with flying kit and went on his first operation: a search for the German Fleet in the Channel. He was now in his 30s when the average age for aircrew was 21. He was later posted to 15 Squadron operating on Stirlings and then 214 Squadron at Stradishall where he completed a tour of thirty operations.

From there Johnny was posted to No. 619 Squadron at Coningsby and flew with the officer commanding 619 Wg Cdr Jeuwine, later Group Captain Jeuwine. After he had completed twenty-nine operations he was recommended for and awarded the DFC. In his recommendation it mentioned that he had damaged a Ju88 which had attacked his Lancaster and on another occasion shot down an Me109. On an operation to Berlin his turret went out of action but he manipulated it by hand and was able to keep up a search upon which he sighted a Ju88 which was closing in for the attack. It was his directions to the pilot which enabled them to avoid the fighter attack.

On 29 January 1944, now a Flying Officer and again on an operation to Berlin, his oxygen mask failed and he was given a replacement which he was able to put on. However, when the pilot received no reply from Johnny on the intercom he sent the flight engineer back to see what the problem was. He found Johnny unconscious and removed him the turret and laid him on the floor of the aircraft, but when fitted with another mask Johnny tore it off again. On landing he appeared very confused and staggered slightly as he left the aircraft; his right cheek and right lower eyelid were frost bitten. He was taken to the station sick quarters, given oxygen, his cheek treated with warm cotton wool and given treatment for shock and then transferred to RAF Hospital, Rauceby. He also went on to live into his 90s only dying in 2007. After the war he became a London black-cab driver.

Prior to joining the RAF Peter Twinn worked in a factory making war material and he was also a member of the Adventure Corps and then the Air Training Corps. He went to the Air Crew Recruiting Centre in London in April 1941 and was called-up in September 1941 to became 1396800 AC 2 Peter Twinn.

After initial training he sailed from Liverpool to Canada for air gunner training. On return in 1943 and after posting to an OTU he crewed up in a rather bizarre way but one that seemed to work. He wandered around a hangar and looked at the various huddles of prospective aircrew, some he knew from training or in the mess, Those he chose to crew with was by an inner feeling that you and they would mould together as a crew. He and his crew were posted to No. 9 Squadron at Bardney in July 1943 and then in September No. 514 Squadron at Foulsham.

Being a rear gunner when you were locked in a turret for anything up to 20 hours was not only lonely but very dangerous, often you were the one the fighter came after to make the aircraft very vulnerable. It was also cold, draughty and noisy.

In July 1943 came the three raids on the city of Hamburg. On the raid of 27/28 July, the raid known as the Firestorm. On the second night 'window' was used (strips of metalised paper cut into lengths that matched the German radar wave length) which meant the German fighters and searchlights were chasing bits of paper instead of bombers. On 29/30 the target was again Hamburg, There were fifty to sixty searchlights waiting for the attacking force. Peter remembers that the fires were still burning from the night before. On this night Peter's aircraft was hit by lightning and lost an engine, it didn't always need fighters or flak to do this the elements were quite capable of making life difficult.

The Air Battle of the Ruhr had just finished and the Battle of Berlin was about to begin: sixteen raids on the German capital between November 1943 and March 1944. On 1/2 January 1944 the 100th raid on the German capital since the war began. Then in February 1944, the largest losses since the war began: seventy-six aircraft lost on an operation to Leipzig on 19/20th. Then on 24 March ninety-eight bombers failed to return. The route to Berlin

Peter Twinn. *Peter Twinn*

A crew on return from operations, Peter Twinn second right. *Peter Twinn*

varied, sometimes up the North Sea and around Denmark and then into
Germany or other times around Sweden. On 15/16 February 1944 Peter's
heated suit packed up while flying along the northern part of Denmark.
It was plugged into the aircraft's electric system with inner gloves and
slippers attached. He should have reported it to the skipper as the outer
suit in temperatures of 40° below outside was not sufficient to keep him
warm. He also knew that aborting would not be popular with the rest of
the crew: it meant they had to do another one towards their tour. As they
went on he got colder and colder and was soon numb from the waist down.
When they finally landed back at base he could not get out of the turret
and had to be hauled out, he soon recovered but the pilot was furious
when he found out the truth. He reminded Peter that if they had to bale
out he would not have been able to.

Peter's navigator would say on crossing the enemy coast, "On our way"
and always sang, 'It's the same old story'. Peter himself carried a pink
stuffed-horse in his pocket as a good luck charm. You were afraid but did
not show it and being an air gunner soon took over and the fear subsided.
Luck and a good crew were the ingredients of survival.

In April 1944, Peter finished his first tour and was commissioned. He
had completed ten operations with No. 9 Squadron and finished the tour
with No. 514. In January 1945 after a rest period his old skipper, Sqn Ldr
Colin Payne DFC, rang him up and asked if he was willing to join him as
his rear gunner on a second tour; Peter having just completed his Gunnery

Leader's Course at Catfoss. He said, "yes" and joined No. 149 Squadron on 25 January 1945. Colin was to be the senior flight commander at 149, and on occasions acting CO. Because of this he and his crew were restricted to the number of operations they could take part in per month. The mid-upper gunner in the crew F/Lt Pugh had flown on Defiants in the Battle of Britain and was on his third tour, all the rest were experienced with at least one tour under their belts.

On 28 January 1945 came their first daylight operation. An attack on Cologne.

On 2/3 February 1945, their first night operation with 149. One aircraft did not return and it had the CO W/Cdr Kay as second 'dicky'. On 13/14 February the infamous attack on Dresden and on 11 March the biggest daylight raid yet: 800 bombers and an escort of 200 fighters.

In April came Operation 'Manna'. It meant dropping sacks of food supplies from 500 ft to the Dutch at Rotterdam and there was uncertainty that the truce with the German would work or be honoured, but it was and all went well. Between 29 April and 7 May over 2,000 Lancasters and 124 Mosquitos dropped 6,672 tons of food. A total of 355 sacks dropped was enough to give breakfast dinner, tea and supper to 3,280 Dutch men, women and children.

On 16 February 1945, Peter was recommended for the DFC; at the time he had completed thirty operations and later went on to complete forty-three before the war ended. This award was approved. His war ended with the bringing back of prisoners of war on 10 May 1945 from Europe. And in July 1946 he was demobbed. He was 24 and had served in the RAF for 5 years.

Sgt Edgeley was an air gunner with No. 15 Squadron at Mildenhall flying Stirling BK-611-U. On 25/26 May 1943 they were detailed to attack Dusseldorf. During the flight both starboard engines were hit by a flak burst and put out action, but Sgt Wilson, the pilot from Sydney, Australia, was able to hold the Stirling straight and level on the two remaining port engines. The mid-upper gunner, Sgt Seabolt, from Canada, asked for permission to bale out and Wilson agreed. Rear gunner, Sgt Edgeley, opened his escape hatch at the starboard back end of the aircraft and was preparing to bale out when he realised that the aircraft was flying fairly level so he returned to his position plugged in his intercom and told the pilot. Wilson replied, "Good, we may make it to the sea and then ditch". They were now down to 7,000 ft and still losing height. When their height was down to 700 ft Wilson said they would have bale out. The rest of the crew started to bale out but when the last man went they were down to 200 ft and he was killed. Edgeley stayed with the aircraft and somehow Edgeley survived the crash with only a small cut on his head. He and the wireless/operator evaded the Germans for about 6 weeks but then they were captured and spent six weeks in the notorious prison Fresnes in Paris. From there they went to Stalag IVB.

Harry Brown took part in an operation to Turin on 12 July 1943. As they flew over the Alps and were running into Turin they were attacked by a single-engine fighter. During their briefing for the raid they had been warned to look out for the single-engine Italian fighter the Macchi, but Harry was convinced it was a German Me109. Harry's fire power hit the fighter and it went down and away to starboard. The next day he had an argument with the gunnery leader who was adamant that night fighters could be seen and recognised as the posters on the gunnery-section wall. On this raid Bomber Command lost thirteen aircraft which was a lot for an Italian target. He believes one of those he saw lost was Wg Cdr John Nettleton VC of 44 Squadron.

John Short joined the RAF in May 1942 and soon became 1625903 AC2 J Short. His air gunner training was carried out at the Elementary Air Gunners School at RAF Bridgenorth. He had been in the ATC prior coming into the RAF so he had a head start in aircraft recognition. From there he was posted to No. 11 AGS Andreas, Isle of Man and trained on Anson aircraft. His last training flight was on 22 January 1943, after 17.55 hours flying. He got high marks in the written/oral exam and was promoted to Sergeant and awarded his coveted air gunners brevet. He was now set for OTU at No. 12 OTU at RAF Chipping Warden, Near Banbury. From there he went to No. 192 Squadron at RAF Foulsham, Norfolk.

On 16 August John and his crew attempted to take off at 11.10 hours and within five minutes the aircraft was a blazing wreck on the ground. The port engine started to misfire just after take-off and the pilot soon tried to return and land. As they hit the runway runway hard John opened the doors and saw the right tyre burst and the brake-drum created sparks as it went along the runway. Then the undercarriage collapsed followed by more sparks and the first flames appeared as fuel began to run from the ruptured tanks in the wing. John soon got out by dropping from the aircraft backwards but forgot he was still connected to the intercom and he soon unplugged and ran like hell.

Shortly after this incident he was commissioned Pilot Officer with a new number 184073. He was soon off for a gunnery leader's course at RAF Catfoss. With the course finished and having passed he returned to Foulsham where he was allocated to a Sqn Ldr 'Guy' Fawkes Halifax III aircraft. His first operation was 3 March 1945, this time with the squadron CO supporting a No. 5 Group raid on the Dortmund-Emms Canal at Ladbergen. As they flew out over the North Sea they found they were in amongst hundreds of Lancasters which promoted many rude gestures and the raising and dipping of guns. Over the target John saw three Lancasters go down but the major losses were over the UK. This was the night of 'Gisella': the *Luftwaffe* master plan for 200 fighters to follow the various bomber forces to the UK. The records how that eight bombers were shot down over Germany and the sea but twenty were shot down over the UK. Back at base, as John's aircraft circled to come into land he saw a long burst of cannon fire under the aircraft followed by a train of flame of another aircraft which had been on another operation and returned before the others. All the airfield lights went out and the WAAF radio operator, possibly Noreen Dunbar, screamed over the radio, "Bandits, Bandits, proceed to diversion airfield" This was Weston Zoyland and a long haul. Many other airfields in Lincolnshire and Yorkshire were also attacked. Never again did John relax or uncock his guns until having landed and in dispersal.

At the end of the war John was sent with a party of six air gunners to RAF Watton, which was designated the 'Radar Warfare Establishment' to set it up for the Gunnery Section.

It had been vacated by the US Army Air Force and they had left all manner of kit behind. They took off their RAF caps and jackets put on the US issue fatigues. John stayed in the RAF and is now a retired Group Captain.

Ernie Reynolds was one of ten children and his father died when he was 11. He left school at the age of 13 and started work as a rivet catcher in Furness Shipyard on the River Tees. One brother served on airfield runways, another served in the medical branch of the RAF, one in the Royal Navy and two in the Army. He joined the RAF in 1943 and flew on twenty-nine operations with No. 195 Squadron: the longest a 9 hour 35 minutes trip to Berlin, and the last a 1,000 aircraft operation to Heligoland, he was still only 19.

Once, over the North Sea, when returning from a daylight operation, the pilot said the controls were being 'awkward' and when Ernie looked down the fuselage he saw that the back door was open. In no mean terms he was told to shut it. He tried to push it shut but it would not go so he decided to open it fully and then slam it but found himself hanging onto the door out of the aircraft! If he had fallen he would not have survived as he had no parachute on. Perhaps in a state of fear he became so mad that he was able to shut the door.

On another night trip he smelt burning but no one else in the crew could. Then he got a pain in his ankle which became vicious and then he realised his electric suit was on fire. He switched it off but then began to shiver so he switched it on again; immediately his ankle again began to hurt and so it went on off, on, off. He then took off his gloves and unplugged the electric sock and found he had a burn on his ankle but he made it back to base where he found a large blister on his ankle.

The danger of collision was always a factor on a bombing raid. Once, on a night trip, Ernie looked up and saw four exhaust pipes of another aircraft and yelled to the pilot who immediately dived. They missed a collision with another aircraft, which hadn't even seen them, by a fraction of a second.

Before the war the pilot had been a London Policeman, and the flight engineer had been a Sergeant in the Tyneside police: now the ranks were reversed. At the end of their tour the mid-upper gunner became an RAF policeman, or 'Snow Drop' as they were known and when he left the RAF went into the police in London. The bomb aimer worked for the telephone service, as did the wireless operator in Australia and Ernie became a fireman and ended up in charge of two fire stations and forty-six men in the Cyprus Fire Service. When he returned to the UK he became a station officer at a Middlesbrough Fire Station.

On the long Berlin operation of 14 April 1945 they were told, in the briefing, that there was a 17 mile belt of searchlights. When over this area, suddenly both gunners were blinded by light from the searchlights. Ernie suddenly knew what it was like to face a firing squad. The lights went out after three or four seconds and they were not attacked by flak or fighters but Ernie saw his life go before him for that short time. Today, apart from the wireless operator in Victoria, Australia, the remainder of Ernie's crew have departed for the big airfield in the sky.

On 14 February 1945, and the day after the infamous raid on Dresden the target was Paderborn. F/Sgt Fred Whitfield, flying with No. 9 Squadron was in his rear turret as they were returning from the target area and were now over Allied territory. He did the normal sky search but as he swung the turret fully to port he caught a glimpse of the mid-upper gunner F/Sgt Frank Stebbings rushing down the fuselage, he had a stomach chill and had the runs. He was in urgent need of the toilet which, in a Lancaster, was the Elsan, a portable, chemical toilet at the rear of the fuselage.

He waited until Frank had undressed out of his flying kit which, because of the temperature, was considerable and was sat on the Elsan with a look of complete satisfaction on his face. Fred switched on his intercom and said to the pilot, F/lt Ron Adams "Fighter, Fighter, port quarter prepare to corkscrew, port, go". On receiving this instruction Ron threw the Lancaster into the famous but awesome corkscrew, involving a sudden sharp dive and then at the bottom of the dive a sudden sharp climb back up it was used many times and saved many lives but not to be recommended if you were sitting on the Elsan. One second he was sat on the Elsan, the next on the roof of the Lancaster followed by the contents of the Elsan. When Ron heard the laughing on the intercom he came out of the dive and levelled out. On landing and the debriefing the WAAF intelligence officer took one sniff of Frank and excused him from the briefing. For some time after he was known as 'Stinker'. Frank did get some of his own back later when he fired a fire extinguisher over the top of a toilet being used by Fred. In 1983, at an Air Gunners Association dinner in Manchester, they met up for the first time since 1945. At about 3.30 am in the morning Frank turned to Fred and said, "After all these years I have decided to forgive you for the dirty trick you pulled over Paderborn". He had always vowed he would never forgive him but time heals. Such is the bond between air gunners.

On one occasion in June 1944 they were attacked by fighters and Fred's rear turret was hit, one fin and part of the rudder on the port wing had been shot away, and one of the port engines had stopped. Despite the controls being sloppy Ron was able to get the Lancaster back to base at Bardney. The aircraft never flew again as every rivet and spring was lose and the rear turret was left with only two BA bolts holding it on, the remaining bolts had sheared off by the violence of the corkscrew. Both Frank Stebbings, who had fired upon an Me109 as it came into attack and retired without firing its guns, and Fred were awarded the DFM.

On 25 April 1945 they took part in the operation at the end of the war that everyone in Bomber Command wanted to be on: the attack on the Berchtesgarden, the Eagles Nest and Hitler's mountain retreat. They all thought on return that Hitler had been there but found he had moved to Berlin just hours before.

Tom Hales flew with 50 Squadron and flew on twenty-four operations, his last operation to Flensburg on 23 April 1945.

Returning from one operation Tom also needed to visit the Elsan and the wireless/operator took his place in the mid-upper turret and he made his way to the back and the Elsan. He had only just arrived and been seated for a couple of minutes when over the intercom came, "Fighter Port Quarter, Corkscrew Port, Go." Clinging on for dear life to the Elsan seat whilst the Lancaster went through the corkscrew process he could feel the liquid in the Elsan splashing against his buttocks. After two dives to port the W/Operator said to the skip, "False alarm skip, must have been a bit of dirt on the Perspex". It was, as before, a put up job between the wireless/operator and the pilot.

When Allen Hudson received his brevet and stripes he was not permitted to wear it on No. 7 Air Gunnery School at Stormy Down so they had to sew the new insignia on to their second uniform tunic and change into it in the railway waiting room. As they did they were interrupted by the station porter who said, "Don't worry every course did the same on passing out and he had seen it many times before".

At a briefing for an operation to Berlin an elderly intelligence officer opened his report by saying, "Tonight, gentlemen, we are going to Berlin". Suddenly came a voice from the back, "Which aircraft are you flying in". He then said, "Gentlemen you are going to Berlin". Take-off was okay but when they got to the Beachy Head area the mid-upper shouted to dive to starboard and then said, "Barrage balloon on port side". They had missed it by 50 yards thanks to the mid upper gunner. A short while after the pilot asked the navigator for a time to the French coast but did not receive a reply. The flight engineer said that the navigator was sprawled face down on his table and nothing they did would bring him round. They then linked him up to the emergency oxygen bottle and this brought some signs of movement. There did not seem anything wrong with his intercom or oxygen so there seemed to be no reason for him passing out. The pilot had no option but to abort and return to base. They sent out a mayday and then went to the Wainfleet bombing range to drop the 'Cookie' and incendiaries they were carrying. On landing the navigator was taken to the sick bay by ambulance An enquiry followed and the outcome was that the navigator was whisked away in the early hours of the morning and not seen again. The chapter

Sgt Flowers during 1944. *H.J. Flowers*

John Lawrey's Crew of 50 Sqn in 1945. Mid-upper gunner Sgt Flowers. *H.J. Flowers*

on Lack of Morale Fibre will explain why. It was the crews first operation and they felt let down.

James Flowers formed up with his crew at No. 85 OTU at RAF Husbands Bosworth. His pilot was F/O John Lawrey from New Zealand. James was the mid-upper gunner and came from Wales. After leaving OTU he and the crew were sent to RAF Wigsbley and No. 1664 CU for training on the Stirling bomber. The training consisted of mock fighter attacks and on one occasion after a fighter had made several passes the aircraft levelled out in the middle of a corkscrew and the pilot said, "Put on parachutes, jump". Then he repeated it. Not quite believing what he heard but having to obey James swung his rear turret to the beam position, dragged open the sliding doors behind him, undid his seat belt and began to climb out of the turret. They were flying at about 200mph at the time and the wind force was tremendous. As he looked down he saw cows in the fields and he then took off his helmet. But then he heard a faint voice in his now hanging intercom; he could not hear what was being said but decided he had better go back in to the turret and find out what was being said. What he heard was the voice of the Instructor Engineer shouting "don't go, don't go", on hearing this he closed the sliding doors behind him and settled back in his turret. This made him feel very shaky and he wondered if his parachute would have opened so when he got into the fuselage he decided to pull the rip cord, to his relief the chute opened and spilled out all over the fuselage floor. It cost him 2/6d to have it repacked, a lot of money in those day when you consider his weekly pay was £2, of which £1 went to his wife. On the ground John the pilot said that with the aircraft under extreme stress caused by the violent manoeuvres of the corkscrew a window behind his left side of his head blew out. The lead weighted curtain was banging violently against the aircraft's steel fuselage causing a loud noise behind his head. At the came time, but by sheer coincidence, the starboard outer engine developed an overspeed fault.

On 9 April 1945 the target was Hamburg. James was now with No. 50 Squadron in support of 617 Squadron, who, because of the 10 ton bomb they were carrying, had had the weight of their aircraft reduced by taking out the mid-upper turret. No. 50 Squadron were told to surround 617 and take on the fighters if attacked. A large force of RAF fighters were also present. After they had dropped their bombs, James told the pilot that as they were well to the rear of the bomber force they were a sitting target for fighters and gradually they eased forward towards the centre of bomber stream. Suddenly, a group of small fighters was seen approaching at great speed. They were climbing faster than any fighters he had seen yet. One of the fighters came straight at them firing its cannons; James pressed the firing button in return and just when it seemed the fighter was about to crash into them it swung to starboard between them and another aircraft close by. It passed within yards and James could see the pilot's face as if he was in the same room. James kept firing as it flashed in between the other Lancaster and them. He then lifted his arms off the turret controls in alarm, he appeared to have fired along the nearby Lancaster's fuselage but all was well as the aircraft's speed bent bullets away from the object they are aimed at. To hit a moving target it is necessary to aim in front of it. They later found out that the enemy fighters were Me262s, German jet fighters. As he stopped firing James looked to the rear and saw a back marker aircraft flown by F/O Berriman burst into flames, break in half and begin to fall. At 2,000 ft he saw the rear gunner jump out of his turret, open his parachute and begin to float down slowly. Suddenly, to their horror, it suddenly burst into flames and fell further and further and to his obvious death. James knew this man well but for some reason had forgotten his name, they joined up together, trained together and were on the same squadron together.

A short time after one of the escort Mustangs appeared behind looping the loop, which indicated he had shot down a German fighter. The rear gunner turned out to F/Sgt Norman Felton, aged 21, from Kettering, and now buried in Hamburg, as are F/O Berriman, aged 25, from Scarborough, West Australia and F/Sgt Anthony Jones the mid-upper gunner.

On 4 March 1945 James was scheduled for a night operation to Bohlen. After the usual briefing James was talking to another rear gunner who, when asked how he had fared on previous operations, and what he encountered. Sensing James's obvious tension he said "Don't worry, there's nothing to it, I'll soon be on my last trip". This was his 31st operation and he went on to say he had not even seen a fighter, leave alone been attacked by one. Ten days later this rear gunner and his crew did not return.

It was a ten hour trip to Lutzkendorf on 14 March and this operation proved to be a very difficult one for James who certainly saw his share of fighters on this occasion. At the debriefing the Gunnery Leader asked if James had anything to report and he replied yes a long combat with two German fighters: an Fw190 and a Ju88. The Gunnery Leader said that we shall be here all night as I have to fill in six pages of reports for every attack. Then he went on to say how he could put it all on one page. All James wanted to do was get to bed and sleep so he did not care very much how the report was produced. Two weeks later James and the rest of his crew were instructed to report to the CO's office. Wg Cdr Jimmy Flint, the holder of the DFC, DFM and George Medal, was sat at his desk, with him a number of other officers including the Gunnery Leader were sat alongside. Jimmy Flint said to the pilot, "You had a 10 second attack by two fighters during which the rear gunner fired 10,000 rounds. This is not possible. What did happen?" With that everyone turned to James and he in turn looked hard at the Gunnery Leader and thought he has reported this incorrectly what should I do? His way was to say he could not remember, and it worked, because all as he received was a ticking off for wasting bullets. James felt gutted having fought off two fighters time and time again and he ended up with a telling off because of an officer who could not take down the facts correctly.

The last time James flew with John Lawrey, was, in some ways, a sad time. Operation Dodge was picking up PoWs from Italy. The route was the same each time over the Corsican mountains and straight for Rome. As they made their way to their destination the flight engineer was flying the Lancaster with John standing next to him, James was sitting with his back against the starboard side fuselage near the mid-upper turret with his legs dangling over the edge of the bomb bay. On board were eighteen Italian PoWs and a spare Lancaster landing-wheel which they were taking to Bari for an aircraft whose tyre had burst. It weighed about a ton and should have been strapped down, but it would appear it was not. Suddenly James was thrown up in the air banging hard against the roof of the fuselage and a large steel drinking-water tank floated up against him. Trapped on the roof he saw the spare wheel doing a circle around the fuselage, it smashed against the Autogyro on the left, then swung over and around the fuselage crashing and twisting the machine-gun bullet ducts, fortunately it missed the rudder bar controls. He then pushed the water tank away from him and was thrown to the ground. The Italians had panic in their eyes and began to get to their feet. James pushed one down and by waving indicated to the rest to sit down. He then decided to climb into the mid-upper turret. They had fallen from 11,000 to 500 ft. John later explained what had gone wrong. As they climbed through 10/10 cloud they flew straight into the centre of a cumulus nimbus tropical storm, the tremendous upward current hit the underside of the aircraft throwing it straight up. It then stalled dropping straight down. He was also thrown up to the roof and thought they had been hit. He got down from the side of the fuselage and stood alongside the flight engineer who was fighting with the controls. He then assisted the flight engineer in pulling out of the dive. He then changed places with him strapped himself in and somehow got full control of the aircraft. At the debriefing all the other crews were talking about the aircraft that had looped the loop.

Andy Black remembers that the feeling of those days was, 'that nothing will ever happen to me, the other Guy, yes! But not me'. He flew in a strike against Essen in March 1943; the Air Battle of the Ruhr had begun and would go on until July attacking the Ruhr cities and towns in Germany, the heart of German industry. It was 12 March 1943, and when the curtain was rolled back revealing the target that night, it was the Krupps Works at Essen.

They arrived over Essen on time and the pilot asked them if they should go straight in and be first to bomb or stooge around for a couple of minutes. The decision was unanimous to go in and get out but as they made the bombing run a white searchlight, the master searchlight, found them and about twenty or thirty more followed; they were well and truly coned. As the pilot went into a corkscrew manoeuvre the rear gunner F/Sgt Jacques Barsalou RCAF opened fire, then stopped. Again and again they were coned but somehow got out of it although they were hit eighteen times. The rear gunner had been severely wounded but refrained from informing his captain but, the captain, sensing the rear gunner had a problem sent Andy back to the rear turret and he found him slumped over his guns and the turret a mass of blood. Andy somehow got him through the doors of the turret and into the fuselage and to the rest position. Andy got him out of his bulky flying kit and administered first aid. The rear gunner was in great pain and bleeding profusely. His spirits, however, were high and he said he would bear up until the English coast was reached. On landing he was rushed to hospital and for some time critically ill. He was awarded the DFM after this operation. The Essen raid was their 21st operation and they went on to complete nine more and finish their tour. However, a number of air gunners in Bomber Command completed many more operations that one could expect.

P/O Edward Lacey was serving with No. 90 Squadron when awarded the DSO in 1943 after completing sixty-four Operations. After the war Edward went on to be come a Wing Commander and was awarded the OBE in 1970. He had served in operational squadrons from 30 July 1940, and had taken part in many operations in 1941 against enemy shipping and since then against many of the most heavily defended targets in Germany and the occupied countries. By the end of July 1941 he had completed forty sorties on Wellington aircraft, this included twenty sorties against targets in the Mediterranean, including the formidable centres of Benghazi, Taranto and Tripoli. During this time he was involved in two serious crashes, both when returning to base after his aircraft had been damaged by enemy action. He later successfully completed twenty sorties against targets in Western Europe , mainly the Ruhr area and German ports. He had served with many squadrons which was the reason given for him not being decorated earlier. He was at first recommended for the DFC but this was upgraded to the DSO by Air Vice Marshal The Hon Ralph Cochrane the Officer Commanding No. 3 Group.

Another air gunner awarded the DSO was Fight Lieutenant John Whymark. He had been awarded the DFC in July 1944 after flying on sixty operations. He was at the time flying with No. 101 Squadron and had with this squadron flown twenty operations. In April 1945 he was awarded the DSO, he was now with No. 103 Squadron and had completed seventy-six operations. He was posted to 103 on 3 October 1944, and since then although being the Gunnery Leader had completed sixteen operations. He often flew with the crews that were rather below standard against heavily defended and difficult targets. On several operations he flew with a crew who were exhibiting signs of temperamental weakness with the object of raising their confidence. By his example the subsequent improvement was most noticeable. Sadly, John was killed on 4 October 1945 when a Lancaster he was flying in, and taking nineteen ATS and Queen Alexander Nurses to Italy, disappeared off Sardinia. His name is now recorded on the Runneymede Memorial, Panel 266.

Peter Davis graduated from No. 4 AGS at Morpeth in 1944 and the comment about him in his log book were, 'keen and reliable should make a good air-gunner'. He eventually joined No. 115 Squadron in February 1945, flew ten operations over Germany, three on Operation Manna and a number on Operation Exodus bringing back prisoners of war from Europe. He remembers the unusual situation of a flight commander called Morrison, also an air gunner, who was, at the time, probably in his 40s deciding to fly with them as mid-upper gunner. Over the target area came a voice with what Peter described as a very classy Oxford accent, "I say rear gunner do you see what I see?" The point of this was that the terminal velocity of a 4,000 lb 'cookie' is slower than that of a 500 lb bomb and therefore it comes out of the bomb bay last. Peter described S/L Morrison as a classy but also gutsy guy, who he thought may have been too old to be a pilot but still wanted to fly, and that not too many air gunners made Squadron Leader. Peter's memories of Manna are worth describing.

As they crossed the Dutch Coast they saw the German AA guns and the German helmets. There had been agreement with the Germans that they would not shoot as the aircraft only had supplies and not bombs on board. They were at 200 ft and dropped the supplies in open fields, not on parachutes but out from the bomb bay went drums, sacks and boxes and as they went out the Germans were running in all directions. As they went over The Hague on another Manna trip, Peter, sitting in the rear turret of his Lanc, had a long piece of cord 200 to 300 ft long and had cut it into four pieces, then tied on bits of coloured rag every 8 to 10 ft or so and tied each cord on each of his four guns. As they left the DZ (Dropping Zone) he pushed out the streamers so they flew behind the Lancaster.

After a period in Egypt with 214 and 37 Squadrons he came back to the UK in April 1946 to attended the Central Gunnery School at Leconfield. By now he was a warrant officer and passed out as an instructor. He then went back to Egypt and here he finished his service. While in Fayid, Egypt and on duty in the admin office with another air gunner he took a look at his personnel file. He found that he had been recommended for pilot training but he was a borderline case and he was good material for Air Gunner training. Peter lost an elder brother, F/O Derek Davis in June 1943 with No. 51 Squadron on a raid to Gelsenkirchen. He was flying in Halifax JD 261 which crashed at Wanrooi. He is now buried in the cemetery at Eindhoven with the rest of his crew. Today Peter lives in California, has three children and five grandchildren.

Denis Over joined No. 227 Squadron at Metheringham in October 1944. It was a new squadron being formed. It was the practice for new skippers to do their first operation with an experienced crew and sadly Denis's skipper Jack Barlow went missing on his trip to Bremerhaven, leaving them without a pilot. Squadron Leader Meagher was just starting his second tour as flight commander of B Flight and adopted Denis's crew a his crew. Their new base was at Balderton. On his 6th operation, a ten hour trip to Piliz on 8 February 1945, came an incident that he was unlikely to forget. As they flew over the north of Denmark they suddenly encountered tracer coming upwards and to the rear and assumed it was the fire from an Me210 or 410 with an upwards firing cannon. Evasive action was taken but then Denis noted the tracer was coming from the ground. A few minutes later the mid-upper gunner W/O Jock Breckenbridge shouted on the intercom "rear gunner don't lean back your turret doors are open." Denis felt back to close the sliding doors that indeed were open. The latch was faulty and kept opening throughout the trip.

As well as the flight commander of B Flight Johnny Meagher was also deputy squadron commander. The Squadron Commander was Wing Commander Millington who was held in the highest esteem. The reason for this can be seen from one example: during one station 'booze-up party' Denis cut his hand on broken glass. When Millington spotted this he took him in his car to hospital and stayed with him while it was stitched, took him for a coffee and then back to the party.

Crews became convinced that all trips carrying a 'second dickey' (new pilots gaining operational experience) were jinxed and often did not return. To remedy this Johnny Meagher carried a 'second dickey' on most of their operations, he also carried the Station Commander and other station aircrew admin officers who were obliged to do one trip a month. Sadly, the gunnery officer, Monty Banks, normally flew with them but when they were on leave he flew his routine trip with another crew and went missing.

Denis and his crew paid a large sum to have a caption painted on their aircraft 'Jane' of Daily Mirror fame, seductively reclining and pouring little bombs from a champagne bottle into a glass and naming it as 'PIMM's No. 1', the W/Op's surname being Pimm. But on two occasions aircraft PA 214 and PA 280, normally their aircraft were lost with new crews in them and when Dennis and his crew were on leave.

On 19 February 1945, the target was Bohlen. Dennis and his crew found themselves over the target area before the Master Bomber Wg Cdr Benjamin in a Mosquito. But having made his first call over the target there was silence from Benjamin and the deputy master bomber took over. Unfortunately, Wg Cdr Benjamin was shot down by flak and is now buried in Berlin.

On the mess dining-room tables were placed bowls of 'help yourself oils' that were referred to as 'wakey wakeys' (Benzedrine tablets). Denis would put a small handful in his turret tray taking two or three at a time to combat tiredness. Denis and his crew rarely went to bed. On return from an operation they would go down to Newark on their bikes to the Salvation Army Services canteen for a meal and then back to the Mess ante-room, for a snooze in the armchairs. Both Denis and Johnny Meagher had careers in British Airways after the war. Johnny retired as a senior captain after helping in the development of the Britannia and Comet 1.

'Buck' Buckley of No. 57 Squadron returned in the early morning from an operation over Germany. After a few hours' sleep they were told to report to the operation section to discover they had again been included on the crew list for that night's operation. It was customary that when a crew was lost and after their kit and personal belongings had been removed a fresh crew from a training unit would arrive the following morning to replace them. On this occasion a new crew had just arrived only to discover they were on the list for that night's operation. A member of the new crew came over to 'Buck' saying he felt he knew him. It turned out that they had worked in the same firm in Dagenham, 'Buck' a Ford car distributor and the new man a mechanic. He suggested they meet the following day when they were not on operations. That night 57 Squadron lost two crews and one was the new crew. This shook 'Buck' so much that for the remainder of his time on the squadron he wondered what his fate was. Three years later and after five and half years service 'Buck' returned to civilian life, this time as an insurance agent with the Prudential in the Dagenham area. After a few weeks he called at a house to discuss some new business. A man came to the door and greeted 'Buck' by saying "fancy seeing you". When 'Buck' asked how he knew him he recalled the time at East Kirkby three years previously. He now had a beard which is why 'Buck' did not recognise him. He was the sole survivor after being shot down over Germany. He had managed to jump out of the side door of the plane and in so doing collided with the tail plane of the Lancaster, was knocked out and in a coma for two months. When he came around he wrote to his mother and asked her to send £5 to the WAAF who had packed his parachute. In the WAAF's letter of thanks for the money she asked for the man's PoW war camp address. During 1945 there was an agreement with the Germans to exchange severely injured prisoners and he was lucky to be included in this. He then called his wife and introduced her to the girl who had packed his parachute. The name of Buck's house is called Silksheen which was the call sign for No. 57 Squadron at East Kirkby.

When Harry Irons arrived to join No. 9 Squadron at Waddington in 1942, he found that Squadron 44 was sharing Waddington with No. 9 Squadron. No. 44 was still recovering from heavy losses at Ausgberg and the losses continued throughout the time Harry was there. In fact only one crew finished a full tour on Lancaster's during nine months at Waddington, and of the fifteen new air gunners when No. 9 changed over to Lancasters he was the only left after four weeks. One of the reasons for the losses was the early warning system in the rear turret of the Lancaster that the Germans had found out about and had perfected their own equipment that allowed them to home in on the out going signal. He experienced proof of this on 19 September 1942 when returning from Munich, and flying in 10/10 cloud for some hours and then breaking cloud to find a Ju88 tailing them only yards behind. The Ju88 opened fire with cannon but being so close the shells overshot and they were able to escape back into the cloud cover.

For some days they were practising low-level cross-country flights over Lincolnshire, known always as bomber country with forty Spitfires simulating fighter attacks on them. One came in too close and flipped over in the slipstream from the Lancaster and crashed.

When the announcement came that that they were to conduct a daylight raid there were no signs of joy from the crews who would have to fly on this raid. On 17 October 1942 the Lancasters, each carrying six × 1,000 lb bombs, set off for the Schneder Armament Factory at Le Creusot in France. The height for the whole operation was 50 to 500 ft and they were so low that French civilians were waving at them on the ground. The plan was for 100 Spitfires to escort them, but like all good plans and intentions the escort did not materialise. The operation, much to the surprise of those on it, was a great success and feeling pleased with themselves they decided to 'beat up' Jersey on the return to the UK and took a pounding from German anti-aircraft gunners. It became known as one of the greatest low-level daylight raids of the war.

Another daylight raid was organised on 22 October 1942, this time to Milan, in Italy. After climbing to 16,000 ft over the Italian Alps 90 Lancasters came straight in on Milan and people were seen running in the streets as air gunners started to fire at around about roof-top level. They flew the same route over France on the return trip as Le Creusot and apart from a pigeon hitting the windscreen and knocking out the flight engineer and again going too near Jersey it was uneventful.

A further raid was organised, this time by Halifaxes, and the city of Milan was destroyed. The next day the Italian press called the aircrew 'English Gangsters' and when they were reprinted in the English newspapers the crews pinned them up around the mess. Years after the war Harry met an Italian living in the UK and told him he had been on this operation, he shook his head and said his grandmother was still talking about that day. Harry flew many of his thirty operations with 9 Squadron under F/Lt Stubbs DFC and Bar who Harry later found out had finished his second tour but was killed flying a Spitfire. After Stubbs left Harry was assigned to Sgt Doolan's crew, whose previous rear gunner had been blown out of his turret and killed. Harry went on to complete two tours which, today he finds amazing considering the many who didn't even complete one. In 1945, now a Warrant Officer and flying on Halifaxes with No. 158 Squadron he was awarded the DFC, the recommendation showed that he flew fifty-one operations, thirty-one on his first tour and twenty on his second.

Gordon Smith finally joined 76 Squadron as an experimental air gunner. The experiment was for Gordon to fly as a mid-under gunner in the H2s position. Once on the aircraft a trap door was lifted and down John went, taking all his equipment, including oxygen and parachute, and lay on his back with his head propped-up to line up with a 1.5 gun and 250 rounds of ammunition to fire out of an open space at the rear of the H2s to combat enemy aircraft firing up from under the bomber while it on the bombing run. On the operation they were attacked from below but John never saw the fighter only tracer bullets sailing by, the pilot then announced that the port-inner engine had been hit and was out but apart from that all was well. If he had to bale out Gordon was to release the ammunition from the gun, take out a split pin, push out the gun and then bale out of the same place as the gun had gone. They were able to get home, although an hour and a half late. After a few operations they decided to do away with the idea of an under-belly gun and Gordon was sent back to crew with another crew who were short of a mid-upper gunner. He was then posted with his new crew to No. 10 Squadron and went on to complete his tour of thirty-four operations. During his six months rest period spent at RAF Shepherds Grove he was employed in the MT Section and here he met a WAF Driver and within sixteen weeks they were married.

In WWII many aircrew, including air gunners, were very young looking, perhaps because many were young, but some looked younger than others. Alex Gamble was one.

When on parade during his initial square bashing the Flight Sgt who was inspecting him said 'Hullo Baby Face, does you mother know you are out? We've lost the war.'

When Alex went into a pub and not in uniform they refused to serve him as he looked under age. His first crew was with an Australian, Arnold Kemp and all of this crew were posted to No. 103 Squadron; they had recently converted from Halifaxes to Lancasters. The training on Lancasters started with fighter affiliation exercises; Squadron Leader Jake Kennard used to borrow a Spitfire from a nearby station and, using films, he attacked Alex's aircraft twice and each time Alex gave the order to his pilot to make a diving turn into the Spitfire's angle of attack. However, when the films were examined they showed that they had been shot down on both occasions. Alex realised he had given the orders too soon. It was a lesson well learned and he never made the same mistake again. This lesson saved their lives over Esbjerg on the west coast of Denmark when a Ju88 attacked them and Alex waited until he made his attack before giving instructions to the pilot. Alex went on eleven operations to The Ruhr or 'Happy Valley' and the most defended targets in Germany. The flak was so thick the aircrew said you could walk on it. This was followed by three operations to Berlin. On a trip to Bremen they were hit by flak and the next day the Engineering Officer found that their aircraft, Z–Zebra was full of holes and the oxygen to the mid-upper turret had been cut, but Alex somehow did not know. It would appear a piece of flak had cut the pipe. Alex was lucky because the flak must have just missed his behind.

Coming back from Spezzia in Northern Italy on 18 April 1943 they were followed by an Italian fighter, a CR42, after some while of this the pilot said that they would attack it and turned to engage the fighter but it soon took flight and disappeared. Were they the first Lancaster or the last to chase a fighter? When they reached twenty-eight operations they were screened and taken off operations. Alex was sent to Lindholme and given a commission and then sent to Faldingworth as an instructor.

His second tour began in August 1944. At Alex's request, once again it was to No. 103 Squadron that he returned. Under the rules he was due to fly twenty or more operations. His pilot on this occasion was Canadian F/O Birch. After the first operation with him he told Alex that he had not wanted an officer in one of his turrets but as he kept him moving he was pleased and wanted him to stay in his crew. On one occasion Alex flew with Sqn Ldr Van Rolleghem, a Belgian who had escaped from Belgium to Spain and then to the UK. When he had severe stomach pains he was told it was because he had eaten so many oranges in Spain. Despite the pain he was able to fly two and half tours until the doctors finally caught up with him. After the war he became ADC to the King of Belgium. At the end of his second tour Alex had flown twenty-one operations making a total of forty-nine, But for one aborted trip he would have made fifty. The most tragic sight he saw was a four-engine bomber, when hit by cannon shells, burst into flames and then disintegrate into two pieces and the rear gunner in the separate back part of the bomber still firing until it disappeared into cloud. From his first tour crew, the bomb aimer, wireless operator, flight engineer and rear gunner were all killed on their second tour. The pilot was sent back to Australia and killed in a motor accident. The navigator survived and now lives in Australia.

Despite heavy losses the spirit and sense of fun was always there. Black foot prints on the ceiling of the mess, passion buses to the nearest town and the usual, "If you go for a Burton or get the chop can I have your bacon and eggs?"

John Kimber joined the RAF in 1940 and joined No. 2 Squadron (Army Co-op) as a ground gunner at Marshalls Airport, Cambridge. In 1941 he remustered as an air gunner. At No. 15 OTU, Harwell. He did one operation to Essen and they were coned over Cologne by a searchlight and then peppered with shrapnel. The pilot went into a vertical dive to get out of the lights. John tried to get out of the turret but was unable to open the turret doors so he relaxed and accepted that he would crash with the aircraft. He then passed out and when he came round they were 30 minuets from base. The rest of the crew thought he had been killed. They were due for leave and then to be posted to Malta but when they came back off leave another crew had taken their aircraft and so they stayed in Bomber Command. In December 1942 he joined No. 57 Squadron and flew twenty-seven operations.

On a trip to Cologne in June 1943 the pilot passed out. Luckily they had a second pilot on board who was able to fly the aircraft back but he afterwards admitted this was the first time he had handled a Lancaster at night. After a rest John went back for a second tour with No. 49 Squadron and flew a further fifteen operations including daylight operations against French and German targets. He flew on this tour as spare 'bod' and instructor on AGLT code name 'Village Inn' and nicknamed, 'A gut load of trouble.' With a small aerial below the rear turret they could pick up a signal of an enemy aircraft approaching from the rear. Using foot pedals one could frame the blip and the W/Operator could call out the range. In theory one could open fire long before one could see the fighter. By then all main force bombers were flashing an ultraviolet signal which they could pick up with a telescope fixed to the gyroscopic sight. It worked well in training but they never had a chance to try it out on operations. In November 1943 John was awarded the DFC and been given a commission.

Gerald Stevenson joined the RAF in 1943 at first he trained as a wireless/operator/air gunner but after six weeks a call went out for straight air gunners and he gained his air gunners brevet in June 1944. In October 1944 he joined an OTU and after long cold night flights in training he joined No. 51 Squadron. He went on to fly twenty-one operations, his first to Mainz on 1 February 1945, six hours, Gerald remembers, of being scared stiff of to what to expect, cold, very cold, ice on your oxygen mask. He is now 78 and still remembers how intensely cold it was in the rear turret and how he would willingly have closed his eyes and fallen sleep to avoid the bitter pain of his body being so cold. He was demobbed in 1947 after a tour in India. Then in 1951 he rejoined Bomber Command flying tail gunner on Lincolns for 3 years with No. 148 Squadron from 1951 to 1954. This time it was not as cold but cold enough.

Bill Green was in the last No. 207 Squadron crew to bomb Germany in WWII. The target was Berchtesgarden on 25 April 1945. The aim was to bomb the SS Barracks while No. 617 Squadron attacked Hitler's Eagles Nest. Their Lancaster was RE 128-X and flown by Flt Lt Verralls DFC. Over the target the bomb aimer could not see the target so they had to go around again; this time they did drop their bombs but as the bomb doors closed all hell let loose and the German flak gunners opened up. After the pilot had thrown the aircraft all over the sky they found themselves on their own. The aircraft was badly damaged: the main plane, fins, rudder and

Sgt Olson. *George Olson*   George Olson. *G. Olson*

Bill Green's turret were all damaged. The Perspex was split by shrapnel and he had a bloody eye, which was congealed. When they arrived back and as he got out of the aircraft a photographer was there from the Air Ministry. Bill went to the sick bay and, in fact, his eye was hanging on his cheek and he had frost bite in his feet. His eye was put back in its socket then they cleaned and stitched his eye and his feet were soaked in olive oil, although even today his toes are still deformed. Although they did a good job on his eye he still has only 30 to 40% vision in it. He was told that he had been recommended for the DFM but nothing came of it. Bill has investigated the so called award but all to no avail.

George 'Ole' Olson was born in a farmhouse in Alberta, Canada. His training was on Fairey Battles at MacDonald in Manitoba in 1943. It was a smelly aircraft and on one occasion after being air sick he had to clean up the turret on landing. In the UK he flew forty-eight operations with No. 98 Squadron of the 2nd Tactical Air Force. His first operation was on the 7 June 1944, his pilot was an Australian, F/Sgt Thurston, and because they had so many war correspondents on board they flew without parachutes. He wrote fifty-six poems about his forty-eight operations. During his operations he flew with eight different pilots; each time replacing gunners who had not made it.

Dan Brennan was one of a number of Americans who before America came into the war joined the RAF and served with them from 1940 to 1943. In 1943 he joined the USAAF as an air gunner and when he went back to the USA he had flown a total of sixty operations, had been awarded the

DFM while with No. 10 Squadron RAF, and from the US he was awarded the Silver Star, and Purple Heart: twelve medals in all. His wife was in the ATS, a Captain predictor officer on 570 Mixed Anti-Aircraft guns shooting down doodle bugs and German fighters.

Many memories have stuck over the years and Alex Duke remembers, in particular, one on 21 January 1944, during the Battle of Berlin. When over Berlin he saw another Lancaster being attacked by an Me109 fighter, The Lancaster was hit a dozen times by cannon fire and was soon burning from end to end. Somehow the rear gunner was still firing back and kept on firing until it passed out of sight. A few days later he learned that a lad from Alconbury village had gone missing on 21/22 January 1944, over Berlin. It was his first operation with 101 Squadron. Alex was a member of No. 156 Pathfinder Squadron at the time and has lived in Alconbury for over 50 years. On a plaque in the church there is an inscription for Sergeant Peter Searle, killed on operations over Germany 21 January 1944. Out of the thirty-five aircraft lost that night sixteen were Lancasters. Peter was flying with F/O Perry that night in Lancaster LM 387-O and he and his crew have no known grave but are remembered on the Runneymede Memorial. Today, and especially on Remembrance Day, Alex wonders if this was the aircraft and Peter the rear gunner whom he had seen acting with the highest courage anyone can witness. We shall never know.

On 24 March 1944, was the last heavy bomber raid on Berlin, and was also the night that seventy-six prisoners escaped from of Stalag III. Sadly, fifty prisoners were later shot. Alex's aircraft was detailed for this operation and as they made the run-up to the target there was a series of thumps: the port wing was hit and there was a gaping hole behind his mid-upper turret. The order to bale out came from the pilot and Alex left his turret, put on his chute and went back to open the rear door. His idea was to tumble out but when he looked down the sight he saw was horrific, bombs were bursting all over Berlin, flak and crashing aircraft were all around. Seventy-two aircraft were shot down on this operation. Having seen this he went back into the fuselage plugged in his intercom and asked again if the bale out order had been cancelled to find it had, they thought he had baled out but had not seen his chute. The pilot had serious frostbite on his hands and Alex was asked to come up and shield him from the sub-zero wind but the rear gunner said as he was wearing a Kapok suit it would be better if he came up and Alex went in the rear turret and so this is what was done. There was a gaping hole in the fuselage and as the rear gunner went forward to shield the pilot he was nearly sucked out of the aircraft; it was only the quick reaction of another member of the crew who grabbed him. The navigator was also suffering from frostbite as did everyone in the crew but his was the most acute. Slowly they fought their way to the Dutch Coast against the gale strength wind and a safe landing was made at RAF Upwood, the home of No. 156 Squadron. They had been hit by a number of bombs from above and were all given a week's leave. Alex's hands were that bad that he had to stand his dominoes upright when playing in the local pub.

While flying on a high level bombing practice from No. 11 OTU at RAF Westcott Jeff Brown was flying in the rear turret when suddenly they flew into a towering bank of cumulous cloud, hidden behind it was a thunderstorm cloud and as they entered the cloud the world changed to various shades of ever darkening grey until the daylight had almost gone and they began to buck and weave most violently. Suddenly Jeff was lifted into the air and like a man in partial weightlessness and then slammed down back on his seat and then held fast by the grip of the 'G' Force as the aircraft was propelled by a massive current of rising air, rushing madly upwards. The turret's interior suddenly became white with frost. All the tools in the turret were rising upwards and then sinking down again like a puppet on strings.

The second pilot was standing by the astrodome hanging on to a rope handle which came down from the roof of the fuselage, he was watching with utter disbelieve the ammunition boxes, the six foot ladder, axes everything else that was not nailed down floating around the fuselage. The navigator was covered in maps and all his instruments and he were they floating upwards and when he came down many of his instruments were lost until the flight was over. The wireless operator had forced himself out of his seat and in doing so broke the arm off the chair. The pilot and bomb aimer (the aircraft had dual controls) were in the cockpit fighting with the controls. The airspeed indicator had spun around madly until the instrument broke leaving the pointer hanging loosely downwards and swinging to and fro like a small pendulum. The pilot decided to turn the aircraft around and fly out of the cloud but as he did so ice began to build up on the wings. Over the intercom came the order, "Fix parachutes and standby". Jeff pulled on the cable which operated the sliding doors behind him and reached inside for his parachute at the same time they started to descend and he ripped off the 'bungee' elastic rubber cords which retained the parachute in its holder and it fell to the floor and there it stayed. Suddenly after what seemed a hopeless situation they were out of the cloud and into the daylight but in an uncontrollable spiral dive. As they dropped the ice on the wings started to come off and the aircraft became controllable. Nobody was hurt but the wooden ladder had gone through the geodetic construction of the aircraft and some of the ammunition boxes had fallen down and punctured the fabric covering. There was immense relief in the crew but they still had the problem of a broken airspeed indicator which would make the landing difficult.

When RAF Westcott heard of their problems they were diverted to RAF Wittering, near Stamford. There they had a pierced-steel planking runway which formed an emergency landing strip of 3,000 yards. The crew padded themselves up for a bumpy landing and they were given radio instructions for landing by RAF Wittering. The landing was made and all was well, although on the steel runway it was a rather noisy landing. The aircraft was repaired and they took off later for RAF Westcott.

At the time of Operation Manna Jeff was now with No. 576 Sqn at RAF Fiskerton. He flew on five Manna operations: four to Rotterdam and one to Valkenburg. As they crossed the Dutch coast all they could see was muddy water, only the tops of embankments and trees could be seen. Jeff saw that some of the food sacks burst on opening and a large sheet of tin had wrapped around the leading edge of the starboard tailplane; this stayed there until they got back to Fiskerton but when they landed it dropped off on the runway as they slowed down. It was half of a 50 gallon oil drum with the ends cut off, then split along the length and opened up to make metal sheets roughly the shape of the bomb doors; the sacks of food were manhandled on top of the sheets, propped up with lengths of wood and the bomb doors closed under them. To drop the supplies the bomb doors were opened and everything fell out. By the end of the Manna operations all the bomb doors were distorted and had to be changed, the sheer weight of the supplies on them had put them out of shape and left 2 to 3 ins gaps at the centre, and the outer skins were wrinkled. The crew would make small parachutes and throw them out loaded with sweets, chocolates and cigarettes. Over Rotterdam people were waving messages and were on the roofs of houses thanking them. Pilots were flying through farmyards although there was a regulation height order, but it was VE Day.

Bob Hughes did not start his flying with Bomber Command but with No. 23 Squadron on Blenheims at RAF Wittering. Their first role was Ack-Ack and Searchlight Co-operation Flights. He then moved to Ford in Sussex patrolling the South Coast to the Thames Estuary. While with 23 Squadron he witnessed what he described as a grim disaster and which has never left his memory. A ferry pilot was bringing a new replacement Blenheim when suddenly it crashed into a nearby railway siding and burst into flames. The pilot was pulled out by a combination of the then Local Defence Volunteers and Bob, who had run across the field. The pilot was put on a stretcher and taken to a waiting ambulance but he was certain to be dead. This was his first experience of death and he now admits it did him a lot of good later in the war.

He then went to the Middle East and flew on Wellington bombers with No. 70 Squadron where he completed a full tour of operations. He was then shipped back to the UK, which took two months on a troopship, going out to the Middle East via Malta had taken 16 hours and 10 minutes. After some time as a screened air gunner he was commissioned and joined No. 12 Squadron at RAF Binbrook. At the time they were still operating with Wellington bombers. Over the Ruhr on one operation he saw no less than five bombers shot down. No. 12 Squadron then converted to Lancasters and were over Essen one night when they were attacked by two Ju88s. He fired sixty rounds, enough to deter the fighters from continuing the fight.

When he had completed seventy-two operations he was again rested and sent as an instructor to No. 8 Air Gunners School at Evanton, and from there he went to the Central Gunnery School at Sutton Bridge for a gunnery leader's course. Then he was posted as a Gunnery Leader to Bishops Court in Northern Ireland. While on a liaison trip to Skellingthorpe he went on a trip with No. 50 Squadron to Magdeberg as a mid-upper gunner. On the way back the pilot asked Bob if he would like to see Berlin but the crew outcry over this suggestion soon dissuaded the pilot, however, Bob did see it from a distance, including the flak defences at Berlin! The Lancaster he flew in was LM 429-C. This was his last operation over German. In 1943 he was awarded the DFM.

Mike Henry started his military career as a dispatch rider in 1938 with the Royal Corps of Signals TA. He transferred to the RAF in March 1939. On 7 October 1940, and with No. 110 Squadron, he took off for an attack on Boulogne, it was his tenth operation. The operation went well until they arrived back at RAF Wattisham, the home of 110 Squadron. The pilot decided to go around again. As they came in for another attempt at landing they touched down safely but as they ran along the runway the port wing dropped and there was a blinding flash, stars and then stillness. Mike found himself standing in the fuselage with his feet in the turret cupola which was on the ground. It started to get lighter and Mike realised this was because they were on fire and flames were licking down the fuselage. He was strapped in his turret, the exit ladder was wedged across his back barring the exit through the camera hatch. Looking around he saw a jagged hole in the fuselage side which was big enough for him to get his head through, he pushed and pushed and with his shoulders protected by a thick leather Irvin jacket and the parachute harness the metal skin gave way and he felt into the night air. He was soon grabbed and put in an ambulance as were the pilot and navigator who, although their faces were covered in blood, were alive. As they drove away the ammunition and oxygen bottles started to explode. The pilot and navigator were taken to a civilian hospital in Ipswich: the pilot had a broken jaw and the navigator concussion. Mike had a deep cut at the back of his head and a torn thigh which was caused when he broke out of the side of the Blenheim.

In August 1941 he went out to Malta to join No. 21 Squadron. The Squadron returned to the UK in January 1942 having accounted for over 30,000 tons of shipping sunk and a further 16,000 damaged. After leave he was posted to No. 13 OTU for his first rest since October 1941. He was later commissioned and sent to London with a £45 allowance to purchase his officers uniform. In August 1942 he was posted to No. 114 Squadron at West Raynham and crewed-up with S/Ldr Thompson B Flight Commander. He was posted to No. 107 Squadron for the third time in September 1943. In December 1943 he was awarded the DFC after forty-nine operations.

Tony Winser of No. 626 Squadron had a very exciting start to his operational career. On one operation, when over the target he looked out and saw smoke on the starboard side and reported it to the pilot who found an engine was on fire and feathered it successfully. However, when Tony

Tony Winsor on the left. *Clare Hardy*

looked around the other side he again saw smoke and as before another engine was found to be on fire. The aircraft then suddenly went into a dive and Tony thought this is my lot but with the combined strength of the pilot, flight engineer, and navigator they pulled out at 2,000 ft. The pilot then was able to limp back to the UK and make a crash landing at Woodbridge in Suffolk.

As his mum and dad did not know he was aircrew he was keen to stop any message getting back to them that he was missing. The next day a Dakota came down and took them back to their Squadron. In Tony's crew were three Australians and four from the UK. When they arrived back from an operation and went into the debriefing room a table had been set up for them and on the table were cigarettes, coffee and biscuits. His father somehow found out that Tony had been on operations but Tony never found out who told him, although everyone but his parents knew. Tony hid his tunic under the table so they would not see his AG brevet. His father told Tony he knew he was on operations and that he must tell his mother. She was shocked but also delighted to hear that he had finished his thirty operations. His father took him down the pub to celebrate.

His tour had not been without incident and included having to ditch in the sea and spend 8 hours in a dinghy.

Douglas Mourton spent a summer to remember in August 1940 at Gunnery School and at the end of the month he was awarded his air gunner brevet and promoted to sergeant. He had passed out as an 'Average Air Gunner'. After OTU at Abingdon he reported to B Flight of No. 102 Squadron and he thought of all those operations to come (thirty) to complete a tour. Then, if he made it, he would have 6 months rest as a flying instructor and then back for a second tour. The average loss on an operation was 5 to 10 per cent although it was often more. At the time No. 102 were operating with Whitley Mark V bombers, two engine and a very tough aircraft on landings. But they were slow and could not climb to any great height so were vulnerable to fighters and flak. His first assignment was as part of a funeral party for an aircraft that had been hit by a fighter while landing and five of the crew were killed. The policy now was that fighters from Northern France would wait for bombers returning to base: with a tired crew and being tense they were easy prey. One aircraft in the hangers had its whole side blown out and the pilot had been awarded the DSO, he was F/O Leonard Cheshire later to be awarded the VC.

Douglas's first op was in November 1940 to Duisberg, he was flying with a Sgt Rix who had three ops to go to finish his tour. All went well until, on the return trip, one of the engines failed and they began to lose height, it was winter time and the North Sea was cold, rough and not at all welcoming. But as it was Rix was able to make Bircham Newton and land safely. That night No. 102 had sent out five aircraft of which one was missing, the CO Wg Cdr Groom. The next operation was to the Fiat works in Turin, Italy. Not the best target for the Whitley with its height problems and the Alps to get over. As it was they flew across France and then neutral Switzerland with all the street and house lights on. They flew through the Alps instead of over them and attacked the works which was poorly defended. On the return, the weather was bad, contrary to the forecast, but they made it back to the UK but were not sure where they were (navigation then was not a precise science). Suddenly the anti-aircraft guns opened up and they were hit, they had in fact flown over Portsmouth in the middle of a German raid. Then, having run out of petrol, the order came to abandon aircraft. Douglas had been in his turret for 12 hours in a temperature of about −30° F. He made his way forward to the cockpit where Rix was still flying the aircraft and he told Doug to jump. Of the seven aircraft that took off from 102 three never even made it to the target, one force-landed near Brighton and a third ditched in the sea off Plymouth. When Doug landed he thought he was in France but when he knocked on the door of a house he found the owner was English and he had landed in England. The remainder of the crew survived. On the way to the local police station they passed the crashed Whitley. Thinking they were over France Doug had put all his letters, photographs and other personal things, which he had forgotten to leave behind and were still in his pocket, in the stricken aircraft before baling out. He then went back into the crashed aircraft and found his things still where he had left them and put them back in his pocket. Having used a Parachute made by the Irvin Parachute Company he became a member of the Caterpillar Club and he received from them a gold caterpillar broach inscribed Sgt D R Mourton. Parachutes were made of silk, and the silk worm is actually a caterpillar hence it being called the Caterpillar club.

On 21 December they had an engine fail when they were 30 miles over the Dutch Coast so they turned to return to base. Later in the war the bombs would have been jettisoned but in 1940 they were not so plentiful so they were brought back. Having got back to the UK and their own base Sgt Rix was just able to pull the aircraft over the boundary hedge, however, parked on the other side was another Whitley and they went straight through the middle of it and it was literally severed in two. The undercarriage wheels of Doug's aircraft were also ripped off so they had to make a belly landing; not the best thing to attempt with bombs and petrol aboard but if you don't have any wheels there is little option. Having got down and stopped they all made a hasty retreat from the stricken aircraft expecting it to blow up at any time. Leonard Cheshire saw the crash and was certain that Rix and his crew were dead. It turned out that it was Cheshire's aircraft they had just cut in two, the one that on a previous operation had its side blown in.

Soon Sgt Rix finished his tour and the next time Doug saw him was 12 months later and he was a Squadron Leader, promotion was swift in the wartime RAF and if you survived you soon went up the tree. His next pilot was Sgt Stevens who was small in stature being only 5 foot 5 ins in height. On 17 January 1941, Doug flew with the CO of 102, Wg Cdr Cole, on a practise formation flight. Doug flew in the rear turret and it turned out to be a frightening experience with other aircraft coming within a foot of his turret. He also found at 102 the gap between the old soldier ground crew and the aircrew was widening because there were some ground crew who resented the rapid promotion that aircrew were receiving.

After a trip to Hannover to bomb a non-military target Doug's conscience started to prick him to the extent he considered refusing to fly because he had not volunteered to bomb civilian women and children. But this he found would take more guts than facing the German defences. In April 1941 when a flight commander went missing Doug was assigned to the new one, a Sqn Ldr Burnett, who soon got the reputation for being a 'press on at all costs' type. Also in the crew were rear gunner Philip Brett, who only recently has met Doug after nearly 60 years through the Air Crew Association newsletter, *The Intercom.*

After twenty-seven operations Doug was again crewed up with a new and inexperienced pilot, Sgt Dougall. But thinking he had three ops to go he was called into the flight commander's office and told he had finished his tour. It would appear that if you completed 200 hours your tour was finished; this was a new Air Ministry Directive and a very pleasing one for Doug. He was also recommended for the DFM but the sting was in the tail in that Wg Cdr Howes the CO would not countersign the recommendation and Doug never did get his well earned DFM. He had crossed swords with Howes over a radio that would not work and the aircraft being scrubbed from an operation which meant that the maxim effort Howes had promised was one aircraft short and he blamed it on Doug.

Doug was posted to Driffield and promoted to F/Sgt where his role was to instruct wireless operators on 104 Sqn but once when an aircraft was short of a wireless/opt/ag he was assigned to a P/O Jones as his front gunner in a Wellington to attack Cologne. He had never flown in a Wellington and soon realised that once in the turret you could not get out unless another member of the crew let you out, also your chute was left behind in the cabin.

While at Driffield he was assigned a classroom and desk and taught the new recruits the dos and don'ts about flying on operations. In November his non-operational spell finished and he was assigned to Sgt David Warnock's crew for a raid on Emden. It was his 30th op and it turned out to be the best operation Doug had taken part in. Sadly, Warnock was killed a few months later while on a period of instructing; perhaps it's no wonder that men would rather stay on ops than instruct. Warnock was known as Doc because he always carried a black overnight bag and was killed on 8 April. OTU courses were losing as many as 25 per cent of their trainees, and many instructors with them. The raid on Emden turned out to be Doug's last operation until May 1942.

He reflected how lucky he had been while flying Whitleys because they were known as 'Flying Coffins'. In winter they were the coldest place on earth. They had four Browning .303 machine-guns and they had a cruising speed of 180mph and a fabric body that was vulnerable and caught fire easily. The role of bombers was bombing and they were supposed to avoid fighters, not to take them on and that was the prime task of an air gunner.

At the end of May the newly appointed C in C Bomber Command Sir Arthur Harris realised he had no more aircraft in Bomber Command than when the war started and he realised he had to show what could be done if a large bomber-force was built up. With this in mind he set about a 1,000 bomber raid which, because of bad weather was homed in on Cologne which was not too distant. Doug was not on the original crews' lists but when a good friend was crewed up with a crew of Canadians who had yet to pass out he refused to fly and Doug was put in his place. Once in the air Doug realised that the reservations that his friend had were coming true: the rear gunner was not keeping the pilot briefed as to where the flak was coming from and the pilot, because of his inexperience was flying straight and level. Doug shouted to him to corkscrew, which he did and the pilot then told the bomb aimer to drop the bombs and so that they could get out as soon as possible. They arrived back at 5am. Doug's friend having been found guilty of LMF (Lack of Morale Fibre) was never seen again. His F/Sgt Stripes would be stripped off his arm and he would be given the most menial and demeaning jobs wherever he was posted. He was not a coward and would have been happy to be posted to another squadron and fly with an experienced crew but it did not work that way; if, for whatever reason, you refused to fly the consequences were mapped out.

In 1938, with war imminent, Jim Goldie joined the RAF; he had been in a gunner in a Territorial Artillery unit and wanted to avoid being called-up for the army. He became an engine mechanic and was posted to No. 224 Squadron at RAF Leuchars. Having hit the towed windsock target several times he received the brass flying-bullet badge which showed he was a qualified air gunner, or the full title of AC1 Flight Mechanic/Air Gunner and received 1/- per day on top of his trade pay. The promotion in 1940 to Sergeant for all aircrew did not go down well with the regular old sweats of the RAF but also there was no room in the sergeants Mess for all these newly promoted NCOs so they dined on the top floor of the Mess.

Jim went on to complete thirty-eight operations in the Lockheed Hudson with sixteen different crews. He and his pal 'Hank' Harrington were then posted to No. 97 Squadron at RAF Coninsgby, they shared a room in the Mess very near to bar which they thought was superb. After a while they were billeted out at Woodhall Spa with a Mrs Baxter and her family. It has to be said that he was not pleased to find out that four previous aircrew lodgers had been lost on operations and Mrs Baxter was none too pleased to have more aircrew thrust upon her. She soon relented and she and her husband became good friends with Jim.

One night Jim crewed up with a crew of a Manchester bomber which crashed the same night and Jim had to spend a few months in RAF Ely hospital. When he returned No. 97 had converted to Lancasters but the string of bad luck continued when Hank, or to give him his correct name, David Harrington age 23, failed to return from the Augsberg raid on 17 April 1942, he is now buried in the Durnbach War Cemetery. The pilot of his aircraft was thrown clear when the aircraft crashed and survived to become a PoW. During his time as a PoW he contracted German measles. Jim then joined 83 Squadron and went on to complete a tour of operations with that squadron making a total of 52 with both 97 and 83 squadrons.

He was then posted to an OTU and became a gunnery instructor and then was posted back to No. 7 Squadron at RAF Oakington and began flying with a crew on its first tour. But after he had completed five operations his wife, an Ex WAAF, who had given birth to a son found out Jim was back on ops and wrote to the commanding officer who immediately took Jim off operations; he had more than done his share!

His operations with 97 Squadron included the low-level daylight raid on Danzig, the 1,000 bomber raid to Cologne, the daylight raids on Le Creusot and Milan and a night attack on Genoa. In June 1943 and now having completed fifty-two operations he was awarded the DFC, he had flown to Berlin three times, to Pilsen, to Italy six times, to Essen, to Duisberg six times, to Hamburg four times, and to many other targets in the Ruhr. At the end of the war he was discharged at Hendon and given £100 and a civilian suit. He had been awarded the DFM in 1942.

Angus Robb was 16 when the war began; he left school at 14 and became a Post Office Telegraph Messenger. On 31 March 1941, his 18th birthday he presented himself to the Recruiting Officer in Glasgow in a bid to become a member of the Royal Air Force, and of course, a pilot. However in the examination he only got enough marks to be accepted for training as a Wireless operator / Air Gunner and had now to face the rigours of an Air-Crew Medical Board. This took 8 hours, and if you were passed fit at the end of it you certainly were as fit as you will ever be in your life. At the end of it he was told "Congratulations, you are a very fit young man. The Board has passed you A1-Fit for Air-Crew". He was sworn in and received the famous 'King's Shilling'. However as there were many waiting to fly with the RAF he was put on 'Deferred Service' and went back to the Post Office until he was called up for service. This came in September 1941.

After Gunnery School he went to OTU and crewed-up. The pilot was known as 'Pop' Haynes as he was 37 years old and had a seven year old son. In civilian life he had played trombone in Henry Hall's orchestra. He had already completed one tour on Whitleys and the ill fated Manchester. Angus was the rear gunner in the crew. In 1942 he was and his crew were posted to No. 431 RCAF Squadron at RAF Burn, Yorkshire. The town of Selby was the nearest to the camp and it had thirty-six pubs but the Albion became the 'Squadron pub'; it was owned by three sisters, one a spinster and two were widows, one of their daughters later married a pilot from No. 431 Squadron. Part of their flying kit consisted of items to help them if they had to escape or evade capture if shot down. Photographs taken in civilian clothes, compasses in all manner of shapes and sizes and concealed in a button that one could screw the top off, or concealed in combs or a pipe. There were also silk scarves that doubled as maps, and key chains that were chain saws. Each man was given a box code named Pandora. This had many interesting items including a fishing line and artificial bait, a razor and shaving soap, plus the usual Horlick, Adrenalin, and Caffeine tables and small tins of compressed cheese with ham. It measured about 7 to 8 ins by 3 to 4 ins. They were give a small, sealed pouch containing about £50 of the currency of the country they would be flying over on operations.

The first aircraft they received from the Vickers factory at Driffield in East Yorkshire but on its first flight the fabric started to peel off and it had to go back. The excuse was that some of the glue they received was not up to the required standard that one would expect, 'there was a war on!'

It was a chilling thought but at that time the average life of an air gunner was 11 hours; Angus went on to complete 56! When getting ready for ops it was the air gunners role to hand out the parachutes and Mae Wests and generally help in the crew dressing room. On one occasion as they were in the crew dressing room the door was flung open and an air gunner came in drenched in sweat and as white as a sheet. He had been standing at the rear of his aircraft when a 4,000 lb 'Cookie' had dropped out of the aircraft, more or less at his feet, not waiting to be told it was not fused he took to his heels across the runway, he had run the a mile or so to the crew room in record time and ended up in hospital with heat exhaustion.

In the aircraft they carried two homing pigeons which were used if they had to ditch. The idea was that if the aircraft was shot down the pigeons were released with their position written in the message container and the pigeons would arrive back at the station with the details of where they had come down. It was always intriguing why the crew required oxygen to survive and yet the pigeons did not. The carrying of pigeons seemed to peter out in 1944.

They had stated their tour at the beginning of the Battle of the Ruhr. On 5 March 1943 was the first operation of the Battle and Essen the target. When the searchlights came up over the Ruhr Valley, or 'Happy Valley' as the aircrew knew it, Angus began to realise he had made a mistake in volunteering for aircrew and should have taken up the offer to help man an Air Sea Rescue Launch. Angus believes it is not possible for anyone who was not there to fully comprehend the sheer weight of metal that was being thrown up into the air over the skies of Germany. Bombers were exploding in a shower of red hot debris when they received a direct hit from a flak shell. It was so terrifying that Angus admits that if there was some way he could get out of flying on operations, without losing face or being branded LMF (a polite term for a coward) he would have taken it.

The aircrew were compiled in lists of six and every six weeks a crew received a weeks leave , which was double leave of the ground crew personnel. If the crew above you on the list went missing your time between leaves was reduced by one week. The losses were that great that Angus and his crew went on leave about every 3 to 4 weeks.

On 18 July 1943 Angus moved to a new home with No. 431 Squadron at RAF Eastmoor, but still in Yorkshire. On the day of the move a WAAF driver had just been posted in from a Halifax Squadron where the room between the top of the bus she was driving and the wing of the Halifax aircraft gave plenty of room. However, No. 431 was still flying Wellingtons where the Wellington wing was much lower. As the WAAF tried to drive under the wing the top of her bus hit the wing and took off part of the wing. The CO was not at all pleased!

The social life in the RAF during the war was as hectic: pubs in Leeds and York were frequented as well as the usual watering hole at Selby. Social functions such as Mess dances and poker games were common. However, the CO of 431 Squadron, being a devout Christian, was trying to organise church parades but without great success, his rear gunner being anything but a church going person. Whilst over the target on one of their trips a gunner reported that there was a fighter on the port quarter but the pilot said, "Never mind, son, the Lord's with us". To which the gunner replied, "He might be up your end but I'm here on my F—- own". For which he was confined to camp for seven days for insubordination.

On another occasion the pilot of P-Peter had been given the message that he was number one to land and was given permission to land. But before he could do so another aircraft reported, "Wounded on board" and P-Peter was told to go around again. This went on for some time as two

A Stirling after a sortie over Essen. *Norman Didwell*

other aircraft also had problems. At last in great desperation a cry came, "this is P for Piss, may I trickle in please?". The WAAF on duty in the control tower came back and said, "Yes P-Piss, trickle in".

On one occasion a ground crew man decided to speak to a rear gunner in his turret. To hear him better the gunner leant forward, depressing his guns as he did so. But as he kept them depressed for some time, the hydraulics built up in the system and oil finally went to the weakest point in the system the triggers. The guns started firing of their own volition but the gunner did not realise what was causing the guns to runaway so kept them pointed at the ground, which trapped the poor ground crew chap between them. The guns fired most of their 350 rounds before stopping, leaving two deep holes at the feet of a petrified airman.

One gunner, a Canadian, had gone out for a drink during the day when he was flying that night and came back the worst for wear. The other crew members put him in his flying kit and smuggled him onto the rest bed in their aircraft. The bomb aimer took his place in the rear turret but, when over the target, left the turret and dropped the bombs and then went back to the turret. The drunken rear gunner was only heard to say that it was the worst take-off the pilot had ever made when in fact they were landing.

Superstition played a very large part in the aircrews' life. For example: the 'Wings for Victory Week' was a drive to raise money for the RAF. As part of this drive, one aircraft made low runs over Pontefract and in the aircraft were five wooden dolls, a gift from the children of Pontefract. The

Crew returning from a sortie to Berlin. P/O Downes and crew of 78 Squadron.

Crew room after a sortie to Berlin. *Albert Dicken*

dolls were later sold as part of the children's effort. However, the loss of
the dolls caused the aircrew great alarm and they were greatly concerned
about their safety on their next mission. All squadrons had what was
known as the 'chop-song': a song that if heard before a flight was supposed
to bring bad luck. In 431 Squadron it was *Dreaming About the Wabash*; no
one ever sang or whistled this song, if it came on the radio it was
immediately turned off. It seemed to start with songs being the favourites
of crews who did not return. Many aircrews had small good-luck charms;
Angus had a small enamelled figure of an old man who was once the
advertisement figure for Mc Ewans Ales. He carried this through fifty-six
operations and still has it today 60 years later.

During his initial training in the RAF Lawrence 'Nick' Nicolson and the
rest of the recruits were taken to Bridlington for the day, thinking this was
a rest day they were looking forward to it. But as it turned out the PTI
(Physical Training Instructor) had other ideas. He told them to jump off
the end of the pier and swim out to the dinghies that were there. It was a
good 20 ft drop and the sea had quite a swell at the time. For 'Nick' it was
an even bigger problem as he could not swim. When he told the PTI he
could not swim he was handed a Mae West and asked, "What will you do
if your plane crashes in the sea? Now are you going to jump or do you
want me to push you in!" He jumped and somehow made it to the dinghy.
They arrived at a Conversion Unit in March 1944 and on one of the training
flights the pilot urinated over the wireless operator who was below him.
This happened on another operation and the crew refused to fly with him
again. They were brought up in front of the CO, who was also a wireless
operator. They were, at first, facing a charge of Lack of Morale Fibre but
when the CO heard the reason no charges were brought. However, they
were able to fly with a different pilot, a P/O 'Kiwi' Lawson. He was older
that the rest being about 30 years of age. And so in July 1944 they arrived
at No. 35 Pathfinder Squadron based at RAF Graveley in Cambridgeshire.
On an operation over Cologne on 23 December and in blue sky a wall of
flak came up and one of the crew, Alan Card, was hit in the face by flak
and became temporarily deaf and dumb. The wireless operator, Ted Herod
went up in the astrodome and was immediately hit in the head and fell to
the floor covered in blood. The Lancaster was now on three engines and
an emergency landing was made at Manston. The aircraft had 100 holes
in it and was a write-off, The crew had flown thirty-three missions in 5
months. Alan and Ted were taken to hospital and the whole crew decorated
with the DFC or DFM. Nick's 52nd operation was with a master bomber,
Gp Capt Le Good, and on this occasion he flew as rear gunner with the
station gunnery officer Sqn Ldr Frazer-Petherbridge in the mid-upper
turret. After being posted to 16 OTU at Heyford he was summoned to the
CO's office; fearing the worst he knocked on the door and marched in. The
CO stood up, returned his salute and then shook his hand. He told him
he was delighted to have a Pathfinder instructor on his base and promoted
'Nick' to Warrant Officer.

Sgt Mayers. *R Mayers*

Bernard Mayers was one of a family of eleven and he grew up with a talent for music. An accomplished violinist and he won the prize of Young Violinist of the year in his home town of Blackburn. Today it is believed there is still a Bernard Mayers trophy for young musicians and is presented annually. Bernard went on to play the saxophone with the famous 1930's Oscar Rabin band and later formed his own band, 'The New Astorians' with whom he won the Melody Maker award in Dublin, and while playing at the Grand Hotel in Grange Over Sands, Lancashire he met his future wife Mary. They later married and a son Robert was born in 1938, by which time Bernard was now the Director of Music at the Ritz Hotel in London. When war broke out in September 1939 he volunteered for the RAF, and after training as an air gunner he served at a number of Air Gunnery Schools reaching the rank of F/Sgt in 1944. And in the same year he was awarded a commission. In November 1944 he, with his crew was posted to No. 1 Aircrew School, a holding unit for No. 1 Group Bomber Command, here they spent two months kicking their heels. On 12 January 1945 they were posted to 1662 Heavy Conversion Unit flying Lancasters. On 19 March 1945 they were again posted, this time to No. 103 Squadron at Elsham Wolds.

On 9 April 1945 the target was Kiel Docks and after being hit by flak they could not close the bomb doors. Then on 11 April their target was

F/O Eric Candler and his crew. Left: Sgt Mayers. *R Mayers*

Plauen, a ball bearing factory south east of Dresden. The rear gunner, Tommy Lincoln, had reported sick with a heavy cold and they picked up an inexperienced air gunner so it was decided that Bernard(Benny) would go in the rear turret to let the new man use the mid-upper turret. The operation went well but on return, with Elsham Wolds under fog, they were diverted to Sandtoft, near Doncaster, but as they were being marshalled to a dispersal area for parking and the pilot was shutting down the engines, turning off the navigation lights and the gunners disarming their guns, they heard a crash and the Lancaster shuddered. A message came to the pilot on the intercom that another Lancaster, piloted by a Canadian F/Sgt had run into the back of them. Perhaps his brakes failed, or the wheels were not chocked, the reason is not known. At the court of enquiry there was no blame attached to their pilot for not warning his crew to keep and eye out as they parked, but it also said that he may well have been confused by torches of the ground crew which were necessary because there were so many aircraft parking on the airfield. The crew was taken to the sick bay for a check up and there later were told that Benny had been killed when the propeller of the other Lancaster had hit the rear turret. He became the last operational fatality of No. 103 Sqn in WWII. He was remembered by his crew as a happy-go-lucky chap who often accompanied them when they went out in the evenings to places such as the Five-Nine café in Lossiemouth, and a pub called the Gladiator in Brigg and others in Scunthorpe. He was buried in Grange Over Sands Cemetery with full military honours. There were wreaths from three RAF stations, a flight commander and his crew. Bernard was 32 at the time of his death and only five foot five in height an excellent height in particular for the rear turret. To die in such a way was no less than a tragedy.

Bernard's crew was largely composed of ex-instructors: F/Lt Len Self was a former navigational instructor in Canada and married a Canadian girl, F/Sgt Pat Westrup, later W/O, was a W/Opt instructor in Scotland, Bernard was the mid upper gunner and with the rear gunner F/O Tommy Lincoln RAAF had both been gunnery instructors and the pilot was Eric Candler, a staff pilot at Nos 1 and 10 gunnery schools. Sgt Johnny Yarr, the flight engineer, had trained as a pilot but later remustered as an engineer. A very accomplished crew it has to be said.

In 1990, in a second hand shop in Gainsborough, a lady, named Mrs Smythe, noticed some badges on sale in the window. As her husband, Frank, collected badges she told him and he went to have a look at them. He found a Distinguished Flying Medal and other world war two medals, and an RAF bandsman's badge; they had all been acquired from a house clearance in the area. The DFM still had a small pin on the back of the ribbon and it turned out that it had been put there for the King to pin the medal on the recipient, and the medals had been sent to the man's widow at the end of the war. The DFM belonged to a Sgt Ronald Jolly who hailed from Brighouse, Yorkshire. He joined the RAF in 1935 and became a qualified musician in the RAF band. When the war started he volunteered for aircrew and became a W/Opt/Air gunner with the then rank of LAC. After obtaining his AG brevet he joined No. 144 Squadron at RAF Hemswell and while there he married a local Gainsborough girl, Doris, the daughter of a police sergeant. On the night of 11/12 May 1940 his aircraft, Hampden P 1236 flown by Wing Commander Arthur Luxmoore was detailed to attack Monchengladbach and as they approached the target they were hit by flak when flying at 6,000 ft. The starboard engine was put of action and the rudder controls were damaged. After flying for over an hour and losing height the crew, including Jolly, were ordered to bale out. All three of the crew left the aircraft with Luxmoore still flying the aircraft and they landed on the French side of the Maginot Line and returned safely to Hemswell two days later. Sadly, Wg Cdr Luxmoore crashed with his aircraft near Finnevaux in Belgium and is now buried there. Sgt Jolly was awarded the DFM on the 23 May and it presented to him by the King, hence the pin, on 27 May 1949 at RAF Hemswell. His citation said that as well as the engine and rudder controls part of the mainplane and tailplane were also shot away. He kept his wireless working and maintained communication and obtained fixes of the aircraft's position to assist the pilot and navigator. He also fired his guns at searchlights which were picking upon the stricken aircraft and was able to knock one out. Before abandoning the aircraft he destroyed papers, locked the wireless transmitter leaving the transmitter turned on and then jumped at a very low height. The other two members of the crew, Sgt H Wathey the observer and P/O R E Alitt the bomber aimer/navigator, were also awarded the DFM and DFC respectively. On 12/13 June 1940, Jolly's aircraft, Hampden P 4343 flown by Wing Commander Joseph Watts DSO, was detailed to take part in a communications flight over Germany. On return they collided with a barrage balloon cable at Felixstowe Docks and crashed on to a flour mill at Felixstowe killing all the crew including Jolly and a mill employee. At the court of enquiry it stated that the aircraft was flying below the operation's height and the wing of the Hampden struck the cable of a balloon at the cross over and was wrenched off. The aircraft dived into the ground and the petrol tanks exploded. It also said that the balloon was at a greater height than the pilot expected. The whole crew was buried at Harpswell Church cemetery with full military honours on 26 June 1940. Sgt Jolly was aged 23.

Mrs Jolly remarried and died before her second husband and when he died the house was cleared by the shop and the medals found. Today they are on display in the Air Gunners Memorial Room at the Yorkshire Air Museum: the former RAF Elvington, near York.

In Bomber Command 7,764 Air Gunners were killed on operations and 908 in training flights.

A GUNNER'S SONG

At night we fly to Hamburg
To Berlin or the Ruhr
Another trip another 'Op'
Will I ever end this tour?
Another flare another fight
Another airman died
The pungent air's our battlefield
Our blood has stained the skies.
    And it was just three months ago
When I was young and green
While now they call us veterans
Though my age is just nineteen.
Still I'll just go on flying
I guess my turn has got to come
How long Oh Lord, How long.

Victor Cavendish (83 Sqdn)

AVM Don Bennett DSO. *Mrs L.Bennett*   Mike Henry DFC. *Mike Henry*

Place	Date	Time	Summary of Events	Page No. Referer to Append
			Patient appeared to be badly shocked and was a bad colour. General first aid and anti-shock treatment was carried out on the spot, after which the patient was placed on a stretcher and carried half a mile to the ambulance over difficult ground. When settled in the ambulance the Rt. leg was slung up and elevated by means of a bandage under the limb and passed over the framework of the upper stretcher carriage. General condition of the patient throughout was good. Patient was taken direct to R.A.F. Hospital. Rauceby., arriving there at approximately 10-50Hrs. Placed on the S.I. List on admission.	
Germany. (Berlin).	29/1/44.	Approx 02;40Hrs.	F/O. Johnson-Biggs (51532.), Air Gunner of No.619. Squadron was rear gunner of Lancaster aircraft engaged on operational sortie over Berlin on the night of 28/29/1/44. Some time after take off oxygen failed and he was given a fresh helmet which he was able to put on himself. As no reply was received by the pilot over the intercommunication, investigation by the F/Eng revealed that he had removed the mask and was unconscious. He was taken from the turret and layed on the floor of the aircraft and fitted with a fresh mask which he also tore off. Was brought back at 22,000 feet in 4 hrs. On landing it was found that his Rt. cheek and Rt. lower eyelid was frost bitten. He appeared very confused and staggered slightly on leaving the aircraft. Taken to SSQ Coningsby and given oxygen, cheek treated by applying warm cotton wool, and shock treatment given. Transferred to R.A.F. Hospital, Rauceby 29/1/44.	
			T. F. McCarthy. Flying Officer, Medical Officer, R.A.F. Base Station, Coningsby.	

Operation Record Book of F/O Johnson-Biggs of 619 Squadron. *Alan Cooper*

CHAPTER EIGHT

Coastal Command

W hen war began in September 1939 Costal Command had only
183 aircraft, the Anson, Hudson, and the Short Sunderland
Flying boat, plus various obsolete aircraft such as the Saro
London and Supermarine Stranraer flying boat. Their duties were
reconnaissance, convoy escort and U-Boat spotting, and thrown in with
this was the occasional attack on enemy shipping. The so called 'phoney
war' was not phoney for Coastal Command who were heavily engaged in
convoy escorts and reconnaissance.

Jim Savage lived in Australia and his father was badly gassed, but
decorated, in WWI. He died in 1930 when Jim was 9 years old. His uncle
died in 1932 from TB which he contracted in the trenches so when WWII
started Jim was definitely not serving in the army and the trenches. With
this in mind he developed a passion for flying, boys' heroes were not only
pilots but observers. Also, the technicalities of photography and air
gunnery appealed to Jim. As a consequence in 1939 he volunteered for the
RAAF. However, at the time they were only training a few observers and
pilots. They were desperate for technicians and he was asked to enlist as
a flight rigger, with the option later that he could remuster or transfer to
aircrew.

In early 1940, having undertaken all his square bashing and an
engineering conversion course, he was posted to a Maintenance Depot but
was very disappointed to hear that all transfers to aircrew was cancelled.
But in June 1940 he heard that replacements were being required for No.
10 Squadron in the UK with fitters, riggers, and wireless electrical
mechanics who were aircrew who were fit and willing to be trained and
fly as air gunners. Jim grabbed the chance and volunteered; he sailed for
the UK on 17 November 1940. Three months later he joined No. 10
Squadron at Mount Batten. Within days he was on a train to RAF Manby,
Lincolnshire.

All those on No. 1 Special Air Gunnery Course were former ground staff
and trained on Fairey Battle and Wellington bombers. They did very well
in achieving the highest marks as a group recorded up to that time and
AC1 Mike Scott, a flight rigger, broke all records for gunnery scores. Back

A Catalina Flying Boat. *Alan Cooper*

in Queensland he had been a bushman. On arrival back at 10 Squadron, and now wearing the air gunner brevet plus an extra 2/6d in his pay, but no increase in rank, Jim began as a rear gunner and in 1941 he remustered as Fitter 2A/Air Gunner. This seems rather strange because all regular air gunners had the minimum rank of sergeant but one assumes that his main role was as a Fitter and not an air gunner despite the fact that he wore the air gunner's brevet!

When Jim was gazetted as aircrew the RAAF did not have a tailor in the UK so he had to go to an RAF tailor who unpicked the brown wreath and stitched in one of blue in the centre of the brevet and enlarged the AG letters. He also had 'RAAF' below the AG. He continued to wear this rather than the one that was officially issued later.

A Short Sunderland Flying Boat. *Alan Cooper*

His flights covered the Atlantic, North Sea and the Mediterranean and after the war he was awarded the Atlantic Star, also the Malta Medal which was instituted a few years ago and given official status by the Queen. A number of Jim's type of air gunner were lost, for example, AC1 Francis Tipping age 36 from Western Australia was lost and Neville Cuddiky, age 22, was lost off Spain in 1942, he was only one a of a number of LAC Fitter/AGs with 10 Sqn who were lost. He is now on the Runneymede Memorial.

When the Empire Training Scheme began the ground crew type air gunners became somewhat redundant. They were flying as LACs, Corporals with men who had been through the ETC and were Flight Sergeant, Sergeants and some officer air gunners.

Because of this Jim returned to ground crew duties and in December 1944 he returned to Australia.

Charles Maton was in London in 1939 and was private secretary to Sir Abe Bailey, a South African millionaire. When war came his wife went back to Cape Town and he volunteered for the RAF. He was 35, and older then the average aircrew. After training with No. 8 Bombing and Gunnery Scholl near Inverness he was posted to No. 500 Squadron in Detling, Kent as a pilot officer. He remained with the squadron for five months flying convoy escorts on Anson aircraft.

In January 1941 he was posted to No. 85 Squadron, whose commanding officer at the time was Peter Townsend, and Charles flew night-fighter patrols on Havocs with Sqn Ldr James Wheeler who had flown in WWI with the RFC and been awarded the Military Cross. In October 1941 they were both posted to No. 219 Sqn at Tangmere and flew Beaufighters until February 1942. After a short period with No. 29 Sqn he was posted back to Coastal Command operations room and promoted to squadron leader. In November 1942 he was promoted to Acting Wing Commander and awarded a mention in dispatches.

In 1943 he joined No. 502 Squadron and reverted back to his war substantive rank of squadron leader. In May 1944 he was appointed commanding officer of 502 Squadron. He was the first air gunner in Coastal Command to command a squadron and went on to lead them on many attacks. However, the night before he was to be posted back to Coastal Command HQ he decided to undertake one last operation with a mainly Canadian crew. The pilot F/Lt Patrick 'Mac' McManus RCAF was flying Halifax HR 686-J. He recalled being called in by Jim Maton who said, "Mac, I'm going to fly with you tonight". He was the type of CO that never asked his men to do something that he was not prepared to do himself. He was a straight air-gunner, having started on the Anson with its Vickers gas operated machine gun. He once told a story of how he had forgotten to take the machine gun along and hadn't told the pilot". The fact that Jim wanted to fly with him caught 'Mac' off guard. Jim explained that it would be his last trip with 502 and he was being posted; although he did not want to leave he knew at his age he would be chained to a desk at Coastal

Command HQ. He loved the squadron and thought it was the best squadron in the RAF.

His parting shot was that he had recommended 'Mac' to be promoted to Sqn Ldr and flight commander of E Flight. All the crew were on their second tour.

The mission, on 3 October 1944, was to patrol the Skagerrak and Kattegat for enemy shipping, particularly enemy troop-ships taking German soldiers back to Germany under the cover of darkness. They had just approached the turn for their next course when they picked up a contact on the radar set. Suddenly in heavy rain and at 800 ft they saw a ship ahead and brightly lit up. Because of this they thought it was a neutral country ship but suddenly when it opened fire they knew it was not. 'Mac' felt a searing burn on the inside of his left knee and right calf as bullets struck home. A shell hit the port inner-engine which caught fire and the aircraft swung to port. He grabbed the intercom and told the crew to prepare for a ditching and for the wireless operator to send out an SOS. He could not hold the aircraft and it was going over on to its back. He was unable to take his hand off the column to open up the throttles nor work the intercom, F/O Lyttle, the co-pilot and also Canadian, was looking out of the right-hand window and had not heard the order to prepare to ditch, he thought 'Mac' was turning to make another attack. 'Mac' then shouted as loud as he could and Lyttle grabbed the column on his side, with both pilots pulling he was now able to take a hand off long enough to open his port engine the result the port wing came up a little. The sea was coming up fast and the glow from the flaming aircraft lit-up the waves which appeared to be reaching up for them. 'Mac' again grabbed the inter-com and said, "We are Ditching". As he put his hand back on the column the wing tip touched the waves, it peeled back and the three propeller blades bent as they hit the water. The aircraft slewed to port, settled on top of a wave and they were down.

'Mac' unhooked his safety belt, stood up on the seat and found the cockpit cover had already gone. As the crew clambered out he counted them and they were all out. The dinghy was stored in the rear port inner-engine nacelle which of course had burned along with the engine. He reached down for the one-man dinghy, which also formed part of his seat but that too was gone and by now most of the aircraft was under water. Soon they were all in the water with their Mae Wests open as the CO_2 bottles had been pulled or activated by the rough sea. If they were to survive they had to get together. The whistle carried by aircrew on their battledress blouse was for this purpose and 'Mac' blew his which brought a reply from most of the crew but two or three did not reply. One crew member was not moving and his face was down in the water; he was F/O La Palme also from Canada and was dead.

Wing Commander Maton was now in difficulty because his flying boots were dragging him down. They were all trying to get them off and 'Mac' was finally able to release the boots. Sgt Allen was in bad shape and seemed to be in some pain to the extent he was not attempting to swim. After half and hour the cold was beginning to get into their limbs. The waves were running at 15 to 20 ft and one by one they were losing men: now down to four. Suddenly 'Mac' saw a small boat but thought he was dreaming, but it was no dream, it was a small coaster with a crew of five. The war diary of the German Leader of the 8th Security Division for 4 October 1944 said, 'Steamer *Amisia* downed one Halifax, five prisoners including two wounded'. It would appear this was the ship that had shot them down but as it was lost at the end of the war it was never verified.

They were taken aboard and wrapped in towels, Allen and 'Mac' had head injuries which were still bleeding. F/O Conlin, and F/Sgt McLaughlin were lost at sea, they are now remembered on the Runneymede Memorial. F/O La Palme's body was washed ashore and he is buried in Mandal Churchyard, near Kristiansand on the coast of Norway. After a couple of hours they landed at Kristiansand, Norway and were taken under armed guard to a railway station and put into a compartment, here they had met W/C Maton, F/Lt Sid Winchester RCAF, and F/O Lyttle who had arrived earlier. They discussed the crash and one of the crew said he had seen the left fin and rudder fly off and the left aileron break away. Bill Allen, not having heard the ditching warning, was still at his navigator's table when they hit the water and, although he didn't remember, it was very likely that he was thrown through the nose of the aircraft. They must have been in the water for about five to six hours. They finally pulled into Oslo and were taken off the train and put on a truck and driven to a large castle. When they entered they found themselves in a large room where an officer wearing the uniform of a *Sturmbannfuhrer* (Major) in the Gestapo, a *Feldwebel* (Sgt Major) and three soldiers came into the room. They were told they were now prisoners of the Third Reich and had, according to the Germans, been on an espionage mission and so would not be given the rights of a prisoner of war. They were then taken to individual cells and locked up but not before they had made an unavailling case for Sgt Allen to be taken to hospital. The next day 'Mac' was interrogated by the Major who said, "Your stupid bosses thought they could disguise a spy as an airman, but it didn't work. Why did they dress him (Charles Maton) in the uniform of a Wing Commander and an Air Gunner. Everyone knows that no Air Gunner ever reached that rank." This was only the start of many interrogations.

On 22 October the guards came early and took 'Mac' outside where a small truck was standing, F/O Lyttle was already there with two guards. The truck took them to the docks where they were put on to a small ship, down into the hold and into a cattle pen. The boat took them to Denmark and then on a train to Frankfurt. This was the main interrogation centre of the *Luftwaffe* Intelligence and Evaluation centre for all Allied aircrew, here they were put into a cell 6 ft by 6 ft and 8 ft tall. They were then sent to *Dulag Luft* prior to being sent to a PoW camp. Here interrogation started again but this time the interrogators were members of the *Luftwaffe*. Much later 'Mac' heard that Wg/Cdr Maton had been taken to a barber who gave him a shave and had made his moustache look like Hitler's, darkened his hair and combed it forward in the same style as Hitler which made him a look like the Fuehrer. It was the Gestapo's idea of a joke.

Wg/Cdr Maton spent over a month at *Dulag Luft*. (Aircrew Interrogation Centre). Eventually 'Mac' and Sid Winchester were sent to *Stalag Luft* III at Sagan, 83 miles NW of Breslau which is now in Poland. When they arrived they found Lyttle already there and that Wg/Cdr Maton had arrived on 13 November. But, their journeys still had not ended as on 20 December, Wg/Cdr Maton, F/Lt Winchester and F/Lt McManus were taken by train to Berlin, here they spent the night in the railway station. The next day they were taken by train to another city and then again by a small truck to another camp, Marlag Milag Nord 33 miles from Bremen. As before, they were put in separate cells and poor 'Mac' was interrogated again, this time by a German naval officer. 'Mac' was asked the nature of his operation and, as before, he replied with his name, rank and serial number.

On 4 January 1945, he was told that he and the other two were going back to *Stalag* III. In the last days of January 1945 the weather was atrocious: frost, snow and biting winds. The prisoners were put on the march to various other camps in the east but on 27 January they could hear the Russian guns attacking Breslau. After six days marching they arrived at a railway station and were loaded into cattle trucks with standing room only and taken to Luckenwalde and *Stalag* IIIA 12 miles south of Potsdam in East Germany. It was an old and long established camp in which were 40,000 Russian PoWs who were starving. It was April 1945 when the first signs of American troops were seen when flares went up in the western sky. But then on 23rd a Russian tank came bursting through the fence and into the camp followed by Russian soldiers who soon captured the Camp Commandant and shot him.

'Mac' and his crew were once again free but they were told to wait for American trucks to come to pick them up but suddenly the wire fences were covered by Russian guards where there had been German guards; they were prisoners again. However, Mac and Winchester found a hole in the fence and told Maton they were going to escape, he wished them well and off they set. They soon contacted American troops and the next day they were taken by plane to Holland, then Brussels and finally London. 'Mac' found out that Sgt Allen was in hospital in Oslo, he had a fractured skull, three broken ribs and a vertebrae at the bottom of his spine was dislocated. It was 6 May 1945 before Jim Maton was finally released.

On 20 August 1944 he had been recommended for the DSO and this was upheld and supported by ACM Sholto Douglas the C in C Coastal Command and gazetted on 10 October. He had flown 138 sorties and flown 510 hours. On 5 June 1945 F/Lt Patrick McManus recommended Wg/Cdr Jim Maton for the DFC. The full account of what happened on the last sorty was in the recommendation. F/O Alexander Lyttle was also recommended for the DFC at the same time and both awards were granted. In September 1945 Jim Maton was posted to HQ Air Command, South East Asia, in Ceylon. Here he was assigned to administrative duties on Lord Mountbatten's staff and in due course he was appointed Deputy Secretary to Lord Louis.

In January 1946 Jim was released from the RAF and returned to civilian life, but not back to South Africa where he had come from. He joined a London firm of stockbrokers and then in 1955 was appointed General Manager of the Guide Dogs for the Blind Association. In 1960, and only 57, Jim Maton died; perhaps that last operation and the time as a PoW had taken its toll.

Robert (Bob) Scott joined the RAAF in March 1941 in Melbourne. After a trade test, which he passed, he was sent to Laverton RAAF base for initial training. He was then posted to RAAF base Point Cook for a 12 week fitter/armourer's course. On completion he was posted to No. 10 Squadron RAAF at Pembroke Dock, South Wales. His rank was Leading Aircraftman. In 1942 he commenced an air gunners course when the squadron was transferred to Plymouth, Devon, undertaking patrols over the Bay of Biscay. His training was carried out on the Fraser Nash hydraulically operated turret. After class room instruction and workouts on the rifle range, they were introduced to the most interesting part of the training: operating from all positions on the Sunderland flying boat. Bob found the tail turret rather difficult while moving from one beam to the other because of the very heavy vibration of the turret caused by the force of the terrific slipstream. His main worry was that the turret appeared to be separating from the aircraft. Once over this fear his confidence grew and he spent many hours in the tail turret. His position in the aircraft was armourer/tail gunner and he was responsible for fixing any stoppages on the small fitters bench situated in the port side towards the tail of the aircraft. He was also responsible for altering the settings on all the depth charges. The pilots would keep the gunners awake by asking the them about the wing spans of various aircraft and how much they would fill the ring sight at 400 yards. It seemed to work as no gunner got any 'shut eye' whilst in a gun position.

Bob's aircraft W3983-R for Robert flew many patrols of 12 hours over the Bay of Biscay and from Gibraltar on patrols over the Mediterranean Sea and towards Malta. On one occasion they had to force land in the sea about 20 miles off the coast of Spain with a fuel shortage. The aircraft was towed in to Gibraltar for repairs and Bob became a member of the Goldfish Club awarded to all aircrew who have to ditch. Flying from Gibraltar towards Malta they attacked an Italian submarine on the surface, they damaged it but were themselves damaged in the action. A Hudson aircraft came out from Gibraltar to finish off the submarine. During the action the bomb rack was damaged and the pilot was unable to drop the depth charges from the damaged rack. Bob organised the change over from the damaged rack to a serviceable rack which enabled the pilot to make another attack which resulted in many of the submarine crew jumping overboard because of the serious damage that was incurred on the submarine. The pilot, F/Lt Graham Pockley RAAF, was awarded the DFC and Bob the DFM, both awards being immediate. Bob's rank AC1. recommendation of 12 June 1942 also went on to say that he had cleared, in action, many major gun stoppages which meant dismantling and assembling the guns, and in spite of four guns being unserviceable, 2,600 rounds were fired at the enemy. The recommendations were approved by AOC of 19 Group on 15 July 1942. The RAAF records show that only four LACs were awarded the DFM in WWII. He was given a few days leave to receive his medal from the King at Buckingham Palace. His big problem that only being an AC1, with AG Brevet and the ribbon of the DFM it attracted the service police's attention as all aircrew in the UK had the minimum rank of Sgt, but when he got his third stripe things got better.

On 2 August 1942, in Sunderland W3983 R, Bob took off from Mount Batten en route to Stranraer. F/Lt Pockley was at the controls and Robert Scott at his guns. The flight plans were in sealed orders and not to be opened until they were airborne. From Stranraer they were heading for Reykjavik in Iceland. Their passenger was no less than Air Chief Marshal Sir Phillip Joubert De La Ferte, the Commander in Chief of Coastal Command, hence the secrecy: his capture by the Germans would have been quite a prize. He was going to Iceland for a high level conference, which was said to have an effect on the shortening of the war. It revolved around the new filling of bombs and depth charges to be used in the future with Bomber Command raids and Coastal Command in the war against the U-Boats, it was called Torpex. The journey took 10 hours during which they saw many icebergs and they thought of the sinking of the *Titanic* by such huge icebergs. During their time in Reykjavik it was bombed by seventeen long-range German bombers which destroyed a number of American P38 aircraft on the ground.

On 9 August they returned to Mount Batten via Invergordon and Stranraer arriving at 1605 where Sir Phillip thanked each individual member of the crew. On 2 September in Sunderland 3985 they took off at 0200 to escort HMS *Ramillies* that had been torpedoed below the water line.

On 7 September 1942 they took off with a crew of ten and a full load of petrol, 2,240 gallons, for a full 12 hour patrol, plus a full bomb load. As they were about to take off the wind changed and Graham Pockley received a red light to abort the take-off until the flarepath could be changed into the new wind direction. However the take-off had not been reported or cleared with the balloon regiment at Plymouth Hoe in order that they might pull down the balloons which were suspended at 500 ft over the Hoe, and directly in their flight path. They were at 200 ft when the aircraft collided with the steel cable between the barrage balloon and the cable winch on the ground. Robert remembered it felt like a giant hand had grabbed them and for just a second all forward movement stopped. They were about to stall and spin into the ground when suddenly they were released from the grip and Graham was able to regain speed and control of the aircraft. They then continued on their Anti-U-Boat Patrol. On landing 12 hours later they found the aircraft's starboard inner engine had picked up the steel cable and the three bladed propeller had cut the cable which had imbedded itself one inch into each blade.

On 17 September Graham Pockley DFC was recommended for an immediate bar to the DFC. In his recommendation was mentioned that he had destroyed two U-Boats and one other craft, damaged three U-Boats and a motor vessel. Sadly on 25 March 1945, after Robert had left the crew and was now with No. 41 Squadron, Graham was lost in Malaysia and is now commemorated on the Labauan Memorial. He was 32 years of age.

Arthur Davies trained as an apprentice fitter at RAF Halton. On completion of his course he was posted to Scotland and as a fitter flew in Sunderland Flying Boats and, later, in Catalinas at Lerwick. In 1942, when the new aircrew category came, in he applied for Flight Engineer training and was posted to St Athan for training on Lancasters. But he was soon posted to a Coastal Command OTU at Ivergordon. On leaving St Athan they were given AG brevets until the official FE brevet was ready. At Invergordon he crewed up but after week it was found that he had never had a gunnery course. In Coastal Command flight engineers had also to be trained as air gunners so he was sent down the road to a gunnery school at Evanton and assured that he could return to his crew on his return provided he passed both boards. When he arrived at the Sergeants' Mess with an AG brevet eyebrows were raised and at first they tried to make him take down his AG brevet until it was established that AG brevets were officially worn by Flight Engineers. The aircraft used at Evanton were Blackburn Bothas, and as the course went on they did air-to-air firing but the Botha got quite crowded with the pilot, gunnery instructor and three pupils crowded into a small space. The way down to the mid-upper turret was down a very narrow passage and it was not unusual for at least one parachute to be snagged and pulled which added to the confusion. One pilot was testing his engines when Arthur noted a rather large drop in revs as he cut one magneto so he tapped him on the shoulder and shouted to him that he had magneto trouble on that engine so he taxied back and changed aircraft (an advantage in having an engineer on board). On completion of the course Arthur asked to be excused the passing out parade, but this was refused so when it was his turn to be presented the Group Captain looked a bit surprised and then decided he didn't need the stripes or brevet. He returned to Invergordon and completed OTU with the same crew and finally the official Engineers Brevet was approved and the AG brevet was ditched although he was qualified to wear both.

Doug Stallard had been in the army before transferring to the RAF. Doug started his RAF flying with No. 415 Torpedo Bomber Squadron in Tain, Ross-shire. The squadron's aircraft were originally Beauforts but they soon lost these to the Middle East and they were replaced by Hampden bombers from Bomber Command. Doug remembers that the Hampdens were never suited to torpedo dropping.

On 7/8 August 1942 a panic call came from Coastal Command HQ outside Edinburgh, for all available aircraft and crews, it was the German Battleship *Lutzow* making for the open seas. Five crews, twenty men, headed for Leuchars to get kitted out. On 10 August 1942, with *Lutzow* ready to slip moorings the aircraft started to take off led by Doug Stallard's Hampden, however, one caught fire on take-off and one had hydraulic failure and could not retract the undercarriage or flaps, on returning to base it lost its brakes as well and ended up over the bank at the end of the runway but the aircrew were unhurt. The remainder of the formation flew in loose formation at a height of about 30 ft, hoping to escape the ships radar. The two twin Vickers guns were tested , and they settled for what was a long flight. After an hour, as Doug braced his back against the main fuel-tank and looked out of the little portholes which were over the wings, he noticed a rivulet of oil on the starboard wing. The pilot thought the ground crew had overfilled the tanks. But as they went on this rivulet became a stream and the pilot now saw a drop in pressure. This was followed by the starboard engine packing up, now at 30 ft and with a full load they were certain to ditch. The order came "Dinghy, Dinghy, prepare for ditching" and then, "Get to hell out of there(the nose) I can't keep this thing up". The sea was running at about 8 to 10 ft and the tail dragged on the surface, they bounced off the top of the swell, then into another, it was like running into a stone wall. The fuselage broke off just aft of the wireless position, and the nose caved in and in came the water. The poor pigeons had no chance and went down still in their cages. Doug was first out followed by the rest of the crew and as the pilot stepped onto the port wing he noticed the dinghy drifting away in the wind, the immersion switch had been activated when they bounced off the first wave and that caused the tether-cable to break after the dinghy had automatically inflated. Somebody cried, "get the dinghy". Doug dived in and, after swimming for a while, he caught up with the dinghy, which by now was about 100 ft away. It was upside down and when Doug righted it he found they had lost the patching kit, pump and all but one flare. Somehow they all got in but the four-man dinghy was not made for comfort and had no leg room.

As morning broke they heard the sound of an aircraft but they did not spot it. However, when they looked towards landfall they saw a launch running parallel with them. By this time they were in an almost totally submerged dinghy but somehow they were able to support the pilot, Wing Commander Ron Denis from Ottawa, who was standing up waving his battledress jacket. Soon the launch was alongside and the launch's crew threw a scramble net over the side. Two of the crew jumped into the water and they were hauled aboard the launch. Apart from being cold and stiff they were all in reasonable condition. They stripped off and climbed into warm dry clothing and then into bunks and headed full speed for

Aberdeen. The launch was HSL 126 and which had just picked up its first live customers. At the dockside in Aberdeen they were given porridge and a hefty shot of the pursers rum, then off to Dyce and a hospital check up. They were told by the ASR crew that Group had received a signal giving their ditching position and after a few calculations they did a square search until they found them. Their Hampden AN 124 M-Mother had gone in at 2000 hours and were picked up at 0700 the next day. Another aircraft had seen them ditch and watched the training antenna that they had forgotten to wind in, a Cardinal sin, and looking like an outboard motor.

One crew in 415 Squadron were in a dinghy for 14 days. The operation was on 4/5 June 1942 and was a convoy strike off the Frisians. When they had to ditch Bill Peebles, one of the air gunners was killed, and is now remembered on the Runneymede Memorial. The remainder of the crew made it to the dinghy but it was a week before they were spotted by a Ju88 which circled them until bounced by a Beaufighter and driven off but, unfortunately, the Beaufighter did not see them. That night the other gunner, Eddie Thomas, died and his body committed to the sea and he is now also remembered on the Runneymede Memorial. A couple of days later another member of the crew, Jim Stirling, died. After 11 days at sea the pilot, P/O Holbrook 'Hoke' Mahn, who came from Denver, Colorado USA, caught and ate a seagull that had landed on the dinghy, and later he obtained a quantity of rain water, the first water they had had in a week. On the 14th day they heard voices nearby and managed to utter something in return. It was the crew of a Royal Navy MTB; they soon got Mahn to port and hospital where part of both legs was amputated due to gangrene. He later returned to the squadron for a short while but died in 1944 from his ordeal.

On 2 June 1943, Sunderland aircraft BU 968-M of No. 461 Squadron with Doug Stallard in the crew were on an anti-submarine patrol when they were attacked by no less than eight Ju88s. The Ju88s took up an attack formation, three on either side and two on the tail. They attacked in pairs, the first shells fired set the Sunderland's port outer-engine on fire. The crew put out the fire but another shell broke the compass which was in front of the pilot, Flt Lt C G Walker, and set it ablaze. He and his second pilot, Pilot Officer Dowling, were slightly burned. In all there were twenty attacks but one of the enemy fighters on the starboard side was hit by the fire from the Sunderland's gunners. Its cockpit and one engine burst into flames and dived into the sea. The rear turret hydraulics were shot away in the next attack by the second pair of Ju88s. The rudder and elevators were peppered and dozens of holes appeared in the helm. Another Ju88 was shot down as it turned away from an attack. In another attack the Sunderland's galley was hit and the galley gunner, Sgt Miles, was wounded and died 20 minutes later. The tail gunner, F/Sgt Goode, was knocked unconscious but later came to and in another attack he and one of the mid-ship gunners shot down another Ju88 which broke away and crashed into the sea. The port galley-gunner drove off another of the enemy aircraft with his fire power. The navigator, Flying Officer Simpson, who had acted as fire controller was also wounded in the leg. Walker was awarded the DSO, Simpson the DFC and Goode the DFM. Sadly, Ray Goode who was later promoted to Warrant Officer was killed on 13 August 1943, he was 34 and has no known grave. He had excelled himself on 13 February 1943 against two Ju88s and two Fw190s, remaining at his unserviceable turret but continuing to fire whenever fighters crossed his sights. He probably destroyed one Fw190.

After the war as there was no RAF reserve in the area Doug joined the Cape Breton Highlanders who are affiliated with the Seaforth Highlanders. After he had left he was approached and asked to be an Honorary Colonel of the 1st Battalion which he accepted.

F/Sgt Wallace Mackie, an Australian wireless/operator/air gunner, serving with No. 461 Squadron had already flown thirty-seven operations when he was recommended for the British Empire Medal. On 29 May 1943, his Sunderland aircraft crashed while attempting an air sea rescue. The second pilot, F/O Gipps, was thrown out in the crash and, in a badly injured condition, was floating away from the remainder of the crew who were standing on the mainplane of the aircraft. Owing to his injuries Gipps was unable to inflate his Mae West and began to sink some distance away from the aircraft. Without hesitation F/Sgt Mackie dived into the water and on reaching F/O Gipps supported him for 30 minutes until the dinghy was inflated. By this time the wreckage had sunk and it was only with some difficulty in manoeuvring the dinghy that they were able to pick them up.

Flying Officer Hilton DFC set out to attempt a rescue in a minefield. A pilot of a Whirlwind aircraft had been attacked by enemy fighters on the afternoon of 31 October 1942, and had to bale out a few miles from the French coast. His gunner was F/Sgt 'Dizzy' Seals a former dirt-track rider in Australia. While on the surface, and after carefully paving a path through the mines Hilton was able to throw the downed pilot a rope and they managed to attach the dinghy to the Walrus. However, the aircraft began to drift towards a mine, so Hilton had to let go the rope and go back to the controls. They managed to travel through the mines safely, dragging the airmen and dinghy after them. It took some effort to lift the man who was unwounded, but weak, out of the dinghy and aboard the aircraft. As Hilton was accelerating up to take-off speed he saw a mine right in front of the Walrus. He pulled back the stick and hoped for the best. The aircraft responded and came up out of the water to a height of about 15 ft. It came down again and bounced a few times before finally lifting off and into the air.

On 18 February 1942, F/O Bernard Bannister of No. 120 Squadron took off in Liberator AM 925 but as he did it came down again and crashed. Sgt John Waite, wireless/operator/air gunner, found himself lying on the grass about 20 yards in front of the aircraft which was by now in flames. Another survivor from the crew told him to run from the scene as fast as possible as there were eight depth charges on board and likely to go off at any minute. Although Waite himself was seriously injured with injuries to his face, back and leg he went back to the blazing aircraft and pulled out the navigator, P/O Densham, who was lying on the floor of the aircraft and surrounded by flames. Waite carried Densham clear for about 100 yards, including through a barbed-wire fence and behind a ditch for shelter just as the depth charges exploded. For his actions he was awarded the George Medal. Sadly P/O Densham died 3 days later of his injuries. In the crash three other members of the crew were killed. P/O Bannister had been awarded the DFM in 1940, then a F/Sgt and pilot with No. 201 Squadron.

F/O Moore of the RCAF and serving with No. 224 Squadron took off at 2214 in a Liberator on 7 June 1944. At 0211 a U-Boat was sighted on the surface; an attack was made and the nose gunner opened fire and claimed hits on the conning tower which contained about eight members of the crew, two of which were seen to fall down. The nose gunner fired about 150 rounds in the engagement. Then three depth charges were dropped each side of the conning tower. The U-Boat reared out of the water and slowly disappeared. When Moore returned over the area only oil and wreckage was seen. A second U-Boat was seen at 0240 and, once again, an attack was made and the nose gunner again opened fire, with a further 150 rounds and claiming hits on the conning tower. As before, depth charges were dropped, four on the starboard side and two on the port side. The U-Boat was next seen with a list to starboard and then the bows reared up out of the water and then slid back into the sea and disappeared. The Leigh light was switched on and three dinghies were seen in the water, also oil and wreckage.

On 2 August 1943, and now with a Flt Lt Hanbury, and while on patrol in the Bay of Biscay, another U-Boat was sighted on the surface, this U-Boat was the new large ocean going type. A Sunderland of No. 416 Sqn was also in the area and both dropped their depth charges, upon which the U-Boat stopped with smoke streaming out aft and the deck a shambles. The crew started to jump overboard when suddenly there was an almighty explosion and the middle of the submarine was blown out and it sank immediately.

On 1 December 1943, and now with F/Lt Grimshaw, Don Norman, in the mid-upper turret, saw no less than eight Ju88s flying at right angles to them. At the Ju88s started to head for them the leading Ju88 attacked on the starboard bow and came in very close before breaking away. In the attack the second pilot was hit in the arm but both Don Norman and the rear gunner got in several telling bursts with tracer seen to enter the Ju88. This caused the Ju88 pilot to take evasive action and, in trying to follow him, the belt feeds jumped off the rollers in the rear turret which put all four rear guns out of action. Just before the action took place Don had been handed a cup of tea from the galley, after the action it was now swilling about on the floor. Although Don did not see the Ju88 hit the water it seemed to have an effect on the other fighters as they were reluctant to come in close to attack but would attack from a distance of up to a 1,000 yards away and their rounds fell short. They were able to get away and below them saw the Ju88s were circling a large patch of foam on the surface which was some evidence that they had probably shot down one of the Ju88s. They had a wounded second pilot and a few holes in the hull. It was later learned that the wounded pilot had suffered greatly and later lost his arm.

Don was flying in a Sunderland again on 17 January 1944 at 0500 and soon after take-off when the starboard inner-engine developed a persistent knock and then caught fire. All efforts to extinguish the fire failed and a distress signal was sent out by Don. After three great bounces on the water a successful ditching was made, although a float was lost leaving the aircraft leaning to port at a steep angle. The flight deck was full of smoke as the fire took hold. They all made it into the dinghies safely with Don sending out emergency messages right up to the last moment and was the last to exit carrying a portable transmitter and two pigeons in their metal containers. Halfway up the astrodome steps he dropped the pigeons and was not able to retrieve them. Still today he thinks about those pigeons and their potential for life saving. The Sunderland eventually blew up and sank. The cruiser HMS *Adventure* arrived at their position first but with its speed over shot them. An aircraft of No. 228 Sqn, flown by F/Lt Squires, had also found them up and circled them until they were picked up and finally deposited in Tenby. It was ironic that Don ended his tour and 600 flying hours with No. 228 Sqn.

Many an air gunner has been the only survivor of a crash and Andrew Jack was such an air gunner. On 23 August 1942, he was flying as rear gunner in Sunderland W4026-M-Mother of No. 228 Squadron. One of its passengers was the Duke of Kent, an Air Commodore in the RAF. Ostensibly, he was going on a welfare tour of Iceland but it is now known that he was going for a meeting with regard to becoming liaison officer with the US Forces. The pilot was F/Lt Frank Goyen aged 25 from Victoria in Australia. Also aboard were his commanding officer, W/Cdr Moseley. In all there were fifteen men aboard plus depth charges in the event of sighting a U-Boat. But it never reached its destination and crashed into a 900 ft hill in Scotland. The aircraft went over on its back and disintegrated on impact and all but Jack were killed. The tail section had been broken off and, although badly burned to his face and arms and suffering other injuries he survived. He had been dragged along half in and half out of the turret and the soles of his flying boots had been torn back at the heel. He looked for survivors but they were all dead, he then lost consciousness. When he came to he walked across the moors trying to find some life but decided to bed down in the bracken for the night and started off again the next morning and it was the afternoon before he came across a cottage and help. In the meantime a doctor had arrived at the crash site and found that the Duke's watch had stopped at 32 minutes after taking off. The crash site now has a memorial with the names of all the men killed in the crash.

There were other air gunners in the crew apart from Jack: P/O the Hon C.V. Michael Strutt RCAF buried in Nottinghamshire, F/Sgt Edward James Hewerdine buried in Lincolnshire, F/Sgt William Royston Jones buried in South Wales, Sgt Arthur Rowland Catt buried in Middlesex and Sgt Edward Francis Blacklock RNAS buried in Scotland. The Duke of Kent was buried at Frogmore in the grounds of Windsor Castle. Although there was an enquiry no real solution has been found for the reason that this aircraft crashed with such experienced people at the helm. Perhaps we shall never know.

Rick Pearson joined the RAF in May 1940 and was trained at No. 7 Bombing and Gunnery School, Porthcawl in South Wales. His training he now describes as appalling. He was told to fire a single shot Vickers Gas Operated gun from the rear of a boat and told to pick a wave in the water and shoot at it. This he did until the gun jammed, which he now says taught him nothing. Next, again, using a VGO, he fired from a truck-mounted turret at a model aeroplane mounted on a trolley running on a circular track, but was not told to fire at the model as it would be destroyed and it was the only one they had. Again he learned nothing. When sent up in a Fairey Battle aircraft and told to shoot at a towed drogue it was impossible to ascertain his score as three of them were firing at the same drogue. Various lectures followed, including the one on the VGO, which he was never to use on operations and then given a rating of 79 per cent and passed with a logbook entry of 'Sound Air Gunner.' He was then posted to No. 201 Squadron as a rear gunner and after several operations on Russian convoys, for which he found the Sunderland flying boat totally unsuitable, he was posted to No. 228 Squadron and spent some time collecting new Sunderlands from the Shorts factory at Rochester in Kent and delivering them to Pembroke Dock in Wales. This meant flying up the Channel with a high risk of being jumped by enemy fighters operating out of France. On one occasion he saw a Spitfire but as it was making what looked like an attack Rick gave it a long burst just underneath it from 100 yards, it had the desired effect as the Spitfire broke off like a scalded cat. He was then posted to Africa during which time he flew through the Bay of Biscay several times and was once attacked by a Ju88 but as they only had daytime tracer in the guns and at night this dazzled the Ju88 it broke off the engagement. After a year in Africa he returned to the UK for a rest and was posted as a gunnery instructor to an OTU and then to the Empire Air Navigation School as a wireless operator although he still knew nothing about the wireless set he was to operate, but with the help of a very friendly wireless mechanic he became very proficient on the T1154/R1155 set so much so that he was posted to a Liberator OTU and crewed up for service in Burma as a first wireless operator. However, the war came to an end and he did not have to fly with his crew from Canada, to Burma via South America, Nigeria, Central Africa and India. Lastly, on one occasion Rick asked his CO for permission to make a parachute jump but the reaction was not what he expected, in fact the CO was furious at such a suggestion. The answer was short and sweet, No! Since then Rick has made over 100 jumps and became Captain of a free fall team and is now a Firearms Dealer specialising in the Luger pistol. But as Ex -Warrant Officer Rick Pearson always said the RAF taught him nothing. Having always been interested in firearms he was able to work out for himself how the Browning .303 and later the .50 calibre guns worked.

Sandy Blamire was one of twelve new AGs posted from Dalcross to Blackpool and then on to No. 179 Sqn. They were just converting from Wellingtons to Warwicks, an all-night low-level search aircraft. The Warwick had the latest radar, Leigh Lights, and a low-level bomb sight and the search was made for U-Boats at a height of 200 ft on patrols for between 12 and 16 hours. Sandy's crew were all experienced and had a tour under their belts so he being a mere boy was put in the rear turret. One summer afternoon, when airborne, Sandy saw a thick plume of white smoke coming from under his turret and he told the pilot who asked him to look in the bomb bay and there was the problem: a smoke marker had ignited in the bomb bay. The bomb doors were opened and out went a bunch of grey canisters. As they turned towards base at St Eval Sandy heard the Skipper being told what to do on landing. When they touched down a Ford Fire engine, and an ambulance followed them. Once they were stationary they were told to abandon aircraft and as they did a Hillman car pulled up and two non-flying commissioned officers got out and began to question them. To Sandy, "Where were you when the float ignited?" To the Second pilot, known as Doc, "How did you know it was a smoke float?" To the Skipper, "Did you know exactly where you were when you dropped your load?" The Warwick was towed away and they all went to the Mess. The next day the three of them were taken to the pyrotechnics store in an attempt to identify the smoke float. On the door of the brick shed were the words 'Pyrotechnics.' And 'No Smoking' in red paint. The ground crew could not understand why they thought this was funny.

CHAPTER NINE

The Far East

Peter Caldwell was trained on Wellingtons as were many of the crews he trained with at OTU at Wescot. At first he found it a bit frightening in the rear turret doing circuits and bumps (take-off and landings) but the pilot soon learned to control the Wellington in such a way as to make life easier for the crew. The turrets in the Wellington were excellent training for what was to come. The this entailed shooting at a Drogue towed by a Martinet aircraft, which some claimed was a suicide job for the pilot. It appeared that the night-flying exercises were for subsequent operations over Germany but the pilot had volunteered for service in India.

Peter was then posted to India and when he arrived he joined up with two other gunners, a bomb aimer, a second wireless operator and second pilot. When these people were added to a pilot and wireless/operator, who came with him from Wescot, they made up a crew for a Liberator, the aircraft in which they were to fly. It had two Emmerson turrets in the nose and tail, a mid-upper turret and a Sperry ball turret in the bottom centre of the aircraft. Each of the two Browning 0.5 machine guns fired 750 rounds per minute. This was supplemented by a waist-gun position on each side of the fuselage which was fired through a large beam hatch which could be opened and locked into position, revealing a panoramic view of whatever you were flying over.

When he arrived at a Heavy Conversion Unit (HCU) at Kolar, India, the fact that the other three gunners were either too tall (over 5 foot 8inches) or declined to become the ball-turret gunner, meant that Peter, at just 5 ft 8 ins, despite having trained on the rear turret of a Wellington, was delegated to this position. For him it turned out to be the most interesting position on the aircraft, although it was featured in a television series called *Suicide Missions* on the History Channel.

Although never directly attacked by fighters they did quite a bit of strafing at low level. Because he was sitting in a legs-apart position, when they dived onto shipping, his first reaction was to close his legs to protect that part of his body he felt was most vulnerable to the resulting tracer bullets aimed at their aircraft. Indeed, the most frightening time in the turret was when they flew through flak, under which circumstances he was tempted to get out of the turret into the relative safety of the aircraft. The first time they experienced heavy anti-aircraft fire was on his third trip. He had entered the area of the aircraft containing the turret knowing they were not in the target area but as he stood in the rear of the aircraft between the two open hatches waiting to be instructed to enter the turret he saw on the starboard side many puffs of smoke. All of a sudden there was a series of crumps around them and then puffs of white smoke. The noise was so loud you could hear it above the noise of the engines. Somehow they survived, although it was quite a shock to the system.

On occasions it was decided not to use a ball-turret gunner in order to save weight. Then Peter either went to another turret or stayed behind. On one operation, a trip to bomb Bankok from a height of 500 ft and made more dangerous with the known presence of balloons in the vicinity, the opposition was light tracer and several searchlights. All the gunners including the beam gunners (2nd Wop and Engineer) had a go at the searchlights and the engineer reported, "One searchlight out Skipper" but Peter reported, "One searchlight back on Skipper", when the light came back on Peter opened fire on it. It was the mid-upper turret that he hated the most, if the sun was shining the 'Green House effect' was almost unbearable.

In India he met two of his brothers, one, a Flt Sgt fitter who hiked from Akyab by Harvard aircraft to Salbani where Peter's squadrons, Nos 355 and 356 were based. The other brother was an Able Seaman, whose ship had shot off its own guns when shelling Java after the war, and it had come into Bombay for repairs, came all the way by train to Bengal to find Peter. Sadly both have now died but wonderful memories of those times and the bond between brothers remain. His eldest brother, a wireless operator/air gunner on Wellingtons was killed on the 1,000 bomber raid to Cologne in May 1942, having completed a tour with No. 9 Squadron; he was at the time flying with a 'sprog' crew from Wellesbourne OTU. He had just received a commission as an officer and was due to be married five days after the trip to Cologne.

Eric Kightley joined the RAF at 18 as a General Duty airmen but soon became frustrated with the mundane life and volunteered for aircrew. He was sent to Cardington for medical, education and aptitude tests, before going before a selection board. His preference was to be a flight engineer but as there was an 8 months waiting list that was discounted. From Cardington he was sent to the Air Crew Reception Centre at St John's Wood which consisted of swimming at Seymour Street, PT at Lord's Cricket Ground and various inoculations. He was then sent to Initial Training Wing at Bridlington. Here he did dinghy drill, Aldis lamp/Morse code, aircraft recognition, firing a sten gun, Lee Enfield rifle, and Clay Pigeon Shooting. From there he was posted to the Elementary Air Gunners' School at Bridgenorth, and was first introduced to the Boulton Fraser-Nash and Blenheim turrets with its four .303 Browning Machine guns, and very importantly the use of the parachute. From there he went on to the

Gunnery School at Bishops Court in Northern Ireland, here they started air-to-air firing from an Avro Anson at Drogues pulled by Lysander aircraft. The bullets were coated with a coloured dye which enabled the marksmen to be identified. They were then awarded their air gunner brevets and told to report to Blackpool and be issued with tropical kit before embarking for India.

It was to Bangalore via Bombay and Kola and a Heavy Conversion Unit flying B24 Liberators. This was for a familiarisation course firing twin .5 Browning machine-guns in an Emerson and Martini turret. After crewing up he was posted to No. 355 Squadron at Salbone, Bengal, where he went on to complete a tour of operations.

One of a number of operations carried out was an attack on the bridge at Katcenbura. This bridge was the now famous Bridge Over The River Kwai which actually consisted of steel and concrete and was not a wooden one as shown in the famous film. The task was to take out the anti-aircraft gun positions by whatever means they could, strafing and bombing whenever a gun position was spotted. They were successful and this enabled the bridge to be taken with minimum resistance.

On 1 May 1945, the CO of 355 Squadron took the unusual step of informing everyone on the station, ground and air crew that the invasion of Rangoon by Allied troops was about to take place. It meant a maximum effort and an 8 hour return trip followed by refuelling and rearming and off again. Eric flew in Liberator KH 210-R Robert with S/L De Souza and the most experienced crew on the squadron. W/C James Nicolson VC DFC was flying with them as an observer: he was the only man in the Battle of Britain to be awarded the VC. He was seconded to the squadron to develop ideas to increase safety when flying in appalling conditions such as a

No. 6 Course converting to Liberators in 1944. *H.G. Sforcina*

219/12 Sqn Camp Area in Darwin during 1946. *H.G. Sforcina*

monsoons when aircraft such as the Liberator would be thrown about easily. They had already completed a round trip to Rangoon when Nicolson boarded the aircraft for the second trip of the day. The take-off was 0050 hours en route for targets in Rangoon. At 0250 hours and 130 miles south of Calcutta problems occurred on the starboard outer-engine, flames were noticed and then the starboard inner-engine caught fire. All efforts to extinguish the engine failed. The aircraft flew with one wing low while everything that could be jettisoned was thrown overboard but to no avail as they were forced to ditch and the Liberator was not noted for its buoyancy. The aircraft struck the sea and sank within 15 seconds. Four of the crew of eleven clambered out, but in the darkness it was difficult to see who was who. But Eric did recognise Mick Pullen, the second pilot, Larry Helsby, another gunner, and someone else who could have been Nicolson. The dinghy seemed to have vanished and Eric's Mae West would not inflate. He then saw the nose-wheel floating by and made his way towards it and managed to attach himself to it with the tapes of his Mae West. He spent the day on his own looking for searching aircraft and worrying about sharks so he made as much noise as possible to deter them. After 16 hours tied to the wheel he was spotted by a Catalina seaplane which landed and taxied over to him, only for the float of the plane to force the wheel to which he was attached to submerge which nearly drowned him. A man appeared who turned out to be American and with a knife cut the Mae West and dragged him clear and into the aircraft. Then another Catalina landed some distance away rescuing Mick Pullen. No one else was found although a search continued for several days. Mick had been thrown out of the aircraft and suffered several injuries. He returned to Australia after the war but died of a heart attack. The remainder of the crew including Nicolson are now commemorated on the Singapore Memorial which stands in Kranji War Cemetery, 18 miles from Singapore.

Bob Denton volunteered as a wireless operator in June 1941 but was put on hold for a year waiting for a training slot so he joined the ATC to familiarise himself with Morse.

He finally went into the RAF in June 1942 and went straight to Blackpool for Morse training but because of severe dental problems he failed the medical tests and he was sent south to Hampshire and put on a crash tender where he attended a few crashes in the time he was there. However, a USAF Squadron started to operate on Coastal Command and he found he would be able to fly with them. He then enrolled as an air gunner and prior to sailing for India he was selected to join F/Sgt Trevor de Nett's crew at 15 OTU Harwell. He trained on Wellingtons before sailing on SS *Stratheden* to Bombay arriving mid-March 1944.

The initial gunnery training was at Bhopal, No. 1 AGS where flying training was done on Blenheims. They then went on a 5 day journey by rail to the Kolar Gold Fields. The train had slatted wooden seats to sleep on and a hole in the floor for ablutions. When they arrived at Gold Fields he rejoined his crew and two crews merged to make one Liberator crew. His crew was led by F/Lt W. Jackson.

Their first trip with No. 355 Squadron was to Akyab, an island off north-west Burma. During the flight the flight engineer reported that they were short of fuel. How they had lost the fuel remains a mystery. The rest of the crew were sure the readings on the fuel gauges were inaccurate but the skipper overruled them and gave the order to bale out, so out they went. Bob, the navigator and another gunner went out as one from the rear compartment. The navigator ended up in the Bay of Bengal, but Bob fell into a high tree in a mangrove swamp and the other gunner into a paddy field. Bob and the navigator found each other by using the escape whistles worn by all aircrew on their battledress. After wading through the swamps and swimming a river they arrived at a solitary hut. Later, Bob found out that there were crocodiles in the river. They were escorted to a nearby village where the headman took them by sampan to a steamer station terminus that took them to Calcutta. Here they were met at RAF Headquarters by an Air Vice Marshal who thanked them for surviving!! A Liberator was sent from Salbani to pick them up.

Stan Willis joined the RAF in April 1943 and after being accepted for a course he decided to change his mind and remuster as an air gunner. He was sent to the AG School at Stormy Down in Wales for a 3 month course that ended in July when he received his air gunner's brevet. His flying on the training course was 10 hours and 45 minutes on an Anson aircraft firing at Drogues and with a cine-gun fitted to test how successful he had been. From there he went to an Initial Training wing at Bridlington and then to Blackpool awaiting departure for India. He sailed from Greenock in

Scotland in June 1944 and arrived in India in July and was posted to RAF Kolar, and No. 1673 HCU. He was there assigned to No. 99 Squadron who were converting from Wellingtons to the B24 (Liberator). He joined F/Lt Anderton's crew and from 31 July to 6 September flew eight operations; a total of 43 hours which included all manner of exercises and cross country flights. They then flew to Dhubalia where they lived in huts made of bamboo, it was a case of do as the natives do; at least the runway was made of concrete. During this time a cyclone hit the base and the only building left standing was the station cinema which was made of brick. Operations against the enemy started with attacks on rolling stock at Honpladuk and train busting at Bangkok when one locomotive was damaged and six trucks destroyed when attacking from low level. Attacks on supply dumps, enemy installations, and store depots followed. One operation was to attack the Japanese Headquarters at Rangoon. On another operation they attacked a bridge at Anin. They completed thirty-two operations covering 305.55 hours. Stan was the ball-turret gunner for half of those operations and when the rear gunner was sent home he took over for the rest of the tour. It was only when on the last few trips and 300 hours flying that he was given a seat type parachute. When the war in the Far East ended he was sent home and demobbed in January 1947.

Richard Hyams joined the RAF in February 1943, he was 19. He had volunteered at 17 but was not called up until 1943 so during that time he joined the ATC and had tuition in Morse code, aircraft recognition and all

617 Squadron India in 1946. Third from left is John Flynn. *John Flynn*

No. 12 Squadron RAAF ground staff at Darwin in 1945. *Jim Bigelow*

other aspects of life in the RAF. He joined on the PNB (Pilot-Navigation-Bomber Aimer) system. After the usual initial weeks spent in Edinburgh he was posted to the ITW at Paington, Devon. On the morning of the Dams raid, and thinking the war would not last too long, they asked Richard and a few others if they would remuster as air gunners for, with the bomber offensive getting into its stride, there was a shortage of air gunners. Having agreed to become an air gunner Richard was first sent to the Isle of Sheppey, a transit camp. Then it was off to Bridlington and learning how to dismantle a .303 Browning machine-gun with his eyes closed and then put it back together in a record breaking time. This was followed by a trip to a beach to fire at moving targets while sitting in a turret. Having passed various tests he was posted to Morpeth in Northumberland where he started flying on Ansons. This aircraft did not have an automatic retractable undercarriage and it was the duty of the gunners, once airborne, to wind up the wheels manually, this was with a handle and meant squeezing along the fuselage on your stomach and then turning the handle until the wheels were fully up. The last gunner in of the three got this task. Richard had hoped on completion to be posted to Bomber Command and operate over Europe but he contracted German Measles, missed his slot and was down to be sent overseas. He did try to bribe the orderly room sergeant without success and so it was an anti-climax when he was presented with his AG brevet. It was then off to India via the SS *Maloga* an experience he did not wish to repeat.

After training on the ball turret he was posted to No. 159 Squadron at a place called Digri 60 miles west of Calcutta, the CO was a Wing Commander Ercolani of the furniture family but was soon replaced by Wing Commander Blackburn. During his time with 159 he hardly used the ball turret and it was not until he was posted to No. 355 Squadron at Salbani that, in his opinion he really entered the war. In Nidia they had no assistance from armourers and so had to arm the guns, and look after their own turrets.

Once when he was on an operational flight off the coast of Malaya, attacking shipping, he lowered his turret 15 minutes before reaching the aiming point and he saw what he first thought were black clouds in a perfectly clear blue sky it was only when he heard the thumps that he realised it was anti-aircraft fire from below: people were shooting at them. It was a good job he washed his own clothes back at base. The flak was quite severe and very accurate and he was hoping the bomb aimer would release the bombs before they got a direct hit. He finally watched the bombs leave the bomb bay and fall all the way down to the sea exploding very near a ship but not actually hitting it. His skipper, Warrant Officer Campbell from New Zealand had only twelve flying hours to go before completing his tour so the trip home was stretched out. On landing at Salbani the first job of the ground crew was to check the remaining fuel left in the tanks. As nothing showed up on the dipstick they rocked the aircraft from side to side and it soon became apparent that the accurate anti-aircraft fire had caused them to lose a great deal of fuel. The whole port side of their aircraft was sodden in petrol and if they had been in the air any longer they would have run out of fuel and probably had to crash land.

Each year Nos 355/356 Squadrons have a reunion at Blackpool and many friendships are renewed and many tales told with some variation as the years go by. Len Moore was trained in Canada as an air gunner and also served with No. 159 Squadron at Digri and in eighteen operations flew 3,7826 miles in 213 hours 30 minutes flying time.

Flight Sergeant Stanley James Woodbridge was a wireless/operator/air gunner in a Liberator of No. 159 Squadron that crashed in the jungle in Burma on 31 January 1945. He was 24 years old at the time and had been born in Chelsea, London. In 1945 his parents were living in Chingford, Essex. Woodbridge had been personally selected by his Commanding Officer to go on an important mission to locate Japanese radar installations in Bangkok, Mandalay and Rangoon. Having successfully completed the operation the Liberator turned for home when it developed engine trouble and the order to bale out was given. Of the eight aircrew six were able to locate each other on the ground. Before baling out Sgt Woodbridge was able to send out an SOS and the Bay of Bengal was searched for four days. On locating a small village and despite giving the headman a large amount of money to get them a small boat he later turned them over to the Japanese. They were taken down river to the

Bassein district and handed over to an Engineering Regiment. The skipper had a piece of paper written in Japanese with an extract from the Geneva Convention stating that they were only obliged to give their name, rank and serial number. But, although the Japanese had originally signed the convention history shows that they did not stick to its rules. The skipper refused to say what base they were from was then subjected to a severe beating. It turned out that they wanted the name of the wireless/operator. All four NCOs were beaten in turn but when they found out Woodbridge was the W/Opt he bore the brunt of the blows. He was beaten with belts and a sword about the head and repeatedly kicked. They then bound him and kicked and slapped him. A Lieutenant Kano encouraged his soldiers to kick Woodbridge where he lay, defenceless. Three of the airmen F/Sgt Bellingham, F/Sgt Woodage, and F/Sgt Snelling were then told to undress and the Japanese lined up with fixed bayonets and formed a circle around them and were told to beat the three if they so wished. The beating and kicking lasted for about 15 minutes. They were then blindfolded and led to a trench where Lieutenant Matsoi drew his sword and, handing it to a corporal, he told him to execute the first man, as he did so about eight to ten Japanese soldiers charged the dying airmen, yelling, shouting and bayoneted his body. A Sergeant then executed the second man with the same reaction from the other soldiers and then the Japanese Corporal followed killing the third and fourth airmen. Stanley Woodbridge was the last man to be executed and when he reached the spot where the other three had been killed he paid them a silent tribute. While being taken there he had managed to get some family photographs out of his pocket and bound them into a handkerchief in his clenched hands but at one point he dropped it and despite all the actions of the Japanese guards he went back and picked it up. Before being killed they had been forced to dig their own grave, a trench about 2 ft deep and long enough to take four bodies. Stanley was then executed by Lt Okami and pushed into the grave. Woodbridge refused to answer all questions regarding codes. equipment, and wavelengths. The two officers were taken away and spent the rest of the war in Rangoon jail.

The graves were discovered in July 1945 and at the village of Myaungana where they had been tortured a memorial was erected over their graves. The bodies were later exhumed and reburied in Rangoon. The two officers in Rangoon jail returned to the UK unaware of what had happened to their four comrades.

At a 1947 War Crimes trial in Rangoon Lt Col Murayama, Lts Kanno and Okami, and Corporals Joko Katayama and Tsukomoto of the 55th Engineering Regiment were all found guilty and Kanno, Okami, and Katayama were sentenced to death. Murayama was also sentenced to death but this was later commuted to 10 years rigorous imprisonment. Joko and Tsukomoto were sentenced to 2 and 1 year rigorous imprisonment respectively. The death sentences were carried out on 27 June 1947. Lt Matsui was killed in action during the Japanese retreat from Burma.

Woodbridge's father James came out to Rangoon for the trial which took two months and the records were eighty-nine foolscap pages long. Before he left to return to the UK he paid a last visit to his son's grave at Rangoon War Cemetery and left a wreath with a simple telling message "From Stanley's dad. Boy, I'm proud of you". On 28 September 1948, it was announced in the London Gazette that Flight Sergeant Woodbridge had been awarded the George Cross. He was only 24.

Jack Lyons served in Burma with 110 Squadron in 1943. The squadron had just been re-equipped with a brand new American aircraft, the Vultee Vengeance, a single-engine dive bomber with a crew of two. It was shipped in crates by sea to India and assembled, tested and delivered to the squadron ready for use. The Vengeance carried two 500 lb bombs in the belly of the bomb bay and two 250 lb bombs on exterior racks under the wings. Most the targets at the time were Japanese troop positions at the battle of Kohima and Imphal. The method of attack was a vertical dive and Jack would cock his twin Browning machines and strafe the anti-aircraft positions that were doing their best to knock them out of the sky.

On occasions the bombs in the exterior racks would hang up and a solution was being sought to rectify this because the pilot and air gunner could not see if the bombs had gone or not and sometimes would land with the bombs still in the rack and primed to go off. Jack's pilot, Roy, came up with the solution: tie a piece of string six foot long to each bomb on the rack and the string would flutter out behind for them to see. This worked well until an operation on 21 January 1944, the target, a Japanese held village in the Imphal valley called Pinlebu. At the time they were operating from an airstrip on he Assam/Burma border and were short of ground crew. The Indian Air Force had sent some of theirs and among them was a young armourer called Ahmed; his job was to help with the bombing up and arming of the guns. They took off and formated crossing the Naga Hills and flying down the Imphal Valley to Pinlebu. Over the target they went into a dive with the two strings fluttering behind them . The flak was quite heavy and as they pulled out of the dive they sustained a few bullet holes in the tail section, for which Jack repaid with interest. It was then that they realised the two strings were still fluttering behind.

When close to the landing strip and because at the time they were on radio silence they waggled their wings and out came a jeep which was the fire tender armed with fire extinguishers and buckets of sand, the crash tender was a lorry with a small crane bolted to the back. The landing was successful, but a frightening one. However, as Jack dived under the mainplane he saw that Ahmed had tied the strings to the bomb rack and not the bombs.

Frank Allworth served in the RAAF and completed his gunnery course in six weeks. The course in Australia was much the same as in the UK, firing from the turret of an Anson at a Drogue towed by a Fairey Battle: both aircraft had been front line aircraft in 1940 but were now obsolete. The gunsight technique was surprisingly hard to master. When switched on a centre dot with a surrounding circle appeared but it was not simply a matter of placing the dot over the target. The deflection had to be calculated together with the range by the gunner and the dot placed well ahead of the target and in its direction of flight so that in an extreme case it might be nowhere in the sight. But there was an alternative method when tracer ammunition was belted up with the ball and by positioning the target along the visible trace and using similar mental calculations the best results were obtained. With a combination of the two methods results were improved. To move the sight one had to move the turret by two handgrips which also had a trigger on each to fire the two guns. Automatic co-ordination between the eye, hand and fingers was essential plus some mental agility so that it was no mugs game and only constant practice and experience could maintain a high level of accuracy.

The flying conditions when operating at about 4,000 to 5,000 ft were awful due to the heat and smoke from bushfires. The air was bumpy and in the turrets the smell of leaking hydraulic oil and cordite that propelled the bullets was able to turn the strongest stomach. Every trainee carried a tin can rather like a small billycan knowing he could be carrying his last meal back in it. If this happened there was another smell to add to the rest and the thought of having to clean out the turret on return when you were so weak you could hardly stand. A number of trainees who could not get into the turret begged others to fire their rounds for them. Frank wanted to get as much practice as possible so did far more than he need to. Stoppages in the air could cause bloody fingers cut by projecting bits of metal in the turret. All this took part at the Air Gunnery School RAAF West Sale, Victoria, Australia.

Having been discharged after service in the UK Frank was again in uniform in 1948. This was because of the Chinese Communists heading south for Korea and Malaya. Frank returned to Sale once again and after gaining an above average rating he was posted to Singapore for a year and he managed to clock up fifty-five operations flying as a navigator, bomb aimer and front gunner. He was then posted to Perth, Western Australia flying on Neptunes. Then to Transport Command in Sydney.

He then joined QANTAS and after 30 years service as a flight controller in the control centre at Mascot he finally retired. A lifetime in the flying game which he would not have missed for anything.

On 22 August 1943, James Bigelow received his call up to the RAAF Medical Centre in Brisbane for a medical examination and then departed for the Initial Training Service at Kingaroy Queensland on 10 September 1943. He had served in the Air Training Corps in Queensland prior to being called up and during this time visited a number of American Air Bases at Amberley and also Eagle Farm, Brisbane. He had worked at the County Press Section of Queensland Newspapers in the early part of the war in the Pacific. It was on 11 November 1943, that he was posted to Maryborough, Queensland to undertake a wireless course to qualify as a wireless operator / air gunner. It was pointed out to him that he could not

F/Lt Frank Casalegno and crew at R.A.A.F Darwin. Casalegno is back centre and front far right Jim Bigelow. *Jim Bigelow*

An aerial photograph of the Cecil Plains airbase and airstrips, South-East Queensland in 1945. *Jim Bigelow*

Liberator A72-316 and air and ground crew. In the front Jim Bigelow with the dog.
Jim Bigelow

be considered for a pilot's course as he was left handed! Some of those that were selected for a pilot's course eventually turned up on the wireless training course. A number of flights in a Wackett trainer and Anson aircraft followed. In June 1944 he qualified as a wireless operator and was now posted to West Sale, Victoria to undertake a gunnery course. Here at No. 3 Air Gunnery School they flew on Ansons with three gunners on each trip. On the previous course there had been a horrific accident. A young lady was walking along the Ninety-Mile beach when a tow line was cut by machine gun fire and being low level it cut into the young lady amputating her legs. Sadly, she died a few days later.

On 18 August 1944 James graduated as a wireless/air-gunner. It was while at Sale that the famous Avro Lancaster 'G for George' landed at the base with Wg Cdr Issacson at the controls, however he miscalculated his approach and braked into a nearby ditch. At the time all the RAAF personnel were lined up along the runway to witness this historical moment. James was put down for a posting to Canada under the Empire Air Training Scheme but within a few days this was cancelled and he was posted to No. 7 OTU at Tocumwal, New South Wales. Here they were trained on Liberators. He was approached by the Chief Wireless Operator and asked to join the crew of Flt Lt Frank Casalegno and on 17 November they had their first flight as an operational crew. The co-pilot, WO Johnny Wade-Brown, had been trained by Frank when he was a flying instructor, F/O Tom Worsley, the second wireless operator had a tour in the Middle

East under his belt. The navigator, Flying Officer David Price had just returned from the UK having flown operations on Lancasters. On the 19 December 1944 they graduated for operational service.

On 8 February 1945, six Liberator crews assembled at Cecil Plains, QLD as the initial force for the re-formation of No. 12 Squadron RAAF which had been disbanded. Flying practice started on March 1945. During this time Jim was posted to Maryborough with other ball-gunners to undertake a radar course, as the new aircraft was fitted with this equipment and on his return full time operations commenced.

When he arrived back and had to crawl into the ball turret with his parachute on he was soon told, "Nobody wears that monster in the turret; leave it in the aircraft". The only person who did not know this practice took place was Frank the pilot. And it was many years after the war that it slipped out. In April 1945 they were attached to No. 24 Squadron in the Northern Territory. Here they had excellent food including an evening meal of steak and eggs and a ration of two bottles of beer per day. On 29 April they took off armed with 1,200 lb bombs and several cases of empty beer bottles as they had been informed that empty beer bottles falling from an aircraft would create a weird and frightening effect.

On 20 May 1945 they were awoken by a loud banging noise and were told that an aircraft had crashed. However, when they all tried to get to the crash site they were stopped by the military police. A few had managed to get quite close and could hear the trapped and doomed crew inside the aircraft banging from the inside. One of those that got quite close was Aussie Jones who volunteered to identify the crashed crew and was quite ill for some time afterwards. It would appear the aircraft had instrument problems and in trying to re-level the aircraft the pilot actually banked one wing into the surrounding scrub. The airfield was covered with U.S. Army landing mesh and was very bumpy, and noisy on take-off and landing.

In May 1945 they received a brand new silver Liberator which was named "Casa's Clueless Crew". The logo depicted a giant Sherlock Holmes towering over a 'little Japanese'. Prior to this they had operated on a borrowed aircraft. When on a patrol far from their own base and were required to undertake some strafing Jim found both his twin guns were useless due to the feed-line not being free. This should have been picked up during an inspection by the armourers. When the bins were reloaded, the ball-gunner always had the opportunity to check on this situation as the turret always had to be lowered to perform this operation. Once in the raised position the ball-gunner could not operate or get into the turret until the aircraft was airborne and that was too late to rectify any mistake.

On 1 August 1945, Jim and his crew took part in a six aircraft raid on the strong Japanese base at Maimere. Jim looked down from his ball-turret and counted the bomb hits. On one occasion they strafed a Lugger close to the shore at such a low height he could observe his own gun tracer near the target before they buzzed over the top of the Lugger.

On one occasion when at 10,000 ft Jim thought he would walk along the cat-walk to the rear before the bomb doors were open. He disconnected himself and started towards the rear or so he thought. Next thing he remembers was being on the flight deck floor and coming out of deep sleep. It transpired that when he disconnected his oxygen he started to pass out but the navigator David Price who had been watching grabbed Jim by his flying suit jacket which saved him going out into space. On 8 October 1945 they flew down from Darwin to Amberley with ten recently released PoWs from Singapore, they were on stretchers and housed in the bomb bay compartment. On one occasion while on a patrol a small island was spotted where it was discovered a small radio outpost was positioned on a cliff edge. Jim got into the ball-turret in record time and waited for the forward and mid-upper turrets to fire, as he sighted the target Jim took aim and pressed the trigger but nothing happened. He then realised that he had not heard the other gunners fire also and when the skipper came through about clueless gunners it became evident that the guns were inoperative, they were defenceless. It transpired that the ammunition was faulty. On another occasion when strafing a Lugger and carrying an RAAF officer as an observer the officer suddenly became very scared and screamed for the action to stop. They never carried a stranger again. On another occasion a blip on the radar screen turned out to be a school of whales.

When in October crews were reduced to four (a gunner, the pilot, navigator and wireless operator) the remaining six were sent by Dakota to Townsville. Here they picked up a troop-train heading south. The Dakota by now was fully lined inside, unlike the aircraft they had been used too. Jim had now been commissioned pilot officer and the next day to flying officer.

The friendships built in the war continued and Frank, Aussie Jones, David Price, and later Russell Glenn have kept in touch and with Tom Worsley's widow Josie. Then in 1997 they again contacted Benny Benjamin the Chief Radio Operator. Sadly, Johnny Wade-Brown and Johnny Moore, the bomb aimer who was also a fine clarinet player and studied under Artie Shaw, had died.

Freddie Ewatski joined the RCAF in Winnipeg in 1942 with two other school friends. His gunnery training was at Mont Joli, Quebec from May to July 1943. Later as part of a group of 450 RCAF personnel he set off for gunnery and flying experience to the UK. On his report card from the OTU gunnery school course it stated that Sgt Ewatski was 'A good hard working and intelligent gunner'. However, of the 450 men 449 were posted to an RCAF Squadron but Freddie was posted to the RAF (why is still a mystery). In the UK he began a diet that was to become his way of life for the rest of war: jam and cheese sandwiches from the NAAFI wagon. His flying training began on Wellingtons which had a lonely and cold rear turret but on one occasion, because of a malfunction of the heating equipment, he found himself in hospital for 10 days with pneumonia. This was followed by ten days leave in London. It was then that he found out that his two school mates, Kenny Smith and Jimmy Waters, who he had joined up with had been killed in action. Freddie said, "I died with them".

It was the winter of 1943 when his skipper P/O Goody an Australian told him that two crews were wanted to go to the Far East, he thought highly of Goody so he readily agreed to go. It would appear that Freddie was the only Canadian on the squadron. The journey took 29 days on an Indian ship and reached Bombay on 7 April 1944.

On 14 April 1944 there occurred two huge explosions on an ammunition ship and hundreds were lost, including sixty-six firemen who were fighting the fire. No less than twenty-seven ships were sunk and the whole docks was a mess.

His first op was with No. 159 Squadron flying from Digree, about 120 miles from Calcutta. The accommodation was a thatched hut with no windows, the food was miserable and the heat even worse, 135° Fahrenheit. On top of this there were snakes and Mosquitos. The main problem was the distance to the target: between 1,000 and 1,100 miles. On 11 December they dropped 6,800 lb of bombs on shipping at Heinz Ban and also strafed ships from a height of 500 to 600 ft. Railway stations, radar installations and locomotive sheds, stores and a fuel dumps were the targets. Altogether a 12 hour trip.

His last operation was the longest and most frightening and was complicated by Allied PoWs being in the vicinity. The intelligence officer was comforting when he said, "Gentlemen, there are six of you going out

A reunion in the Gold Coast in 2001. Left to right Jean Bigelow, Frank Casalegno, Joan Casalegno, Barbara Jones and Austin Jones. *Jim Bigelow*

but only three of you will come back, because it's a heavily fortified Target". After bombing the target, Rajburi bridge, they went on to strafe a merchant ship. It was the first time Freddie had used .50 calibre bullets and saw sparks flying off the deck. They suffered seven holes in the aircraft; one bullet had knocking out his intercom and because he could not contact the rest of the crew they thought he had been hit. The trip took 14 hours 40 minutes.

He flew eleven operations as a nose or rear gunner on a Liberator. In total he logged 91 hours and 20 minutes by day and 38 hours by night and was assessed as 'above average' as a gunner. In November 1945, and now a Warrant Officer, he was demobbed. Many years after the war he became one of the founders and the first President of the Canadian Air Gunners Association which, as he himself said, "Not bad for a Ukrainian/Canadian boy from the North End of Winnipeg".

On 22 September 1943 P/O Joseph Cohen, age 21, of the Royal Australian Air Force took off from Ceylon for an operation to the Car Nicabar. He failed to return and the Japanese reported having shot down F/L-939. But it did not go down without a fight because two Zeros had been shot down by the Liberators gunners. The crew have no known grave but their names are recorded on the Singapore Memorial.

At the end of the war many bomber aircraft were sent out to the Far East in preparation for the bombing of the Japanese mainland to end the war with Japan. One of those was the now famous 617 Squadron who had breached the Ruhr Dams in 1943 using white painted Lancasters.

CHAPTER TEN

The Middle East

Gil Graham joined the RAF in 1938, the start of 32 years service. He trained as a pilot but an accident early in the war in which he sustained a head injury resulted in his career as a pilot being over, but he could continue flying as an air gunner. He was, at the time, flying Hawker Hinds out of Carlisle.

Gil was posted to the Middle East and on the sea journey he met and became good friends with an Irishman, Sgt 'Paddy' Francis Hendron, who came from Co. Tyron, Northern Ireland. When they arrived they went their separate ways and lost touch, but after about 3 months Paddy paid a visit to Gil on a day he wasn't flying and gave Gil a small crucifix which had

Top W/C Maydwell. *Gil Graham*

Gil Graham. *Gil Graham*

been given to him by his grandmother just before he left home. Although Gil was reluctant to take such a personal item Paddy insisted he take it and that they had their photographs taken together. Sadly, he never lived to see it printed for only the next day on 28 October 1942 he was killed on a bombing raid with No. 233 Squadron to Tobruck harbour, he was 24 years of age. It was several weeks before Gil heard of his death and he wondered if Paddy had a premonition he would be killed. Had the crucifix protected him on previous operations? Why did he give it to Gil the day before he died? Questions Gil has asked himself ever since. Paddy has now known grave but is on the Alamein Memorial in Egypt.

Gil put the crucifix on his identity discs around his neck and there they stayed for the whole of his 32 years in the RAF. Most aircrew have some form of lucky charm and this was Gil's. One South African pilot with a huge handlebar moustache had it cut off each year and the whiskers placed in a packet and carried in the breast pocket of his battledress tunic. He referred to it as his 'Ju-Ju' or African magic. A number of the experienced pilots would not wear flying boots because they felt that they made baling out that much more difficult. Instead they wore ordinary boots.

In 1942 Gil was a rear gunner with No. 14 Squadron flying Marauder aircraft in the Western Desert. At that time air gunners were only surviving six or seven trips on average. His first flight was on 6 November 1942 as Gil recounts:

At 11.50 hours we took off from Fayid to carry out a low level reconnaissance on enemy shipping in an area to the North of the island

B26 Marauder Dominion Revenae. *Gil Graham*

of Crete in the Dodecanese Island. To avoid the enemy radar the flight was to be carried out at 50 ft above the sea, and at times, I felt sure it was much less because we were creating a wash behind the aircraft. The trip was uneventful until we were off the North coast of Crete which was German held territory when we sighted a number of large barges carrying troops towards Crete: a good target for us. We flew low over them and I opened up on the barges with my guns. One could not assess how many were killed or wounded but the large number who dived overboard was quite remarkable and they probably expected us to do a second run but we had other important work to do and we headed north.

Immediately after the encounter with the barges we sighted a lone Junkers Ju52 transport plane but on going into attack we saw Red Cross markings on it, so we allowed it go on its way towards Crete. We then sighted two ships which appeared to be merchant ships, with a Heinkel He115 seaplane in attendance. On going in to investigate we were met with a hail of anti-aircraft fire and we were badly holed at the rear end of the aircraft. The top gunner was wounded in the legs and I was completely deafened by exploding shells, one of which burst within a few feet of my head, and it was only on return to base that I discovered my parachute harness had been severed in two places by shrapnel. There was a bit of panic on board because one of the internal petrol tanks had caught fire but somehow this was extinguished by the wireless operator. Hardly had we recovered from that encounter when we sighted a shipping convoy heading South escorted by five destroyers and seven Junkers Ju88s. Three of the Ju88s came in to attack us but with the top turret now out of action we decided to avoid confrontation and took rapid evasive action. After a few anxious minutes we escaped without further damage.

His accommodation in the desert was, to say the least, primitive: he shared a tent with three other gunners and his bed a groundsheet on hard sand. His kitbag was his pillow, and he had two horse-hair blankets to try and keep him warm during the cold desert nights. The toilets were buckets with a board on top and set out in the open. For washing they used old petrol cans cut in half. The dress of air gunner on operations was a flying helmet, battledress blouse, khaki shorts, and flying boots.

Gil also flew on Liberators and on one operation had the left earphone of his flying helmet shot away. He then took to wearing a steel helmet over his flying helmet for protection.

On 10 June 1943 they took off for a low-level shipping reconnaissance south of Sicily. Soon Gil spotted two enemy fighters, they were Me109s and he was prepared to let them come within range but the tail gunner opened fire with a long burst in the general direction of the fighters. The fuses in the top turret had blown and would normally be replaced by the wireless operator but he had climbed into the astrodome to give a running commentary. The gunner carried on asking for his fuses to be replaced. Gil put a short burst into one of the Me109s and white smoke began to pour from the underside of the aircraft. This aircraft dropped back and took no further part in the action.

The 13 July 1943 was a day that Gil will never forget for many reasons. He took off with then Wg Cdr, later Group Captain, Maydwell at the controls. They were to reconnoitre the harbours on the west coast of Italy and the south coast of France. On the north coast of Corsica they sighted an Me323, a six engine aircraft, the biggest used in WWII. In its huge cabin was nine tons of flak, a half-track vehicle and two VW personnel carriers. It had a crew of nine, a mechanic in each wing and carried four vehicle drivers. Gil's aircraft immediately attacked the Me323 and put its nose guns out of action. Gil's Marauder kept in front of the Messerschmitt and Gil shot at it continually with his rear gun. Three bits of the enemy's engine fell off and it made for the nearest possible landing place: Corsica then occupied by the Germans. This they did on a rocky shore. Gil thought all the crew had been killed but in fact they had survived. The pilot was Walter Honig and now lives in Pforzheim. He was at the time flying to an airfield just north of Rome. He had experienced engine trouble before take-off and so the rest of the formation took off and he was caught by the Marauder while trying to catch them up. The rest had a fighter escort. After crash landing they sent up a flare to signal where they were but this came back down and set the grass on fire around them. On seeing this the other aircraft thought they were dead and their kit was sent back to their families with a note saying, 'Killed in Action'! Walter had hurt his knee and spent two weeks in hospital. He was later caught by the Russians but escaped and walked 300 miles but was again captured by the British in Berlin. The outcome is that Gil and Walter have now become firm friends after being brought together after a newspaper article. Gil has a propeller tip from the ill-fated German aircraft as a souvenir.

On 19 July 1943 they set off on a reconnaissance of Rome. A decision had been taken that vital targets in Rome should be bombed by the combined forces of RAF and USA, however, the problem was that the Vatican and other most holy places in the city were not to be touched. Much planning went into this and even the weather had to be perfect. On this day Gil was again flying with Wg Cdr Dick Maydwell in Marauder FK 142 R-Robert and named 'Dominion Triumph'. They took off from Protville in Tunisia at 0300 and flew at 50 ft across the Mediterranean heading for Rome. The first surprise was flying across an enemy airfield at 260 mph near Anzio and to their surprise seeing a neat row of Heinkel III bombers all lined up alongside the runway. So surprised that Gill did not open up on them much to the annoyance of Dick when he got back. However Dick later apologised as alerting the Germans may have caused the *Luftwaffe* to look for them before they had completed the mission. When they arrived at the target area they radioed back that the weather was perfect for the operation.

Having done so they flew up to Lake Bracciano where a number of seaplanes were anchored. Now that the reconnaissance mission was over they decided to knock out one or two seaplanes. Several strikes were seen and the next day a reconnaissance showed that three were badly damaged and lying on their sides. The next target was a train which they duly strafed. The actual raid took place with 169 P-38 aircraft and 107 B-26 aircraft in what was probably the biggest raid ever carried out in the Mediterranean Theatre.

Barry Lillywhite joined the RAF on 4 September 1939 and served as an accounts clerk until October 1942 when he undertook his gunnery course at No. 2 AGS Dalcross from 10 October to 14 November 1942, flying on Defiant aircraft. In his 8 hours and 30 minutes flying he fired 2,350 rounds at Drogues towed by another aircraft. He finished second in his class with 79.3 per cent. He then joined No. 107 Squadron and flew with them on Boston aircraft until February 1943.

On 18 March 1943 he flew out to North Africa on Bostons with No. 114 Squadron and joined No. 18 Squadron and flew Army Co-operation bombing raids until 30 April 1943. On the 30th he was flying in Boston AL 738-G, with pilot Sgt Greenwood and their target was Ragouret Souissi which they successfully attacked from 7,500 ft. On the operation Barry was wounded by a $2^1/_2$ inch piece of shrapnel in his left shoulder and taken to an American hospital in Oran. The shrapnel also cut his parachute harness in two. He remembers that one of the nurses looked like Dorothy Lamour the film actress. He found lying on his stomach uncomfortable but apart from that he was very well treated. Later in the year he returned to the UK and joined a new crew and went to No. 20 OTU at Bitteswell flying Wellington aircraft, then on to No. 1660 Conversion Unit for training on four-engine aircraft, from there he went to No. 5 Lancaster Finishing School on 23 July 1944. After that he joined No. 44 Squadron and flew day and night operations on Lancasters as a rear gunner until 30 October 1944 when his tour ended, he was now a warrant officer. He was then commissioned and finished his service as a flying-control officer, first at Croydon airfield and then for his last six months at Oslo airfield in Norway.

There are air gunners buried all over Europe, the Middle East, Far East and in the UK. Flight Sergeant William Porritt DFM RCAF of No. 462 RAAF Squadron came from Vancouver, was only 20 years of age and was flying with F/L A.E. Hacking. His previous squadron, No. 227 had been amalgamated with No. 10 and No. 76 to form 462 RAAF Sqn. On 6 September 1942 they set off in Halifax W 7679 on the new squadron's first operation to attack Heraklion airfield in Crete. At 6,000 ft and over the airfield they were hit by light flak and the order given to bale out. They crashed at Kastelli Pediada and three of the crew, including Porritt, were killed and were buried by local Greeks. All three are now buried in Crete at the Suda Bay War Cemetery. He had previously flown with No. 10 Squadron and had distinguished himself in August 1941 on daylight attacks on the German Battle Cruisers *Scharnhorst* and *Gneisenau*. During an attack by four Me109s, he shot down one in flames, riddled another which was last seen in a vertical dive, and in a running battle he fought off the remaining two until fighter help arrived. In this combat he was wounded in the face and hands and spent several weeks in hospital. On the morning of 6 May 1942,

on his 14th operation and returning from Saarbrucken he suddenly shouted that an Me109 was 200 yards astern. The pilot went into a dive and as the fighter overshot F/Sgt Porritt gave a fierce burst right into it from underneath. It was then seen to plunge vertically to earth and a few second later a flash was seen and then flames. It was claimed as destroyed. For his actions he was awarded an immediate Distinguished Flying Medal.

Sergeant Air Gunner Papenfus of No. 21 Squadron SAAF is now buried in the Knightsbridge War Cemetery, Libya. Before the war he played cricket for Joberg Pirates. He used to cause havoc when the officers played the sergeants because his ability to make the ball jump about on the sun baked and flaky soil.

Herbert Dodson DFM. *Joan Dodson*

Pappy, as he was known, set off on 18 November 1941 to attack enemy vehicles and tanks in the Western Desert. In the target area they were attacked by Me109s and one was shot down but two No. 21 Squadron aircraft were shot down and of those killed one was Papenfus.

Sergeant Thomas Westwood of No. 37 Squadron was attacking aircraft dispersed at Kastelli Rediada landing ground, Crete on 23 November 1942 but failed to return and he is now buried at Suda Bay, Crete. Also buried at Crete is P/O Carroll Durant of No. 160 Squadron RNZAF. His aircraft was attacking aircraft dispersed at Maeleme airfield Crete in a Liberator and also failed to return.

Herbert Dodson DFM at Buckingham Palace with his mother and father in 1941. *Joan Dodson*

P/O Herbert Dobson joined the RAF as soon as war was declared in 1939. After training he was posted to Egypt as a Sergeant and served there for over a year. He also flew with No. 37 Squadron in 1941 when he took part in attacks on Benghasi and El Aden. He was awarded the DFM after completing thirty-six operations against targets in Crete, Cyrenaica, Syria, Greece, and the Dodecanese as well as targets in North Africa. His recommendation went on to say that as gunnery leader he set a fine example to the rest of the flight. On return to the UK he was commissioned and took part in the 1,000 bomber raid to Cologne with No. 15 OTU, and for a while was the gunnery leader at Harwell. With No. 83 Squadron he served with the Pathfinder Force but on 20/21 January 1944, during the Battle of Berlin, he was shot down and is now buried in Berlin, he was 25 years old. He was flying with a Sqn Ldr A P Jones in Lanacster ND 414-K. On this night thirty-five aircraft failed to return.

F/Sgt Foot was flying with F/Sgt Evans of No. 55 Squadron and the target was Capopichiono in Italy when they were hit by anti-aircraft fire over the target and crash landed at Monte Cassino. Foot was killed in the crash. He is now buried in Monte Cassino War Cemetery. Another air gunner buried at Monte Cassino is Sgt Rodd Campbell from Canada. He was flying with No. 420 Squadron in Wellington HE 334 flown by F/O East.

Sergeant John Blair was awarded the DFM in 1940 after operations over Derna. On one occasion the pilot was killed when they were attacked by enemy fighters and, while the air gunner fought off the fighter attack, John took over the controls and flew the aircraft 350 miles and landed safely.

Flt Sgt Peter (Jesse) James was flying with No. 624 Squadron in June 1944 when operating out of Blida in the Middle East when he was awarded the DFM. His first tour had been with No. 78 Squadron of Bomber Command and when awarded the DFM he had flown some fifty-nine operations. This was followed by special operations in the Balkans and Italy flying out agents and dropping supplies. On return to the UK he flew with No. 226 Squadron of 2nd TAF on Mitchell bombers and then Washingtons (B29s). On finishing his flying he had completed over ninety operations.

William Wynn in September 1939 was serving with No. 99 Squadron and based at Rowley Mile Racecourse, Newmarket. He had trained as a wireless operator and an air gunner. He now had the flying bullet badge. Eleven days before Christmas they were conducting a search for the German fleet in the Heligoland area. However, what they did find was some German fighters and the cost was high. Of the twelve aircraft that had set out only six returned, one overshot the runway and was written off and five did not make it back. From the other two squadrons who took part twelve crews failed to return. In 12 months he completed thirty-six operations. This was followed by a spell with the RAF Regiment recruits teaching them to handle the Lewis machine-gun. Then came a posting to the Middle East. He was to fly out with S/L Samuels and second pilot P/O Payne an ex-99 Squadron pilot. There were also two VIPs on board: AVM Boyd and his ADC F/Lt Leeming plus a brown paper parcel of £250,000 worth of Pirates, the wages for those living in the desert. On 21 November 1940 they set out in a new Wellington bomber. Their destination was Malta. When they arrived over Malta, however, it was covered in sea fog, a decision was made to make for Sicily. Samuels landed the aircraft with the greatest of skill on what was no more then a rough pasture. The money was scattered all over the sea in their descent to land. All the kit was unloaded and the pilot then discharged a Very cartridge into the field near the aircraft and up went the new Wellington. After about half an hour a soldier of what was a sort of local home guard arrived. They took the service revolver off each member and they were taken away to Catania Air Force Base in order of seniority with the sergeants at the rear. After a week at Catania they were taken by taxi to Messiah and then a ferry across the straits and then by train to Rome. After interrogation they were taken by train to Salmon from there by jeep to a village Font Damage at the foot of a mountain and PoW camp No 78. Here William, along with 4,000 PoWs was to spend the next 2 years and 9 months. AVM Boyd was kept in a house at Salmon. In early 1942 the Italian authorities decided to implement one of the Geneva Conventions, i.e. the identification of all camps for PoWs from the air upon which a group of workmen arrived with large wooden tubs, pails, long handled brushes, ladders and a supply of slaked lime. Having filled the pails they climbed to the first roof and whitened one half and proceeded through the whole compound. At the end of the week the work was completed and the workmen were setting off for home when the barrack doors opened and out dashed two fellow prisoners wearing clothes similar to the workmen; they rushed to the tubs, a quick dab with a brush and with bags similar to those of the Italian workmen they sauntered out of the gate. But not having allowed for the terrain or for the help they may get from the local people they were soon brought back having begged food from the wrong house. They were thrown into the cell block without any clothes except for socks and no bedding to sleep on. By the next day the temper of the commandant had cooled and he gave them a two week sentence. The prisoners including William were formed into a hollow square and told at some length how ashamed they were of insulting them by trying to escape which was greeted with laughter.

About this time William had a period of solitary confinement. He had sent home in a weekly letter verbatim information from the notice board on details of how Italian PoWs were having their privileges restricted and so those prisoners in the hands of the Italians would also have their privileges restricted. About six weeks later and along with two other PoWs he was summoned to the Commandant to explain. The other two got various terms of solitary but William got 30 days. The cells held three people so it meant exercising by numbers, four paces from the door to the wall and four paces back between 8am and 4pm. When the Italians capitulated in 1943 the guards deserted and the Allied officers took over the camp. They were issued with rations and told to walk south. After about 25 miles they were captured again, this time by the Germans. The AVM had been ferried by fishing boat dressed as a nun to Allied lines. An order came for 1,000 PoWs to be taken by train to Germany. This journey took some days with three stops per day, for water and the usual ablutions. Some times they were met by the Italian Red Cross ladies who dispersed cups pf tea. When they were nearing the German border William decided to jump from the train. After a few days he heard Italian voices and came across an old farmer who sent off and got a young man named Franco Fortunato who invited him into his cottage and Franco's mother made him breakfast. William told him that his plan was to make for Switzerland to which Franco said there would be too many problems and suggested he stay in the area. This he did through the Winter and into Spring. While he was here they came upon a small band of former PoWs: two New Zealanders, two Australians, one Cypriot and the remainder were Scots and English. Some weeks before Easter shots were heard in the distance so, thinking they were in danger, they were taken to a rocky area and secure caves. They then decided to break up into small groups and William's group was him and three soldiers. At the end of July they heard that a band of local partisans was being organised by a British officer, who was a Flying Officer with the honorary rank of captain, so they set off to locate them. After a number of near misses and others joining the party they reached a flat open ground guarded by Tito's forces, to which the RAF brought in supplies and within a week they were uplifted to Bari, Southern Italy. Here he was kitted out and given a rail warrant to Naples and a transit camp for two days. From a post office he sent an important telegram home, "Free and coming home, love to all". His trip home was via Tunis, Algiers and Casablanca finally landing at St. Eval, Cornwall. Here he ran down the steps of the De Havilland Dove that brought him home and kissed the ground. After being medically checked he was able to catch a train to London. He found he had built up a credit of £400. He then caught a train to Manchester and as the only bus to Bury meant a 4 hour wait he was able to get a lift on a newspaper lorry.

Jimmy Wright was commissioned into the RAF in 1942. He became an air gunner and wore the brevet of an air gunner so as he could fly, although he had poor eye sight. Before the war he had been trained as a cameraman in a film studio and so became an aerial cameraman and joined the RAF Film Unit at Pinewood Studios. After operations over Europe he was posted to the Desert Air Force. He joined No. 223 Squadron flying Baltimore bombers and had a few scrapes before the one that changed his life.

On 15 October 1943 his aircraft was hit by enemy fire over the mountains in central Italy and he had to bale out. This had its difficulties as it appeared he had put the parachute on back to front but was somehow able to pull the rip cord and land safely. He immediately returned to operational duties. In October 1943, he was recommended for the DFC which was approved. The recommendation said that he had taken part in thirty-five sorties in Mitchell, Boston, and Baltimore aircraft. In that time he had produced many excellent films, many of which today still reside in the Imperial War Museum. He often filmed two sorties in one day and carried out experimental camera-work on night operations. He contributed greatly to the film archives of the Italy, and Sicilian campaigns. Although on his recommendation it stated he had flown thirty-five operations it was in fact thirty-eight.

On his last operation in a Marauder the aircraft crashed on take-off and, although he survived, he was badly burned on the face and hands. He was so badly hurt that he had already, in anticipation, thought he would die and be put on a casualty list. His father was a war correspondent having served in the RFC in WWI and as it happened was in the Mediterranean theatre and flew over to see his son. He was transported home wrapped in bandages on a Liberator bomber to the UK and into the hands of Sir Archibald McIndoe who specialised in treating burns and his patients were all known as Guinea Pigs. On one occasion, previously, he had filmed men who had been in the situation he was now in. Despite being blind and having spent many years as a patient of Sir Archibald he went on to carve out a very successful career in the film world and in 1981 was awarded a BAFTA. Whenever you saw Jimmy he was happy and smiling, a great example to others who found themselves in this situation.

Bill Gausden joined the Civil Defence as a messenger at the age of 16 and attended many bomb and shelling incidents with an Air Raid Warden. On his 17th birthday he joined the Air Training Corps at Dover. Six months later he enquired about going into the RAF Air Sea Rescue but was told he had to wait until he was 18. In the meantime he was accepted as an ATC Cadet awaiting training in the role of supernumerary crew. He was appointed to a launch, the skipper was a Flying Officer. After six months he was accepted by the crew as a trained member. One thing he had learned to operate was the .303 Browning machine gun mounted in a turret on the launch.

On 30 August 1943, aged 18 and 2 days he reported to RAF Cardington, Bedfordshire for duty. After initial training all the airmen were assigned trades, Bill expected to be assigned to ASR but, to his surprise he was assigned as a radar mechanic despite showing the officer in charge his certificate of competency. He then decided to volunteer for air crew training and was accepted. He wanted to be a navigator but this was changed to air gunner. But as he could not start his air crew training until he was $18^1/_2$ he went back to complete his recruit training. He was the only one there with the white flash in his forage cap After that he was posted to a Training Command Station on General Duties.

In December 1943, while pushing a wheelbarrow load of coke, the Commanding Officer came by in his car to which Bill gave an eyes right but when the car stopped and reversed he wondered what he had done. The window was rolled down and the driver said "Airman, report to the Group Captain. 1400 hours today." It turned out the CO was not happy about an aircrew candidate pushing coke around and said he was to be given jobs that would be useful for his flying career. The remaining weeks on General Duties were the best he ever spent in the RAF. The Armourer taught him all about guns, cleaning, assembling and firing most types on the ranges.

When in the Initial Training Wing he became a member of the Bridgenorth gymnastic exhibition team who performed at local fund-raising functions. This would be a half an hour exhibition of box vaulting, and Swedish drill with sticks accompanied by the Station Band. He was finally issued with his flying clothing, helmet and oxygen masks which were checked by the Equipment Warrant Officer to ensure that everything fitted properly. They were then issued with two kit bags, one filled with flying clothing and marched to the railway station. His gunnery training was at No. 12 Air Gunnery School, RAF Bishops Court, Northern Island. All the instructors sported the brevet of AG, navigator, signaller, and were all Sergeants or Flight/Sergeants having completed a tour of operations so he could not be in better hands.

On 15 June 1944, and wearing full flying kit he clambered aboard Anson LV 237 for his first training flight, in fact his first flight in an aircraft. The flight was out over the Irish Sea and he was beginning to think he had made the right choice until the pilot made a violent surge to starboard and commenced a series of manoeuvres that tore their stomachs apart. Having spent a lot of time at sea in small boats and being immune to sea sickness he fared better than his colleagues: all the faces changed to a pale shade of green and one violently sick. The pilot looked at Bill and gave the thumbs up and continued to throw the Anson all over the sky. One man lay on the floor in a pool of vomit. As Bill had occupied the second pilot's seat it was his duty to wind down the undercarriage which was quite a strenuous and sweaty task in flying kit. On landing the pilot told Bill he must have a good stomach, and that he will have no problems. The others were told that they should be okay as most flights did not incur such violent actions, but the one lying on the floor did not get off lightly; he had to go up again later that day. As the Anson door opened they were confronted with a grinning airman carrying a bucket of disinfectant and a mop. He said, "Half a Crown to mop it up, or do it yourself". The man who had been sick gladly paid up. The pilot said (tongue in cheek) that he hated doing this but it had to be established early on if potential aircrew could cope with air-sickness. It had to be established if the man who was sick had eaten a bad breakfast or had a stomach upset. He went back up with three others and when they came back the airmen with the bucket collected four half-crowns. In all he had collected about a £1 that day. The next day the four handed in their flying kit; unfortunately for them they had a condition that was out of their control.

The dinghy drill was carried out at Belfast Swimming Pool. Those that could not swim (Bill not being one) had to have confidence in their Mae West's keeping them afloat. Bill had to take one of the non-swimmers to the deep end where they jumped in head first. Bill came up straight away but the non-swimmer was half submerged so Bill pushed him to the side where the remainder of the crew pulled him out. After more practice the non-swimmer got over this but the next test was jumping from a 10 ft spring board which they all were able to do. Various tests with the dinghy followed including coping with an upside down dinghy. They all passed and they went for a pint that night.

After passing out and receiving his AG Brevet and Stripes he was told they were being posted overseas. They departed from Liverpool on the troopship *Monarch of Bermuda*. Ten days later they docked at Port Said, Egypt and entrained for Cairo. However, he was later assigned to No. 34 (SAAF) Squadron at Foggia, Italy. The accommodation was in tents and Bill, having been in the Boy Scouts, was the only one who knew how to pitch a tent and build a ditch around the tent. Bill also dug a large hole which acted as a soak away. When, a few weeks later, came torrential rain they had one of the driest tents on the site. One air gunner in their tent, Sgt Bowdens, was reported missing. At this stage air gunners were flying as spare 'Bods' and he failed to return from an operation. His father had gone down on HMS *Hood* when it was sunk and he was the only child. His mother, having lost her husband and son, was devastated.

Bill's first operation came on 13 October 1944, flying in a Liberator as mid-upper gunner with Lt Cullingworth of the SAAF whose officers had army ranks. Bill did not have the courage to tell him he had never seen a Liberator and had no idea how to operate or fire the .5 Browning Guns. The target was the marshalling yards at Budapest. The mid-upper turret was located above the flight deck and he stood looking up wondering how he could get up into his turret which was 8 ft above him. The wireless operator came to his rescue and told him to put his foot on his table and then he gave him a push up. As he got into the turret came a loud click as his seat was snapped into position. Suddenly came a voice "Power on", all the switches had been operated and as he applied the pressure to the controls he felt the turret move. The pilot said on the inter-com "Ok. Gunner, the best of luck on your first trip." But as they took off the pilot had a problem with the undercarriage which would not come up. Nothing they did got the rogue undercarriage up so, as they had full fuel tanks and a full bomb load, they were told to land on the grass away from the runway. The crew were told to get into crash position which for Bill was near the main spar. Fortunately, when they hit the grass the undercarriage held. It was the shortest trip an air gunner could have on his first flight, he had not even loaded the guns. Perhaps it was lucky for Bill as he had not been able to find the switch which operated the ammunition booster motors and also could not find the switch for the reflector sight. The next day bill spent all day crawling all over the Liberator and a ground-crew sergeant showed him how to switch on and off the engines and transfer fuel between the various tanks.

His next operation was on 15 October, this time as a rear gunner with Major Demaris, the squadron commander. The target was in Northern Italy. The Major gave him instructions on what to do if they came across enemy fighters, and the bomb aimer told him to remember the area where the bombs hit as he was the only one in the crew who would see the bombs hit. The navigators then asked Bill to give him the wind drift readings. Drift was the lateral movements of the aircraft caused by strong port or starboard winds and the navigator had to take a degree of drift into consideration when plotting and maintaining courses. The rear gunner had a graduated chart painted on the top of the Perspex of his turret and a box of flame/smoke floats stowed within reach outside the turret doors. A float was thrown out and flame/smoke appeared on impact with the sea/ground and the gunner centralised his turret and laid his gunsight on the float. The gunner turned the turret slowly to maintain the sighting and after one minute, read off the degree of deflection on the graduated chart. Bill was sure to be busy on his first operation.

The Liberator had a tricycle undercarriage and the rear gunner could only take his place after the Liberator was in the air, he, therefore, sat on the flight deck and he would pass along the catwalk between the bomb load to the rear gun. The catwalk was about 12 ins wide and everywhere there was a mass of electrical leads which activated the bomb releases. He was the smallest member of the crew and could not negotiate the cat-walk with ease. The target was bombed without any problems and Bill saw hits on the railway tracks and nearby buildings. On landing the pilot said he was satisfied with him as did the navigator with his drift calculations and the bomb aimer for plotting where the bombs had hit.

On 1 August 1944, the Polish Army began Operation Burze the codename for the uprising of the Polish Army in Warsaw against the German Garrison. Within weeks the Poles were asking for arms and supplies. Winston Churchill responded and instructed that an airlift was to be staged without delay. However, with the distances involved the weather and the strength of the German Defences casualties were heavy on aircraft and crews.

On 16 October 1944, Bill was again detailed to fly with the CO, his former pilot Lt Cullingworth, remarked laughing that the 'Old Man' had stolen him but wished him the best of luck. They were to take arms, ammunition and food to the Polish partisans who had been forced out of Warsaw and deep into the surrounding woods. The dropping area was a difficult one because the partisans were constantly on the move. A plan was devised that when they were overhead the reception party leader would signal by flash light the Morse coder letter 'D' and the drop would be from 500 ft. The pilot called the crew together and stressed that this was a 'Naughty One', but still possible. As they crossed the Danube they knew that they were now leaving all the normal targets and that the Germans would soon deduce that they were on their way to drop supplies in Poland. Almost immediately a series of explosions nearby illuminated the sky for about a minute. Bill turned his turret expecting a fighter attack any minute but none came. A warning came from the navigator that they were obliged to pass near a well defended town and there would be opposition. About a dozen searchlights suddenly came to life followed by heavy anti-aircraft fire. Bill told the pilot that the gunners had got their range and were close to a direct hit. He put the nose down and swung away to starboard. Having lost 2,000 ft he resumed his course. The gunners had lost them and stopped. Fifteen minutes from the drop zone the pilot took up his position and they all started to search for the drop zone. They were now down to 500 ft but still no signal then suddenly there were a series of twinkling lights but they turned out to be the flashes of small arms. They were now on reduced fuel and should prepare to return to base when the signal was seen flashing the Morse code 'D'. A pass was made and the canister dropped. When they arrived back at base the news was not good, two Liberators were missing. One of them was Lt Denis Cullingworth, Bill's first pilot with 34 Squadron. It turned out that he had been the CO's best friend and they had trained together but war is war and one must go on. He came from Pretoria, was 27 years old and is now buried in Krakow Rakowicki Cemetery. The airlift was suspended because of the losses and no guarantee that the supplies being despatched were reaching the right hands.

On 19 November 1944, Bill was down to fly as third gunner on a raid on a bridge close to a small town, Visegrad, 80 miles east of Sarajevo, Yugoslavia. It was daylight low-level flight hence the third gunner was told to keep the opposition heads down during the run in to the target. As they came over the target they could not see the bridge for spray because two Liberators had just bombed. They had to try and make an identification as there were seven liberators behind and turning to make a second run would be tricky. Suddenly, the anti-Aircraft gunfire commenced and was too accurate for comfort. The skipper called to all gunners to open fire and try to keep the enemy quite. Several long bursts of .5 Brownings from the rear turret and beam positions aided by the glowing tracer bullets thudded into the sites. They were successful and one hit and several near misses were recorded.

On Christmas Day 1944, the squadron was told that volunteers were needed for a special supply-drop mission. A groan went up, but when the CO added that included in the supplies to be dropped were toys and sweets for Yugoslavian partisans' children, that did it and every hand in the briefing room went up. The supplies were dropped on snow covered ground and the people below rushed forward to pick them up.

The New Year 1945 brought torrential rain and occasional hail stones the size of golf balls. The word went around that the CO was allowing twenty-four men to visit Rome on leave. Bill put his name in the hat and was, for once, lucky. For the next ten days he would be living in a proper building and not a tent. When they arrived back, of the original twenty-five air gunners posted into Nos 31 & 34 Squadrons only fifteen remained.

The end of Bill's time in Italy came when the SAAF had trained sufficient air gunners of their own to man all crews and accordingly the RAF air gunners were to be posted to a neighbouring RAF Squadron which was due to convert from flying Wellingtons to Liberators. They were to act as instructors and then fly as the additional members of crews, because a Wellington had only one regular air gunner, having no mid-upper turret.

Jack Wakefield came from New Zealand and trained there as an air gunner on Swordfish aircraft and Vickers Vincents which the RAF had given to the New Zealand air force before the war for service in Iraq and India.

He arrived in England in May 1940 and began further air gunner training on Defiants. He then joined No. 75 New Zealand Squadron and completed thirty operations, with, as he said, the usual searchlights and flak damage. He also served for a year at No. 23 OTU and on one occasion they crashed on the Great North Road near Finningley when both motors on the Wellington cut out, they went through a hedge and the aircraft broke in two and burst into flames. The pupil rear gunner was killed in the crash. Jack was then posted to the Middle East and No. 38 Squadron whose aircraft were fitted with radar and their duties were mine laying, torpedo strikes, and anti-submarine patrols carrying depth charges. He found this the most satisfactory task of the war; homing in on U-Boats who were threatening convoys and forcing the submarines to crash dive and in the four months that he was involved they did not lose one convoy ship. The radar would pick up the convoy and the escorting destroyers several miles ahead and anything else on the radar was an enemy submarine.

On one occasion, at evening time but still light, they left Shallufa, Egypt and flew out looking for shipping when they observed a storm that caused seven waterspouts and although the pilot, a well decorated Squadron Leader, tried his hardest to fly around it they were thrown around like a straw in the wind. With a full load of petrol and two torpedoes they decided to return to base whereupon Jack suspected that the landing was going to be a touch and go affair so he removed the hatch of the astrodome of the Wellington. On touchdown one of the undercarriage legs gave way, and the aircraft slid to a halt with a broken back. The torpedoes tore out of the aircraft hissing air, and with concern that the casing might give way Jack ran for about 100 yards away from the aircraft. However, the rest of the crew went to the rear turret to see if he was okay but Jack, having been a Boy Scout, 'Being Prepared' was always his motto.

F/Lt Leonard Vaughan, in December 1941, and with No. 148 Squadron had been awarded the DFC after taking part in fifty-four operations, including twenty-eight on Germany and German occupied territory. On one occasion during a mine-laying mission in the Corinth Canal his aircraft was subjected to fire at close range from two anti-aircraft guns which he silenced and so averted a very difficult situation. He was a qualified gunnery officer and carried out a great deal of the instruction on new crews. In December 1942 he was going back to the UK for a rest period having now completed 100 operations and 691 operational hours. He was serving with No. 40 Squadron at Shallufar, Egypt where he had moved to from RAF Alconbury. On 17 December 1942 he boarded an aircraft, Halifax

The grave of F/S Porritt DFM in Crete War Cemetery. *Alan Cooper*

War graves in Cassino War Cemetery. *Alan Cooper*

DT542, of 138 Sqn which had come out from RAF Tempsford to route to Libya, and was now on its way back to the UK and flown by Flying Officer Dubromisski. At 0400 hours they took off but following an engine fire they tried to return and land but undershot the runway and crashed in Tas Sis Quary. If it had carried on its flight path it would have crashed on a children's orphanage. All aboard including the all Polish crew were killed. On board were seventeen people including ground crew from 138 Squadron and are now buried in Capucciu Naval Cemetery, Kalkara, Malta which is situated above Valetta Harbour. It has 726 graves of which 394 are airmen. In the Middle East Vaughan had taken part in operations to Bizerta, Tunis and Sicily. He had been recommended for the DSO, a high award for a junior officer, this was approved and gazetted on 5 January 1943, only two weeks after his death.

CHAPTER ELEVEN

Prisoners of War / Evasion / Casualties

There were a number of men in the RAF aircrew who did not return from operations and there were over 12,000, of which 9,000 were from Bomber Command, who became prisoners of war. They all heard the phrase 'For you the war is over' and ended up in a prisoner of war camp.

There were others who, through good thinking or circumstances and a lot of luck, were able to evade capture and eventually get back to the UK. Many were air gunners.

When an air gunner took off from an airfield there was always the possibility that he would not return. In the terminology of the day: 'nothing further heard' but they could end up as a 'guest' of the Third Reich.

Roy Child joined the RAF at the age of 17 and after training was posted as an air gunner to No. 90 Squadron, flying Stirling bombers. On 9 November 1943, and having completed ten operations he requested a transfer and in December was posted to No. 7 Pathfinder Squadron, a former Stirling Squadron now operating with Lancasters. Including himself his new crew had completed 400 operational flights over Germany between them. It was now the period of the Battle of Berlin and on 20 February 1944, his aircraft was attacked by a German fighter that shot them down at Wittenberg. Three of the crew were killed, the remaining four including Roy were able to bale out and became prisoners of the Germans. For them the war was over.

After capture Roy was taken to *Dulag luft* and interrogation centre for captured aircrew and manned by the *Luftwaffe*. In the early hours of the morning he was taken for interrogation by a German officer who insisted on calling him Mr Child. He said he knew he was an enemy agent and had been sent to blow up a bridge at Halle. It was up to Roy to prove differently and if he failed to do this the Gestapo would come and take him away. Somehow the Germans knew a lot about No. 7 Sqn, in fact more than Roy knew. He was taken to a barren compound to begin his life behind the wire. No one who has not gone through this can really imagine what it felt like and, in fact, what it was like. The prisoners came from UK, USA, Poland, Belgium, Canada, Australia, New Zealand, Russia, South Africa, South America, India, and many more places. They shared each other's grief and sorrow and helped each other over the obvious depression that soon set in. RAF prisoners were not allowed to work, as did army prisoners so there was no contact outside the wire.

When the mail arrived morale went up but in some cases soon went down when the Dear John letter was opened telling them that their wife or girlfriend had met someone else. The separation for what could be an unknown period was just as hard for those left behind. *Stalag* 357 at Fallingbostel, and the home of many of the men captured at Arnhem, became a very unpleasant camp. In April 1945 the camp had some 10,000 prisoners and with the guns of the Allied troops only 30 miles away they were put on the road and force marched to the River Elbe. Orders had come out from an insane Hitler that they were to be shot rather than liberated by the Allies. The march had its tragic consequences: they had stopped to rest outside the village of Gresse where a lorry turned up with welcome Red Cross parcels. They had lived on stolen potatoes and sugar beet, slept in barns and fields and were shattered. As they rested a flight of Typhoon fighters came over which soon brought a cheer of comfort to the bedraggled men. But suddenly they peeled off and one by one attacked the column of prisoners. As the cannon fire came down the road so the prisoners fell. Roy took cover behind a tree but he suddenly felt a terrible pain in his leg. Once more a fighter attacked and more men were hit. Next to him was a dead prisoner who had a huge hole in his back, but for some reason no blood could be seen. Roy decided to make a run for it along with hundreds of prisoners. As he did so another fighter came roaring across the field and Roy knew he would not make cover so he just stood there, but for some reason, perhaps the fighter was out of ammunition it did not fire. He had left back on the road over fifty dead prisoners. After being shot down and held prisoner for many years they were killed by their own men: pilots of the RAF, the force they had served. A rare experience of 'Friendly Fire' in WWII. They were all buried in a hurriedly dug mass grave at Gresse. Roy found it hard to understand how the Typhoon pilots could not see that they were PoWs, men in old clothes and on foot. It was a terrible day for all and today Roy still has a scar on his leg to remind him of that day in 1945.

In April 1945, Fallingbostel was liberated by the Allies. Men who had been taken at Dunkirk and Arnhem, a South African who had been taken at Crete in 1941, they were all now free. All the PoWs, including Roy, were picked up by Lancaster bombers and flown back to the UK, but many fellow prisoners, were left dead, killed or even as in the case of the Great Escape murdered and are buried all over Germany.

WO Nicholas Alkemade, a F/Sgt, was serving with No. 115 Squadron as a rear gunner on Lancasters. On 24 March 1944 the target was the 'Big City' and the capital of Germany: Berlin. Just after the words "Bombs Gone" came from the bomb aimer the aircraft was hit and there was a big explosion, it shattered Nick's turret and he was hit by splinters of Perspex. They had been attacked by a Ju88 fighter and it was coming in for the kill. Nick aimed at the fighter and fired at its port engine which exploded and the fighter turned away. By now the hydraulics of the Lancaster were non-existent and the aircraft was on fire with flames coming past Nick's turret. The order came to bale out. There was a rack behind his turret and on it was his parachute but the fire prevented Nick from reaching the parachute. It was jump without it or burn to death. He chose the former; he took off his melting oxygen mask and he was able to get himself into a position to fall out backwards. He knew that having no parachute he stood little chance of surviving. It was then that he passed out. When he came to he could see the stars above and he felt very cold. The trees had originally broken his fall and then he had fallen into more than a foot of snow after dropping some 18,000 ft. Apart from a twisted knee and his burns he was unharmed. He was soon picked up by the Germans and taken to hospital. When they realised he had no parachute and he tried to explain that he had jumped from an aircraft they thought he was mad. He heard that his aircraft S-Sugar had been found and hoped that the remains of his parachute would be there and substantiate his story. When the Germans searched the remains of the Lancaster the harness of his parachute was there, where he said it would be. They brought it back and he tried it on and they also found the scorched handle of his ripcord in the wreckage and it was then that they believed his story.

It was his 13th operation and he had survived. At *Stalag III Sagan* he was presented with a signed witness testimony that proved his story. He also received a supply of cigarettes from other prisoners for autographing their 'line books'. Four of the crew had been killed in the crash, only the navigator, the wireless operator and Nick survived. He died in Cornwall in June 1987. His feat of dropping so far without a parachute is recorded in the Guinness Book of Records.

When an airmen baled out his only hope of help was from people on the ground such as the French or Dutch resistance or Escape Lines, but in the case of Denis Salt it was a different matter. He was an wireless/operator air gunner with No. 578 Squadron when on 15 March 1944 he took of with his pilot, F/Sgt Lyon to attack Stutgart. He was just 20 at the time and came from Birmingham. His aircraft was shot down by a Ju88 night fighter and five of the crew lost their lives. Denis had lost both legs below the knee and was resigned to dying. He lay in a snow covered field which helped to stem the bleeding from his legs and probably saved his life. A group of German villagers came out and helped to make a stretcher from his parachute. It has to be said that there were some villagers who were not keen on helping him because the RAF was still bombing Stuttgart so one can see their point of view. However, there were three young girls who decided they would try and save him and they succeeded. He was then taken away by the military to a hospital. When released from hospital he was taken to *Stalag* IXC and became friends with Norman Jackson, who, when he returned from captivity was awarded the VC. Norman Jackson would carry Denis around the camp on his shoulders. Dennis came back to the UK in 1945 and took up a very active life. In 1993 he again met up with the three young ladies who had helped him when they flew to Birmingham for a civic reception. Denis said, "I was the enemy but they treated me like a German". Six years later, 1999, Denis died.

On 24 June 1944, Harry Garratt was the rear gunner with No. 9 Squadron detailed to attack the rocket sites in France. The Lancaster aircraft, flown by Eddie Holdsworth, was attacked by an upward firing Me110 known as the '*Schrage Musik*.' The Lancaster was, on this occasion, carrying an 8th man; he being a belly gunner added to the crew to combat the upward firing fighter. When the order came to bale out Harry disposed of the belly gun and dropped through the space where it had been. Harry knocked on a farmhouse door only to find it occupied by German troops; for him the war was over. After interrogation he was taken to a PoW camp at Bankau and then *Stalag* IIIA at Luckenwald, a new camp which was still being built, despite the fact the Russians were already advancing through Poland. It was May 1945 when he was liberated by the Russians and then taken in a US Marauder aircraft flown by an American Colonel to an area where he picked up a Lancaster bomber for a flight to the UK. The only other man to survive was the belly gunner, the mid-upper gunner had been seen with his parachute on waiting to bale out but somehow he did not jump and was killed. Out of twenty-two Lancasters lost on that night three were from No. 9 Squadron. At the time Harry was 19 and remembers a young Welshman being full of excitement because he was going on his first operation that night. It was to be his one and only operation as he failed to return and became one of 56,000 men killed serving with Bomber Command.

Jim Everson was from Wales and was a Wireless Operator/Air Gunner with No. 78 Squadron in 1940 when on the night of 28 November 1940, his aircraft made a forced landing on one of Frisian Islands and were soon picked up by the *Luftwaffe*. Jim had to say that they were very well treated and taken by launch to the mainland and then by train to Frankfurt-on-Main and then on to Obersal and the infamous interrogation centre. Jim had flown mainly in the rear turret but found the cell here at the centre much more enclosed. The heat was turned up full during the day and off in the night. The dim electric light was kept on day and night, the bed hard and conditions Spartan. From here it was by train to *Stalag Luft* 1 at Barth situated on the Baltic Coast where he arrived just before Christmas 1940.

Classes were started and text books supplied from Oxford. Much 'good baiting' went on like walking behind the Germans who came into the compound. An escape committee was formed and Don Bristow made a radio receiver. For security reasons this was called Canary and BBC News bulletins were compiled. The winters were bitterly cold and there was snow which set hard. In March bitter winds resulted in dust storms. Despite the news of the war not being at all cheerful morale was high. Some of the German interpreters who came into the camp would sell their birthright for chocolate and soap so maps, railway timetables, ink for making passes, and even a small camera were produced. A jar of coffee could work wonders when blackmail became the order of the day.

While at Barth one PoW, Sgt John Shaw, was shot and killed in an escape attempt. He and a Lloyd Evans attempted to cross a sports field covered in deep snow when a guard spotted them, challenged them and then fired. Lloyd stood up and was taken to the 'Cooler' but John did not get up and was buried at the cemetery in Barth. For over a year, Barth was closed so Jim and the others were sent in cattle trucks to *Stalag Luft* III at Sagan, a nightmare journey with shortages of food, water, fresh air and no proper sanitary arrangements. The camp was set in the middle of a gloomy pine forest. When at Barth they could see the church and some of the houses but at Sagan the view was gloomy and depressing. A space was cleared to play rugby, one other Welshman there at the time was Peter Thomas, later post-war Home Secretary for Wales who came to Newport to visit Jim after the war. In October 1943 they returned to Barth and were glad of it.

On 3 May 1945, they were liberated by the Russians and after a few hectic weeks flown home by American B17s and landed at Ford in Sussex. Then to RAF Cosford for a debriefing, kitting out and then home on leave. After the war Jim said that being a prisoner taught him to live with some of the best men he was fortunate enough to meet. They were boys when they became prisoners and men when they got back.

On the night of 22/23 April 1944 Bernard Warren took off with No. 103 Squadron as a mid-upper gunner to attack Dusseldorf and arrived over 30 minutes late over the already burning city with the distinct sense of being alone. Suddenly Bernard's inter-com went dead, the hydraulics ceased to function and his guns were useless. He rotated the turret by manual control but from there on they were a sitting duck. More flak followed and the aircraft was now on fire so he decided to leave the turret and came face to face with the wireless operator who had been sent to look for him and indicated that they were to bale out. He put his parachute on and went out of the rear door. He pulled the ripcord and counted to ten. The parachute opened with a jolt and he passed out and landed still unconscious. When he regained consciousness he found he was completely unhurt. He released the parachute and buried it. Then he just sat there but soon he heard a stream of German words and someone approaching him. He had been captured by an old farmer and young boy. The farmer gave the boy the shotgun and then went to the phone. Shortly afterwards the German army turned up and Bernard was taken to an army camp. The next day they moved to Dusseldorf and while there an air raid took place and they had to move to the cellars and share this with the civilians who were not too happy about this and started to lash out with sticks and umbrellas. The guards intervened and protected him from serious damage.

After the usual interrogation he spent a year at *Stalag* VI East Prussia, then to 357 at Thorn and finally to 357 Fallingbostel until released on 16 April 1945 by members of the 7th Armoured Division, Monty's Desert rats.

It was 27 October, 1939, the first year and the second month of WWII. The conditions outside the No. 51 Squadron's Whitley bomber were freezing. For 27 year old Alfred Griffin in his rear turret it was even colder. Their operation was a raid on Munich, normally a round trip of 1,400 miles, but on this occasion they had flown to Villeneuve in France, on to Munich and were on their way back to Villeneuve and were over northern France. Alfred got on the inter-com and said to the pilot, "Aren't we getting a bit low". But there was no reply, only the noise of the two Armstrong–Whitworth Tiger Engines. He could now see the hills getting closer and closer, what he did not know was the crew had already baled out. They had flown to Munich, which even from France was 700 miles, to drop not bombs but leaflets. The pilot was Johnnie Bowles, who had been an engine fitter before becoming a pilot. They took off in K 8984 at 1805 and at 7,000 ft it started to get chilly despite the flying suit, scarf, helmet and gauntlets that the crew were wearing. The further they travelled south-east the colder it became and snow was pouring into the front turret and the snow went through the aircraft and was piling up around Sgt Griffin. On the engine cowlings ice was building up to 6 ins, the windows were thickly coated and they were surrounded by cotton-wool-like cloud.

There were 15 parcels of leaflets to drop, each had 12 bundles making 180 leaflets in all. At 2115 the last bundle was dropped. To do this they had to lower the central turret, or 'dustbin' flush with the floor then fit the chute through which the bundles were dropped. When the last one had gone Bowles turned for home and ordered the turret up but when they tried to they found it had been frozen in the down position. Griffin suddenly noticed a blue flame escaping from the exhaust stub which could only mean one thing: the rocker gear had broken on one cylinder. They were now 99 minutes from base in France. Then came an explosion and the cylinder head blew off leaving no power in the starboard engine.

After summing up the situation Bowles decided to abandon the aircraft and shouted out the order no aircrew wants to hear, "Bale out, Bale out". When he gave a last call to Griffin and got no reply he was happy that Griffin had left the aircraft. But Griffin thinking all was well stayed with the aircraft until it crashed and turned over leaving Griffin in his turret upside down. Somehow, apart from a bang on the head he was unhurt. He thought the crew were still in the aircraft and tried to get into the cockpit but was beaten back by the flames.

He was picked up by three French soldiers who thought he was a German and marched him to the nearest village but when he was reunited with his crew all was well. Alfred was not taken prisoner but if the accident had happened a few months later he would have been.

For some such as Percy Carruthers DFM, on one occasion life as a PoW was harder than others. He and the other prisoners left Heydekrug on 15 July 1944 for an unknown destination, all they were told was that the journey would take one day. At the railway station they boarded cattle trucks and set off, all they could deduct was that they were travelling north. Their journey, which actually took three days, ended at a seaport, Memel, and a cargo ship, the 7,000 ton *Insterberg*.

On board they were soon pushed down into the forward hole and, although they had food with them, there were no facilities for cooking. It was, as they described it, a hell ship: one bucket was for ablutions and one for drinking water but the problem was the buckets soon got mixed up.

At the end of the journey their boots were removed and they were chained and handcuffed. The journey continued once again in cattle trucks, this time, thankfully, it was a short one to *Stalag Luft* IV at Gross Tyshow about 80 miles from Danzig. On arrival at the railway station they were given the good news that they would have to spend the night in the cattle truck, it was stifling hot and there was a shortage of drinking water.

The next day their boots were returned. The guards now were Kriegsmarine, (naval cadets), and the *Luftwaffe*. They all, according to official reports, had something with which to hold a grudge against the British.

They formed into one column and the guards were told by an *Hauptmann* Picard that they were 'Air Gangsters' and the favourite saying 'Terror Flugers' or 'Terror Flyers', and these were the men who had bombed Hamburg, Berlin and Cologne etc.

The order was given to march, with the German officer in a car a short distance in front of the column. Then they were ordered to march at the double and their guards used rifle butts as well as bayonets to encourage slackers. The prisoners were chained in pairs so if one fell the other man had no choice but to remain with him and suffer more attacks. Sometimes shots were fired with the idea of making the prisoners try to escape. Most of their kit had now been abandoned and those that still had their possessions were forcibly encouraged to drop them. The Germans also used dogs to attack and bite the prisoners. When they arrived at the camp gates 150 prisoners had bayonet wounds, dog bites or injuries from rifle clubbing. They were then searched and all Red Cross food, cigarettes and personal clothing was removed and pens, watches and rings were stolen. All photographs and letters were destroyed in the search.

Not all PoWs were shot down in Germany, some were captured in other European countries. Peter Skinner, flying with No. 158 Squadron, was shot down by light flak near Esbjerg, Denmark. Peter was the only member of the crew to survive, although one other crew member was wounded and died four days later. Those who died are buried some 20 miles from Esbjerg.

Peter was soon taken to Germany and, after the usual interrogation, he ended up in *Stalag* 8b, Lamsdorf, which in 1944 changed to *Stalag* 344. After registering, and delousing, he found himself in a compound with 800 airmen all wearing manacles on their wrists attached to a chain 15 ins long. The compound was run by a German named 'Ukraine Joe'. At the end of the war he was handed over to the Russians who were looking for him as a traitor and persecutor of Russian PoWs.

On 22 January 1945, nearly 1,000 PoWs were marched out of the camp. Those that could not march were left to tend to the sick. It was freezing with snow on the ground that became hard and slippery. At 10pm that night they were herded into barns, sheds, pigsties and lean-tos for the night. Overnight, the temperature dropped and those that had taken their great coats off to use as blankets were frozen stiff and those that had taken off their boots could not get them back on in the morning. In some cases their boots had been stolen.

Peter was on the march for 81 days during which he had only three 'rest' days. He saw absolute depravity, which caused fear among ordinary decent people and death became commonplace, but he found courage and comradeship which taught him much about how to live one's life and even today he still tries to attain those ideals.

Sgt Reginald Luce was born on the 17th, his flying licence number, gained when he learned to fly before the war, was 1777, his squadron No. 77, service number 911370 and on the seventh month in 1941 he was on his twenty-seventh operation as a wireless operator / air gunner. As he crossed the Dutch coast and he sent the routine signal informing base that they had crossed the enemy coast. On venturing near the cockpit he was amazed to find that the pilot's seat was empty and just saw a figure leaving the aircraft though the escape hatch; he was, it would appear, alone in the aircraft.

He soon grabbed his parachute and opened the mid-fuselage hatch, outside the wing tank was on fire. As he crawled along towards the escape hatch he felt a stabbing pain in his body: the fighter that had made the first attack was now making a second and a cannon shell struck him in the left hip which went clean through chipped his spinal column en route and then left his body leaving his back with a large hole. He was now paralysed down his left side with no feeling in his left arm and leg. He had to get out, particularly before the blazing tanks blew up. Somehow he got out of the aircraft and pulled the rip cord, missing the tailplane by inches and landed in a tree in a forest at Leuwarden where he hung there. However, he realised he only about 3 ft from the ground so he knocked his release gear on the parachute and dropped to the ground and here he lay for about two days until found by three Dutch foresters.

They could not speak English and he had no knowledge of Dutch. They found out he could not walk and made attempts to tie branches on his legs as splints. His RAF buttons were cut off by one of the men who, Reg heard say, "We must get the Bosche". This they did and a German Captain asked him for his weapon but when he found Reg did not have one his manner changed and Reg was soon in a hospital. From there he moved to thirteen prison camps and hospitals in Holland and Germany. It was a German doctor, aged 77, who saved his life; he practically rebuilt his bowel passage which the cannon shell had torn through. He was also helped by two British army doctors who had been captured at Dunkirk. In 1943 he was repatriated and in 1944 discharged with the rank of warrant officer. It would appear that his fellow crewmen had jumped facing the nose instead of the tail of the aircraft and all must have struck the tail of the aircraft as none survived.

Stan Reed served with No. 78 Squadron in Yorkshire. On 10 April 1945, with 21 year old Jack Adams at the controls of Halifax DT 775 F-Firkin they set out for Frankfurt am Main in Germany. Stan, also aged 21, was the rear gunner and the mid-upper gunner was Joe Enwright, he was 28. Stan never saw the Me110 night fighter that hit them and they became one of twenty shot down that night. One of the crew was hit in the leg and another had burnt hands. There was nothing from the rear turret so he could not have seen the fighter either. The order came to bale out and Stan opened the rear door upon which he was met with a mass of flames so he sat on the floor with his legs outside the aircraft. As he prepared himself to bale out he was suddenly sucked out and found himself falling and the tail of the Halifax going over his head. As he moved his hand up to operate the ripcord he found to his horror it was not there; he had no parachute, just the harness straps. He must have he left it on the floor of the aircraft. This was it, he felt, and having survived the fighter attack he was now going to die in this way. However, and thankfully for Stan, it was just in the panic of the moment that he had thought he had no parachute. In fact, his parachute had somehow opened and in his own words, 'hit the ground like a sack of wet potatoes'. His knees came up and struck him under the chin. He rolled over and realised he was somewhere in darkest France. He had got away with it no broken bones, only a sore nose and very painful chin. He threw his parachute into a ditch and stuffed his flying helmet and Mae West life jacket up a large drain pipe he found in the same ditch.

He set off to look for help and soon came across a large house with a smaller one alongside but when he looked inside he saw the biggest German soldier he had ever seen, it was a guard house with rifles and German helmets hanging inside. He was soon found by a German Dobermann Pinscher dog which did not actually bite him but came too close for comfort. He shot out of brambles where he was hiding and was told to put his hands up; he was faced with two German soldiers and a civilian. He was reunited with other members of his crew who had also been caught. The usual aircrew interrogation followed at Frankfurt am Main. They found out that one body had been found in the crashed Halifax, it was Joe Enwright, the rear gunner. His first name was actually Jethro but became known as Joe, he came from Durham and is now buried in Briey Cemetery, France.

Stan's flying kit and uniform were taken away and he was given a rough khaki uniform with many brass buttons to wear and on his feet clogs. A German officer produced a book all about No. 78 Squadron with photographs of crashed Halifaxes and dead crews lying alongside, some of which Stan knew and had played football with or drank with in the mess. Stan and his crew were taken to *Stalag Luft* 1 at Barth in cattle trucks with seventy-five to eighty men in each one. He found out that Jack, his pilot, had been the last to leave the aircraft and later reached Paris with the help of an escape line for Allied airmen. Jack was in Paris for 10 days but was then captured in a Gestapo search of the 'safe house' they were in. Jack and other prisoners were taken to Fresnes prison in Paris where they spent six weeks and during this time many PoWs were taken out and shot in the courtyard. He finally arrived at Barth but it was many weeks before he became anything like his normal self.

Not all airmen who had to bale out were captured, some evaded and got back to the UK. Donald Brinkhurst began his RAF career as a flight mechanic and after training was posted to Egypt. It was 1940 and he was 19. His first flight was in a Valencia aircraft and it so impressed him he volunteered to became a full-time air gunner with the rank of AC2 and earned 2/- a day flying pay. He later reverted back to ground duties and it was January 1943 before he was accepted for aircrew duties and sent to Rhodesia for training at Gwelo. He passed out from here on 31 March 1943 and returned to the UK. His advanced air gunnery was at Binbrook.

He joined No. 101 Squadron flying Lancasters and flew on his first operation to Munich on 6 September 1943. Six weeks later on an operation to Kassel they were attacked by a Ju88 and although the Ju88 was beaten off without casualties the aircraft suffered damage to the fuselage and the mid-upper turret which was manned by Donald. Having completed twenty-four operations, including six to Berlin, he was on a further operation to Berlin when he was hit by a piece of shrapnel which pierced his arm just below the elbow. He was given first aid and helped out of the turret. During this time they were again attacked and the rear gunner Sgt Jim Goodall and the wireless operator, Sgt Ryland Luffman, now a substitute mid-upper gunner sent the fighter down in flames. On the return journey Donald recovered enough to allow the wireless operator to get back to his set for wireless duties. On landing he was taken to hospital and was off flying for six weeks.

His last operation, as it turned out, was the infamous raid on Nuremberg on 30/31 March 1944. They were the 7th aircraft shot down of a total of ninety-six, the heaviest losses since the war began. They were not shot down by an enemy fighter or flak but by a Halifax bomber. The Lancaster DV 264 was hit on the port side, and both engines caught fire and the intercom was put out of action. With the fire starting to spread down the fuselage Donald left his turret and came across Jim Goodall who had also left his turret and was sitting on the lid of the Elsan portable toilet. They made ready to bale out and Donald successfully baled out. Sadly it would appear that Jim Goodall did not get out and is now buried in the Durnbach War Cemetery near Munich. Also, F/O Marrian, a special electronics operator, baled out but his parachute failed to open and he was killed.

Having landed safely Donald hid his parachute and started to walk, but coming across some villagers he hid in a ditch until they went back to their homes. Later he tried with sign language to seek help from two middle aged women who promptly ran off. On coming to a weir he decided to cross it and was up to his knees in water. On arriving at the other side he took off his flying boots and emptied them of water and then wrung out the bottom of his trousers. After half an hour's walking his trousers began to freeze and his boots became stiff. Then he found an empty house and bedded down for the night and was awoken the next day by the voices of children, he was on the edge of the village of Roetgen. After dark he again began walking and having walked for about six hours he came across another village and on turning a corner he found himself not in a village but a town square. Across the road were two German sentries who saw and shouted at him, they burst out laughing but he never did find out what was so funny about his appearance. However, as he thought he was about to be captured he just kept walked away from the square. He later found out that the was Eupen, 10 to 15 miles south of Aachen.

Near a village called Herbestal he found a barn and again settled down for the night. The next day he again set off and came across a farm where a woman was putting out her washing, he approached her, telling her he was an airmen and could she help him, upon which she grabbed him and took him to a shed where she locked him in. He heard footsteps and expected it to be Germans but it was the woman with her husband and son. They shook his hand and gave him a glass of cognac. He was put to bed and woke some hours later to find a doctor and the local priest and a young man who spoke good English. His name was Joseph Bovy. Various safe houses were found for him until one day the Germans turned up so he was led to the bathroom by his hosts and a small trap door in the ceiling which he squeezed through and the door was closed behind him. He was up there for over two hours until the Germans had left and the door opened and he climbed down. He was now moved from place to place and finally to Liege where he stayed with the wife of an American for about two weeks. In the crypt of a large church were housed a number of RAF and US aircrew about twelve in all.

One day they were all told it was time to move and climbed aboard a lorry with five resistance men wearing red cross bands on their arms. En route they lost their way and ended up at a Ju88 German airfield, the sentry was kind and redirected them to the right road. Some five miles from the Belgium/French border they got out of the lorry and walked to the border in pairs. But the news was bad, the escape chain had been broken and they would have to return to Liege and start all over again.

Donald, with an American, Charlie Westerland whose wife was expecting their first baby, decided to make a break for it across the French border and hopefully be picked up by the French Resistance. They were joined by four other Americans, and one of them, Philip Solomons, spoke good French. They crossed the border without any problems when suddenly a man came out of the bushes and asked, in an American accent, if they spoke English. It was a Tim Holten in full USAAF flying kit. He joined the party and off they went.

Later, they were trying to catch a bus to Charleville-Mezieres and they asked Philip Solomons to ask a Frenchman for information but as they did Tim Holten stepped forward and his best American accent said, "Say Bud, where does the bus for Charleville leave". This had the effect of dispersing the crowd that was at the bus station and it was left to Philip to speak to a small Frenchman who had stayed. The Frenchman, although shocked, but still took Philip around the corner and into a back street where the bus they wanted was waiting. Philip purchased the tickets and they all clambered aboard. As they went along the road the air raid sirens sounded upon which the bus driver stopped the bus and told them all to jump out and promptly drove off. And so they broke up into pairs and started to walk again.

After they had walked through a village a boy about 11 years old came up to them and said, "Come" and pointed back down the track. Don and Philip, who had paired up, went back to a cottage where they were welcomed and given pancakes. This was the Hourrier family, the husband worked on the railway at Mahon. This was helpful as he was able to get them railway tickets from Mahon to Befort which was near the Swiss Frontier. By now the others had turned up and they were again nine in number. There were no problems on the first part of the journey but at Nancy they had to detrain and spent the night in the waiting room. Early the next morning the Germans turned up along with the French police. The Germans were only interested in checking work cards but the French police wanted to check ID cards. They all had forged ID cards but Tim did not have a work card. The seats were slatted and they devised a plan whereby the last but one man could pass his work card under the seat to Tim who was on the end, and it worked with the Germans not realising that they had looked at the same work card twice.

They boarded the train for Belfort but had an uneasy time when two Germans entered the compartment and tried to talk to them. Don replied in French saying they did not understand and pretended to go to sleep. Later to their relief the Germans left the compartment.

At Belfort they were asked by the local Resistance chief if they wanted to join the Resistance or go to Switzerland, Don explained that none of them were trained in ground combat but aerial combat. It was now late May 1944, and the chief told them that they would not able to go to Switzerland until the end of the war in Europe. But after a meal they left for the Swiss border and were then left by their French guides. They then contacted the Swiss Army who took them to the local barracks where they were detained before going into quarantine for a month. They then went back into France and in Grenoble saw the American troops enter the city. Don was then taken to Marseille in a jeep and told to go to an American Field Hospital that flew the wounded to Italy daily. Within a day he was on a Dakota aircraft bound for Rome. From there he went to Algiers and Casablanca and finally to the UK in a Liberator bomber, landing at Newquay in Cornwall.

On 5 December he rejoined No. 101 Sqn with a new crew and on 2 January 1945 took off again for his first operation to Nuremberg; a further twenty followed.

On 11/12 June, 1943, Bill Bailey was flying in a Wellington of No. 429 Squadron, the target Dusseldorf. Being twin-engine aircraft the Wellingtons were wedged between the Lancasters and Halifaxes. In the early hours of the morning they were attacked by a Heinkel night fighter. At the time and with a full bomb load they were flying at 17,000 ft. The starboard wing was badly damaged in the attack and, despite being only 50 miles from the target and the markers of the PFF having lit up the target area, they turned for home but as they turned the fighter came in for a second attack. This time the damage they sustained meant they had to bale out. the pilot failed to jump but the remaining four in the crew baled out successfully.

Bill landed safely and walked for some while until he hid in a copse. At about 6am he saw a young girl and spoke to her. The result was that two men came from the nearby village and he was taken into the underground network. He was in Belgium near the border with Holland. It was here that he learned of the death of his pilot and two of the crew had been taken prisoner but that the other two were safe, although one was wounded.

In Brussels he was astonished to find another pilot from No. 429 Squadron: Gerry Conroy a Canadian and a pal of Bill. Four aircraft from 429 had been shot down on this operation. They then moved towards Liege where they remained hidden for about two weeks. One morning at 5am the Gestapo raided the house they were in so they jumped over the garden wall. That night they returned to the same house. They were then moved to a house that had two escaped Russian PoWs and five members of a Jewish family. Despite another raid by the Germans when all the fugitives were moved to a cellar and spent a week there. Later, Bill and Gerry were moved to another safe house in Brussels and then on to Paris via Mons. They also had a new travelling partner; an American air gunner, Sgt Beverley Geyer. From Paris they went by train to Bordeaux and here changed trains for Dax, where they rode on bikes for 60 km. After a night spent in a café in the Bayonne/Biarritz area they then led by Basque guides across the Pyrenees which was very tiring in the condition they were in. In Spain they were placed in semi-internment in a *pension* café in Irun. Finally they arrived in Madrid and after a day left in a minibus with twelve passengers which took them to Seville and from there finally Gibraltar. Bill described the Madrid, Seville and Gibraltar trip as a hilarious riot. The final stage was from Gibraltar to Cornwall in a Warwick aircraft, the civilian version of the Wellington. Bill remembers he was terrified. From Cornwall he went by train to London.

Stephan Bulmer was trained in Rhodesia and Kenya and back in the UK he joined the crew of Frank French a 22 year old. Stephen recommended 'Buck' Buchanan, an Australian, for the mid-upper gunner spot. Stephen had already been asked if he would fill the rear gunner slot and he accepted. They were posted to No. 90 Sqn at Tuddenham and began operations by dropping mines or 'gardening' as it was known in Bomber Command. Later, their role changed to dropping supplies to the Maquis (French Resistance). On 4/5 March 1944, they set off but only the pilot and navigator knew their target. However, it would appear that there was an error in navigation because they flew directly over a German airfield. Immediately six searchlights came on and cannon fire came up. Both Stephan and Buck fired back but the aircraft was badly damaged; the port engine and wing were on fire. Soon the crew heard the command, "Jump, Jump Jump", and Stephan replied on the intercom, "Rear gunner baling out". He got the turret into the central position opened the tiny doors behind him and somehow got back into the fuselage. On the starboard side there was a separate escape hatch especially for the rear gunner, it was about 20 ins square. He took of his helmet and gauntlets pulled back the lever and off went the hatch. As soon as he got his head and shoulders through the hatch he was pulled out at about 200 miles an hour. He was spread-eagled against the fuselage with his right leg at right angles and his left firmly wedged across the hatch. Each time he tried to get free he was forced back. His mouth was tightly shut and his face distorted and his eyes felt like they were coming out of their sockets.

Somehow he was able to bend his body towards the wind sufficiently to grab the side of the hatch with his left hand and pull himself backwards, just enough to release his leg. He let go and pulled the rip-cord. There was the usual terrific jerk and within a second or two the ground came up to meet him and he found himself on all fours in 6 ins of snow. The aircraft crashed in a huge fireball about 2 miles away.

His eyes were streaming and his leg was sore but other than that he was unhurt. For a while he walked and spent the night in a haystack and woke to find not a cloud in the sky. But then a door opened and a man came out wearing clogs. Stephan stood up and said, *"Bonjour Monsieur, Je suis aviator Anglais. Je tombe par parachute saveidi soir et Jai faim"*. The man looked terrified but said he would bring something and came out with a large white bowl of black coffee and some bread which Stephan dipped in the coffee. He thanked him, put his finger to his lips, waved and set off across the fields. As he got to the middle of the field a German army truck came in sight. Stephan realised he could not run for it, so turned his back to the road and pretended to be attending to something. It worked as the lorry went on its way. He then came across a farm house and risked making contact with the farmer. He turned out to be very friendly and took him indoors.

Here he spent a few days until he waited for a car to come from the Resistance. He was given a piece of ribbon which had been cut in a random way, the driver of the car would have the other piece and when the car turned up he showed the driver the ribbon and the piece the driver had matched perfectly. He did not speak English and drove very fast. Suddenly he stopped the car and a young girl of about 8 came up to the car and said in English "We welcome you to the resistance and we shall try to get you back to England safely" He thanked her and off they went. It turned out to be the driver's daughter.

They next stopped at a chateau and they met by a very elegant and well dressed man who said, "Hello old chap, how are you?" They both burst into laughter. The man was a Count and the head of a very noble French family. Here Stephan was able to get a wash and shave and a change of clothes. The meal was superb, hare cooked in red wine, vegetables and a carafe of wine. In the morning he was awoken by the butler with coffee and rolls. He was told by the Count that after lunch he would be taken to Paris. The car was driven a by woman of about 30 with a studious expression on her face. She told him they were driving to Nevers and then catching a train to Paris and went on to say that the other members of his crew had been captured. One had knocked on a door with his parachute under his arm, the owner of the house had taken fright and called the police. She also told him that the pilot had been killed in the crash. The local Mayor had asked for a French funeral and the Germans agreed. He was buried in a small churchyard in the tiny hamlet of 'Laverdine' many French people attended the funeral but not one German.

The station at Nevers was packed but when the train came in they found two seats sitting opposite each other. All went well until two *Luftwaffe* officers came in but were so engrossed in their own conversation that they never even gave them a glance. They arrived in Paris and caught the Metro and then out into the streets of Paris. They arrived at a house and the door opened and there was his navigator Harry Yarwood. Here they spent three weeks during which time they were taken out shopping by their host Monsieur Gilbert but only one at a time. They then set off to catch a train to Toulouse, his false identity card said he was Antonio Rosini an Italian.

They were taken across the Pyrenees during which time Harry slipped and hurt his ankle badly. They reached the border with Spain at about midnight. It was exactly four weeks since they had been shot down and it was now Easter Sunday. They took one last glance at France and said goodbye to the guide. As they crossed a bridge in Spain four Spanish guards jumped out shouting and pointing their rifles at them. They were taken to a village and thrown in a dungeon. They decided to try and bribe the guards and when the officer came in he took money from a fellow prisoner, a Belgian who spoke Spanish, and the next day a representative from the British and Belgium Embassies arrived. They were soon on their way to a hotel where they were given a meal and a bed for the night. At 3am in the morning Stephan pulled back the bed clothes to find the bed full of bed bugs which were feeding on him, the rest of the night was spent in front of a log fire with coffee and a bottle of brandy. With in a short time they were in Madrid. An RAF lorry was sent from Gibraltar to pick them up. They then flew to Whitchurch, and were interviewed by the Air Ministry in London in which Stephan told them that the pilot, Frank, had given his own life to save the rest of his crew. They were given three weeks leave and Harry the DFC. But nothing for Frank. The only award that can be given posthumously was the VC or a mention in dispatches.

Gerry McMahon was born in 1920 and joined the RAF in August 1938. He trained as an armourer between September 1939 and September 1941 and was employed in aircraft salvage and the repair of armaments, which later became one of the Bomb Disposal Squadrons. In October 1941 he remustered as an Air Gunner and then joined No. 97 Squadron. In 1942 he was awarded the DFM and in his recommendation was mentioned the now famous raid on Danzig on 12 July 1942. During the low attack on the target his aircraft was held by many searchlights, but showing great skill and resourcefulness he was able to dispose of seven with machine gun fire.

In 1943 he was given a commission and joined No. 620 Squadron flying on Stirling bombers. After completing twenty-one secret operations over Western Europe he took off on 5 June 1944, carrying a full complement of paratroopers. As they crossed the French coast they were hit by light flak and some of the paratroopers received minor wounds. Despite this all of them were able to leave in order and on the drop zone. It was later learned all went well and they all landed safely.

On 6 June they again took off, this time towing a glider that they were to drop in an area between the French Coast and the French city of Caen. The glider was released in the drop zone and they headed for the wood at low level where they had seen a gun position. However, the Germans in the gun position saw them coming and hit them first, this blew out the petrol tank on the port wing which blew the wing up and the aircraft on to its back. Gerry as rear gunner, had the first indication that there was something wrong when the ammunition came out of the chutes and hit him in the face. But because of the G force they were not in a position to do anything. The pilot, Flt Lt Gordon Thring, had given up trying to fly the aircraft in the normal way so had his feet up on the dashboard, pulling back on the stick with the hope that he could pull out. Then came a miracle: the aircraft turned over the right way up and a perfect belly landing was made in a ploughed field. Gordon was, within a week, recommended for an immediate DFC. They all got out and ran 25 yards into a wheat field before the aircraft exploded and caught fire. The Germans soon turned up but the crew were able to find good hiding places and the Germans soon left.

Later, they saw two soldiers on bikes and thought they were Americans but they turned out to be Germans and, for the time being the war was over for them. One of the Germans, who because Gerry had a decoration ribbon, thought he was the captain and told him he was educated in England. Gerry and the rest of the crew were interrogated and searched. They were told that they had to retreat to a position near Caen and Gerry and his crew were surrounded by about 200 soldiers and later by a company who had been in combat; one of the soldiers having a badly broken leg with the bone sticking out. Gerry and his crew were chosen to carry the wounded man at first by crossing hands and then on a stretcher. They later disposed of the wounded German and the officer decided they would look after their own wounded.

They marched all night until arriving at a Chateau, this had been a German HQ at one time but was now a fighting garrison. They were put in a barn and some hours later a German Captain arrived with several bottles of champagne and sausages. He explained that this was the only drink available as the water had been polluted. The crew had constantly had thoughts of escaping and plans were afoot to do this. During the next day the Chateau was reduced to rubble by Typhoon attacks and the German morale was low.

The Germans moved out into slit trenches and advised the prisoners to do the same and only three minutes after they had left it the barn received a direct hit, and it was said that some of the German sentries were killed.

Then came a surprise: the Captain sent for Gerry and said to Gerry's astonishment, "I wish to surrender to you, myself and sixty-one men". Gerry accepted their surrender but only if the crew were fully armed and the Germans agreed to march with them to give themselves up. This they did for three miles until surrounded by Canadian soldiers who took the prisoners off Gerry. Gerry was given a receipt for one German officer and sixty-one other ranks. In four days flat they were back in the UK, having been taken back on a Royal Navy destroyer. They were given some leave and then within days they were again flying and took part in the Arnhem drops in September 1944.

On 21/22 June 1944, the target was Wesseling in Germany. Lancaster ME 795-G was piloted by P/O Rackley RAAF of No. 630 Squadron. They were attacked from below by a Ju88 but the mid-upper gunner was able to hit the intruding fighter and it disappeared. However, the Lancaster had been damaged by the fighter attack and they were left with no aileron control and the rudders were sloppy. It was decided to turn for home and jettison the bombs. As they turned the rudder control gave way but by considerable effort the rudder bar was brought back to the central position and tied with a piece of rope, where the rope came from is a mystery.

When they crossed the coast near Ipswich the crew prepared to bale out. There was a huge hole in the fuselage and the rear gunner had to have some assistance to negotiate past it but then it was discovered that his parachute had been damaged by the cannon fire. Without hesitation the flight engineer volunteered to take him down on his parachute. They were tied together and dropped through the escape hatch but, sadly, the wind forces outside the aircraft caused the lashings to give way and the gunner fell to his death. The gunner's name was 'Taffy' Davies. He had escaped death once before when on take-off his aircraft crashed and all the crew apart from him were killed. F/O 'Blue' Rackley was the last to leave but as he landed his parachute caught on the engine of an express train. The parachute finally fell off the engine but not before 'Blue' was badly injured. He was picked up by the guard of a goods train. This crew was not taken prisoner nor had to escape but nevertheless they had to bale out and face the perils of landing.

F/O Steve Nunns and his crew, also of No. 630 Squadron were detailed to attack the railway yards at Kaiserslautern on 27/28 September 1944. The mid-upper gunner was Sgt Keith Nelson and the rear gunner was Sgt Jim Elliott.

After just over two hours flying the port outer-engine caught fire, all efforts to put it out failed and the flames started to spread along the wing. The order to bale out came but Jim reported that he was stuck out on the port quarter and needed help. The engine that was on fire controlled the hydraulics to his turret and, obviously, the hydraulics had failed and his parachute was still in the fuselage. Keith, his fellow gunner, came back and operated the dead man's handle which turned the turret inboard and out Jim got. By the time he got his parachute on the only one left was Steve the pilot. Jim reported to him that he was free, sat on the bomb aimers hatch, threw off his helmet, to avoid being strangled, leant forward and was dragged out by the slipstream.

He landed in a beet field, threw off his parachute and ran across the field, when suddenly he realised he had forgotten to bury his chute. He went back and buried it as best he could, and from time to time blew his whistle to see if anyone else was around. He then heard voices which were obviously not English or French but German. He decided to stay in the field until dawn. He was awoken from a doze by the sound of aircraft and looking up he saw the silhouettes of Lancasters above. He started to walk and came across a barge moored on the other side of the canal. A man appeared throwing something into the water so Jim whistled and shouted to him, he then came across in a small rowing boats. He took Jim across a field to a railway crossing and left him with a large elderly French woman who gave him a hug and kiss and some food. The barge man returned with four other men all wearing the arm band of the Free French. They stopped a train and travelled for some distance on the train until disembarking and walking across the fields until they came to a town called Laone on the St Quentin to Rheims road. Here he was handed over to the French police who were busy and not very interested, so he just sat there waiting. Suddenly, he saw an American on a motor bike, a Military Policeman, to whom he told his story. The American said he would help him to get to the base at Rheims but things were fluid and the Yanks were moving fast. A truck was hailed and along with a few GIs he was taken to a sort of airfield. Here he was fed and interrogated by an American Captain. They checked his story and said it checked out and he was to be given a lift home in a Dakota aircraft. He was flown to Le Mans, and then back to the UK. He arrived back in just over 24 hours after leaving East Kirkby the home of Nos 57 and 630 Squadron. There he found that Steve the pilot having seen Jim leave the aircraft had flown it home alone and had been awarded the DFC. Jim's kit had been handed in, thinking had got the 'chop'. The discarded flying helmet had been found still in the hinges of the bomb doors by the inter-com cord. The result was that pilot type parachutes were issued to gunners. As this parachute had to be sat on and being six foot tall Jim became a mid-upper gunner because there was not the room for him now in the rear turret. It was also decided that for good publicity for 630 Squadron they should go back on ops that night, but, unfortunately, bad weather meant that operations were aborted for that night and for the next few nights so they did get a few days of rest. Having said that they did go on and complete eighteen operations, one of 11 hours to Gydinia in Poland. In March 1945 Jim finished his tour having completed thirty-six operations. Today one of the crew has passed on, two have lost touch but the rest are in touch with each other.

Tom Maxwell left Belfast to become a fighter pilot in the RAF, but he was not the only one: every young man joining the RAF wanted to fly a fighter. He was told they wanted navigators or air gunners but he turned this down and went back to Belfast on leave. But after a week he decided to return and become an air gunner.

On 15 March 1944 and flying with F/Sgt Thompson RAAF of No. 622 Squadron he set off in Lancaster LL828-J to bomb Stuttgart. After bombing the target and still in the target area they were hit by flak and, although they continued on track for base, they were using petrol rapidly. A route was plotted to reach the coast in the shortest possible time but as they passed over Paris they were hit again over the area of Beauvais and given the order to bale out. Tom came down in a ploughed field, near Baxancourt. He lay low for about 10 minutes then ripped off his chute and buried it along with his Mae West and outer clothing in a ditch. It was a young boy who recognised him as a British airman and took him home to his family, they gave him a bed and food, despite the fact that, at the time, the Germans were only 3 miles away and if they had been caught they would have been shot. He was given plain clothes and they set off on bikes to Menerval and the home of a farmer. Here he stayed in a barn until 19 March when he was taken back to the original house and stayed there until the 22 March. Eventually he was helped back to the UK arriving on 23 May 1944. Four of the crew managed to escape and three were taken prisoner including the pilot F/Sgt Thompson from Australia. Both Tom and Peter Jezzard, the wireless/operator, returned to operations. Peter finished his tour in November with thirty-five trips and Tom finished with thirty-two on New Year's Day 1945. Sadly W/O Peter Jezzard DFM died on 5 April 1948 when his Wellington aircraft crashed into the North Sea.

The recommendation for an immediate DFC for Tom was dated 25 October 1944. It gave a full résumé of his being shot down and evading capture. And it also mentioned that, despite having been away for some months he returned immediately to 622 Squadron. His recommendation was endorsed by the AOC of 3 Group on the 30 October 1944. Six months after his return the AOC 3 Group was Air Commodore Andrew Mckee, later Air Chief Marshal Sir Andrew McKee, at a briefing for an operation at Kopertayion Top, Hamburg, sat down beside Tom and handed him two pieces of P/O Ribbon and the ribbon of the DFC. Tom at the time was 19, today he is in his 80s but still remembers the occasion as if it was yesterday.

Len Clarke was shot down on 14 May 1940. At the time he was an AC1, the minimum rank of Sgt came in after he had been shot down. But promotion did come through to him in a prisoner of war camp, and on 1 May 1943 he was promoted to F/Sgt and then later Warrant Officer, some promotion. What was unusual about this was he still did not have the half brevet of air gunner but was wearing the flying bullet badge. One wonders what the other PoWs thought of his rank and lack of an air gunners brevet!

On 14 May the target for his Fairey Battle L-5188 of No. 12 Squadron was Amifontaine Near Reims, France. The pilot was Sgt Reg Winkler who had joined as an apprentice in 1930 and retired as a Squadron Leader in 1973 and died in 1992. The observer Sgt Maurice Smalley, also a regular, later became the Vicar of Chelmarsh Salop and died in 1980. Len stayed in the RAF until 1948 and went into the Civil Service retiring in 1982.

It was a bad day for 12 Sqn: besides Len's aircraft another aircraft of A flight was shot down when leaving the target and two of the crew were killed and another one became a PoW. In B Flight two aircraft were shot down with four crew killed and two becoming prisoners.

Len's aircraft received a direct hit in the engine which threw the aircraft upwards and with the resultant flames sweeping back into the cockpit. The order was given to bale out and Len was given a push from behind and out he went. He landed on the towpath of the canal leading from the River Meuse. He was the first airman the Germans had seen but they looked after him by bandaging a cut on his head and giving him cigarettes, fruit and coffee. As he was escorted through the streets of a small village he really saw what the war was all about with dying French soldiers and German soldiers everywhere.

As they walked along shells started to fall and they all jumped into a ditch. A German he was next to asked him if he had a helmet and when he said no the German said get underneath me. When the shelling was over he thanked the German, he replied it was nothing, and that Len was lucky, he would survive the war, but for him and his comrades, no one knew the future.

He was taken to the local HQ and handed over to some officers who invited him to get into their staff car and drove for about half an hour to a large house which turned out to be a form of HQ. The next day he was interrogated by an officer who spoke perfect English, he had been to England and spent the summer at Stratford-upon-Avon the year previously.

The next day he met up with other members of his crew and they were taken by lorry through the Ardennes, staying a few days in a warehouse at Libremont in Belgium before moving on for two days in a coal truck to

Stalag IV and a number of other camps ending up at Fallingbostel. There he stayed until March 1945, when all prisoners were ordered out of the camp and on a march. However, Len managed to escape and made it back to the UK on 23 April 1945, nearly five years after being taken prisoner.

Len Manning was trained at No. 1 Gunnery School at Pembery in South Wales. His initial training was at Bridlington and included dinghy drill in the harbour by jumping into the water with a Mae West on and swimming to a single dinghy, climbing aboard, then rolling out and swimming further to a large bomber-type dinghy, again climbing aboard, and finally rolling out and swimming to the harbour wall.

In June 1944 he joined No. 57 Squadron at East Kirkby, on his 18th operation, the 1,000 bomber raid to Caen. Having returned safely they were told they were going again that night, this time to Revigny. On the way to the target there was an explosion in the port wing caused by cannon fire. Flames were streaming past his turret which had by now stopped working because of the damage to the engine. The fuselage was a mass of flames and the aircraft was in a steep dive. His parachute was stowed on the port side and already starting to smoulder. He pulled it out and clipped it on his harness which was not easy to do with the 'G' force he was experiencing. He managed to jump out and he pulled his rip cord but found himself hanging to one side. Something brushed past his face; it was his inter-com lead attached to his helmet which was whipped off when the parachute opened. The lead became entangled in the silk shrouds and he grabbed it and hung on. This helped to take his weight and somehow balance the parachute. The parachute was beginning to burn and he hoped he would get down in time before it fell apart. The Lancaster hit the ground and blew up.

On the ground he quickly put out the fire in his parachute and staggered off into the darkness. He walked for about 8 miles and then collapsed in the doorway of a farmhouse. The farmer realised Len was in great pain from the burns on his face and took him in and put him to bed. The next day he was given civilian clothes and moved to another farm in the village. To his amazement he was interrogated by the local Resistance group to make sure he was not a plant. He was taken across country by a member of the Resistance until he reached a café in the village of La Treoir where he was made very welcome and given a room in the hotel across the courtyard. He had the run of the orchard behind the hotel but was kept away from the front of the café. Some while later Len was told that German tanks were seen coming towards the village. But all was well as they soon left.

Some weeks later the Americans arrived and Len ended up in Paris, but before he left he was able to get coffee and tinned food for his French friends and a big liberation party was held. Len's battledress reappeared, it had been darned where the fire had burnt it and pressed. In Paris at the Hotel Maurice a reception centre for RAF evaders had been set up. The next day he was flown to Hendon for interrogation and then taken to a hotel at Marylebone where he completed a report for Bomber Command Intelligence. Because he lived in London he was home before the telegram from the RAF was delivered saying he had arrived in the UK. He was given nine months sick leave and discharged in 1945. In 1991 he learned the name of the German pilot who had shot down his aircraft: Herbert Altner. This pilot had in fact shot down five Lancasters that night in the space of 30 minutes. In 1996 Herbert invited Len over to Germany as his guest and broke down in tears when he met Len. Sadly four members of Len's crew were killed and are now buried in a cemetery at Basseville. The mid-upper gunner Sgt Fred Taylor and the navigator F/O Rushton survived. In 1999 a memorial was erected at Basseville, it is a 6 ft high piece of local stone, carved with the names of the crew on a plaque along with remnants of the crashed Lancaster and it was unveiled by Len.

Sgt Pearce reported to the RAF Reception Centre at Lord's Cricket Ground. He was kitted out and given the now famous white flash to slot in his forage cap to show he was trainer aircrew. Here he spent three weeks in all manner of initial training. The first time he went into the west end of London he was stopped by an RAF policeman wanting to see his evening pass.

His air gunner training was at No. 11 Gunnery School at Andreas, Isle of Man. When the training ended the Group Captain presented them with their AG brevet and the three stripes of a sergeant. To receive these they had to mount a platform, salute, take the insignia, step back one pace, salute, about turn and return to their place on the parade. One cadet having received his badges etc , stepped back, did an about turn and saluted not the Group Captain but the rest of the parade.

At No. 29 OTU at Bruntingthorpe, Leicestershire he crewed up with an operational crew. The pilot was F/Sgt Peter Reaks from Wimbledon. The rear gunner was Sgt Geoff Bamforth, Pearce was the mid-upper gunner. He never remembers wanting to be a rear gunner. There was no mid-upper turret on the Wellington so he spent much of his training time sitting in the body of the aircraft except for the occasional change with the rear gunner. To reach this position you had to walk along a cat walk and at the end was a triangular metal panel, this was the emergency parachute exit. On one occasion an air gunner when trying to swap places with another gunner stepped on to the panel and fell through. The other gunner grabbed him and pulled him back in giving the rescuer severe shock. Pearce and his crew were finally posted to RAF Bardney, the home of No. 9 Squadron. The air bomber in the crew was P/O Edward Bates whose father was Sir Percy Bates, Chairman of Cunard Shipping. Edward had a Ford V8 Pilot tourer car and was soon asked to stop parking it next to the CO's RAF Hillman Minx.

After climbing up into his mid-upper turret he would reach behind to clip himself to a suspended, padded seat. He had a perfect all-round vision from the top of the aircraft and was visible from outside from the waist up. His elbows rested on the tops of the ammunition tanks, which reached to the base of the turret. There was a handlebar grip for each hand to activate the rotation of the turret and the elevation and depression of the guns. They also had handlebars on the firing triggers. The rear end of the two Browning .303 machine-gun breach blocks were about 2 ft in front of him and at about shoulder level. Suspended mid-way between them was the gun sight, a green ring with a dot in the centre, the illumination of which could be varied and allow him, not only to aim , but to estimate the distance of any approaching aircraft. Between his knees, fixed to front of the turret on a metal plate, were the switches for all the electrical power and two plugs to connect the intercom and oxygen supply. The ammunition belts were loaded in sequence with explosive, tracer, incendiary and armour piercing rounds. Fixed to the rotation shaft under the turret was a metal cylinder with channels and studs which prevented the guns from firing should they point to any part of the aircraft. The turret was driven by a drive-shaft connected to the starboard inner engine. His parachute was stowed in a special retainer fixed to the port side of the fuselage just behind the turret.

The clothing worn by aircrew in WWII is well worth a mention. Normal under clothing, and more waist high underpants and high necked vests. The normal uniform shirt and tie, white polo sweater, battledress top and trousers. A one-piece flying suit with zips, fur collars and cuffs and parachute harness clipped tightly under the groin. Thick woollen socks, electrically heated slippers and fur-lined knee-length flying boots. Silk gloves, woollen mittens and leather gauntlets. There was also a flying helmet balaclava style and in leather, parachute, coffee, sweets, Horlick tablets and chewing gum and you were ready to go.

On New Year's Day 1945 Pearce left his mother and girl friend, who had come to visit him at a bed and breakfast house in Bardney, for an 0600 hours briefing. The target was Ladbergen on the Dortmund Emms Canal. After dropping their bombs there was a sharp explosion and flash in the area of the cockpit. The pilot yelled for them to bale out. He pulled off his helmet and disconnected the intercom and oxygen supply and lastly pulled out the plug that wired him to his heated suit and exited the turret. As they made their way to the rear exit behind them was a mass of flames and some smoke. He and the navigator baled out and Pearce landed in snow in the corner of a field. A civilian turned up with a hand-gun pointing at him. He was shouting and it appeared he was saying stay where you are. A corporal from the *Luftwaffe* turned up on a bike asked him, in good English, how he was and helped to pile his parachute on to the carrier of the bike and they set off towards the a nearby tow path. It turned out the corporal had studied at Hull University.

On arrival at a control point a junior officer came out and asked him his name, when he said 'Pearce' the officer asked him to repeat it and then said with a wide smile, "We have been waiting for you". He was then taken to a high wooden tower where a more senior officer came down to him and started to hit him around his arms with a swagger stick. From there he was taken to a large building, inside several officers sat around a table and on the facing wall was a picture of Hitler. He was the locked in a cell. In the late afternoon the rear gunner was brought to see him, he had been to hospital having injured his groin on landing or when the parachute opened.

Between the time of being captured and arriving at PoW camp *Stalag Luft* I at Barth he remembers being on trains and passing through heavily bombed towns and the guards pulling the blinds down so he could not see out. Once when the train was stopped at a station the guards asked them if, on their honour, they would not escape. It was night time and snowing outside and the guards then went off and left them with a carriage full of passengers for some time. One of the German guards was elderly and said, *"Deutschland Kaput"* more than once and tried to ask why England was fighting Germany and not Russia. They were not given any food but did get coffee and a thin beer to drink.

They then spent some time at Frankfurt and the interrogation centre where they had all the details of his RAF service and postings. A short time followed at a transit camp and then in cattle trucks they were taken to Barth. The camp was between Lubeck and Tostock and they were marched from the train to the camp through the streets lined with people jeering at them and insulting them.

In the camp there were about twenty to a room, it had a table, and a couple of stools plus a small coal-burning stove. The beds were three tiered shelves with straw palliases, a straw pillow and one blanket each. He got the top one where he could not even sit up in bed. They were warned about stepping over the warning wire; one PoW had been shot for stepping over it to pick up a football. There was a compound shop where goods were bought on a points and cigarettes system. The Americans were generous with their cigarettes except for Lucky Strike, Camels and Chesterfields. He did experience Canadian Caporals, but only once. It consisted of dark tobacco wrapped in grey paper attached to a short cardboard tube. When he applied a match there was a quick fizz and the tobacco disappeared in a wisp of smoke. On one occasion they saw a *Luftwaffe* corporal approaching. As he drew near, one of the PoWs said, "Watch this one, he speaks English". At which the corporal, as he passed, said with a grin on his face, "Yeah! I swear like a son-of-a-bitch". He was a German/Canadian or Canadian/German. In the last days of the war civilians started to turn up and one morning they found the guards had left overnight and all the gates were wide open. The Russian army had arrived in the town. Their first sight of a Russian soldier was a female who turned up in a jeep. She was immaculate and had ammunition belts, grenades, side-arms and over her shoulder an automatic rifle. Then came a tank, followed by a herd of cows. The Russians had been told that what was needed more than anything was meat. The British CO said, "Fresh Meat, to eat", upon which a Russian soldier shot all the cows. The Russians wanted to send all the prisoners to Montgomery's 21st Army Group in trucks but the British CO held out for aircraft to fly them out. The roads outside were littered with furniture, bedding, clothes and crockery and the Russians were looting every house they could find. One Russian boy of 16 had been with the Russian troops since they broke out of Stalingrad. In a German training camp across the field were abandoned uniforms, caps, badges, and so on and abandoned American cigarettes. One long standing prisoner ignored official advice not to eat too much too quickly after so long on meagre rations but he did and was immediately taken ill and died.

About a week after liberation the Russians agreed to allow Allied aircraft to use an adjacent airfield. The next day American Fortresses arrived and eventually Pearce got aboard and ended up in the Perspex nose facing backwards. One RAF man had been in the camp since 1941 and when he saw the British coast tears came to his eyes. They landed at RAF Ford and were greeted by WAAFS with all manner of cakes and sandwiches. From there they went to RAF Church Fenton in Yorkshire for kitting out, leave pass and railway warrant. Having arrived on a Friday within two days he was walking in the front door of his home. He was on leave until September and was paid fortnightly by postal draft. He was offered various jobs in the RAF and finally decided on a General Duties clerk at RAF Records in Gloucester, it was here that he met his wife a WAAF at Gloucester. His pilot, Peter Reaks, is now buried in the Reichswald Forest War Cemetery, as are the air bomber, Edward Bates age 31 from Cheshire, Thomas Scott, the flight engineer, age 19, from Selkirk and Bill Currigan, age 23, the W/Opt/AG from Dagenham, Essex.

Sgt Harold Allen enlisted in December 1943 and after air gunner training he joined No. 576 Squadron at RAF Fiskerton. He had been in a reserved occupation and had a struggle to be released. Two of his best pals had been killed flying with the RAF. His training was at Bridgenorth, Bishops Court, Northern Island and Desborough before joining 576 on 13 March 1945.

On 4/5 April, when returning from an operation to the oil refineries at Lutzkendorf in Lancaster ME 671, under skipper Sgt Douglas Hogg, they were hit by a bomb from above which hit the port wing and port-outer engine. The order soon came to bale out and Harold shouted, "Rear Gunner Gone". The remainder of the crew stayed with the aircraft and survived the following crash. They searched around for Harold but failed to find him. After avoiding capture for six days they were eventually captured and taken prisoner. Harold's body was not found until July 1950 and then buried at Eckolstadt, but later reburied in the Berlin War Cemetery. It would appear from extensive searching that he died after his parachute failed to open.

Donald Stevenson always wanted to fly but when he was 11 he developed a problem with his lungs. However, he was determined to get into the RAF and when he was 17 he tried to enlist but was told to come back when he was 18. However, he finally managed to join the RAF while only 17. This was in 1940 and by the time he was 18 he was training in Manitoba, Canada. He had wanted to be a pilot but came back to the UK

Donald Stevenson at No 3 Bombing/
Gunnery School in Manitoba, Canada.
Donald Stevenson

in January 1943 as a rear gunner. He joined No. 101 Squadron and on 25 May 1943, in Lancaster ED 775, they took off for Dortmund but because first one engine overheated and later another engine overheated they decided to abort the operation and return to base. As they came into land at RAF Coltishall the engines caught fire and the Lancaster crashed into a ploughed field at Westwick two miles from the airfield. The navigator died later of his injuries but the remainder of the crew were unhurt, apart from the pilot who received slight injuries. Donald and the others were taken to Norwich hospital, he had burns to both arms, and he persuaded the driver that took them to take him to his home for a while. This was the last time his sister, who was the only one at home, at the time, saw him. After the visit to the hospital he was then taken back to Holme-upon-Spalding Moor, Lincolnshire and the base of No. 101 Squadron. His last letter arrived on the day that the telegram arrived saying he was missing. In this letter he spoke of his friend a navigator being killed and seemed to accept that death was never too far away.

His last operation was on 8 July 1943. He was the mid-upper gunner in Lancaster ED697-V which took off from Ludford Magna at 2022 hours for an operation to Cologne. The pilot was a Fl/Lt Fleming and the rear gunner Sgt J W Johnson. They were missing for some time until a Mr Val Grimble was able to work out that they had crashed between Beachy Head and Dungeness at 0045am. Donald's name is now recorded on the Runneymede Memorial, panel 165.

After a few operations with No. 158 Squadron Trevor Aris was posted to No. 148 Squadron in Italy. They first had to go to SOE Headquarters in Mayfair, in London. Here they were sworn to secrecy and not allowed to make a phone call and under no circumstances allowed to spend the evening at home. Later that night they were taken to Oxford where they boarded a Dakota which then landed at Gibraltar, here they found eggs and plenty of fruit. The next morning they took off for Naples where they entrained for Brindisi and 148 Squadron all in 48 hours.

The squadron is still remembered in Warsaw for attempting to drop supplies to the Polish Resistance who were being overwhelmed by the

German Army. The flying time was 11 hours 55 minutes, much of it over enemy territory and with no fighter escort. After the war they were awarded the Warsaw Cross at the Polish Embassy.

On 6 November 1944, they were required for an operation to drop arms and supplies on a target close to the Yugoslavia/Austrian border. Nearing the dropping zone they became aware that the outer-starboard engine was losing power and there were signs of fire, the skipper set off the extinguisher and ultimately feathered the engine, by this time they were very low and urgently trying to gain height. Trevor in the rear turret checked his parachute and escape route. As they tried to gain height the inner-starboard engine also started to fail and the pilot ordered them to the crash positions having decided they were too low to bale out. As they hit the ground huge cracks appeared in the fuselage, then there was bumping, swerving, tearing, scraping and finally they stopped.

Trevor picked himself out of the debris, it was 12.45pm. They then saw armed men racing towards them and it seemed logical to surrender, but the men were Yugoslavian Partisans allied to Tito. The partisans quickly surrounded them and took them into custody. They were given a form Schnapps made from fermented potato skins but the guards were not friendly and heavily armed. After a 300 odd mile walk, mostly over mountains in rain, hail and a foot of snow, sleeping in barns and the floor of houses and covered in fleas and lice they arrived at Split and, at night, were rowed out to an awaiting destroyer and freedom. After a time in hospital in Naples and then RAF Halton he was posted to Binbrook and became Camp Commandant to 250 German Prisoners of War.

Peggy Stephens was a WAAF MT driver and her fiancé was Reginald Stephens who served as an air gunner with No. 38 Squadron. He was born in 1912 and was one of nine children living at Charlton Kings, Cheltenham, Gloucester. He worked in the motor trade in Cheltenham and was a well known local sportsman in the town. He volunteered for the RAF prior to the war and was called up immediately war broke out.

After air-gunner training he was on active service from January 1940. He was posted to No. 38 Squadron at RAF Marham, Norfolk. He flew on his first mission on 16 August 1940 attacking targets in the Ruhr. On 7 October 1940, he was a member of Wellington P9287-HD, under Sqn Ldr Taylor, which took off from Marham to bomb Berlin. Nothing more was heard from the crew after take-off. The crew were all buried in Berlin.

John Blair joined the RAF in May 1940, and had formerly worked for LMS Railway. After training he joined No. 103 Squadron and in August 1941 he was awarded the DFM having flown operations. On a raid to Brest on 24 July 1941 he was rear gunner in the leading aircraft of a section of three which was attacked by an enemy fighter whilst over the target area. The enemy fighter was destroyed by the combined efforts of the gunners in the formation.

In 1943 he was now a F/Lt and flying with No. 97 Squadron when awarded the DFC. On 21/22 May 1944, and now with No. 156 Pathfinder

S/L Blair DFM MID. *Mike King*   Sgt Ian Blair. *Mike King*

Squadron his aircraft was detailed to attack Duisberg in the Ruhr, he was by now a Squadron Leader and his pilot a F/Sgt Ward. The aircraft was shot down by a German night fighter near Molenaarsgraaf. The aircraft exploded and the pilot was blown out of the cockpit. Wounded and in need of urgent medical attention he was surrendered by Dutch locals to the German forces and became a prisoner of war. The remaining crew, including Blair, were buried in Molenaarsgraaf Protestant Churchyard. Out of the eleven aircraft sent out by 156 Squadron F/Sgt Ward's aircraft was the only one that failed to return. On 22 May his wife, Selina, received a letter from Wg Cdr Bingham–Hall, the Commanding Officer of 156 Squadron, and on 14 November 1944, a further report had been received from the International Red Cross confirming that her husband had lost his life on 22 May 1944, and that he was buried in Molenaarsgraaf 12 miles east-south-east of Rotterdam, Holland. This was confirmed by the Air Ministry Casualty Section in 1950.

On 26 April 1942, Reg Adams was posted to No. 405 Squadron flying Halifax bombers. He was now a F/Sgt and took part in the 1,000 bomber raid on Cologne on 30 May 1942 and Essen 1 June 1942. On 30 June 1942 his aircraft was shot down by a German night-fighter, *Oberleutnant* Rudolf Sigmund of II/NJG 2, and crashed at 0148 at Noorewolde. Reg and the rest of the crew are now buried in Westellingwerf. His aircraft was one of thirty-five Squadron aircraft shot down by German night-fighters.

Arthur Fowler, an air-gunner, was serving with No. 320 (Netherlands) Squadron of 139 Wing, 2nd Tactical Air Force. On 24 October the squadron were briefed to carry out bombing attacks on road bridges over the River Maas in Eastern Holland. Their target was the bridge at Hedel south of Venlo and far from the German border. This bridge was considered to be the gateway to the Ruhr. The air defences were very effective and well organised with 75mm anti-aircraft, radar predicted guns which, once they locked on to an aircraft, were lethal. As the message, "bombs gone" came over the intercom there also came a crump and a very loud explosion and the nose went down with the pilot fighting with the controls the order to 'bale out' was given but before Arthur could get clear of his turret another heavy explosion occurred and all power went and the intercom was dead. The air gunner and wireless operator in their B.25 North American, or Mitchell as it was known, were located aft of the bomb bay and therefore out of physical contact with the pilot and navigator; they could not see the pilot and navigator who, equally could not see the air-gunner and W/op. If the order to bale out came they both had to act as a separate entity if they were to escape. Arthur vacated his turret and clipped on his parachute. The wireless operator jettisoned the outer hatch which had a sliding/folding arrangement and a retaining strap which was clipped to an adjacent bulkhead. This arrangement was meant to keep the hatch open so that they just drop out, however the strap was not there. This had been overlooked in previous checks and this left a huge problem. The escape hatch opening was the whole width of the aircraft at the aft end and was longer than it was wide, in order to get out one had to sit at floor level on the aft end of the opening and drop out. But to do this safely the inner hatch had to be held upright. Somehow the WO/Opt got out, then Arthur held the hatch upright with one hand and at the same time sat astride the opening at the opposite end facing the inner hatch. His outstretched arm was not long enough and as he began to drop through the hatch his fingertips lost contact with the hatch and it slid closed trapping Arthur's left arm in the opening. He was left suspended by his neck inside and the rest of him was outside the aircraft. One of his flying boots and the a sock came off in the slipstream. He managed to push his left arm into the opening under his chin and hanging on to the opening rim he pushed the hatch sufficient enough for him to drop out. In the process he ripped the sleeve of his flying suit, gouged his arm and hand and broke the strap of his wrist watch and the watch hit the ground before he did.

The aircraft was now on fire and as he saw trees looming underneath him he crossed his legs under him and protecting his face with his arms he fell into the trees and ended up suspended. He decided to take a chance and hit the release on the chute and fell to the earth with a bump. He was unhurt but very cold, but had two socks left on one foot so he took one off and put it on the naked foot. He had landed in a wood between the river and the front line battle and was picked up by a forward reconnaissance unit of the 51st Highland Division. He was taken to a Dutch farmhouse and the farmer gave him a pair of pointed gents shoes. In return Arthur gave them his only surviving flying boot. From there he was taken on the back of a motor bike, sometimes coming under small arms and mortar fire, to RAF Eindhoven where he met up with the rest of his crew; they had landed on the Allied side of the front line but because of the delay Arthur had landed on the German side. They were taken to Melsbroek after commandeering a gas propelled lorry from a Dutch farmer because the RAF at Eindhoven had no transport for them. When they got back the Stores officer was very reluctant to write off their loss of equipment to 'Enemy Action' but more to carelessness on their part!

Doug Fry joined No. 15 Squadron on 13 June 1943. Only days after arriving the gunnery leader came in and said that one of the crews' mid upper was missing for the operation that night and asked for a volunteer. Doug volunteered and started to get himself organised but was then told the missing mid-upper gunner had in fact turned up and Doug was no longer needed. The target was Mulheim and F/O Hawkins and his crew were flying in Stirling BK 656-A. However, the crew, including the mid-upper gunner, failed to return and were later reported killed. 'There but for the grace of God go I'.

On the morning of 30 July 1943, Doug and his crew, having flown the night before, were surprised to find their names down for an operation to Remschied. They were looking forward to a night at the local pub or to Cambridge and a dance at the Dorothy Café. When they turned up for the briefing at 2000 hours they found arc lamps and an RAF Film unit preparing to film the briefing. A few weeks previously 'Bomber' Harris had turned up and in chatting with them had said they would going to eliminate Hamburg and that they would be using anti-radar 'Window' for the first time. He also said that Churchill wanted a film made about the work of Bomber Command and that it should be called *The Biter Bit*. They now assumed the Unit was here to make this film. While they waited the film crew were filming them and it was shown Doug's his mother's local cinema, and when he went missing the Ministry of Information gave her several still shots from the film showing Doug close up.

They took off at 11.42 in Stirling EF 427-A piloted by P/O Judd with a full bomb load. As they got near the target they saw the glow of the first wave attack. As they came in on the bombing run a master blue searchlight locked on to them and this was quickly followed by about a dozen more, they were like a spider in a web. The bombs were dropped and for another ten seconds they flew on a straight and level course. Suddenly Doug heard a noise above the engines: they were on fire. Doug left his turret to see if he could help but the fire was well underway. The flames had now eaten through the bulkhead and consumed the dinghy which was hanging down. As he made his way down from the turret he felt a blow in the stomach and fell to the floor this was followed by a huge explosion in the nose of the aircraft. They had taken a direct hit and they went straight into a vertical dive and Doug was floating in mid-air. Although he must have been wounded, George Judd, the pilot, pulled out of the dive which gave the crew a chance to survive. Back on the floor once again he saw the flight engineer go past and bale out of the rear escape hatch. Somehow Doug got up and went to get his own chute but it was on the floor and so he crawled past the flames and put it on and then jumped out of the rear exit. His parachute opened perfectly and the Stirling continued on its way with four members of the crew who all perished with the aircraft.

As Doug was about to land he saw a wall in front of him and lifted his feet to miss the top of the wall and made a good landing in the back garden of a small house. People came out of the house and started to help him inside, inside a lady shook her fist at him but then pointed to a chair for him to sit down. His clothes were lifted up and disclosed the blood and a jagged hole about an inch in diameter where the shrapnel had hit. The lady then got him a glass of water but indicated he should not drink because of the stomach wound but just wash out his mouth. In the top of his flying boot he had bars of chocolate and thought it would help his situation if he gave them to the children in the house. But when he reached for them, not surprisingly they had gone. Then a man came in wearing a black uniform and waving a pistol at him saying, "Englander Schweinhund". the others argued against whatever he had in mind for Doug and he went off in disgust. They then put him on stretcher and took him to a local doctor. After treatment and an injection he was taken off in a car. He then passed out but thought he could hear the familiar voice of his Canadian rear gunner. He was then taken by ambulance through Dusseldorf and then woke up on a table next to another table and on the other table was his rear gunner. He was then put to sleep and woke up three days later with someone cutting a large blood-stained dressing off his body. It turned out that it had been touch and go and only the fact that he was young and fit saved his life. His doctor was Polish, the Germans themselves had done nothing to help him. An X-Ray showed that the piece of shrapnel was still lodged in his body under his bottom rib. There were many other aircrew with all manner of injuries and wounds in the same hospital. It was *Stalag* 6J, reserve hospital about 3 kilometres from Dusseldorf. It was mainly used for prisoners from various countries who were forced to work in Ruhr factories. His damaged flying boots had not been returned so he was given a pair of boots three times too big to wear. From Dusseldorf they were taken by train to Cologne and then to Frankfurt. At the railway station they were taken upstairs to a large room which was full of RAF aircrew. Some were bandaged and one, a fighter pilot, had his head and hands covered in bandages and his battledress was scorched. The next day they were taken to another hospital set in its own ground and told to strip off. They were going to have a bath. Doug turned on the hot tap and they had about a quarter of an inch of hot water before it turned cold. But even a cold bath was enjoyable after not having washed properly for six weeks.

Soon the interrogation started and a *Luftwaffe* officer who had been educated at Oxford, knew England and said he liked England began the initial process. He had a large file on 15 Squadron, his crew were listed and four names with black crosses. He then went and told Doug when he had joined the RAF, and where had trained. Doug played dumb and said as an air gunner he did not know the answers to questions he was being asked. They were then taken to *Dulag Luft* awaiting passage to a PoW camp. The journey to Heydekruge was in cattle trucks and took five days. After three days the doors of the cattle truck opened and a *Feldwebel* (Sergeant) said in an American accent, "Hi fellow". It turned out that he had been living in the USA when he had been sent a telegram from an official source in Germany to say someone in his family had died and so he went straight back to Germany and was immediately called up, he got them hot water from the train engine to have a brew up. When they arrived at Heydekruge they marched to *Stalag Luft* 6, it was a new camp with two huge blocks divided into twelve barrack rooms with six rooms to a block.

Via the Red Cross Doug received a pair of new boots, great coat and underwear all RAF issue. Soon a batch of PoWs came from *Stalag Luft* 1 at Barth and among them his flight engineer Dick Richards, he was very surprised to see Doug as he thought he had been killed and apologised for not helping him as he went pass to the rear exit as he thought Doug was beyond help. His mother sent him a number of parcels which were things that were of the greatest use, although no food was allowed apart from chocolate and chewing gum. On 15 Squadron there had been a comfort fund to which they all subscribed, this provided all manner of things to any member of the squadron who had been shot down and Doug received, although he did not smoke, three lots of 500 cigarettes. The first parcel had been broken into and 300 stolen.

Later, they were taken by ship to Swinemunde in the Baltic and there put into cattle trucks. When they arrived at a railway station they had to march 2 miles to *Luft* IV at Gross Tychow and here they saw men from the first column still hanging about and a German officer waving a pistol around and screaming his head off. It turned out that the first column had been manacled in twos and forced to run up the road at the end of a bayonet, and bitten by guard dogs. The dogs had been allowed to run amok among the prisoners and one dog who turned on his handler in the panic was shot dead. It was 20 July 1943, and it turned out that the reason for the abuse was that there had been an attempt on Hitler's life.

The huts were small, more like big dog kennels and had been erected in an American compound with ten men to a hut. They slept on bare boards and could not stand up in the hut. One of the huts was struck by a violent thunderstorm and one man who had been struck by lightning died but he might have been saved had the German in charge not refused to take him to hospital. Two days later a German *Luftwaffe* electrician was working on the perimeter lights when he suddenly went stiff and dangled from his safety belt. One of his fellow guards had turned on the power, an eye for eye perhaps.

There followed another move, this time to Fallingbostel *Stalag* 357. Here the accommodation was in huge marquees and sleeping on the ground. It was now April and the Germans with PoWs as hostages started to march across Germany. They slept in barns at night and on once occasion a barn was attacked from the air and some PoWs wounded and one killed. After one march they arrived at another small camp and ten days later on 2 May 1945, and the day before Doug's 21st birthday the German guards fled and soon afterwards the Americans arrived. The PoWs were then taken to Luneberg, in the British area and put in German barracks. Here they had plenty of hot water and showers. While in the barracks ENSA came and gave concerts, one singer was a young Carol Carr and sang the popular songs of the day. They were then taken to Lubeck for transport to the UK and they met the crew of the Lancaster that had come out to pick them up. The mid-upper gunner had nipped off home for two days leave so Doug was allowed to sit in his old position for the journey back to the UK. Doug noticed the crew were not wearing parachutes or Mae Wests. When Doug mentioned this to the rear gunner he said that as the PoWs did not have parachutes or Mae Wests the crew had decided not to wear them. So Doug left in the mid-upper turret of a Stirling and returned in the mid-upper turret of a Lancaster. The route back was over Hamburg and they landed at an airfield in the midlands, when they got out of the Lancaster WAAFs were waiting to take their arms and carry what little kit they had. The hangar they were taken to was decked out in bunting welcoming them home. In the hanger they had a party and danced with the WAAFs. From there they were taken to No106 Personnel Receiving Centre at RAF Cosford. Each billet had beds made up with clean white sheets and a hospital blue suit pending them getting new uniforms. They were kitted out, given double ration cards, normally given to pregnant women and were driven to the mess for a fish and chips meal. When taken to mess bars they were unable to drink their pints that they had dreamed of in a PoW camp, it was all too overwhelming and exciting to eat or drink. Next day they went to London by special train, it would appear the word had got out as all along the route were 'Welcome Home' signs and banners were everywhere. When he arrived at his house he found more bunting and a key signifying his 21st birthday. His had regretted that he had not been able to get forward in the aircraft to help his stricken crew, and had not seen his skipper's father before he died a few days after the war ended. Also, he did not see his Canadian rear gunner before he was shipped back to Canada. His pilot, George Judd and navigator Denis Brown were engaged to be married and Denis had planned to get married on his next leave and had even managed to get a half bottle of whisky from the local pub the Bird in Hand. Two of his boyhood friends Tommy Lucy also an air-gunner with 149 Sqn and another in the army had been killed. Tom Lucy has no known grave, nor has his pilot, George Judd, and the other members of his crew who did not get out of the aircraft. Therefore, during his leave, he went to see their parents. He found it an awful feeling that he was alive and healthy and they were never to see their sons again. He was released in March 1946 and married in October 1948.

Ken Apps flew with No. 12 Squadron and on 1/2 January 1944 failed to return from Berlin. It would appear that his aircraft Lancaster ND 325-G had been hit by flak because it was losing a lot of petrol and he and his crew had to bale out and were all taken prisoner apart from Sgt Denis Smith who was found by the Germans still attached to his parachute but his head had been severed. The conclusion was that in baling out he had not folded up tight and had hit the tail rudder. After the usual interrogation he was taken to *Stalag Luft* IVb at Mulburg. Here he got a top bunk with a straw mattress and a blanket covered in fleas. The ceiling had holes in it and rats used to run about and peep down at them. They got fed once a day and normally kept it for the evening. It consisted of cheese, brown bread and mouldy soup. It was brought in by two men in iron containers and the order of the day was to find the pea in the pea soup. There were no plates or mugs so they had to be made by the prisoners. And there was one toilet for 250 men.

In the winter they took it in turn to steal coal for the stove, if you were spotted you could be shot. On one of these sorties a guard saw two prisoners stealing coal and pulled out his pistol. One of the PoWs hit the guard with the bag of coal and bullets started to fly everywhere and one prisoner was shot in the thigh. The camp was attacked by a German Ju88 fighter on one occasion and a PoW killed, the pilot was later demoted.

One of the RAF chap's mother was married to a German officer and living in Germany. She was smuggled into the camp, given a uniform and her hair cut short so as to pass as a prisoner. She stayed for three to four months. Stealing food was the worst offence and on one occasion when it was found a guard was the thief he was tied up and thrashed with a leather belt. Near the end of the war the 150 per hut went up to 300 per hut.

Roy Shirley has a date that will he will always remember, 23 December 1944. The Germans were mounting an offensive in the Ardennes, Belgium. The target for Bomber Command was Gremburg, a part of the Cologne marshalling yards. Outside it was cold and damp and the briefing at the most unsociable hour of 0530am. The main trouble in supporting the troops on the ground had been the weather, thick fog and ground mist had virtually shut down southern and central England. His crew were quite highly decorated: the pilot had the DFM and the wireless operator and flight engineer the DFC. Roy was the mid-upper gunner. It was some time before they got out of the cloud and into blinding sunshine. As they levelled up for the bombing run up came the flak when suddenly a burst of shells engulfed the port wing which then erupted into flames. The enemy fighters came in head on and out of the sun with cannon and machine-gun fire. As an Me109 came in Roy opened up and it broke away. Then two 109s came in and his gunsight was blown to pieces inches from his face. The bombs were dropped but by now the entire wing was on fire.

His intercom was just a charred mess and smoke was pouring into the aircraft.

The next problem was opening the exit door and it was only by the use of the axe carried in the aircraft that they were able to get it open. They were now down to 5,000 ft and the nose of the aircraft was lifting and he and the wireless operator sank to the floor with the centrifugal pressure pinning them down as if held by a giant arm. They were resigned to their fate and said Goodbye to each other. Suddenly he seem to awake and heard voices and when he opened his eyes saw swirling snow. Somebody was undoing his clothes and he felt the prick of hypodermic needle. He had survived and was taken to a hospital in Cologne. After treatment he was sent to a PoW camp.

In April 1945 the Germans announced they were being marched 150 miles south to Mooseburg a camp near Munich. At the time the Americans were only 50 miles away so it was a way of prolonging their captivity. So he and others decided to make a run for it. As they did they had no idea where they were running to and ended up running in a circle and were soon recaptured and taken back to Langwasser 13 their previous camp. Their second attempt was successful. In the camp were a number of aged senior officers of the Serbian army who had been PoWs for many years so they concealed themselves amongst them on the theory that as they were aged it was unlikely the Germans would move them deeper into Germany and that is what happened. When the Americans arrived they revealed who they were and were soon on their way home to the UK where they arrived 15 days before the war in Europe ceased.

Bob Pearce was born and raised in Toronto, Canada. His father was a vet and he decided that he should enlist to oppose the 'bad guy' but to enlist in the RCAF you had to show proof of age, but the army were not so strict and if you could walk and talk you were in. He enlisted in the Canadian army at the age of 17 in June 1942. Having endured the army for seven months, and 12 days before his 18th birthday, he transferred to the RCAF and began training at bootcamp in Lachine, Quebec. Having tried and failed to get on a pilots' course he went through the shortest route to becoming aircrew, an air gunners course at Mont Joly, Quebec. When qualified as an AG he was transferred overseas and within nine months had the rank of F/Sgt.

In January 1944 and nearing completion at OTU he became a regular member of a crew flying with No. 101 Squadron, an experimental squadron. After fifteen operation over Germany, France, Belgium and Holland he and his crew were asked to volunteer for the Pathfinder Force (PF) and they joined No. 582 Squadron in June 1944.

On one operation over the Ruhr Valley they were caught in flak and the aircraft suffered 180 bullet holes. The hydraulics were shot away and two engines had cut out but somehow they managed to make it back to base. On another occasion Bob saw two Lancasters collide in mid air and fall to the ground in two balls of fire. Equally frightening was the time he saw a

Lancaster caught in searchlights and a fighter following it down firing all the time. No one survived from the bomber.

On 23 December 1944 he was sent on his 31st operation, half way to finish operations for good. The number to complete a tour for the PF was sixty operations.

They were attacked by Me109 German fighters and strafed in the under belly. The gunners did not see the fighters until they had passed, The petrol tank in the starboard wing was hit and then the port wing, the fighters were obviously going for these parts of the aircraft. The pilot was able to right the aircraft and gave the order to bale out. Bob could not get out of his turret as the rear door had jammed, it was also the first time he had worn a seat pack parachute, prior to this it had been a chest pack. Finally he was able to get the door open and standing on the sill of the turret was able to open his parachute. He was not familiar with this process as little parachute training was given to bomber crews.

The aircraft crashed near Cologne and he landed in backyard of someone's home. He was soon surrounded by the German Youth Movement pointing Luger pistols at him. Their main interest was his parachute and when they left he began to be surrounded by a mob of people but some German soldiers arrived and he was taken to the local police station and the cells in the cellar. From there he went to Cologne airfield where all the prisoners from the raid had been rounded up. The next day the RAF bombed Cologne and the bombs came close to where the prisoners were. On Christmas Eve instead of having a party in the mess he was on a freight train to Frankfurt and to solitary confinement. On the floor of the box car were forty prisoners and six German guards. When they arrived after a long journey Bob was asked by an interrogator what was the price of wheat in Canada. The interrogator, it turned out, came from Saskatchewan in Canada. Bob said later it was all he could do not to lean over and catch the man by the throat and cheerfully strangle him. He also found out during this interrogation that the main force on the operation on the 23rd had been cancelled leaving only the Pathfinder Force, this left them on their own and with no fighter escort. It was a daylight, with clear skies and no cloud for cover, the ideal day for the fighters and they made the best of it.

The PoW camp to which he was sent was mainly occupied by Americans. In 1945 they were released by Russian troops and Royal Engineers of the British Army who cleared away the landmines from the *Luftwaffe* base nearby and once this was done the B17 bombers came in and took the prisoners back to the UK. The non-Americans were flown out first as a gesture of courtesy and respect and this did not go unnoticed by the British prisoners. Bob arrived back Canada in June 1945 to a hero's welcome from his family and friends. He found it difficult to settle in civilian life having lost five of his crew, only he and the mid-upper gunner survived. He and the mid-upper gunnery lived only two hours from each other for 30 years but because of sad memories they never could seem to get together. They had been inseparable in their flying days. In 1990 Bob went back to Germany and visited the graves in Dusseldorf where the five members of his crew are buried. He has attended a number of 582 Squadron reunions but the loss of those five men is as acute today and it was when he first learned they had not survived.

The raid went very badly: two Lancasters of No. 35 Squadron collided over the French Coast, and because of the clear skies it was decided to allow the aircraft to break formation and bomb visually, to use Oboe to bomb would have made them very vulnerable to the flak defences, but this instruction did not get through to the leading 582 Lancasters including Sqn Ldr Palmer DFC who was on loan from 109 Mosquito Squadron. He was soon hit and despite bombing the target, the Gremberg railway yard, his aircraft went down out of control and crashed, only the rear gunner survived. Six of the thirty aircraft despatched were lost. It was Palmer's 110th operation and he is now buried in the Rheinberg War Cemetery with those of his crew who were also killed. He later was awarded a posthumous Victoria Cross.

In some cases RAF PoWs were not afforded the protection of the Geneva Convention and killed or in fact murdered. F/Sgt Klucha, an air gunner with 300 (Polish) Squadron, was shot down in June 1944, taken to a police station. He was then taken to a wood and shot not once but twice by different policeman under the guise that he was trying to escape. One of the criminals was put in prison for life but the fate of the other is not known.

F/Lt Sinclair KIA 18/19 July 1944.
Mike King

Sgt Wilfred Ray KIA 18/19 July 1944.
Mike King

On Right F/Lt Sinclair, sitting Sgt Ray. *Mike King*

F/Sgt J.G.Williams of 102 Squadron was shot down in December 1944. He also was taken prisoner by a policeman and was taken to an area and in the conference room of a building, he was maltreated and then shot in the head, his body was taken away and thrown into a stream that ran into the Rhine.

Sgt Norman Wilcock, having baled out, was captured by a civilian who hit him a number times and he then was kicked to death by three civilians including the first man.

Rear gunner Sgt Price baled out of his doomed aircraft in February 1945 and was taken into custody by a policeman and two civilians. What happened to him next is not sure but in 1948 when the body was exhumed and a post-mortem was conducted he had a number of injuries to the skull that must have been sustained while in captivity and not from baling out.

Sgt Freddie Tees was shot down when flying with 617 Squadron to attack the Ruhr Dams in May 1943. He was the only survivor from his aircraft and, although badly burned, having been thrown from his rear turret, he was taken to hospital and then a PoW camp at Heydekruge.

There were many more attacks by German people on captured airmen, and were regarded as War Crimes under the 1907 Hague Convention. Many perpetrators were brought to justice and sentenced to death or imprisonment. However, there were many others that we shall never know about.

REQUIEM FOR A REAR GUNNER

And should you weep for him, if so inclined,
Then mingle knowledge with your gift of tears
Bare not your heart alone-dwell your mind
Upon the history of his nineteen years.
He kicked a ball in narrow London streets
Then pedalled groceries around Walthamstow;
He learnt of love in cheaper Gaumont seats,
Set it to jazz-time on his radio.
He had a wife for seven magic nights,
His eyes grew softer in a small hotel;
they shared a dream of London, rich with lights
And all the things that Woolworths has to sell.
He sat, the sergeant-child, among his crew,
And heard with awe the gross Great Man expound
The cult of polish extol the sacred few
Who'd glistened long and loyally on the ground.
Against his shaggy head he brushed a sleeve,
Within the barber's shop considered 'pride',
Bought contraceptives in the hope of leave,
Then flew to Nuremburg that night, and died.

Walter Clapham

Len Manning in 1944. *Len Manning*

CHAPTER TWELVE

Awards

In WWII many awards were given to men of the RAF, although some would say, on occasions, not enough, or to men worthy of a decoration, in particular air gunners. There were two types of award, Immediate and Non-immediate. They began with the highest award in the land, The Victoria Cross, then the Distinguished Service Order or DSO, and Distinguished Flying Cross or DFC. The VC could be awarded to all ranks of the RAF but the DSO and DFC only to commissioned officers in the Royal Air Force. For the airmen only there was the Conspicuous Gallantry Medal (Flying) and lastly the Distinguished Flying Medal or DFM. An immediate award was for one operation or incident, and the non-immediate for a tour of operations or period of leadership. Lastly, there was a Mention in Dispatches which, together with the VC is the only award that can be awarded posthumously.

In WWII four air gunners in the Royal Air Force were awarded the Victoria Cross, Sgt Thomas Gray was, at the time of his death, in 1940 an observer but on leaving RAF Halton, having been apprentice aero-engine fitter in 1932, he flew with No. 40 Squadron as a part-time air gunner and in 1938, and now a Corporal he won the Silver .303 Bullet prize, an annual firing competition held in the RAF. In 1939 he was promoted to Sergeant and now with No. 12 Squadron he moved to France on 2 September 1939.

On 12 May 1940 he, with his pilot P/O Donald Garland, attacked the bridge at Vroenhoven in Fairey Battle P2204-K and came under intense flak from more than 300 guns and fighter defences. It was not long before he and a number of other aircraft were blasted out of the sky, but not before he had dropped his bombs and the bridge was damaged. Both Thomas and Donald Garland were awarded a posthumous VC, but for the air gunner LAC Lawrence Reynolds there was no award. Donald Garland was one of four brothers lost during the war. All three crew of the Fairey Battle are buried in Heverlee War Cemetery having been hidden from the Germans by the local French until the end of the war. The operation had cost six deaths, seven PoWs and two wounded. Another crew was attacked by an Me109 which set the port petrol-tank on fire but the return fire of air gunner AC1 Patterson seemed to find its mark as the fighter was seen to vanish into cloud, emitting black smoke. The pilot P/O Davy made a forced landing and was awarded an immediate DFC, and his crew including Patterson were awarded the DFM. Although Thomas Gray was not at the time an air gunner, he had served much of his time in the RAF as an air gunner and it seems only right now that he is mentioned in a book on air gunners of WWII.

John Hannah joined the RAF in August 1939 as a regular airmen. After training as a wireless operator he was sent to No. 4 Bombing and Gunnery School at West Freugh for a brief course in air gunnery. He soon joined No. 106 Squadron but after a short spell was posted to No. 83 Squadron at RAF Scampton.

On 15 September 1940, his aircraft Hampden P.1355, piloted by P/O Arthur Connor RCAF, was detailed to attack barges being lined up at Antwerp for the invasion of the UK. The crew were very experienced and Sgt Hayhurst, the navigator, was on his 39th operation. As they approached Antwerp the sky was full of flak and searchlights. At the second attempt they dropped their bomb load but as the bombs went away so the aircraft were hit in the bomb bay by a shell, and from the resulting explosion the wing petrol-tanks were hit and set on fire. The W/Opt/Air Gunner and rear gunner cockpits were also set on fire. Because of the flames the other gunner Sgt George James had no alternative but to bale out, as did Hayhurst who, having checked aft thought that James and Hannah had been killed. In the meantime Hannah had somehow reached the extinguisher and was fighting the fire but he was being suffocated by smoke and heat. He finally resorted to trying to put out the flames with his flying log book and then his bare hands. As well as the flames ammunition was going off all around him and he started to throw out the now red hot pans of ammunition. Somehow he finally put the fire out. He then, on the instructions of the pilot, crawled forward to see if the navigator was hurt, only to find he was missing, he had earlier discovered that the rear gunner was missing. He then went back and informed the pilot and passed him the navigator's log and maps. He told the pilot he was fine although he was suffering from burns and exhaustion from the heat and fumes. His face was burned black, badly swollen and both hands severely burned.

At 0300 hours Connor, with only Hannah aboard, brought the Hampden into land at Scampton. The aircraft was a mess with multiple flak holes. Only one wing fuel-tank had not ignited. The sides of the aircraft had been ripped away. Metal was distorted and the framework scorched by the intense heat. The two carrier pigeons had been roasted alive and John's parachute had been destroyed. He had secondary burns to his face and eyes. For his bravery, courage and determination he was awarded the VC, Connor received a DFC as did Hayhurst who became a prisoner of war. At the time Hannah had flown on eleven operational flights. He was strongly recommended for the VC or Empire Gallantry Medal by the Station Commander at RAF Scampton on 16 September 1940. This was endorsed by the then AOC of 5 Group, Air Vice Marshal A T Harris, later CinC Bomber Command on 17 September 1940. This was approved by the King and gazetted on 1 October 1940. A year before he had been working in a shoe shop in Glasgow and at 18 became the youngest holder of the VC of the war. Connor was soon to die however and is now buried in Brattleby village cemetery. For Hannah his operational flying was over and in 1941 he contracted tuberculosis and was discharged from the RAF in 1942. He died on 7 June 1947 at a Sanatorium in Leicester where he had been for some months and is now buried at Birstall (St James) Churchyard, Leicester. He was only 25 years of age. In 2001 his brother, Jim Hannah presented the Hannah trophy to the 237th Glasgow Company of the Boys' Brigade and this trophy is competed for each year for excellence on the vaulting horse.

On 12/13 June 1944, Lancaster KB 726-A of No. 419 (RCAF) Squadron, flown by Flying Officer Arthur 'Art' de Breyne, took off at 2144 to attack the railway yards at Cambrai, although the operations record book for 419 gives the target as Versailles. This was probably because there were two targets that night for which 419 Squadron supplied aircraft.

The crew: Flying Officer Bob Bodie, RCAF; the navigator, Sgt Roy Vicars RAF; the flight engineer, WO2 later P/O Jack Friday RCAF; the bomb aimer, WO2 Jim Kelly RCAF; and the two air gunners F/O Pat Brophy RCAF; the rear gunner and WO2 later P/O Andrew (Andy) Mynarski RCAF the mid upper gunner.

Andy Mynarski was born on 14 October 1916, in Winnipeg, Canada. For four years he worked as a leather worker until he joined the RCAF at the

Andrew Mynarski VC. *Alan Cooper*

age of 25 on 29 September 1941. In December 1942 he had attained the rank of sergeant and was posted to the UK in January 1943. On 18 December 1943 he was promoted to Warrant Officer II. He was posted to No. 419 Squadron at RAF Middleton St George, on 10 April 1944. En route to the target Pat Brophy warned Andy that a Ju88 fighter was approaching from behind and below. As Art De Breyne started to corkscrew the Lancaster the port wing and aft sections of the fuselage were hit by three exploding shells. Two hit the port wing knocking out both engines and setting the petrol tank between them on fire. The third shell burst between the rear and mid-upper gunners and also started a fire. The intercom went dead and the pilot's instrument panel turned black. The aircraft was down to 3,000 to 4, 000 ft and at the bottom of the corkscrew but with the loss of power the aircraft kept losing altitude. With a full bomb load it was clear the aircraft would soon crash. Art gave the order to bale out by signalling with his hand to Roy Vigars, the flight engineer at his side and to the gunners by flashing a 'P' on the red light in the gunners turrets which Art knew had got through because his own light had lit up. Baling out of the aircraft seemed to take longer than it should have. As Jack Friday pulled up the escape hatch the wind took it and caught him in the head and he sustained a deep gash over his right eye which knocked him out. It was Roy Vigars who rolled him over, clipped on his chute and dropped him through the hole, holding on to his ripcord. He came down in a state of slumber and woke up three days later in Amiens prison. Somehow Art kept the wing up with the help of a searchlight 10 miles away at 10'clock off the port wing. After Roy jumped, he was followed by Jim Kelly and Bob Bodie. When he saw the last one out Art throttled back on the starboard engines to keep the aircraft on an even keel and went out through the hatch and pulled his rip cord without counting. It was no time before he hit the ground landing in a wheat field, the cushion on the seat pack helping to soften the impact. When he baled out the altimeter was reading 1,300 ft.

Unknown to Art Andy Mynasrski was still in the aircraft and as he went forward to the escape hatch he saw that the rear gunner Pat Brophy was trapped in his turret. Without any hesitation he went back to help him and grabbed a fire axe and tried to smash open the turret. As it seemed to be hopeless and by which time Andy's clothes and parachute were on fire Pat told Andy to save himself. Andy then went back to the escape exit saluted his trapped comrade and jumped. Amazingly, it was Pat who had all the luck and survived. The bomber, with twenty bombs still on board, slid across a ploughed field, tore up a tree in its path and caught the left wing alight. However as the aircraft crashed the jammed turret opened and Pat was thrown into the air and onto firm ground unhurt. He fainted for a moment and when he came to he found part of his hair was burned, having lost his helmet in the aircraft, but apart from this he was without a scratch. Unfortunately, Andy burns were so severe he was dying before he hit the ground. The French found him but were unable to help or save him. He is now buried in Meharicourt Communal Cemetery, Somme, France. Pat Brophy was found by a Frenchman, Edmund Brulin who informed the Cresson brothers whilst the Chief of the Resistance in the sector of Arne du Capron was notified. He was taken on a cart and hidden in the vault of a cemetery. During the course of his evading he wanted to see his stricken bomber once again, it was still lying there but now guarded by German soldiers. With the help of the Resistance he was able to dismantle and remove various pieces including a machine-gun. The tail wheel later turned up in the War Museum at Ottawa, Canada. Jack Friday, who was unconscious for four and half days, and Roy Vigars landed safely but were soon taken prisoner. Art, Bob Bodie and Jim Kelly were helped by the Resistance and after three months arrived back in London via Paris.

On 15 February 1946, Headquarters Royal Canadian Air Force, Overseas Headquarters, received a recommendation from Ottawa recommending a posthumous award to Andy Mynarski. The information for this recommendation came from Art de Breytne and Pat Brophy. This was sent to the Under Secretary of State at the Air Ministry. On 30 August 1946, a formal recommendation was made for a posthumous Victoria Cross and signed by Air Marshal Bottomley the C in C Bomber Command. This was awarded on 11 October 1946. The spot in the small village of Gaudiepre, near Amiens, France, where the Lancaster crashed has been marked by a bronze plaque. On 13 June 1981, five members of the crew, including Art, were greeted by a group of Resistance members known as 'Les Passeurs du Nord' who had passed airmen down the line and were affiliated to the RAF Escaping Society. Fifteen hundred people came along to pay homage to Andrew Charles Mynarski VC, and Passeurs who had died.

Previous to the war George Thompson, a certified grocer, had been in the Kinross Branch of the Red Cross detachment and also a member of the Home Guard. He was known to be a kind man often helping old people with their ration books etc. He was born in the small village of Kinneswood, five miles from Kinross, and came from a farming background. After early schooling at a neighbouring village he went to Kinross Junior Secondary School, this has now become Kinross High School. He began his RAF service as an LAC on ground wireless-duties and served 12 months overseas in Iraq, Persia and the Persian Gulf. After air gunnery training he was promoted to sergeant and joined No. 9 Squadron at Bardney in September 1944. His pilot was P/O Harry Denton, a farmer from Amberley in New Zealand, who joined the RNZAF in 1941, and in June 1942, wearing an army uniform with an air force cap, joined the defence unit at Woodbourne. After many lectures and guard duties he was put on pilot training flying Tiger Moths. In April 1943 he was sent to Canada where was awarded his wings and the rank of Pilot Officer. A two month navigational course followed with Coastal Command and then to Bomber Command. He arrived and spent four weeks at Brighton in January 1944. It was at OTU that he got his crew together, then a Stirling conversion course, and in August 1944 they were posted to No. 9 Squadron. His crew was Flying Officer Ron Goebels, the bomb aimer, he had trained as a navigator but transferred to bomb aiming because of shortages, Wilf Hartshorn the flight engineer from Yorkshire, Ernie Potts, the mid-upper gunner, a Welshman from Newport, in Monmouthshire where he had been an agriculture engineer and had also started as ground crew and transferred to aircrew, he was known as the 'daddy' of the crew being the oldest and also the only married man, and Ernie was a keen darts player. The rear gunner was also a Welshman, Haydn Price, and a first class air gunner, he was known at times to sing in good Welsh style until told to pack it in by the skipper or another member of the crew. His great friend understandably was Ernie Potts. The navigator was Edward (Ted) Kneebone, a chemist from Manchester. Last, of course, was George Thompson, the wireless/operator/air gunner, remembered as a highlander with a strong Scottish accent.

On 1 January 1945, the target was the Dortmund-Emms Canal at Ladbergen and Harry took off in Lancaster PD 377-U at 0744. The weather had been very cold for some time and in Lincolnshire there had been a persistent fog. There had been a dance at Bardney on New Year's Eve, however it was not to last too long when crews learned they were on standby for an operation the next day. It was around about 0500 when they were awoken and after a hurried breakfast they made for the briefing room. Outside it was very cold with freezing rain. When they arrived at their Lancaster it was covered in frost and before they took off a glycol bowser came alongside and sprayed the aircraft with glycol and with glycol dripping from the wings they roared down the runway and took off. They soon got to 500 ft but as they did Ernie Potts shouted, "God he's gone in!" A No. 9 Squadron Lancaster had crashed on take-off and burst into flames. As they crossed over Holland it could be seen that the ground was covered in snow.

Ernie Potts asked Harry to move out of the slipstream of the other aircraft as he was being thrown about. They were heading into a wind of 100mph so progress forward was slow. A big barrage of flak was starting to come up and aircraft ahead were being hit. Eventually the crew heard the words they all wanted to hear from Ron, "Bombs Gone". Suddenly there was a loud explosion followed by another and Edward Kneebone found himself at first surrounded by flames and just as suddenly the flames disappeared having been blown out by the 100mph gale coming in threw the shattered nose. The intercom had been damaged and communication was impossible. All Edward's charts and maps had been sucked out of the aircraft. As they approached the Rhine they were down to 4,000 ft when three Fw190s appeared. When the Fw190s did not attack it was assumed that they were out of ammunition. As they flew south of Arnhem they came under intense flak and the port engine was hit. The engine burst into flames and Harry shut down the engine and feathered the propeller and the fire went out.

George was unhurt by the hits on the Lancaster but he noticed fire around the mid-upper turret and the gunner was still in it although unconscious. He went down the fuselage, despite the fire and ammunition exploding and removed the gunner from the turret, and somehow negotiating a large hole in the floor of the fuselage, carried him away from the fire. He then beat out the fire on the gunners clothes and made him as comfortable as possible. He himself had suffered terrible burns to his face and hands. His trousers had been burnt off and his legs were also severely burned. He then saw that the fire was spreading around the rear turret and for a second time went and to the aid of a fellow crew member. He rescued the rear gunner the turret, and, as before, he dragged the gunner to safety and put out the flames on his clothing with his bare hands. George was in a pitiful, in fact he was so bad that Harry Denton, the pilot, did not recognise him.

It was now obvious they were going to have to crash land and Edward indicated to Wilf and Ron to come amidships and take up crash positions. George joined them and at last the bump came but they were down and alive. The Lancaster broke into two pieces which made it easier to leave the aircraft. They had crashed West of Heesh in Holland at 1200. They were taken into a Dutch cottage and given blankets. Soon the whole village turned up and were all trying to squeeze into the cottage to see them; some of the women were crying. Eventually two RAF doctors turned up and the crew were taken to the nearest RAF station and then No. 52 RCAF Mobile Field Hospital in Eindhoven. It was obvious that George and Ernie were in a bad way and Harry Denton had suffered with frostbite during the latter part of the flight as had Ron who lost the first joint of all his fingers from frostbite. Ted Kneebone suffered greatly with stomach nerves and was in hospital for a month. George was able to walk but very badly burned with most of his clothes burned off his body. Ernie Potts only lived for 18 hours but George seemed to be improving when Harry and Ted were flown home to an army hospital at Camberley. Harry had bumped his head in the landing and the frostbite to his face and hands healed up in a few weeks. Haydn Price suffered a head wound but soon recovered.

On 21 January 1945, a recommendation was submitted by Group Captain McMullen, the Station Commander of RAF Bardney. This followed a full report that Harry Denton had submitted on his return to Bardney and the loss of his aircraft. The recommendation was for the Victoria Cross to Flight Sergeant George Thompson. The recommendation was strongly endorsed by Air Commodore Hesketh. No. 53 Base Commander at Waddington of which Bardney was a part. On 9 February 1945, the CinC of Bomber Command, Sir Arthur Harris, said to the Secretary of State for Air, "I entirely agree that Thompson's gallantry was of the very highest order and that it fully justifies the award of the VC". On 17 February it was announced that George had been awarded the VC and it was gazetted on the 20 February. Unfortunately, George had died on 23 January at No. 50 Military Hospital where he was given penicillin and seemed to be on the way to recovery but having contracted pneumonia he was overcome. He never knew that he had been awarded the highest bravery award that can be awarded in the UK. He is buried in in Brussels, Belgium. Harry Denton visited George's parents, not an easy meeting he recalls, but both were very brave and had taken it well. They later made the journey to London for the presentation the VC to them by the King. Ernie Potts had a daughter Christine born in November 1944. Today Christine is 64 and she has a lot of her father's ways including being fond of animals. On 4 February 1945 Harry Denton was recommended for the DSO but on 8 February awarded an immediate DFC.

The rest of the crew have had various reunions over the years, Harry having gone back to Farming in New Zealand, Ron became an architect, Wilf a policeman, Haydn a bricklayer, and Ted an executive with an oil company. In 1968 a VC10 aircraft was named after George, and in 1970 150 former members of 9 Squadron came to Kinloss to present the High School with a replica of the VC10 that was later flown by No. 10 Squadron and is now The George Thompson Memorial Prize. There is also a plaque to the memory of George in the school. At RAF Innsworth, now Personnel Training Command of the RAF, roads in which a number of married quarters are situated are named after holders of the VC and also the Conspicuous Gallantry Medal. One of the roads is called Thompson Way in memory of George, another is Gray Close, and another Hannah Place. In 1978, Margaret Palmer an artist and former WAAF at Waddington, painted a portrait of George, he looked almost baby-faced at the time she said. One other aircraft of 9 Squadron NC 223 flown by F/O Reaks also failed to return from the operation to the Dortmund Emms Canal.

The next highest award after the VC for non-commissioned members of the RAF is the Conspicuous Gallantry Medal (Flying), it was instituted in 1942 and to date only 112 have been awarded. Of this 112, twenty-seven were awarded to air gunners. The first recommendation was in February 1943. Sergeant George Ashplant, a pilot of No. 166 Squadron was recommended for the VC, but later awarded the CGM.

Sergeant Ivan Hazard of No. 101 Squadron with his two gunners Sgt Les Airey, the rear gunner, and F/Sgt George Dove, the mid-upper gunner, when attacked by a Fiat biplane, were able to shoot it down between them. However, their Lancaster, ED 377-SR-X was badly damaged and Les Airey had been hit in the legs and also received facial burns. Although wounded, and with the help of the rest of the crew, he was helping to put out the flames. George Dove who had also been burned on the face and hands was already the holder of the DFM for a tour with No. 10 Squadron in which he had eight different pilots. Both Hazard and Dove were recommended for the VC, and three others including Airey the CGM. The officer in the crew P/O F. W. Gates was awarded the DSO. And in March 1943 all five CGMs and the DSO were awarded, the sixth man, the bomb aimer had mistaken the orders given by Hazard and baled out. Before the awards had been Gazetted Hazard, Bain, the flight engineer, and Williams, the navigator, were all killed when the new Lancaster they were in struck a pill-box on the beach at Hornsea and crashed into the cliffs. Fortunately for them, on this occasion George Dove and Les Airey, having been wounded, were not in the crew.

F/Sgt Norman Williams was an Australian from New South Wales and joined the RAAF in May 1941, and in March 1942 was awarded his Air Gunner brevet. He trained in Australia and the UK before joining No. 10 Squadron in August 1942.

On his 10th operation to Bremen the aircraft was attacked by a Ju88 which came up under the tail and out of the view of Norman. However, when he did see the fighter he immediately called for a steep climb. Norman opened fire and the fighter burst into flames before hitting the ground. For this he was awarded an immediate DFM. And in March 1943 a bar to the DFM followed. By this time he had volunteered for the Pathfinder force and was posted to No. 35 Squadron at Gravely. On 11 June 1943, flying with P/O Cobb and now with forty operations under his belt, they were attacked by two fighters and in the first attack both he and the mid upper gunner were wounded: Norman being hit with bullets in the legs and one in the stomach. Despite this and in the second attack he opened fire with a long burst of 300 rounds, the fighter stopped firing and exploded. In the third attack he again opened fire with 300 rounds and bits were flying off the offending fighter but still Norman kept firing until it was seen going into cloud with large pieces flying of it. He refused to leave his turret and when they finally made it home then, because of the damage to his turret, he had to be cut out of it. Four days later he was recommended for the CGM. After some time recovering he returned to No. 35 Squadron, and, now commissioned, he returned to Australia and took part in the Pacific War carrying out thirty-six operations against the Japanese which, after Germany, he described as a milk run. In 1948 he left the RAF with the rank of Squadron Leader and was one of the most decorated air gunners in WWII. In 1951 he rejoined the RAAF, serving in Singapore and Korea. He resigned from the RAAF again in 1954. His damaged turret now resides in the War Museum in Canberra, Australia.

Sergeant Geoffrey Keen joined the RAF in 1940, and in 1941, after completing a tour, was awarded the DFM. After a rest period he joined No. 427 Squadron RCAF in Yorkshire. On 12 March 1943, and while on an operation to Essen, the aircraft was hit by flak, the navigator was killed and Keen lost half of one foot and received lacerations to both legs. He worked on the damaged radio for two hours and then helped with the navigation. They made it back to make a crash landing safely. On 27 March his pilot and CO, Wg Cdr Burnside, put his name forward for the VC, this was later changed to the CGM, Burnside received a bar to his DFC and two other members of the crew were given DFCs. Sergeant Keen was awarded the CGM and

F/Sgt G.Keen CGM DFM. *Alan Cooper*   two other members of the crew the

Sgt Hall CGM and his crew at Buckingham Palace. *Alan Cooper*

Jimmy Hall CGM. *Miss A Ellcombe*

DFM. After the war, with the help of a special boot, he played football and also cricket.

Sergeant Thomas Hall was a mid-upper gunner with No. 115 Squadron. On 28/29 June 1943 he was flying on an operation to Cologne when they were attacked by two Fw190s, he and the rear gunner, Sgt White, opened fire and the first fighter broke away without opening firing. The second fighter did open fire but the fire passed behind the Lancaster. However, the first fighter then came in and attacked from 200 yards. Both gunners again opened fire but so did the fighter and the rear turret was hit and Sgt White killed. The Lancaster caught fire but despite this Sgt Hall kept firing his guns until the fighters broke off, one of the fighters was last seen on fire and in a steep dive. He then helped the wireless/operator to fight the fire and between them they managed to put it out. It was then that they realised that the rear turret had been completely shot away, sadly taking Sgt White with it. His body was never found and his name is on the Runneymede Memorial.

The now famous raid on Peenemunde was the operation where Sergeant George Oliver of No. 467 Squadron won his CGM. His aircraft was attacked by an Me109 and in its first attack it wounded the rear gunner Sgt Barry, destroyed the hydraulics and put his turret out of action. When the Lancaster went into a dive a fire broke out setting alight the ammunition. Sgt Oliver, in his mid-upper turret and on his 23rd operation engaged the fighter and managed to shoot it down. He then made his way to the front of the aircraft where he met up with the wireless operator and navigator and they informed the pilot, W/O Wilson that the aircraft was on fire. However, as the aircraft was responding to his control he told them to go back and fight the fire. This they did and put out the flames and then went back and chopped the rear gunner out of his turret. George was awarded the CGM and the pilot the DFC. After two more trips this crew finished their tour and other members of the crew were decorated.

Sergeant Walter 'Mike' Cowham, a Rhodesian, joined No. 57 Squadron in October 1943 and within a short time he had five trips in his log book. On 18 October his aircraft was detailed for an operation to Hannover. Minutes after dropping their bombs he reported an Me109 in the area and soon after the German fighter came in for an attack. The fighter came in firing its cannon and Cowham was hit in the attack but continued to fire and saw hits on the fighter. He had in fact been blinded in his left eye by a splinter from a cannon shell which had burst in his turret. Much damage had been done to the aircraft and 120 gallons of petrol lost. They were attacked again some 25 minutes later near the Dutch coast but the Mike's pilot was able to make a landing at the nearest aerodrome in the UK. When they got Cowham out of his turret it was found that, as well as his eye wound a bullet had gone through his flying suit and taken skin off his shoulder. Mike had also lost a great deal of blood. His CGM was awarded in November, in Rhodesia he had been a big game hunter and remarked that he would now not have to squint his eye when he went hunting.

Flight/Sergeant Geoffrey Smith was an Australian and was born near Sydney. On 15 February, while flying with No. 156 Pathfinder Squadron on an operation to Berlin during the Battle of Berlin, he sent a message to the pilot that a fighter was coming up behind his rear turret. A burst of machine-gun bullets went over the top of the Lancaster but then a second fighter came in unseen and fired a burst that struck the Lancaster between the mid-upper and rear turrets. Sgt Clarke, in the mid-upper turret, was hit in the leg and suffered a compound fracture and Smith, in the rear turret, was hit in the ankle by a cannon shell which severely wounded him. Both turrets were out of action after the attack. Geoff reported to the pilot that

F/Sgt Smith CGM.

F/Sgt Smith at Buckingham Palace to receive his well earned CGM. *Alan Cooper*

the Me110 had been hit by their return fire and exploded. After the attack they found that the bomb doors would not open and they, therefore, decided to turn back. By this time a fire had broken out in the back of the aircraft and it was, in fact, Geoff's parachute that was on fire. Despite all pleading he refused to leave his turret and was operating his guns with one hand. Once over the sea on the way back the rest of the crew chopped down the door of the rear turret and extricated Geoff. They landed at Woodbridge and he was taken to Ely hospital where his right leg was amputated above the knee. He returned to Australia and had a very successful life in business. On 6 February 1986, having been ill for some time, Geoff died.

George Downton enlisted in the RAAF in 1941, he was 23 years old. His training was done in Australia, Kenya and then Rhodesia before joining an operational unit in the Middle East.

On 21 April 1943, he took off with his pilot, Lt Ballard, a South African, for a reconnaissance to the Cape Bon area. When they were reported to be overdue they were posted as missing. An intercepted German message came through that a dinghy had been picked up and it was hoped that it was Ballard and his crew but nothing more was heard until July when George Downton was reported as being a prisoner of war.

They had, in fact, been attacked by ten Me109s and in the subsequent battle Ballard and another member of the crew were killed. Another crew member, F/Sgt Hartley, was badly burned and died the next day. George took on the fighters but found that his gun was not working properly so he directed his pilot in the early stages of the attack which lasted 20 minutes. As the aircraft was forced down he was wounded and, finally, when Ballard was hit and killed, the aircraft crashed. George scrambled out and regardless of the flames he was able to get F/Sgt Hartley out. He then went back to try and get out the rear gunner F/O Tassie but was beaten back by the heat. George and a Major Braithwaite, who was a passenger on the operation, were captured and made PoWs. He spent the next two years as a prisoner in Italy and Germany.

Flight/Sergeant William Crabe, from Canada, flew as mid-upper gunner with No. 170 Squadron. Shortly after dropping their bombs on Luftwigshafen on 1 February 1945, William's 11th operation, they collided with a another Lancaster badly damaging the tail of their Lancaster and smashing the rear turret and killing the rear gunner. Crabe immediately left his mid-upper turret to see if he could help the rear gunner and was assisted by the wireless operator. They cut away the side of the smashed turret and tying a rope around himself climbed into the wrecked gun position. He was open to the elements and had no parachute on because of the confined space he was in. He was put up for the DFM but at a higher level this was upgraded to the CGM.

Flight/Sergeant Robert Hartley was an air gunner with No. 9 Squadron at RAF Bardney and after twenty-nine operations (Five operations had been to the German capital Berlin.) he was recommended for the CGM. On 20 February, when Bomber Command lost seventy-six aircraft on an operation to Leipzig his aircraft was attacked by a night-fighter but with good team work he was able return the fighter's fire and it broke off the engagement. When he had completed five operations he had to be taken off flying with a perforated ear drum. After being out for 2 months he returned and in 3 months went on to complete twenty-four operations. After he had been flying for some time it was found that he had been in constant pain as a result of a duodenal perforation caused during an operation to remove his appendix prior to entering the RAF. This was only confirmed after he had finished his tour and he was again in hospital for 2 months.

Flying Officer William Anderson of No. 405 Squadron was flying as mid-upper gunner when attacked by a Dornier 217 which opened fire with a burst of cannon and machine-gun fire. In the attack he was hit four

F/Sgt Crabe CGM. *Alan Cooper*

times in the arm but still continued to fire his guns and during the seventh attack the enemy fighter went down in flames and crashed on the ground where it continued to burn. After first aid he acted as look-out in the lower blister on the return journey. He was awarded an immediate DFC.

Not all awards to aircrew and air gunners was for bravery in the air. Pilot/Officer Charles Patten of No. 70 Squadron was serving in the Middle East on an operational raid when the aircraft crashed and burst into flames. He was able get out of the turret and around to the nose of the aircraft where he saw the front gunner alive but trapped in his turret. With the help of two other members of the crew they were able to wrench the turret from the machine and drag the gunner out to safety undoubtedly saving his life. For his actions he was awarded the George Medal.

Not all air gunners in Bomber Command were in the RAF. Major John Porter of the Royal Artillery flew thirteen operations as an air gunner to observe and advise on German flak. After an air gunnery course he was awarded the AG brevet and wore it on his army battledress. It is thought there were about fifteen RA Officers serving in the RAF in 1943 time and were carrying out a similar role. One was awarded the DFC and another the MC after putting out a fire aboard the aircraft.

Flight/Lieutenant William Gabriel of No. 9 Squadron was the rear gunner on a daylight attack on the submarine pens at Bergen. After dropping their bombs and leaving the target area his aircraft was attacked by four Fw190s. During the attack his turret was hit and put out of action and in the second attack he was wounded above the eye. Along with the mid-upper gunner, whose turret was also put out of action, he kept up a running commentary on where the fighters were, thereby allowing the pilot to manoeuvre away from the fighters. In all, fifteen attacks were made on the Lancaster and they only gave up when out of ammunition. At the time he had completed forty-six operations and was awarded the DFC.

One award worthy of mention was the DFC to Warrant Officer Percy Pope of No. 578 Squadron. When he had completed seventeen operations with No. 578 Squadron it made his total of operations 105! He had joined the RAF in 1931 and flown in the UK and India. When war broke out he was a gunnery instructor and he volunteered for operations and carried out his first Anti-Submarine patrol on 9 March 1940, a $5\frac{1}{2}$ hour patrol.

The operations continued until February 1944 when he commenced flying on Halifaxes with No. 578 Squadron. He flew with the CO of 578, Wg Cdr Wilkinson DSO, and targets included Stuttgart, Frankfurt, Dusseldorf, various targets leading up to D-Day and rocket sites. After the recommendation was submitted he flew on further operations and on 9 September 1944 he had flown 110 operations.

Two gunners were awarded the Military Medal: Sgt John Barr and Sgt A R Evans. Sgt Barr was serving with No. 104 Squadron in the Middle East. His aircraft was detailed to attack shipping at Tobruk. It was severely damaged by anti-aircraft fire and they prepared to land in enemy occupied territory. After two days on the ground Barr and another gunner set off to try and intercept Allied mechanised transport in the area. They heard a vehicle coming which turned out to be a Volkswagen and Barr stood in the road bringing it to a halt. Its passengers were two German officers and an orderly who went for his gun but Sgt Barr had him covered with a revolver and so they surrendered. They boarded the vehicle and ordered one of the Germans to drive down a track to the crashed aircraft, here the remainder of the crew boarded the vehicle and left the Germans to make it back on foot. On the 4th day, and after driving over rough ground, the car broke down and they decided to walk, but not until night time. After two hours walking they found they had wandered into German lines, somehow they avoided the attention of the sentries but later were discovered and disarmed by the Germans. They were taken to a PoW camp for interrogation and on to Tobruck by truck. But on the way a plan was made to overpower the guards which they did successfully and after another 3 days they were rescued by two Allied army-vehicles and taken to safety.

Sergeant Evans was an air gunner with No. 102 Squadron, when on 27 April he set off to bomb the docks at Dunkirk. The aircraft was hit by flak and the order to bale out given. He had been hit by shrapnel while in the aircraft and machine-gunned during his parachute descent. His parachute was holed and he landed heavily breaking a bone in his ankle. After a while he was taken prisoner by a German who marched him across the road. But, believing Evans, to be helpless, the German took his eyes off him and Evans took full advantage of the German's carelessness and hit him with a beer bottle on the jaw. Not knowing if he was dead or not and not wanting to be caught with a dead German he filled the soldier's pockets with bricks and rolled him into the canal. From there by various ways and means he got back to the UK.

On a rare occasion a whole crew, including the gunners, were decorated for one operation. Flight/Sergeant Paul Campbell of No. 61 Squadron and his crew took off to lay mines in the Baltic on the night of 25/26 September 1942. When over Denmark they were attacked with anti-aircraft fire and a shell exploded in the bomb compartment which started a fire in the fuselage setting light to the reconnaissance flares and distress signals. A second shell burst in the nose of the aircraft which destroyed the Perspex nose and the majority of the Perspex showered over the pilot. The bomb aimer, Sgt Frank Bunclark, was blown back in alongside the pilot. The second pilot, Sgt Stanley Gunnell was blown onto the floor beside the navigator, Sgt Ernest Corbett. All of whom received facial burns from the exploding shell. With the cockpit full of smoke, and the pilot unable to see his instruments they were attacked by two fighters. The aircraft was hit by cannon and machine gun fire. Cannon fire entered both the rear and mid-upper turrets. The aircraft stalled and lost 2,000 ft before the smoke cleared and the pilot was able to regain control, he dived into the clouds and was able to lose the fighters and escape the anti-aircraft fire.

The fire in the fuselage had now got bigger and ammunition was exploding all over the aircraft. The rear gunner Sgt Stanley Thompson was hit in the leg by a piece of shrapnel, and his leg was broken. Because of the aircraft being out of control he was unable to fire his guns when attacked by the fighters but was able to report the position of the fighters to the pilot. He was later taken out of his turret by the navigator, air bomber and mid-upper gunner and spent the rest of the trip on the rest bed not once complaining or asking or expecting assistance. Sgt Sydney Smith, who was considerably burnt about the hands, face and body stripped off his flying clothes put them on top of the fire and then fell on top of it. This successfully extinguished the flames. Despite his injuries he returned to his turret for the rest of the trip. All maps, instruments and wireless logs had been blown out of the nose of the aircraft.

The wireless operator, Sgt Cyril Coakley, was able to establish contact with his base from a distance of 400 miles, described as an amazing feat in the circumstance and continued to obtain regular bearings throughout the trip. Despite the hydraulics and emergency gear for the operation of the undercarriage and flaps being completely destroyed the pilot made an excellent belly landing. Sgt Gunnell had flown the aircraft for 2 hours on the return trip which gave the pilot time to rest and to take stock of the instrument readings. F/Sgt Campbell was awarded an immediate DFM and a commission in the field. The remainder of the crew were awarded an immediate DFM.

A typical non-immediate DFM was awarded to Sgt Albert Johnson in 1940; he had at the time flown twenty-three operations with No. 83 Squadron and he was described as a source of inspiration and instruction to all air gunners in his squadron. Air Marshal Bert Harris, then the AOC of 5 Group and later CinC Bomber Command signed the recommendation on 31 July 1940.

F/Sgt Cowham CGM. *IWM*

Flight/Lieutenant Chas Chandler, after flying ninety-two operations was awarded the DFC and Bar. Also, he was the only man in 617 Squadron to be awarded the Medal of Valour (Russia).

Sergeant John Grant was flying a Halifax, DG 396, with No. 295 Squadron, and towing a glider, when attacked in the Bay of Biscay by no less than twelve Ju88s. The glider cast off according to plan and the Halifax sent out an SOS message. Meanwhile, eight of the Ju88s closed in on the Halifax and raked it with cannon fire. Although outgunned, Sgt Grant kept up continuous and accurate counter fire scoring hits on several enemy

F/Sgt L.Airey CGM. *Alan Cooper*   F/Sgt G. Dove CGM. *Alan Cooper*

Left Sgt Addley DFM and right F/Sgt A Johnson DFM at Buckingham Palace in 1941. The awards were for the raids on German battleships at Brest and shooting down two German night fighters. *Alan Cooper*

aircraft. He saw smoke coming from one of the fighters and it probably never reached its base. He fired 2,000 rounds and at the same time gave the pilot, F/O Norman the correct evasive procedure. The action lasted 15 minutes before cloud was reached, it was due to Grant that the aircraft survived, even when his turret was hit by cannon fire. This was a great example of what can be done against overwhelming odds with a determined and courageous gunner. In October 1943 he was recommended and awarded an immediate DFM.

In June 1941, Air Marshal Slessor the AOC of 5 Group, wrote to the then CinC Bomber Command concerning the award of decorations. He got his staff to make a study showing the number of awards to each aircrew category in a bomber. The study covered six squadrons.

In No. 44 Squadron twenty-two out of twenty-seven captains and five out of nineteen W/Opt/AGs were awarded immediate or non-immediate awards. But for straight air gunners nil.

In No. 49 Squadron twenty-two out of thirty-two Captains and six out of twenty-one W/Opt/AGs were awarded immediate or non-immediate awards and again nil air gunners.

In No. 50 Squadron seventeen out of twenty-two Captains, twelve out of fifteen W/Opt/AGs and 2 out of 3 Air Gunners were awarded immediate or non-immediate awards.

In No. 61 Squadron thirteen out of fourteen Captains and seven out of thirteen W/Opt/AGs were awarded immediate or non-immediate awards, and nil Air Gunners.

In No. 83 Squadron seventeen out of twenty-eight Captains and twelve out of eighteen W/Opt/AGs were awarded immediate or non-immediate awards and nil air gunners.

In No. 144 Squadron fifteen out of twenty-four Captains and fifteen out of seventeen W/Opt/AGs were awarded immediate or non-immediate awards and nil Air Gunners.

For the Group as a whole 72 per cent of Captains, 54 per cent W/Opt/AGs and only 20 per cent Air Gunners were decorated.

It thus became evident that the ordinary air gunner was not getting a fair share of awards. One of the troubles was, of course, that so few air gunners in night bombers had let off their guns in anger, and so it was difficult to write them up. But the chap in a lower turret of a Hampden had a pretty mouldy job and nothing much to occupy his mind. He, therefore, deserved more than his fair share of what is going in the way of medals. This was the feeling in 1941.

It is interesting note that out of 112 awards of the Conspicuous Gallantry Medal (Flying) twenty-six were awarded to Air Gunners and of this number twenty-two were awarded to air gunners in Bomber Command.

CHAPTER THIRTEEN

Post War and National Service Air Gunners

ircrew including air gunners had been drastically reduced at the end of WWII but when the Cold War started with the Eastern block, aircraft and aircrew in Bomber Command and Maritime Reconnaissance had rapidly to be increased.

The rapid build up of the RAF was due to the UK's responsibility to NATO which began in 1949. This was to combat the menace of the USSR. But it took some time for the realisation of the responsibilities of being part of NATO. The Defence Chiefs expected an offensive action from Soviet forces in the early 1950s. The expectation was an invasion of the Shetland, Orkney or possibly the Outer Hebrides by 1953, followed by an invasion of Norway. Once this had been implemented it was expected the islands would be used as nuclear submarine bases and launching pads for an invasion of mainland Britain. With this firmly in mind it was realised that the RAF did not have sufficient aircraft or crews to face this, it was Munich 1938 all over again.

Because of this crisis air gunner training was reduced from six to three months. It became apparent during a meeting of the Air Chiefs of Staff of Canada, France, UK and the USA in Washington that the reasons for the working of the system of National Service aircrew in the RAF were not commonly understood. First the various forms of entering the RAF. The flying personnel were and are called the GD (General Duties) Branch of the RAF. There were five Categories of Aircrew in the RAF: Pilots, Navigators, Signallers, Engineers and Gunners. For the first two the policy was that they should all be commissioned officers. But in reality there were a number NCOs in each category.

There were three categories consisting of mainly NCOs, though some signallers were commissioned during their service.

The Cranwell Entry. A total of 130 entrants a year which provided the hard-core of regular long term officers.

Short Service. Eight years regular service followed by four years Reserve service.

National Service Entrants. All boys called up at the age of 19 for 2 years service followed by $3^1/_2$ years part-time service in one of the armed services. The RAF in 1951 received thirty-five per cent, about 50,000 men.

Before the Korean War the RAF was only able to take a very small annual quota for aircrew service. But when the Korean War broke out, 1950/52, this was increased and the planned intake of NS pilots and navigators at the peak of the expansion was 2,275 a year as against 4,050 short service regulars. As per the tradition of aircrew all were volunteers. Although called up for service in the RAF, aircrew duties were by volunteering.

Mo Mowbray was called up for National Service, volunteered for aircrew duties and went to Jurby on the Isle of Man for a six months pilots' course. However, Once the Korean War began it all changed. Potential NS pilots were given the chance to become regulars and sign on for 8 years, or remuster. Mo did the latter and went to Leconfield for three months on an air-gunners course.

His training was undertaken on a Wellington MX X bomber. On this aircraft he learned to fire four .303 Browning machine guns from the rear turret. From an Operational Conversion Unit he was selected to go on to the B29 Washington Conversion Unit at RAF Marham, Norfolk. This was run by the US Air Force and, if nothing else, the food was good. In May 1951 he was presented with the AG Brevet. He then set off for the re-formed No. 57 Squadron at Waddington where he found conditions to be superb. Here he flew with Flt Lt Eric Scott and so began a lifetime friendship until Eric died in1999. At Waddington he had ten months glorious flying and flew all over Europe and the Mediterranean.

In April 1952 he was posted to RAF Coningsby where he found conditions vastly different so he was glad he only had six weeks to serve before being demobbed. Happy days, no medals, lots of laughs and good memories is how Mo remembers his National Service days.

Gerald Oakley spent a time at RAF Leconfield on No. 8 Air Gunners Course from October to December 1950.

Edmund Phillips began his NS days at Padgate on 10 July 1951. After the usual kitting out and inoculations and vaccinations he and eight aircraft cadets went to RAF West Kirby for basic training. Then on to RAF Leconfield for training on AVRO Lincoln B2 aircraft. Sqn Ldr 'Darkie' Draper signed his log book at the end of the course on 16 December 1951. The award of the AG brevets and sergeant stripes followed at a passing out parade. He was only 17, his 18th Birthday was on the 21st Dec 1951. He then went on seven days leave before reporting to Pembroke Dock and Sunderland Flying Boats and then, as he thought, operations in Korea.

However, they were recalled to Leconfield after a few days at Pembroke and then sent to the Maritime Reconnaissance School at RAF St Mawgan. Here he spent 12 weeks training on sonar, etc and the handling of various pyrotechnics and were 'christened' Radar Gunners and then it was off to No. 236 OCU at RAF Kinloss. Here they found the new Shackletons which Edmund found light years ahead of the MR Lancasters at St Mawgan. Four big Griffin engines, twin 20 mm Hispano Cannons with a Gyroscopic computer gunsight, a proper galley, bunk beds, and loads of space. The downside was the loud noise from the four Griffin engines with their stub exhausts for anything up to 18 hours at a time.

He was then posted to No. 240 Squadron which was to re-form at Ballykelly in Northern Ireland. The main problem for the RAF was a lack of crews for Shackletons: each Shackleton needed a crew of ten to twelve. Some of the air gunners from Bomber Command were diverted and after training on sonar and radar the manpower problem eased somewhat.

In 1953 squadrons of Shackletons took part in the flypast for the Queen's Birthday over Buckingham Palace in Mk 18 1a Shackletons on the 5 June 1952 and aircraft of Nos 220, 240, and 269 squadrons took part. In all there were eighteen Shackletons flying down the Mall and over Buckingham Palace on the day of the Trooping of the Colour. Edmund was in the mid-upper turret of one of the 240 Squadron aircraft WG 507. There were many complaints from Newquay to RAF St Eval as the town had been shaken

Air Gunners Course No 8 at RAF Leconfield in 1950. *Gerald Oakley*

to the foundations. On arrival back at Ballykelly they had been in the air for six hours and twenty-five minutes.

It was the first time the new Shackleton has been seen *en masse* by the public. The last time the Shackleton was seen by the public before being withdrawn from service was again over Buckingham Palace after the Trooping the Colour in 1991 after forty sterling years service. It was the last piston aircraft left in service. It was a direct descendant of the Lancaster and had been named after the artic explorer, Ernest Shackleton, who was related to the wife of the Shackleton's designer Roy Chadwick. At first it was known as the AVRO 696. It first took to the air in 1949 and by 1952 there were seven squadrons of Shackleton's in the RAF. A Society has been formed from Leconfield Air Gunners(LAGS). and each year many return to the Leconfield and share memories of the 50s.

Peter Morrey was called up in June 1952 and reported to RAF Padgate. Here, at this enormous camp, he was kitted out and seeded. A sergeant got them all together in a large hut and asked people to step forward when he called out various schools that people may have attended. All the public and minor private schools were mentioned and at the end the grammar schools waited and waited. Those men whose schools had been mentioned were sent off for officer selection and never seen again. Those that had opted for aircrew were sent to the Aircrew Selection Centre at Hornchurch. On the way, via the underground, every time they stopped at a station a corporal was standing to prevent those who had second thoughts from

Gerald Oakley in training. *Gerald Oakley*

leaving. They were at the Centre from 19 June to 22 June and while there they undertook aptitude tests and a thorough and sometimes fierce medical. One consolation was that if you passed this test you were very fit. A number of men were rejected including those with vast ATC experience. Finally, came the crunch day: to be selected or rejected. Peter was called in and told he had been selected to train as an air gunner. Apart from passing the tests he was told by a squadron leader that having been a King's Scout taught him a great deal about Peter's character. He then reported back to Padgate picked up his kit and then off to the Aircrew Transit Unit at Cranwell for a week.

At RAF West Kirby began the square bashing, there were twenty-four recruits in D Squadron and they

Gerald Oakley back right. *Gerald Oakley*

wore a white plastic disc behind the beret badge and white bars on each shoulder. Many hours of foot and rifle drill, followed and then the day of passing out came. One recruit had the idea that putting your belt in bleach would make it whiter; but, unfortunately for him it just disintegrated.

After five days leave it was back to Cranwell and the Aircrew Holding Centre. Here he kicked his heels for a month until finally it was off to the Central Gunnery School at Leconfield where for the first time they saw the aircraft they would train and fly on: the Lincoln. The Officer Commanding was Squadron Leader 'Darkie' Draper and the OC Gunnery Despatch Flt Lt E. Owen, the OC of the Flying Wing was Wg Cdr Smythe. There seemed so much to learn and the sight of the electrical diagram of a Boulton Paul Defiant turret on the wall was frightening to say the least particularly to a former bank clerk. The theory of gunnery was hard and even at meal times the trainees traded questions. Many hours were spent in the gun room learning to strip and reassemble the .5 Browning and the heavier and bigger 20mm Hispano Cannon. If you forgot the correct procedure it could mean a powerful return spring leaping into to your midriff. The only sympathy you got from the instructor was, "it serves you right!" But they became competent and could strip them down blindfolded to the smallest part and reassemble them with gloves on and even with their hands tied behind their backs; not the most useful skill but it became a party piece.

Escape and Evasion was also part of the training. They were given their flying kit: suits, silk gloves, gauntlets, helmets, oxygen masks, boots and parachute and told how to put it all on without damaging your wedding tackle. Then came the first flight in a Lincoln Mk II to get their bearings and then it was flying every day, at least twice a day and sometimes three times. The flying training involved shooting with cameras on the gun sight at Spitfires or Meteors. During this time they were allowed to order the pilot to corkscrew the aircraft during a mock attack. Live firing took part over the sea off Bridlington. This meant turning the guns on the beam and firing and, as the aircraft moved forwards, aim to hit the splashes you had originally created. It was tense stuff and many a cadet was smacked about the head for making the bursts too long ("just boom, boom, boom, boom lads that's all".)

Peter was selected to go on Operation Barrage, a flight of some 6 hours over the North Sea and then into Germany. The pilot was the CO Wg Cdr Smythe. It was cold, and the sandwiches were the wrong choice of tomatoes which froze solid and could be snapped like wood. In order to move around the aircraft they had to clip their oxygen tube to a small bottle until they reached a main source. The bottle Peter had was empty and he passed out. Fortunately for him he was seen by another member of the crew from the observers dome. He promptly plugged Peter's tube into a main source and he recovered. Later, somebody, probably a ground crew chap, was severely reprimanded for not making sure the bottle was full.

They now wore the brass albatross on the sleeve of their uniform which showed they were aircrew under training, final exams came and their marksmanship was carefully scrutinised. The time came for best blue uniform and they were marched into a hanger where they saw a table and on it the brevets of an air gunner with which they were soon to be presented. With it came the rank of sergeant, and new identity cards reflecting their rank and then their first visit to the sergeants' Mess. Peter remembers that the Sergeants' Mess was paradise compared to what they were used to.

He was then posted to No. 57 Squadron at RAF Coningsby and flying on Washington aircraft, or B-29s as they were known. The B29s were on loan from the US until jet bombers came into service. He found them more comfortable than the Lincoln being pressurised, warm and smooth as they flew at much higher altitudes. The pilot was Squadron Leader 'Speedy' Holmes. He was known as Speedy as he was reputed to have flown a Spitfire from Scotland down to a southern airfield faster than anyone else had. The station Commander was Group Captain Willie Tait of No. 617 Squadron fame and the sinking of the German Battleship *Tirpitz*.

Peter was then posted to No. 115 Squadron at RAF Marham where he became a regular member of a crew. One day, having arrived at their aircraft they found tins of duroglit and were told that they had been selected to go to RAF Odiham as part of the Bomber Command representation at the RAF Review by the Queen. After much spit and duroglit the aircraft was gleaming but when the first time the gleaming aircraft flew it rained hard and all the spit and polish began again. The prop blades were simonised and the tyres painted black but when the Queen drove past she was looking the other way as she talked to a senior officer and never even saw them or the aircraft. When the jet bombers arrived it was time for the Washingtons to return to America.

There was much competition to be a member of a crew taking the Washingtons back to America but an officer pulled rank on Peter and he was left behind. At the time he was furious but the aircraft Peter was to fly on, WF 495, crashed into the Atlantic on 27 January 1954 soon after take off and all seven crew members were killed. The policy for National Servicemen was that in their last couple of months they were taken off flying so Peter worked in the Air Traffic Control tower and was then demobbed in June 1954. Today Peter still considers it to be the most exciting time of his life.

Ted Blackwell was called up in September 1951 and demobbed in September 1953. He flew on Avro Lincoln 2B heavy bombers, during which the majority of his time was spent in the UK during the Cold War period, as well as 'policing' areas of local unrest and uprising in the Mau-Mau offensive. On completion of his *ab initio* Gunners' course at the Central Gunnery School, RAF Leconfield and subsequent crewing up at No. 230 OCU at RAF Scampton he was posted to No. 49 Squadron, Bomber Command, and based at RAF Waddington in Lincolnshire.

Early in 1953, while still at Waddington, somebody saw an advert appealing for a good home for a retired racing greyhound. This person then contacted the owner and said he was the CO of No. 49 Squadron and they would like the dog as the squadron mascot. The owner agreed and the dog was delivered to the CO Squadron Leader Alan Hewitt's house. At first he was at first not overly impressed but agreed to keep the dog. The next day he walked it along to the Squadron Offices and introduced it to everyone and named it 'Skipper' and gave it the honorary rank of sergeant. An officer was appointed as i/c Dog.

At Waddington part of the runway was being extended to accommodate the new jet bombers and No. 49 Squadron were posted to RAF Wittering. The dog travelled in Ted's aircraft, RF 444, flown by Flt Lt Worral and Ted was the rear gunner. It was Ted's job to get 'Skipper' into the Lincoln, which was not an easy task, but Ted managed to sit 'Skipper' on the Elsan (Portable Toilet) and kept a tight grip on the dog's lead. By the time take-off came the dog was demented with fear and so the inevitable happed and humane nature took its toll. Consequently, Ted had to put up the smell for the whole 30 minute flight and with no oxygen available as they flying at low level. When they landed at Wittering and the door opened the ground crew were not at all pleased with what they saw. Ted just ran for the crew bus shouting out for them get the dog out and clean up the mess. Sadly, a few weeks later 'Skipper' was run over by a lorry on the base and killed.

Gerry Beauvoisin was called up in August 1951 and travelled by train from Newcastle to Padgate via Manchester and Waddington. As he stock on Newcastle Central Station he could see many tear stained mothers and youths waiting for the train. But Gerry's mum was made of sterner stuff having had one son who had served in the Royal Navy during WWII. Gerry was one of a large family and he had learnt to fend for himself. From Padgate he was sent to Hornchuch for aircrew aptitude training, leading on to qualifying as an air gunner. Others were accepted for the whole range of crew appointments, pilot, navigator, flight engineer and wireless operator. After returning to Padgate it was on to RAF Driffield which was an aircrew transit camp. Along with eleven others he was sent to West Kirby for square bashing: the universal way of breaking new recruits into service life and discipline. Of the twelve trainees seven were destined to be air gunners, and the other five engineers.

As potential aircrew they were allocated their own table in the mess hall and wore white bands on their epaulets and a white backing to their cap badge. The discipline and sense of being smart and well turned out has never left Gerry and has helped him to get on better with his fellow man. The square bashing lasted from September to November 1951. After passing out they were posted to Leconfield, the Central Gunnery School and arrived on 12 November 1951. On the course they learned about escape and evasion, the Bolton Paul Turret, B17 Electric turret, .5 machine guns, 20mm cannons and aircraft recognition. Some of the pilots they flew with were Poles who were very good pilots but sometimes a little crazy. The Lincolns were thrown about by the Poles as if they were Spitfires.

In January 1952, and the heart of winter, they were sent on an escape and evasion exercise. Before going they were searched to make sure they had no cash and were then dropped in pairs about 10 miles from the camp and told to make their own way back. They had to be back by midnight to be successful. Also they had to report to various check-points en route. But nobody accomplished this without being caught, Gerry and his partner John Jennings got within 200 yards of the crew room when they were bounded upon by two instructors.

After passing out Gerry with two other air gunners went to Bomber Command and the remainder to Coastal Command. One was given a compassionate discharge because his father had died and he was the only bread winner left in the family. Gerry was posted to No. 57 Squadron at RAF Waddington. He joined them on 3 March 1952 and remembers being lucky as 57 were flying Washingtons, which in those days were like air liners: pressurised and warm. His crew were the pilot, Flt Lt Hicknolts, 1 second pilot, 2 navigators, a wireless operator, an engineer and four gunners of which three were National Servicemen. In April 1952 they moved to RAF Coningsby and Gerry remained with them until March 1953. He also went on a conversion course at RAF Marham and here he found that the remote control system needed a near genius to invent it but it was very efficient in as much that at any one time a gunner could control three turrets. The senior gunner or CFC as he was known would allocate turrets as required and was in charge of all the aircraft's defences.

A number of the flights were quite long and flying rations were issued: tinned soup, tinned meat, bread, chocolate, wine guns, chewing gum, and coffee. At the rear of the aircraft there was a water heater and it was one of the gunners tasks to heat the soup and meat when required. This also became an excuse to crawl along the tunnel connecting the two compartments to join the five up front in the sharp end and to look out at the world from a different angle. Gerry would stretch his visit as long as possible. One of their pre-flight tests was to climb out of the dorsal escape hatch, straddling the base of the fin and then walking along the top of the aluminium fuselage slipping down on to the wings, checking the fuel and oil levels in each engine. On a nice day it was a pleasure but on a wet night or frosty day it needed a good sense of balance. Before the flight they had to remove the undercarriage-down locks and the bomb-bay door locks. This was operated by compressed air and really snapped shut so one had to be careful not to be chopped in half when they shut.

The late Air Chief Marshal Sir Augustus (Gus) Walker, then a Group Captain, was the Station Commander and he had lost his right arm when Station Commander at RAF Syerston in 1942. It was quite a sight to see him driving and saluting with only one arm. When 57 Squadron converted to Canberras in 1953 the surplus crews and aircraft were transferred to RAF Marham.

On one occasion in March 1953 and flying over the North Sea towards Europe they lost both port engines within a minute of each other. The aircraft dropped from 3,000 to 1,200 ft in seconds. Somehow the pilot, a F/O Stafford, and his co-pilot were able to keep the aircraft in the air. The rest of the crew expecting a ditching and ready to launch the dinghies as soon as they hit the water. The loss of the engines also meant the loss of some electrical power and Gerry offered to go to the rear and try and start the auxiliary power unit which, after a struggle, he was able to do. This helped to reduce the loss. When they reached the coast and not too far from Marham Stafford decided to go for it and land at base. They were given permission to land straight away and saw ambulances and fire engines tearing down the runway, thankfully they were not needed and a safe landing was made. Without doubt this was a superb bit of flying by the two pilots.

Also in 1953 came Exercise Jungle King. This was the biggest operation mounted by the RAF since the end of WWII, every serviceable aircraft in Bomber Command was used. This exercise was mounted in response to the actions of the Russians in shooting down an unarmed Lincoln on a training exercise. The Lincoln RF 531 C-Charlie flown by Flt Sgt T J Dunnell and his second pilot Sqn Ldr H J Fitz, who had just taken over as the Officer Commanding No. 3 Squadron, was shot down on 12 March 1953 and was from RAF Leconfield. It was shot down by a MiG 15 at Bolzenburg just inside the Russian Zone. It had strayed into the Russian Zone because of navigational error and problems when they were trying to get back into the British flying zone. The MiG opened fire at point-blank range, the starboard wing caught fire and the Lincoln broke-up in mid-air. Three of the crew were able to get out but the parachute of one of them failed to open and the other two, although landing safely, died of their wounds. There was indication that one of the two MiG 15s attacked the parachutists' as they came down. The Lincoln was unarmed. The Russians condescended to apologise and returned the bodies and the wreckage to RAF Celle in Germany. On 17 March Sir Winston Churchill said, "Seven British lives including two air gunners were lost because of a navigational mistake which could have been dealt with by the usual reports and an inquiry".

Much of the flying time in 1953 was in preparation for the Coronation Review of the RAF which took place at RAF Odiham on 15 July 1953. Those in the formation could only see the aircraft around them and not the whole picture.

During his National Service he managed $391^1/_2$ flying hours. He did try to stay on for pilot training but did not have the necessary aptitude so was offered training as a wireless operator but it was pilot or nothing and he came out of the RAF. He sometimes regrets this but then looks at his life since and is satisfied. He still keeps in touch with those days and is a regular attender at the Leconfield reunion.

Frank 'Paddy' Flood was a regular but served at RAF Leconfield during the National Service Air Gunner days. He had joined the RAF in 1944 and he thinks he was one of the last wartime air gunners trained. His training was at No. 2 Air Gunners School at Dalcross now, Inverness Airport, and No. 21 OTU at Moreton-In-Marsh flying on Wellingtons. Finally after training he arrived on No. 35 Squadron in November 1946.

In May 1950 he was posted to Leconfield to help set up and run the Air Gunners course for National Service men, he was there for five years and four months. In 1958 he was offered a Navigators course which he accepted and was successful. Paddy completed a tour with No. 205 Squadron in Singapore and No. 201 at St Mawgan. He finally ended up at the HQ Coastal Command. While at Leconfield he flew over 500 sorties as a an Air Instructor and in the Ground School.

For George Gillard it was the reverse. He flew with Coastal Command in 1952 as a navigator when in 1954 he was nominated to undertake training as an air gunner at RAF Leconfield. He had gone on leave thinking he was to attend the Qualified Bombing Instructors course at the same station. He arrived at Leconfield in November 1954 and found himself on a course with a mixture of AEOs and Air Engineers and one other navigator, Flying Officer Huxley, all from Coastal Command.

He subsequently discovered that the Shackleton had mid-upper turrets and in some cases a nose turret which is why the two navigators came in having been selected as Wing Weapons Leaders on future postings. At the end of the course they were both posted to No. 236 OCU at RAF Kinloss and soon became Chief Weapons Instructors. Soon afterwards the mid-upper turrets were removed leaving the nose turrets for use in Colonial Policing duties in the Middle East. George now lives in Australia.

Dinty Moore became a National Service air gunner in 1950 after he had been scrubbed form a pilots' course. He was posted to RAF Kinloss and became a Radar/Gunner. He then attended the Free Gunnery Instructors Course and became the Assistant Gunnery Leader on No. 120 Squadron. He then remustered to Air Signaller and after completing the course was posted to No. 220 Sqn and took the post of Gunnery Leader and was the gunner when they won the Aird White Trophy. He was some years later posted to No. 269 Squadron at Ballykelly to train the squadron for 'Colonial Policing.' He remained in the RAF for 27 years but his air gunnery days were not over. In 1999 he attended a Gunnery Leaders Course at RAF

Benson as the RAF were still training Air Gunners. He left the RAF having been awarded the Air Force Cross.

Sid Johnston began his National Service air gunner training at Leconfield Central Gunnery School and remained here for three months. His course was the first to fly on Lincoln bombers. The Lincoln was equipped with a Fraser Nash rear turret and two .303 mm guns. His first visit to the turret to fire the guns he remembers was frightening, but looking back funny. He and five other PAGs (Pupil Air Gunner) with an instructor took off in a Lincoln and flew out over the North Sea. Here they took turns in firing into the sea. When his turn came the instructor told him where and when to fire. He was to fire a five second burst and seated in the turret with the doors closed he swung the turret, depressed the guns and on the command fired a burst. As he waited for the command to fire again there was a silence which he thought was odd as all the others had fired at least five bursts. He took it upon himself to fire two further bursts into the sea. Suddenly his head was jerked to his left and he discovered the intercom lead from his helmet was trapped in the breech of the port gun. The intercom lead connection was under the seat between the gunners legs, and the lead which was fairly long had looped around the cartridge belt of the port gun, and when he fired his burst the lead became unplugged from the plug hole and the lead lifted up and fed into the breech of the port gun. Because of this the instructor was unable to speak to him, later the other PAGs told him what happened it appeared that the instructor spoke to him but got no reply but the guns began to fire. The instructor then told the pilot he had a madman in the turret who was firing bullets all over the North Sea and advised him to keep away from fishing boats or yachts in the area. When he swung the turret back to line up with the window in the doors behind he saw a not too happy face looking back and gesturing for him to open the doors. When he did the helmet was pulled off his head, and without ceremony he was pulled out of the turret and sat on the floor next to the other PAGs. The instructor then went into the turret was wrestled with the jammed lead and having released it he threw his helmet and chewed-up lead down. On landing Sid thought he was for the high jump but it appeared that as the instructor had not warned them of this possibility nothing else was said, although the instructor told this story over drinks on a few occasions there after. RAF Leconfield is now the forces driving school.

On completion he was awarded his air gunners brevet and new gunners were normally posted to Bomber Command in Lincolnshire. However, six volunteers were asked to go to Maritime Reconnaissance so five, including Sid Johnston, volunteered. They had been together throughout the course and got on very well. They were sent to RAF St Mawgan for another six months (which was reduced to three) to train on radar and sonic equipment on Lancaster Mk 3s. And then on to Kinloss in Scotland for training on the Avro Mk1 Shackleton. When this was completed he was posted to No. 269 Squadron. The threat to the UK at the time was a large Russian Submarine Fleet, but they were not aware of the danger or threat.

STANDARD EFFICIENCY TESTS

...IT DON'T MEAN A THING IF YOU AIN'T GOT THAT SPRING... NOT TO MENTION THE WHOLE GUN.

Efficiency Test Credit. *Alan Cooper*

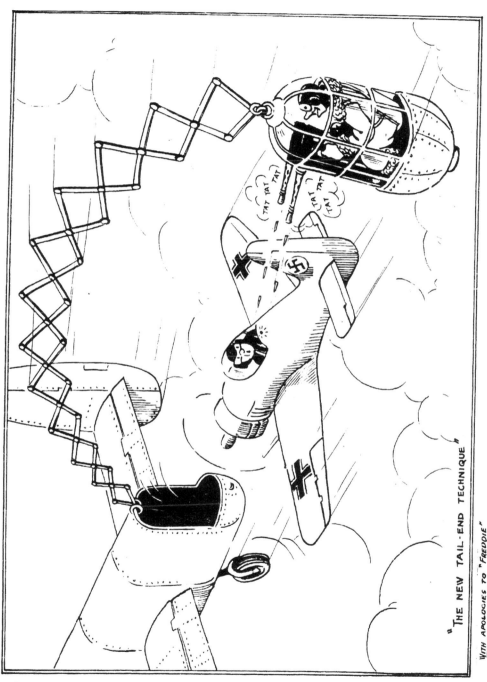

Tail End Technique. *Alan Cooper*

After leaving Leconfield he never flew again as an air gunner but he did keep his hand in firing the .303 guns on the Lancaster, and the 20mm Cannons in the Boulton Paul mid-upper turret on the Shackleton. This turret was removed when the Shackleton Mk II was brought into service. He is now a member of the Shackleton Association that keeps the memory of the 'Old Grey Lady' alive.

'Riv' Rivkins had wanted to fly as aircrew in the Royal Air Force since he was eight. He achieved this twelve years later at RAF Swanton Morley, Norfolk on a winter's morning in 1951. After some years as a Sgt Signaller on Washingtons and B29 bomber squadrons he was posted to Coastal Command and air gunner training followed.

His air gunnery training was undertaken at the Central Gunnery School RAF Leconfield, and then Maritime Operations Training at RAF St Mawgan in Cornwall. The course was No. 87, probably one of the last groups of aircrew to be formally trained as air gunners and to wear the AG brevet. Most of his family were gunners of one sort or another. His father had served as a gunner in the Imperial Russian Army of Tsar Nicolas II during the Russian-Japanese War. In WWI, having come to England in 1905, he served with the Royal Horse Artillery. His eldest brother served in the Maritime Artillery as gun crew on convoys to Russia. Another brother was in the artillery in the Western Desert and later Italy. And not to be outdone his sister served in the ATS as a predictor on anti-aircraft guns during the blitz in WWII.

After training he and Sgt George Heald were posted to No. 210 Squadron at RAF Topcliffe, Yorkshire. He had a slight problem as the RAF had him down as having dual nationality, Russian and British, and in the event of going to war with Russia he was to be given an alternative identity. More than one person on 210 thought he was a Soviet spy.

On arrival at Topcliffe the first person who spoke to them was a flight commander who asked them if they had ideas on the subject of air gunnery. But they replied by saying, "Modesty forbids us to comment adequately, Sir". Upon which they were told to get their flying kit on and get into the Nimrod aircraft as they were taking part in the Aird Whyte Coastal Command gunnery competition air to ground firing sortie. When they pointed out that they had not had any briefing for this aircraft the officer told them no buts just get in and that he would brief them on the way. It took twenty minutes to get to the target area. The target was five canvas rectangles located in line ahead along the length of the beach. They were allowed one dummy run to line up and acclimatise to the area and the on the second run they had to commence firing from the deck turret. On the Nimrod the mid-upper turret was known as the deck turret. This consisted of a Martin twin .50 Colt Browning armed job, fitted with a gyro sight. On the first run George fired, and Riv on the second and final run. It seemed to go well as the flight commander was in good spirits. It turned out they were the top gunners in the competition and they received plenty of back slapping from the No. 210 Squadron crew room.

Air Marshal Tuttle, the AOC asked George how long he had been a crew Sergeant. George came from Manchester so there was no wrapping up things and said, "We only arrived yesterday, Sir, from Kinloss, we have never flown with this crew before". Somebody tried to shut him up including Riv who sensed that this was what the AOC did not want to hear. But, he was in full flow and carried on. In twenty seconds flat and from being the heroes they were now the villains.

During this time one of his best friends whom he had flown with on several Lincoln and Washington crews, F/Sgt Ray Fox, was killed in a Neptune crash with No. 36 Squadron. He had been a second world war air gunner and taken part in many bombing sorties over Europe and Germany as an air gunner on Lancasters. On the morning he was killed his daughter had helped him load his kit on to the aircraft. As he finished he said to his daughter, "Give your Daddy a kiss, and I will be on my way". But being shy she declined. Ray then said "Come and give me a kiss, it will be the last opportunity you will have". With that she burst into tears and ran into the married quarters. Riv then said to Ray, "Why did you say that, you frightened the life out of her?" After a moment's silence Ray said, "I am not coming back from this one Riv, I've had this feeling for some time". He was certainly not his old self. But he was adamant about not coming back. The following morning a message came down that a Neptune had crashed near the Mull of Kintyre, on the Scottish Coast. Somehow Riv knew this was Ray's aircraft and when he cycled past Ray's married quarter and he saw the station commanders car outside his fears were realised. Ray's wife Trixie had met him when he was on a Lancaster crew, she a WAAF on the same station. Most of the crew of the Neptune were buried at Topcliffe but Ray was buried at his home town of Sheffield which was very appropriate as he was a man of steel. No. 36 Squadron organised a bronze plaque to be placed at the site of the crash.

On one occasion, when searching for a missing trawler in the North Sea, Riv was sitting on the newly modified nose section of the Neptune. The Emerson turret had been removed and a complete Perspex observation-type nose section had been fitted in its place. Along with another modified Neptune they carried out the search in foggy conditions so much so that they could not see the other Neptune. One of his friends, Sgt 'Jock' Mackintosh, also a signaller was in the other aircraft. Suddenly Riv saw himself looking directly into 'Jock's' face, he was holding a mug in his hand and had a very startled look on his face. A thought went through Riv's mind, 'What is Jock doing in our crew?' it then dawned that the two aircraft were only feet apart and on a course for collision but somehow the other Neptune just cleared over the top of them.

Most sorties in Coastal Command lasted some 15 hours and on occasions 20. For many years the Lockheed Neptune held the record for the longest non-flight refuelling journey lasting on one internal tankage on a great circle flight from California to Sydney, a journey of $56^{1}/_{2}$ hours non-stop.

The crew of eleven needed at least three meals during the average Costal Command sortie, plus endless cups of tea, coffee and hot soup. In view of

The tail turret of a Washington aircraft. *Jeff Brown*

The view from the mid upper turret of a Washington aircraft. *Jeff Brown*

Washington WF 491in 1951. *Jeff Brown*

Washington in flight 1951. *Jeff Brown*

this the most important item that the ground staff had to load was the ration box, without it on take-off somebody was in for a hard time. On one occasion a rather browned off National Serviceman forgot to load the ration box, he also forgot the parachute of one of the signallers, Sgt Pete Brown. Sgt Brown only discovered this when an engine caught fire and the order to put on parachutes was given by the pilot and to prepare for bale out. Fortunately, the fire was extinguished and they made it back to base on one engine. From that moment on Pete never trusted anyone and made sure that all the safety equipment including parachutes was on the aircraft prior to take off. The cooking was done on an electric oven and two large percolators.

Riv's greatest moment was not in firing his guns in anger but being complimented by the AOC, Air Marshal Tuttle, the same man whom he had met on his first day with No. 210 Sqn when on an anti-submarine recce flight Riv had cooked his bacon sarnies. Mail drops were one way of finding out who your friends were. The mail was for the Ocean weather ships out in the Western Approaches and was delivered by the GPO contained within large rectangular wickerwork baskets fitted with flotation gear. The basket's dimensions were about 5 ft long and about $4^1/_2$ ft in height, and very heavy. The Neptune had a very large hatch located in the floor of the rear fuselage just aft of the deck turret. The man who dropped the mail basket was selected for his ability to fulfil two principal criteria, he had to be small, Riv was, and light in weight causing the least loss to the crew should he follow the mail basket out through the hatch. The drill was to sit with your back against the deck turret structure wearing a parachute harness, and sitting with one's knees bent and both braced against the end of the mail basket, ready to push very hard when given the signal. Two members of the crew grasped our parachute harness by the shoulder straps, and they in turn clung on tightly to opposite sides of the deck turret structure. A third member liaised on the intercom with the pilot who gave the order to drop. The trick was to drop the mail basket as close to the side of the ocean weather ship as possible in order that the ship's crew could and drag it on board with boat hooks and the ships winch. When the hatch was opened an icy blast entered the aircraft and someone always said to the man elected to drop, "Can you lend me a fiver?" and the reply was always, "Afterwards!" With a pat on the head and the order, 'Push Riv' and the pilot put the aircraft into a dive. Riv pushed out the mail and would have slid down towards the open hatch but was held back by two pairs of strong hands. And then the hatch was closed, but not before you saw the weather ship slip away directly below you.

In 1994 Riv had some sad news. His old buddy George Herald had been killed when he was hit by a lorry while riding his moped. On one occasion when the Neptune suffered a complete electrical failure and the pilot, F/Lt Keatley, a WWII Coastal Command pilot, told them he was going to ditch, it was George who did all the organising so that it went very smoothly.

In May 1951, Jeff Brown, who had served in WWII as an air gunner, was now flying with No. 149 Squadron at RAF Coningsby and operating on

A Lancaster crew in 1945. Jeff Brown is second from left. *Jeff Brown*

Jeff Brown. *Jeff Brown*

Washington B-29 bombers. The Americans had loaned the UK seventy of these bombers and they were supplied as part of the Military Defence Aid Programme. They would supplement the ageing Lancaster and Lincoln and fill the gap until the new jet bombers such as the Canberra and Valiant were ready to enter service.

The B-29 was fully pressurised with a large forward compartment in which were the captain, co-pilot, navigator/bombardier, and the wireless operator. In the rear compartment were two waist gunners known as left and right scanners, a top-gunner known as the central fire controller and in a curtained blacked out section the radar navigator and right at the back the good old Elsan toilet. The rear gunner, or tail gunner, was in a

Wellington MF 560 stranded at RAF Digby in a snow storm due to engine failure during January 1945. *Jeff Brown*

separate pressurised section. Any ground crew who were interested could put their names down for a flight and two at a time were taken up. On one particular flight were a very enthusiastic airmen and an older Warrant Officer. The airman wanted to fly up front with the pilot but as the Warrant Officer also wanted to fly up front rank told and the airmen went to the back. The weather was poor and the flight quite a rough one. After a while the flight engineer called up and said one of their passengers was not feeling very well and was coming back to be near the toilet in case he was sick. It was the Warrant Officer who, when he came back, did look at all well, he said he wanted to use the toilet as if there was nothing wrong, not knowing the crew at the back had already been told. The airman was sent up the front and he disappeared down the fuselage like a happy little rabbit. The fuselage was 33 ins in diameter and 33 ft long. Then the gunner sat the Warrant Officer in his rotating seat with his head in a sighting blister which turned out to be the hottest, stuffiest and smelliest position in the aircraft. Then they all lit up cigarettes and blew their smoke up towards him. He was not there long before getting out of his seat making a dash for the Elsan and was violently sick and for the rest of the flight he was on the floor with his head on a parachute pack. For the way he had treated the poor little airman it was a case of, 'Sorry Chum you asked for it'. After his time as an air gunner Jeff remustered and after training in Canada became a pilot. When he left the RAF he became a draughtsman at AVRO HSA and British Aerospace working on armament development for Vulcans, Shackletons, and Nimrods and later Technical Publications until he retired in 1989.

Air Gunners Course in 1951. *Ted Blackwell*

W/C Mo Short and crew including Peter Allen. *Peter Allen*

AIR GUNNERS

On Mother Earth they walked with pride,
Up in the air they fought and died.
They are no more. The Service sees
No further use now for AGs.
Their time is past, their day is o'er,
And we shall see them nevermore;
In modern aircrews there will be
No Tail-End Charlie or Wop/AG
A little box will now compute
How, when and where and what to shoot;
So we invent, advance adjust,
And little boxes will succeed
In firing guns in time of need.
But aircrew they can never be
Like Tail-End Charlie and Wop/AG.
And little boxes cannot breed
The kind of men they supersede;
The men whose place in history
Inviolate will always be.
And when the rolls of fame unfold,
And tales of valour are retold,
Full many a story there will be
Of Tail-End Charlie Wop/AG

Courtesy of Ken Starkie

Air Gunners Course. (Peter Allen)

CHAPTER FOURTEEN

The Celebrity Air Gunners

There were men in WWII who had careers before World War II careers which were far different to being an air gunner. Sportsmen, and actors featured amongst these. William Clark Gable was known as the man who played Brettt Butler in *Gone With The Wind*, and was married to the famous and glamorous actress Carole Lombard. As soon as Japanese aircraft attacked Pearl Harbor in December 1941, bringing the USA into WWII, Gable sent a telegram to President Franklin D. Roosevelt offering his service in the army. The reply was to stay where he was. When Carole was killed in an air crash Gable spoke to Colonel Luke Smith of the Army Air Forces and asked him what was the toughest job in the Air Forces and Smith told him it was recruiting aerial gunners. The MGM press agent begged Army Air Forces boss General Henry H. 'Hap' Arnold to make Gable a Captain but he had no military experience so he could not begin as a captain. Therefore, in 1942 he joined up as a 41 year-old private.

He was sent to Officers Candidate School at Miami Beach and after 13 weeks training became a second lieutenant. He, and his side-kick and cameraman, Andrew McIntyre were then sent for gunnery training at Tyndall Army Air Field in February 1943. On the personal orders of General Arnold he was sent to the UK to shoot *Combat America* a propaganda film about air gunners. He was then assigned to 351st Bomb Group at Polebrook, in the UK, and although neither ordered nor expected to do so, he volunteered to fly combat missions. By the Autumn of 1943 he and his camera crew had exposed 50,000 ft of film. He flew five combat missions, the first to Antwerp when he manned the radio room gun. During the operation the bomber was hit with a 20mm cannon shell, but no one was injured. On an operation to Gelsenkirchen a piece of shrapnel hit his turret 2 ft from his head. His last mission was to Nantes and when his aircraft was attacked by fighters he put down his camera and took over one of the guns. Sergeant Steve Perri remembered Gable as a great friend of the enlisted men, and a great all-around guy. He returned to the USA in October 1943. The film *Combat America* was taken to the US for editing but overshadowed by William Wyler's *Memphis Belle* which was released in 1944.

Because Gable was over age for combat he was released in June 1944 with the rank of Major. His release was signed by Captain Ronald Regan (later The President of the USA). He resigned his commission in September 1947 and died in 1960.

Another actor who was serving as an air gunner was Charles Bronson. He served on B-29s as a rear gunner. John Huston was given a commission in the Signals Corps in 1942 and was given a five-man camera crew. He was sent to Midway and Umnak Island, and then on to Adak. The US Bomber Command was making regular bombing missions and Huston flew with them. He flew in B-24s making combat films.

On one mission his aircraft was attacked by Japanese Zeros and the waist gunner in front of him was killed outright. The belly gunner beckoned Huston to take over his gun and he took over the waist gun. When Huston took charge of the belly gun he opened fire on the Jap planes. Although they were badly shot up Huston and crew made it back to Adak. In his camera crew was a Sergeant who carried the equipment but was not a cameraman but when he pestered Huston to allow him to go on a mission Huston agreed. Unfortunately on that operation two aircraft were lost and ten others badly shot up, including the one the Sergeant was flying. He was able to say he got a good camera shot of a Zero coming directly at them.

Charlton Heston joined the US Army Air Force and trained as a radioman/gunner on B-25s otherwise known as the Mitchell bomber. His service was from Alaska but apart from a few attacks on the islands of Attu and Kiska he saw very little action.

Actor Richard Boone was another who served on torpedo aircraft as a gunner.

Stan Mortensen, who scored three goals in the famous Cup Final in 1953, which became known as the Matthews final, was W/Opt/AG and just before he was to join a squadron he went in a Wellington on a 900 mile flight during which the aircraft crashed into a forest near Lossiemouth, Scotland. The pilot and the bomb aimer were killed and the navigator lost a leg. Stan had twelve stitches in his head but was playing football three weeks later. He played for a number of teams during the war and also a number of wartime internationals including coming on at Wembley as a replacement for Wales as they had no spare players.

George Hardwick was training as an air gunner with Bomber Command when the airfield he was at was attacked by the *Luftwaffe* and he had to be dug out of the shelter he had been in. He was almost asphyxiated and had badly damaged his left leg to the extent that he thought he would probably not play football again, at the time he was on Middlesbrough books. Now being unfit for aircrew duties he was put in charge of an LMF (Lacking Moral Fibre) centre and it was here he got his first taste of

The grave of F/Lt Chalk DFC. *Alan Cooper*

leadership and learnt to revive flagging morale. He said the men here were in an awful state and it was his job to bring them back from the hell they had been through. Eventually his leg healed and he played in wartime cup finals for Chelsea, but no medals were awarded as there was no metal that could be spared to make them. He went on to play again for Middlesbrough and to gain thirty-six caps for England of which thirteen were as captain. In that time they won ten, drew two and lost only one.

Jim Sanders was a professional goalkeeper who, at the end of the war, played for West Bromwich Albion. He served as an air gunner in WWII and completed three tours. On his third tour he received a severe wound after an engagement with an enemy fighter.

Gerry Chalk played cricket for Oxford University and Kent. At the outbreak of war he joined the Honourable Artillery Company (HAC) as a gunner but later transferred to the RAF and became an air gunner and was awarded the DFC. On one operation while over Amsterdam his aircraft was attacked by an Me110, but in the face of cannon and machine-gun fire he fired two bursts which were seen to enter the enemy aircraft and it turned away in flames. He completed twenty operations. Later in the war he retrained as a pilot and began flying operations on Spitfires. On 17 February 1943 he was reported missing flying with 124 Squadron having been shot down near Calais and in January 1944 he was presumed killed.

Pilot/Officer Butterworth was killed on 20 May 1940 serving as a rear gunner on a Lysander of No. 13 Squadron. He was captain of Harrow at cricket and had also made occasional appearances for Middlesex. His aircraft was shot down over France and he is buried at St Martin-Au-Laert.

Flight/Officer Walker RAAF was a close friend of Donald Bradman and was killed flying as an air gunner with No. 50 Squadron over Soltau on 18 December 1942. He has no known grave but is on the Runneymede Memorial.

Reg Taylor joined the RAF at the outbreak of war as an air gunner and was awarded a DFC flying with a Lysander Squadron during the Dunkirk evacuation. He was the first professional cricketer to be awarded the DFC

R.M. Taylor fifth from the left. *Alan Cooper*

in WWII. Before the War he played for Essex and after the war went on to play 300 games for the county.

Douglas Weatherill was not perhaps a celebrity but if he had lived he may well have been. Before the war, being only 5 ft 1in tall he was an apprentice jockey. In 1943 he was awarded the DFC with No. 158 Squadron. His citation said he was an air gunner of high merit and that on more than one occasion, his skilful evading directions and good shooting contributed in a large way to the successful return of his aircraft to base. On 26 June 1944, and now with 35 Pathfinder Squadron, he took off in the rear turret to attack Coubtounne in France in Lancaster ND 734-H flown by S/L Ingram DFC who was the Master Bomber for the operation. Over Dunkirk his aircraft was shot down by a night-fighter at 11,000 ft and crashed. he was killed and is now buried in Coxyde Military Cemetery. He came from South Ascot, Berkshire. S/L Ingram was also killed but the remainder of the crew survived and were taken prisoner.

The Dambuster raid in May 1943 is immortal in the history of WWII and the man who buried Guy Gibson's dog Nigger, just prior the raid on the dams, F/Sgt George 'Chiefy' Powell is also well known for his connection with 617 Squadron and the dams raid but he was an air gunner and wore the brevet of an air gunner in 1940 with No. 500 Squadron, who came under Coastal Command and flew out of RAF Manston. He was a regular airmen prior to WWII and older then than the majority of aircrew at that time. It was for this reason he took on a ground role but was still at that stage wearing his brevet. But when he was posted to X Squadron (later 617 Squadron) in March 1943 as the man designated to put together a new squadron in record time he took down his brevet feeling that if the aircrew coming in from all over the UK to RAF Scampton, found a grounded air gunner in charge he would not get the swift response it was vital he received. It seemed to work as George, along with Sgt Jim Heveron the orderly room sergeant, was able to get 617 settled and airborne in record time. The Dambuster raid followed and the rest is history.

CHAPTER FIFTEEN

The Mighty 8th USAAF

The US 8th Army Air Force were formed on 19 January and activated on 29 January 1942. The US 8th arrived in the UK in 1942 and set off on its first operation on 17 August 1942, the target the marshalling yards at Rouen, France. The idea of combining the 8th and Bomber Command of the RAF was that night and day bombing could be sustained, the 8th in the day and the RAF at night.

The RAF had tried day-time bombing but it was found that the US 8th with its B-17 Flying Fortress and B-24 Liberators were more suitable with their ten .50 calibre machine guns. These were operated by:

bombardier/nose gunner,
Navigator/nose gunner,
Radar operator/gunner,
Flight Engineer/ upper turret gunner,
Ball turret gunner,
Two waist gunners,
Tail gunner.

The composition of the guns on the B-17 was:

Chin Turret with two 0.50 inch guns
Starboard Cheek Gun, one 0.50 inch gun
Port Cheek Gun, one 0.50 inch gun
Upper Turret, two 0.50 inch guns
Lower Ball Turret, two 0.50 inch guns
Starboard Waist Gun, one 0.50 inch gun
Port Waist Gun, one 0.50 inch gun
Radio Compartment Gun, one 0.50 inch gun
Tail Turret, two 0.50 inch gun.

Ten gun positions and 13 guns.

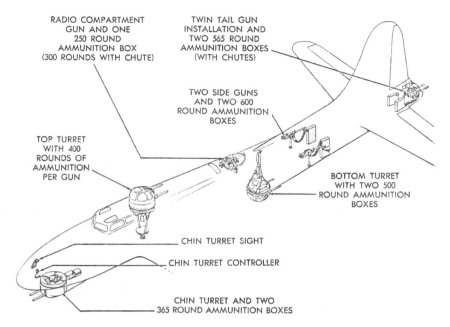

RADIO COMPARTMENT
GUN AND ONE
250 ROUND
AMMUNITION BOX
(300 ROUNDS WITH CHUTE)

TWIN TAIL GUN
INSTALLATION AND
TWO 565 ROUND
AMMUNITION BOXES
(WITH CHUTES)

TWO SIDE GUNS
AND TWO 600
ROUND AMMUNITION
BOXES

TOP TURRET
WITH 400
ROUNDS OF
AMMUNITION
PER GUN

BOTTOM TURRET
WITH TWO 500
ROUND AMMUNITION
BOXES

CHIN TURRET SIGHT

CHIN TURRET CONTROLLER

CHIN TURRET AND TWO
365 ROUND AMMUNITION BOXES

US B-17 bomber layout. *Dick Bowman*

There cannot be a more uncomfortable, claustrophobic and dangerous position than the belly or ball turret position. The whole underside of the aircraft was defended by the ball turret gunner, who, if he was to get in the turret, was to be no more than five foot four in height. The Sperry lower ball operated hydraulically on pressure built up by a constant speed electric motor. It could turn 360 degrees and the guns could be lowered and raised from level 0 degrees and straight down minus 90 degrees. The gunner did not enter the lower ball until in full flight and he exited before landing. It hung down below the aircraft and men had been killed or injured because they did not know the right way to get in, Or were careless. It was a heavy turret and if not in place it could swivel and break a man's leg or snap into him as he attempted to enter. All that was between the gunner and a five mile drop to earth was a canvas safety strap and a glass panel. Also the gunner would pray that his electric suit did not fail as the ball turret would become like an icebox.

Paul Barr, a tail gunner with 436th Bomber Squadron, preferred the gun positions in the B-24 to the B-17, he always felt remote in the B-17 where as in the B-24 the waist gunners were always in view when the turret doors were open and he liked to fly with them open.

The waist gunners in the B-24 could move about and were not cramped like the turret gunners, However the waist gunners had to stand over their gun for hours; there was a very cold breeze and they were thrown around by any sudden changes in flight the pilot made.

Riding tail gunner in the B-24, as in any other bomber, could be rough ride. The whip and acceleration could throw your head onto the gun sight.

Ed Smith of 514th Bomb Squadron said the ball turret was no place for the nervous guy. There were stories of the turret mechanism jamming, the retraction gear failing, being isolated by a fire in the fuselage and the turret dropping off. His greatest fear was not being able to get back up and get his chute on if the plane was going down. When it was lowered over enemy territory it took 10 to 15 mph off the aircraft's speed. Ed prayed the heating did not fail as it would soon become an icebox.

Ted Parker flew with 855th Bomb Squadron as a flight engineer and top-turret gunner. As the 855th did not use a ball turret the gunners were rearranged and he flew top turret with another engineer free to look after the engines and generators. His head was low in the turret which he climbed into once over the sea to test the guns So he did not have much of a view below the horizontal and parts of the turret mechanism blocked his view at that level on both sides. From the point of view of comfort for the gunner it was the best defence position on the B-24.

The gunners whom were not assigned to a crew went into the 8th Air Force Gunner's Pool. Sgt Irving Hirsch upon arriving at 729th Bombardment Squadron(H) of the 452nd Bombardment Group was removed as the 10th man in the crew to create a nine man crew. Sgt Hirsch later went to the 15th Air Force in Italy and flew combat missions as a Belly Turret Gunner. The reason for this was that in June of 1944, the 8th and other commands were short of gunners and found that the inside formation waist gunner, in a 10 man crew, tended to shoot at German fighters when they flew through the formation and often hit other bombers in the formation.

In Lt Gott's crew was a tail gunner, Staff Sgt Herman B. Krimminger. When over Saarbrucken in November 1944 the aircraft was shot at and damaged. Gott and his co-pilot, Lt William Metzger, flew decided to crash land in occupied territory but ordered the crew to bale out. However, Krimminger's parachute opened accidentally and he was pulled out of the arms of the Waist Gunner and Belly Turret Gunner after his parachute had gone out of the escape door and over the tail of the aircraft. He was pulled out of the door and ended up pressed up against the underneath of the tailplane. As the crew baled out they saw him there knowing he was doomed. Both the pilots were awarded the Congressional Medal of Honor. In 2000 the remains of the aircraft were found in France and a Memorial was been dedicated to the crew's memory.

About 297,000 air gunners were trained in the Army Air Force after Pearl Harbor was attacked on 7 December 1941. They served in every theatre of war and were being trained at the rate of 3,200 per week. In WWII 12,700 B-17s were built by Boeing, Douglas and Lockheed-Vega. The first was built in October 1939 and the last in July 1945. Over 30,000 airmen were killed and another 30,000 made prisoners of war. Their casualties exceeded the combined losses of the US Marine Corps and US Navy. The area that the 8th operated from during WWII was East Anglia which became known to the aircrew of the 8th as an 'unsinkable aircraft carrier' having 130 US bases and 75 airfields.

The aircrew ages were much the same as the RAF with the average age being 20, and some men only being 18 and in one case, Sgt De Sales Glover was grounded after he had flown six missions when it was suspected that was only 16 but it later transpired he was 14! The number of operations required to fly was twenty-five, which later went up to thirty and then thirty-five. It is reported that in some cases men completed 100 operations. Anybody who survived became a member of the 'Lucky Bastards Club.'

The fear of to flying on operations was as prevalent as in the RAF with men starting to get petrified as soon as they arrived in the briefing room but when they settled into the aircraft they were okay and did their job as well as anyone.

The ground crew worked the same way as the RAF with a team of men assigned to each bomber as they awaited their charge to return and saw a coloured flare fired from the bomber it meant that wounded were aboard, one gunner who had been wounded was too weak even to be given a blood transfusion in the aircraft. Tails shot away, dead engines and out of thirty-six men in three aircraft twenty-nine were killed. One coming aircraft landed with its nose and bombardier section blown away, and with no brakes or flaps. They took off at 30 second intervals in bad weather, in darkness and with radio silence. Near misses were very common and part of the day's work. When the guns of the jammed, air gunners, forgetting how cold it was, would pull off their gloves and their hands would freeze to the bare metal of the guns. One gunner, Robert Sweatt could only watch the Ju88s fire their 200mm cannons into his plane as he tried to unjam his guns. It would fire two short bursts and then jam, luckily a P-38 Lightning fighter came out of nowhere and knocked the German fighter out of the sky. He took part in seventeen operations over Europe with the 389th Bomb Group and took part in the raid on Ploesti oil fields in Romania, a mission on which the Americans lost fifty-four planes and 532 men out of 177 planes and 1,726 men who took off. On one occasion his aircraft crash landed in a sugar beet field after two engines had cut and another time when his aircraft was shot down he was the only survivor.

Murray 'Big Shorty' Codman was an engineer/top-turret gunner on a B-17. 'Big Shorty's first mission was to Berlin on 19 May 1944 and his 35th and last to Belfort, France on 8 November 1944. Thirty- five missions in 84 days. He was awarded the US DFC, five air medals and a Presidential Citation and credited with two kills and one damaged. The US DFC was awarded to any person who, while serving in any capacity with the United States, distinguished himself by heroism or extraordinary achievement while participating in flight. This had to be a voluntary action above and beyond the call of duty. It was established in 1917 and initial awards were to people who had made record breaking and endurance flights and set altitude records. Captain Lindbergh was the first man to received the DFC in 1927, and later for their previous efforts the Wright Brothers.

Staff Sergeant Richard E. Bowman flew as a Ball-Turret Gunner with the 96th Bomb Group 339th Squadron of the 8th. They were based at Smetterton Heath Air Base Station 29, near Cambridge. They had been stood down since 10 November 1944 after an operation to Weisbaden. A number of the crews had flown twenty-five missions and a few were near that magic thirty-five and a ticket home. They were to have the second highest losses in the 8th losing 190 aircraft between May 1943 and May 1945.

The targets in November were concerned with crude oil for the Me262 twin-engine jet fighter. The plant at Merseburg was the one supplying those needs. Because of this a large number of anti-aircraft batteries surrounded the plant. It was a long way into Germany and not far from Leipzig. The fighter escort had to drop their auxiliary tanks which shortened their range. When confronted the German fighters turned away but returned when fighters had to leave the bombers and return to the UK. The tactics used by the fighters at this time was 'fighter fronts', a head-on attack by several fighters firing cannons in an attempt to hit the crew members and disrupt the formation. The 262 and Me163 were also being used and the 163 was seen climbing vertically into the bomber formation from the ground. It would fly through the formation firing cannons, then

Crew of *Bachelors Lair. Dick Bowman*

Reconnaissance photo on route to target. *Dick Bowman*

after the rocket fuel was exhausted, roll on to its back and dive back through the formation firing its cannons on the way down.

Richard had flown thirty-four missions in 'Batchelor's Lair' and with one to go was having problems sleeping. Would they make it, would his luck run out? Dick was the only crew member on his last mission. He was

Test fire on the ground. *Dick Bowman*

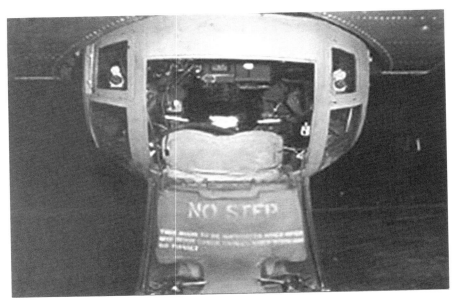

The office. *Dick Bowman*

two missions ahead of the rest of the crew having been ordered to fly two extra missions with other aircraft needing a ball-turret gunner, they were now flying their thirty-third mission.

On 25 November, and with an operation pending, Dick went to his aircraft in order to clean the twin .5 calibre machine-guns in the chin turret for First Lieutenant Reed, the bombardier who would fire the guns when not dropping the bombs. The cleaning took about 3–4 hours because Dick was very thorough; the guns must operate perfectly. He then had a slice of toast and a cup of coffee, and went to the station chapel with the rest of his crew. The briefing was set for 0530 hours and the target was Merseburg. They knew what to expect as the German Air Force had been pulled back to protect Merseburg.

Dick was 5 ft 4 ins tall which was a help as he crawled into his rather small turret. He was not able to take his chest parachute or flak jacket, they were wrapped up and put on a ledge inside the aircraft near the turret opening and easy to grab if required. In his turret he was isolated form the rest of the crew except for his intercom. He could move the turret and see from horizon to horizon and the entire earth below. The engines were loud but with his earphones on the noise was reduced.

Near the target Dick heard the first shells exploding with a sound like a big dog barking 'Wuff', 'Wuff'. Dick was sitting on a steel plate which gave him some protection from below but behind him was a piece of aluminium which was of no use at all. The glass in front was 2 to 3 ins thick but also not much use against cannon shells or flak. In October, on a mission to Berlin, a piece of shrapnel had gone through the glass like a knife through butter. It hit Dick's parachute harness buckle and knocked him out cold. The radioman Bruce Bjornstad saw that he was unconsciousness and his oxygen mask away from his face. He was unconscious for about 2 or 3 minutes and except for a painful chest he was unhurt. A few hours later he had a bruise the size of a basketball and the pain much worse. The doctor checked him out but because the skin was not broken and there was no bleeding he was not awarded the Purple Heart.

He been trained at a Gunnery and Radio School and later he was trained for ball turret gunnery. At gunnery school, Tyndake Army Air Force Base in Florida, he met Clark Gable and found him not only to be a good gunner but also a decent crew member with no airs or graces. Late in 1943 Dick was assigned to a brand new B-17 and they were to ferry it to the UK from Nebraska heading to Gander, Newfoundland and then to the UK.

They arrived in the UK on 5 June 1944. His first mission was on 24 June 1944 and the target was Bremen. Then followed another thirty-three missions and then the last to Merseberg.

An hour before the target was reached they were attacked by Me109 and Fw190 fighters. They came from all directions but were held off by the fighter escort and the guns of the bombers. Soon the German fighters broke off and the escort fighters were having to turn back because of fuel shortage. The German fighters then returned and started to engage the bombers but the group carried on to the bombing run when the fighters again broke away in order to avoid being shot out of the air by their own flak. The flak was heavy and many B-17s were hit and set on fire, one taking a direct hit and blowing up; one minute it was there and gone the next.

Dick's aircraft dropped its bombs and as it turned for home, with the bomb doors still open, a flak shell exploded directly under the B-17 and in front of Dick's turret taking out the No. 2 Engine, the left landing gear and shredding the bomb doors. The propeller hub on engine No. 4 was shattered and the engine died. Although riddled with holes the aircraft somehow was still flying. Dick was taken out of the turret covered in a black substance that resembled soot. It had come from the burst of flak and got into the turret through gun openings. The turret was damaged but Dick, remarkably, was unhurt. The rest of the Group left Dick's aircraft to its own fate.

The co-pilot, First Lieutenant Neal Keyes trimmed the aircraft and then descended to 15,000 ft to enable the crew to come off oxygen. They had several hours flying ahead and had lost some fuel from the damage. Everything that could be was thrown out to lighten the load including guns, ammunition and flak jackets. They flew on two engines and never saw another aircraft, friend or foe, a defenceless aircraft on two engines and flying over enemy territory for many hours. But lady luck was with them and they were not attacked. The pilot, Captain Weaver, gave them the chance to bale out over France or stay with the aircraft but with 50 miles to reach their base they decided to stay with it. But having crossed the coast over Dover and just before Weaver set a course for home the remaining two engines cut. The crew got into the crash positions against the bulkhead sitting between each other's legs facing backwards with Dick in the front. The B-17 was set down on a mud flat which unfortunately had boulders in it and the aircraft hit them and the chin turret and part of the nose were torn off. As they went along they hit another boulder, this pushed the ball turret up with such force as to break the aircraft's back and open it just beyond where Dick and the crew were sitting. When it finally came to rest the tail gunner S/Sgt Troy Thrash and waist gunner S/Sgt Mike Chavez were looking at them from the separate rear section of the broken plane. But somehow they all survived unharmed; their faithful aircraft had protected them to the last. When Dick jumped out he landed in two feet of mud, and did not kiss the ground. But he did look up and thank God.

In just five months, from 24 June to 25 November 1944, and just over 252 combat flying hours, Dick, a young man of 20, went from High School to completing thirty-five missions with the 8th USAAF. Today Dick is in his 80s and is glad to have served his country and insists that a great deal of the courage and strength to fight the war came from the British. Despite facing raids from German bombers day and night for months their spirit was never broken.

In December 1944 Dick was on board SS *Brazil*, a coastal steamer in convoy with many others ships on their way back to the USA. It was carrying a large number of wounded and liberated prisoners of war from camps all over Europe, most of them airmen shot down on bombing and other raids. They were rescued at Bastogne by General Patton's 3rd Army but having been on the march for some time and being short of food they were in poor condition. To those men the march was like the 'Bataan March' but in Europe. On the voyage back home they ran into a storm in which the steamer rolled a lot and many of the GIs were seasick. The conditions on board with cramped space and foul smells was terrible but they were on their way home. When they arrived they were refused access to a train, which was supposed to take them to a camp in New Jersey, because the men were infested with lice. They were instead taken in trucks and on arrival deloused. The ironic thing was that at the camp the food was being served by German PoWs. This was not thought to be appropriate so the Germans were removed and the returning GIs were then served by other GIs.

At Tyndale Air Base Dick was assigned as a gunnery leader where the students listened to Dick, a man who had been in combat and had shot down an Fw190 at Merseberg. Dick explained how the fighter had approached from the rear and low. In this position the fighter's speed was slower and when he was within 800 yards range Dick opened up and fired a burst. The fighter continued to fly straight at him and fired his guns but missed. As theFw190 came nearer Dick's next burst was more accurate and

Dick Bowman in 2004. *Dick Bowman*

he struck the enemy fighter in the nose. Pieces of the Fw190's engine flew off and it began to smoke. It rolled over on its back but the pilot was not seen to roll out as expected.

On 12 July 1943, Sgt Maynard H. Smith was presented with the Medal of Honor, America's highest award. On 1 May 1943, his first operation with 423rd Bombardment Squadron of the 306th Bomber Group the target was St Nazaire, France. He was flying in one of thirty-six B-17s. Just before reaching the target they were hit by Fw190s and flak. The fighters had probably shot down eight or nine bombers in the first attack. A flak hit on the wing cut the wing tank off and petrol poured into the aircraft and caught fire. Sgt Smith was in the ball turret and lost his electrical controls. He manually cranked the turret around, opened the armoured hatch and got back into the fuselage. The radioman jumped out of the window without a parachute. outside it was –50° F. After dropping their bomb load the pilot took the aircraft down fast. When they got down to 2,000 ft one of the gunners got excited and tried to bale out but got caught on a .50 calibre gun. He finally managed to jump but struck the stabilizer and he must have broken it into a dozen pieces. All the radio equipment was on fire, and wires were burning everywhere. However, Sgt smith managed to put out the fires with extinguishers and water bottles. All the while they were being fired upon and while he was not trying top put out the fires he was manning the waist guns. Eventually the enemy fighters ran out of fuel and left. out of the original thirty-six B-17s they were left with just four. The tail gunner had been hit and crawled out of his rear

Dick Bowman's B-17. *Dick Bowman*

turret with blood coming out of his mouth. He had been shot on the left side of his back. Sgt Smith made him comfortable and to relieve the pain gave him two shots of morphine and he went to sleep. Thankfully, he survived.

Both pilots has also been hit and needed first aid which Sgt Smith gave them. He then went back and repaired some of the control cable wires and proceeded to throw out all the remaining ammunition to lighten the aircraft. He had wrapped his hands and face with his scarf to save him from being burned. When they got back the plane had 3,500 bullet holes and the centre was burnt out, all that was left were the four main beams. Only 10 minutes after they landed the aircraft collapsed on the runway. The strange thing was that after a further four missions he was taken off flying with operational exhaustion and reduced to the rank of private.

Maynard Smith died in 1984 and is now buried in Arlington National Cemetery, Washington as is the right of all holders of the Medal of Honor.

In December 1943 22 year old Sgt George Buske was based at Molesworth with the 303rd Bomb Group, he was a tail gunner on B-17s and came from Rochester, New York. Five months earlier he had been wounded in his left hip by a 20mm exploding shell. For this he was awarded the Purple Heart, another Oak Leaf Cluster to his Air Medal and the Silver Star for conspicuous bravery. After 45 days in hospital he returned to duty.

The mission on 20 December 1943 was a return to Bremen which they had already visited twice that week. On previous visits the flak had been moderate and they only encountered a few fighters. Just after dawn they took off in B-17 'Jersey Bounce' flown by Captain Merrle R. Hungerford who came from El Passo, Texas. When they got near Bremen the flak was much heavier than previous and a shell burst knocked out the No. 1 Engine and just after "Bombs Away" came from the bombardier another shell knocked out No. 4 Engine and its propeller was windmilling out of control. With only two engines they then dropped out of the formation.

The fighters were lining up to pick off this easy target but with the .50 calibre guns they were able to knock out four of the fighters. The struggle continued out over the North Sea and the fighters continued to attack the stricken B-17. One after another the crew were hit and Sgt Buske took a bullet through his lower abdomen and then a 20mm shell exploded in front of him blowing his chest and abdomen open, the force propelled him backwards from his tail gunner's seat and into the fuselage. Sgt Vosler, although wounded, took over the tail gun but was soon struck in the chest, face, and both eyes, but even though he could only see vague shapes, he, along with the other gunners, kept firing until the fighters broke off and turned back to Germany. Within sight of the East Anglian coast the B-17 crashed into the sea and Sgt Volser got out on to the wing. The others dragged out the unconscious Buske. They were seen crashing by a Norwegian coaster which transferred them to a fast RAF Air Sea Rescue boat and within an hour they were in Great Yarmouth harbour.

One of Sgt Vosler's eyes had to be removed and in the other he only had partial sight. At Great Yarmouth Hospital Sgt Buske underwent surgery and had several blood transfusions. He had a large hole in his chest in which his right lung was exposed and another gaping wound in his upper abdomen. He had shell fragments in his right thigh, abdominal wall and both lungs, one or two fragments were close to his heart. A machine-gun bullet was lodged deep in the muscles of his back.

When transferred to a US Hospital at Botesdale in Suffolk his wounds were found to be infected and had to be drained. For a month he was unable to take anything by mouth. Many complications followed and his weight fell to 88lb. But finally he began to recover but skin grafts to the wounds on his thigh followed. In June 1944 he was evacuated back to the USA for further treatment. Four months of convalescence and rehabilitation followed. Amazing as it may sound, after three weeks leave he was returned to active duty and was not discharged until September 1945. In 1952 George W. Buske had to have the shell fragments and machine gun bullet removed after developing abdominal pain and a fever. In 1988 he underwent a coronary artery bypass and after the operation the surgeon presented him with an encrusted shell fragment that had been found near his heart. T/Sgt Forest L. Vosler was awarded the Medal of Honor which President Franklin D. Roosevelt presented him with at the White House, he was only one of three enlisted men of the 8th during WWII to receive this award. He died in 1992 aged 69 of a heart attack.

The 3 October 1943 is one day that Sgt Bernard Resnicoff will never forget, although perhaps he would like to if he could. His Squadron, No. 422, had already undertaken a few night operations and 3 October was to be another. They normally flew operations in the day and let the RAF take on the night-time skies. Their own ship was called 'Sam's Little Helper' but as it did not have 'Tokyo Tanks' they were assigned aircraft No. 091. The regular bombardier was on a leave pass, but, although he was recalled for this mission he did not arrive in time and they were assigned Lt Pierce. The regular ball turret gunner, Staff Sergeant Abbott had a cold and was replaced by Staff/Sergeant McCoy. Bernard could also have cried off as he had a stiff back contracted on the raid to Munich the day before. He had already missed several raids having been hospitalised with swollen eyes so he did not want to miss this one. The whole crew were due a 48 hour pass after this operation. The bombardier, Lt Harkavy, did finally arrive but was told he was too late and Lt Pearce would remain in the crew.

The target was Frankfurt and the two B-17s, including Bernard's, were operating with a force of over 200 RAF Lancasters. The B-17s were briefed by an RAF Officer as to the altitude they were to fly and at what times the RAF Lancasters would strike. They would fly above them and bomb on the RAF's flares, their bomb load was six 500lb HE bombs and also a quarter of a million propaganda pamphlets. The coldest part of the B-17 was the waist windows: a pair of long johns, a heat suit and overalls were all worn, not to mention scarf, gloves, helmet, shoes and last, but not least, oxygen mask. They had red lensed goggles for use against searchlight glare, but never wore them because they were impractical. Take-off was 8pm.

Lt Seay, the pilot, decided at the last minute that he needed to relieve himself and went to an outhouse 50 yards away. While he was away the CO of 422 Squadron, Major Price, came out and wanted to know why the engines had not been started and during the furore that followed Seay returned and was told that he could be court martialled but was told to get in his ship and the CO would see him on his return. Considering what was to unravel in the near future Bernard wished this had come true.

Things went from bad to worse when No. 2 engine cut and stopped. After three failed attempts to start the engine they all got out and moved to the standby ship No. 056. Ten men with flying kit on one jeep was a sight to see. On arrival and after checking his kit Bernard realised he had left his oxygen mask behind and went back for it. When he arrived back he found the guns on 056 had not been cleaned, they were soon disassembled and under the headlights of a jeep they proceeded to clean them. Bernard was keen to clean and assemble his own guns having seen what happens when you let someone else do it for you. The guns were cleaned, dried and reassembled. Their problems continued as there were problems with No. 1 engine on 056 so, the problem on 091 having been fixed, they piled into a jeep and back to the original ship. Finally they took off but at least half an hour late.

Bernard and Williams, the left-waist gunner changed the guns twice, and put a round in the chamber. This had a two-fold purpose, first, to be ready for immediate use; second, to prevent the cold air from passing into the case, and freezing the firing pin. To the left were searchlights probing the sky, somewhere there was London but because of the blackout they could not see the capital. They flew over the Channel at 10,000 ft and then entered enemy territory when the gunners stood and prepared to fight. They flew over France, Belgium, Luxembourg and then into Germany.

Over the target the bombs were dropped but one box of pamphlets did not go so it meant going into the bomb bay to release them manually. The searchlights were so bright they could have read a book with fine print. When Bernard looked at Williams he was standing there with this hands above his head hanging on to the roof of the ship and the guns swinging loose. He appeared to be dazed from the evasion tactics and would not let go. At 6 o'clock came the fighters and the ball-turret gun opened up but then the top-turret gunner told the pilot there was a small flame between Nos 3 and 4 engines. The pilot went into a dive and this soon put out the fire.

An Me109 opened fire at them and they were hit and set alight beneath the cockpit where the oxygen bottles were stored and one of the crew began to tackle the fire with an extinguisher. In another attack the whole fuselage from the rear part of the radio room to the tail was raked by 20mm guns. Bernard felt a twinge on his right arm but no pain. However, when he looked at Williams he saw a large red patch of blood was forming across the stomach of his overalls. When he did not fall down Bernard thought he had just been scratched. But when he fell against him and then sagged to the floor Bernard knew it was serious and tried to pull him up but as he did the whole ship started to flounder in the air. The wing of the ship was on fire and the ball-turret gunner was asked if he wanted the bomb doors open and he replied that it was the only way he could get out. For Bernard it was now a question of looking for parachutes, both his and William's, but in the confusion it was not easy. Finally Bernard did find his parachute and he opened the escape door and dived out and he was relieved to see the parachute open. However, his left foot felt cold and when he glanced down he saw that it was bare except for a stocking. Over to his right Frankfurt was on fire and bombs were dropping and exploding and the flak guns firing. His right arm felt cold and the sleeve was saturated with a dark liquid which he knew was blood. But as he could flex his fingers it knew it was just a flesh wound and looked worse than it was. The oscillating parachute made him feel sick and he landed in a field of cabbages and when he pulled in his parachute cabbages came with it. He put the flying boot on his left foot and had an inner shoe on the right foot and a boot on his left.

His back was now hurting quite badly and pains were shooting through his back and sides. Bernard decided that the first person he encountered he would surrender to but when he did confront a man he turned out to be a Polish prisoner. The Polish man took Bernard to a long barn and the first thing Bernard saw was an American 1935 Ford V-8 van. It turned out the area was a country estate and he was taken to the front door where a German woman appeared and he was taken inside, sat in a chair and the sleeve of his overalls rolled up, The heat suit was unzipped and rolled up to expose the forearm. It was, as he thought, just a flesh wound but it looked raw and ugly. In the house was large glass case with rifles and shotgun shells. On top of the glass case was a life sized bust of Hitler in shiny black marble. On the opposite side of the room was a painting of *Washington Crossing the Delaware*, someone must like or admire Americans to have this in their home.

A German came in with a first-aid kit, he was dressed like a sportsman with boots and a slouch hat. The man dressed his arm and then searched him for any weapons. He then asked, "English?" Bernard replied, "No, American". Bernard was asked if he was hungry and he replied no, but a bit thirsty. He was brought a glass of water and later two apples. They went outside and spoke about the American Ford van. Bernard was then told to get in and they drove off. After a little while they saw a parachute in a field but there was no one with it. In a small town a crowd of people was gathered and Bernard was shown an RAF Sergeant lying on his stomach with a parachute under him; standing over him was a big, burly, dumb soldier dressed in the blue of the *Luftwaffe*. When Bernard asked the Sergeant, a Sergeant Smith, how he was the sergeant said he had piece of flak in his ass but as he had been out all night he was frozen. The crowd was very hostile but one old man put his arms around Bernard's shoulders and said what Bernard thought was, "Don't worry, you will be okay".

They were taken away by lorry and when they arrived at a village Sgt Smith was found to have a flesh wound and he asked to see a doctor as his arms and legs were hurting. Again they were taken by lorry, Bernard's back was still hurting terribly but it was nothing compared to the pain Smith was feeling . They finally arrived at a hospital and Smith's clothes were taken off him by hospital staff and Bernard was also told to take off his clothes and he was put to bed. Their wounds were treated and then they were taken by ambulance to *Dulag Luft* where he was marched into a room in which were RAF and US Airmen. One of the men, a Captain Rodgers had been shot down a couple of days before on the Munich raid. He soon met two of his crew, including the pilot Lt Seay, the Major would not be seeing him until after the war. Sadly, four of the crew did not get out and were found in the crashed B-17. From here Bernard was taken to *Stalag* 17B; the Americans had five compounds in this camp.

The treatment at this camp was, at times, brutal. When two men escaped and were caught they were brought back and shot with their hands above their heads. One died immediately but the other was shot in the leg. After he fell the guard ran to within 20 ft of him and fired again. The guards then started to fire at random towards the barrack blocks. One bullet wounded an American who was lying in his bunk. Treatment for the injured man was delayed for several hours. Another man who was mentally ill and dressed in hospital pyjamas was shot in the heart when he tried to climb the camp fence. Red Cross parcels were often stolen and those that did arrive had been opened. On 8 April 1945, 4,000 prisoners from *Stalag* 17B began an 18 day march of 291 miles to Austria. They slept in open fields, or, if they were lucky(on three occasions), cow barns. They finally arrived at a PoW camp for Russians 4 kilometres from Brauna, in Austria. This camp was liberated on 3 May 1945 by men of the 13th Armoured Division and they were evacuated back to France on 9 May 1945 and a few days later they were repatriated to the USA.

Merrle Sieling flew forty operations(408 hours and 10 minutes) and was awarded the Air Medal three times, the European Theater ribbon with four battle stars for the PO Valley, Rhineland, North Apennines and Air Combat over the Balkans with the 97th Bomb Group, 340th Bomber Squadron flying missions from Foggia, Italy. He had enlisted in the Army Engineer Corps and when in hospital with the flu found he had been transferred to the Army Air Corps as a First Sergeant.

His first mission was on 14 October 1944 to Blechammer, Germany, and his last mission was on 19 April 1945 when his aircraft bombed the Railway Bridge at Rattenburg, Austria. Two further missions to Vienna in May were scrubbed just before take-off. On 5 November 1944 he was asked to fly with a Lieutenant Emerson to test a brand new aircraft and after $1^1/_2$ hours of flying the test was completed successfully; the aircraft handled well and Merrle found the weapons on board to be working well.

On the 6th he was detailed with the same pilot to attack a target in Vienna, Austria. If this was clouded over they were to proceed to another target, Maribor, Yugoslavia. Over the target flak was light to moderate. In the briefing they were told there were about sixteen guns but it was possible the Germans could have 88mm guns on railway cars. These guns could read their altitude whereas the static guns could not.

The 6th started at 0300 hours when they were awoken for breakfast and a briefing. When the curtain covering the target was pulled back a groan went up from the crews, Vienna was heavily defended. Later over the target they found there were many more 88mm guns than had been thought. They were taken out to their respective aircraft and started to prepare for the flight: guns had to be checked and after that they all went to the front of the aircraft to start pushing the props through several rotations to draw fuel into the carburettors. As they did Merrle approached the new co-pilot, Second Lieutenant Ernest N. Vienneau who was flying with them for the first time. He had a picture he had just received, a picture of his first baby that he had received day before and wanted Merrle to see it. It was dark so Merrle had to put on his torch to show it to him. The order then came from Lt Emerson, the pilot, to board the aircraft. They climbed aboard and the crew chief in the front of the aircraft gave the 'all clear' call to Emerson who then engaged the ignition and the propellers began to turn, the engines caught and the exhaust belched a large cloud of blue smoke. Finally all four engines were up and running and they waited for the green flare to go, or a red flare, which meant shut down, and scrub the operation. But on this occasion it was a green flare which meant the mission was on and they were going. The first aircraft took off and every thirty seconds an aircraft took to the air. Each pilot had his hands full because often the turbulence from the preceding aircraft would throw them all over the sky.

They soon reached 10,000 ft and Emerson told them to use oxygen and they gradually climbed to the bombing altitude of 32,000 ft. The fighter escort was provided by P-51s and flown by the black Tuskegee pilots, who were known for being excellent pilots. When they arrived at Vienna it was completely under cloud so they set off for the alternative target which sat high up on the Alps on the border between Austria and Yugoslavia. The target area was coming up and the bombardier started to adjust the bombsight. Just as the words "Bombs Gone" came from the bombardier a shell burst underneath them and severed the hydraulic line to the controls of the bomb-bay doors. Then once again another burst below the No. 3 engine, setting it on fire. The fuselage filled with smoke and flames were streaking past the gun position and the tail of the plane. The fire was extinguished by Emerson. At this time Merrle was standing on top of his flak vest and against the armour plate beneath his .50 machine gun and watching chunks of steel flak, some the size of your fist, going through the aircraft. It soon looked like a sieve with other pieces hitting the plane and sounding like hail on a tin roof. He then became aware that he did not have his steel helmet on and called to Vernon Rhoda, the left-waist gunner to throw it over to him but as he did a piece of flak hit the helmet tossing it into the air. He grabbed it out of the air and had he not made this movement he would have been hit by a piece of flak that came up through the bottom and went out through the top of the aircraft. Another shell exploded below the No. 2 engine severing the oil line, which looked like an oil gusher spewing out of the engine. Again Emerson stopped the engine and tried to feather the propeller. The rest of the group were now pulling away from their aircraft fearing that the aircraft would blow up and take them with it. The right wheel had also dropped down and was increasing the wind drag on the plane. With the flight engineer, John Young, Merrle tried to wind it back into its position. Merrle and John went into the bomb bay, straddled the catwalk close to the pilot's door and together they tried to crank up to the offending wheel, but it would not budge. Having failed they then went back to their respective positions, John to the top turret and Merrle to the right-waist gun.

Then Emerson called Merrle on the intercom and asked him to come up to the cockpit with a battle dressing for the co-pilot. Merle grabbed a box of battle dressings and a canister of oxygen but he could not get through the bomb bay area so he went back to the radio room and took a big gulp of oxygen and put the canister down. He knew from his training that he could last close to 5 minutes before having breathing trouble. As he looked down at the snow covered Alps passing beneath the plane he thought, 'if you lose your footing and fall no one will ever find you'. Lt Emerson asked him to get Vinneau, the co-pilot, out of his seat, he was unconscious and his feet jammed under the rudder bars. With the help of Young they took him out and laid him down on the flight deck. Merrle took Vinneau's blood clotted oxygen-mask and replaced it with his own. A piece of shrapnel, 1 inch in diameter had entered his forehead above the left eye and come out above his left ear, leaving a huge hole in his skull. As Merrle tried to attend to him the navigator, Lt MacFarland, pulled his head back and put on his mask to enable him to breath. Emerson asked MacFarland for a course to Switzerland but he was told they would not make Switzerland because of the rapid loss of altitude. He then requested a heading for the Secret airstrip on the Isle of Vis, off the coast of Yugoslavia. All the guns, ammo, flak vests etc were thrown out to lighten the aircraft. All the time that they were doing this Merrle was attending to the wounded co-pilot but could hear clearly all the instructions being given and he put this down to the fact that the two inboard engines were silent.

Emerson then asked the crew if they should bale out or stay with the aircraft. With the co-pilot being wounded they decided they had no option but to stay with the aircraft. Suddenly, in a gap in the clouds they saw the Isle of Vis but as they lined up to land No. 4 engine failed, out of fuel. Then up came a red flare and the nose was pulled up sharply and the order came to prepare to ditch. Back on the cat walk all Merrle could hear was the wind coming through the bomb bay. As he was going to his ditching position his parachute harness snapped into the bomb wires, holding him captive to the bomb racks. He hit the release button, jumped out of the harness, and had just opened the door to the radio room when they hit the water. The wall of water kept him in the radio room and slammed him up against the wall. He got to his feet and removed the escape hatch to climb out of the plane. As he did so he felt someone pulling on his feet and legs and he fell to the floor. It was John Young who said, "Let me get out here". At this Merrle started to laugh as from his training he knew that he was to be first out to release the life rafts from the aircraft. Then the ball-turret gunner, also a crew replacement for this mission, came over and asked him where they kept the spare bulbs, they were wanted for his gun sight which had just failed. Sgt Rhoda from Kansas City told him to follow him and led him to the entry door in the fuselage, and promptly threw him into the water and told him in no mean terms to swim as they were sinking. Rhoda had completed twenty-five missions in the UK and was now on his second tour.

Only one raft was usable, the others had been shredded by flak. MacFarland had stripped off and was swimming ashore. Others were getting into the raft and paddling ashore. Merrle was standing on the wing and called for them to come back for him but they kept going. He then went back in the aircraft and tried to get the co-pilot out when the nose suddenly tilted down below the water. He then heard a scream from the co-pilot who was lying on the lower deck of the plane. Then there was silence. With the movement of the aircraft he dived into the water and swam towards the raft and hung to on the side. In their training they were told that it was possible that the aircraft would stay afloat for about 45 to 90 seconds. In fact it stayed afloat for about 5 minutes because all the equipment had been discarded and the petrol tanks were empty.

They were only 700 to 800 ft from the shore. A British radar unit and a local fisherman came out to help them reach the shore. As Merrle was barefoot the tail gunner Billy Clayton hoisted him on his back and carried him over the sharp pointed rocks to the shore and the radar station building. After one day here they were asked to celebrate a victory with the Partisans of Yugoslavia. A large fire was lit and with a few bottles of wine, and arm in arm, they proceeded to dance around the fire area while the American crew watched. At Vis there was a former Second Bomb Group B-17 bomber and it was in this that they flew back to base. In 1999 the ditched B-17 was found and Merrle sent details via the 'B-17 Combat Crewman and Wingmen Association' this described the found B-17 as having one wheel down, the bomb doors gone, waist guns missing and various other things that meant it had to be his aircraft. In 2001 he received a picture of the aircraft from a scuba diver, Danijel Frka of Croatia who had found the plane at 350 ft and about 800 ft from the shore. But since it was known that the co-pilot's body was still aboard it had been left as a war grave or living memorial by the Croatian Government. Danijel said the aircraft was still in very good condition. Merrle returned to the USA on an Italian luxury liner in 1945. A friend of Merrle also ditched in the water not far from Bari but when they tried to rescue him as he hung on to the barrel of his .50 machine gun he kicked out at them until the aircraft went under the water taking him with it still hanging on to the barrel of his gun.

Wally Hoffman flew B-17s in the UK and took part in the raid on Schweinfurt on 14 October 1943. This was the second raid on the ball bearing factories. On the previous raid in August 1943 sixty B-17s out of 315 despatched were lost. Some 42 per cent of Germany's ball bearings were produced at Schweinfurt. In 1998 Wally wrote his memories of this operation and this is an edited version of it focusing on the air gunners in his crew.

The B-17 was called 'Morning Delight' and his crew were very young, they ranged from 19 to 27 years old. The oldest was 27 year old John, known as 'Pappy' and he manned the top turret and came from Pittsburgh where, in 1942, he had been working as a lead man in a steel mill. In the ball turret was Bill who had, in 1942, worked for GM in Detroit. He would protect the underside of the bomber. Bob manned the left waist-gun and had been about to become a church Minister when called up, sadly he later died when his aircraft crashed in Wales on its way back to the USA. The right waist-gun was manned by Jim from West Texas, an excellent shot. The tail gunner, John, was from Kalispell, Montana and had been driving log trucks in 1942.

At the briefing when the black curtain was drawn back a groan went up and the comments were that this would be their last mission. The battle ahead would be fought 6 miles above the earth and with a temperature of minus 50 to 60 degrees below zero.

Many boxes of ammunition for .50 calibre machine-guns were loaded and would be needed. This was their fourth mission and they had already learned to place a condom over the mike in the oxygen mask to keep it dry.

Not long after they crossed the Channel and were into Europe the attacks by fighters began. There were Me109s and Fw190s everywhere with aircraft blowing up and spinning down in flames and smoke. The thirteen machine guns on board soon opened up. Somehow they got through without being hit and were over Central Germany. The tail gunner was reloading his belts, the ball-turret gunner had a side window hit and could only see straight ahead. The top-turret gunner had a 20mm ammunition box come through the turret knocking out one of the guns and the ammo boxes on each side. He was injured on the leg and the crew tore off his flight suit at the thigh but, although he had a slight red mark on his leg, he was not seriously injured.

All the glass in the cockpit gauges were broken but they were still working. The pilot's windscreen was cracked and the co-pilot's flak helmet was knocked off and, although he was not hurt, there was a huge hole in it. Normally, as aircraft left the target, the bomb doors would open and out would come the cardboard chaff boxes that carried the thin strips of tinfoil to confuse German radar but on this occasion one of the crew had used it for the call of nature and then dropped it on Germany with Lord Haw Haw broadcasting that Wally's bomb group had started 'Biological Warfare'. Twelve hours after taking off there below base, Polebrook.

Below ambulances and fire trucks awaited the returning bombers. As they hit the runway there was a terrific bang, the tail wheel had blown. Later they were told that owing to the fighter attack the total frame just forward of the horizontal stabilizer had been totally torn apart by the fighter's 20mm shells. All that held them together was skin and control cables. This was the last mission of 'Morning Delight', she was scrapped for spare parts. One pilot said in the post-mission briefing, "I had accepted the fact that I was not going to live through this mission. It was for certain that it was only a matter of seconds or minutes. It was impossible for us to survive..."(This for Wally summed it up for everyone). Bob the waist gunner was stumbling along and was crying, obviously thinking of those that had not returned. They had fought to the death five miles up in the air and as one tail gunner said as they left the coast of Europe and the fighters began to disappear. "I bent forward, rested my head on the window and began to cry uncontrollably. I stopped long enough to say, 'Thank You God'. I cannot to this day know from where came the voice 'Trust Me', but in my heart I knew I had not been alone in the tail".

The bomber force was protected over the English Channel by Spitfires and then 50 Thunderbolts as far as their fuel capacity allowed. In all, the force had been attacked by no less than fifty fighters. For the next three hours to the target they were under constant attack and out of the 315 despatched only 229 reached the target. One Group, No. 305 lost thirteen out of fifteen despatched. Although the bomber gunners claimed 138 fighters shot down the Germans recorded only thirty-eight having been lost.

Of the B-17s despatched fifty-nine were shot down over Germany, one ditched in the English Channel and twelve were scrapped or crash landed. On top of this 122 bombers were damaged. Of the 2,900 crewman despatched, 650 did not return of which some were recorded as PoWs. Of those that did return five men came back dead and forty-three wounded and a further 594 were missing presumed killed and would not have a grave.

The citizens of Schweinfurt have erected a monument to this battle five miles up which states:

In memory of citizens of Schweinfurt and airmen of the 8th U.S. Airforce and the German Luftwaffe *who lost their lives in mission 115, October 14, 1943, known to those who were there as Black Thursday.*

The Memorial to the 8th US Air Force at the RAF Museum, Hendon. *Alan Cooper*

CHAPTER SIXTEEN

Lack of Morale Fibre

Lack of Morale Fibre was not only focused on air gunners in WWII, but all aircrew. Firstly it has to be remembered that all aircrew in WWII were volunteers, a man could be called up for service in the RAF but could not be made to fly. What does Lack of Morale Fibre mean? Its meaning in the RAF in WWII was: 'to lose or forfeit the confidence of your commanding officer'. In WWI this would have been known as 'cowardice in the face of the enemy'.

The subject of losing the confidence of your commanding officer first came up at the Air Ministry in March 1940. The cases varied and instructions for dealing with such cases were for general guidance and not intended to fetter the discretion of commanders. The instructions were not intended to apply either to flagrant cases of cowardice that demanded disciplinary action by Court Martial, or to cases where flying personnel were exhibiting symptoms of strain as the result of the conscientious discharge of their duties and no question arose of a lack of courage or determination. There were two cases concerning LMF:

(a) The case of a man who was maintaining a show of carrying out his duties, but, nevertheless, lost the confidence of his Commanding Officer.

(b) The case of a man who had not only lost the confidence of his Commanding Officer in his courage and resolution but made no secret of his condition and that he did not intend to carry out dangerous duties.

It was thought that such cases could be medical and could be handled as such with encouragement and tact. But if there were no such signs and it was just a lack of morale fibre the offenders should be dealt with and quickly disposed of. However, if the Commanding Officer had satisfied himself that a case is not one which can be cured by encouragement or one that can be suitably dealt with either by disciplinary action or as a medical case, he should at once send to the Air Ministry a report initialled by the

officer or airman concerned stating the facts and making one or other of
the following alternative recommendations.

(i)   The services of the individual shall be dispensed with; normally
      those in category (b) above.
(ii) That a note of the report be made in the individual's records and
      that he should be considered for advancement until the confidence
      of his Commanding Officer in his courage and determination had
      been restored.

On 18 July 1940 it was recorded that officers holding permanent
commissions should not waver (LMF) if they were to keep their
commission. After two months on a non-operational unit and if they were
not prepared to go back to operations they would be asked to retire.

On 26 April 1941 airmen graded 'waverers' should be remustered as
AC2s. In September 1941, a memorandum was set up for the disposal of
members of air crews who forfeit the confidence of their commanding
officers. Genuine cases should still be dealt with under an earlier Air
Ministry letter of 4 March 1941, as before in 1940.

There were three categories.

(i)   Those medically unfit and losing the confidence without having
       been subjected to any exceptional flying stress. These men would
       not be given an opportunity to rehabilitate or given non-operational
       air crew employment.
(ii)   Those who are given a permanent medical category solely on
       nervous symptoms and without having been subjected to any
       exceptional flying stress. For airmen it was the same in category (i)
       for officers, they would be invalided from the service and relinquish
       their commission.
(iii) Those not included in (ii) who were given a medical category A1B
       or A3B would follow the normal invaliding or retention for
       employment within the medical category procedure, as may be
       considered suitable in the individual case.

A lot rested on the Commanding Officer and the Medical Officer on a unit.
The action taken was as follows:

The case of moral fibre was to be submitted by Group HQ to the Air
Ministry without delay. The AOC Commanding concerned would make
a personal recommendation in forwarding the case to the Air Ministry.
The full details of the individual was furnished to the AOC by the
Commanding Officer, flights made, their number, duration date of the
last flight and if he had suffered any particularly bad experience on such
flights. The medical officers report was also submitted to the AOC. The
report must be seen by the individual concerned, and the documents

submitted to the Air Ministry must bear his initials and he was entitled to submit a statement which was to be forwarded with the other documents.

If an individual was found to be in either category (i) and (ii) above and was disposed of, permission to wear the appropriate air crew badge was withdrawn under Air Ministry Order A.896/40.

In the case of an airmen remustering the reason was not to be shown in his documents or in Personnel Occurrence Reports but for the guidance of those concerned with the airmen's future movements in the service; his Form 1580 would be marked in the top right hand corner with a large red 'W'. In no circumstances was any reference to LMF to appear on any documents issued to the airmen on discharge from the service.

The disposing of LMF aircrew members was at the Aircrew Disposal Unit. At first this was located at RAF Uxbridge but, because it was a major centre, with the initial selection and training of airmen as its main focus, it proved to be unsatisfactory and was moved to Eastchurch, again this proved unsatisfactory and it moved to Chessington and then Keresley Grange, near Coventry.

One Bomber Command Station Commander was asked if a man was away from a unit and suspected of 'lack of moral fibre' and then found to be fit and completely recovered by the medical authorities would he take him back on his station? His reply was "No!" There were airmen who witnessed the 'ceremony' of a man being stripped as a result of LMF. In October 1943 at RAF Syerston the aircrew of Nos 61 and 106 Squadrons formed a hollow square for the Station Commander, Gp Capt H A Evans DFC, to read out the sentence of the Court Martial on two NCO aircrew who had disappeared to Nottingham when detailed for operations. The Station Warrant Officer ripped off the men's brevets and stripes.

Frank Clarke flew as an air gunner in the Middle East and during a rest period between tours he was stationed at a Bomber Command base, and a F/Sgt pilot who had flown thirty operations and was on his second tour reached breaking point and refused to fly on operations again. At a Court Martial he was found guilty and he also had his rank and aircrew brevet torn from his tunic in front of the squadron and was reduced to the lowest rank in the RAF and given the most menial tasks possible, his previous operational service counted for nothing.

The signs to the ground crew of 'lack of morale fibre' were known as Operational Twitch. This indicated to them that the poor lad was reaching the limit of physical and mental endurance. It showed in a number of ways, uncontrollable flickering of the eyelids, a little tremble of the lips, the hand shaking as they took their cups of tea at dispersal. Trying to do things too quickly causing them to fumble and drop things such as when they pulled money out of their pockets to pay for their tea. The exaggerated good humour that was so pathetically false. The drunken boisterous antics they indulged in as an escape from reality and to numb the mind. Dr David

Stafford-Clark, a station doctor during the war, thought the LMF label was grossly unfair. They had, in some cases, volunteered for something they could not meet in the way of its demands. This was particularly true for men who had completed ten or even twenty operations and in some cases more; a coward wouldn't have done more than one. He had learned that the signs were sleep disorders, changes in personality and short temper. They came in and asked for sleeping pills. He originally saw them as young eager recruits and then later as unspeakably tired veterans. They lived with it and also died with it. An estimated 5 per cent of the 125,000 aircrew who served in Bomber Command in WWII were believed to have been affected mentally, 6,250 men. It was thought that air gunners made up the majority of the cases, and pilots second.

Broken down the figures show 8,402 cases of neurosis and 1,029 of LMF. One third of the neurosis cases were from Bomber Command as was a third of LMF (343 cases). Over 30 per cent of the LMF cases were disposed of without social consultation. Of the 4,059 cases submitted 2,337 were airmen and 389 officers.

One Flt Lt was sent out to help a Cpl Radar Mechanic and the officer told him that the officer's records said he was LMF, which meant he was too scared to get into an aeroplane again. The Flt Lt recounted how he had been flying with a pilot, who was also a close friend, in a Beaufighter which had armoured steel doors that separated the pilot from the Radio/Observer (the Flt Lt), the idea was to protect the pilot from an attack from the rear. On one night they picked up a returning bomber heading for France. They homed in on it but as they were about to attack the bomber's rear gunner spotted them and opened fire. From the cries it was obvious the pilot had been hit, and the Flt Lt called on him to open the door so he could get into the cockpit and help him. But the pilot said he was fine and would fly over land before he would bale out as he did not want to fall into the sea. At 1,000 ft and over the South Coast he told the Flt Lt to bale out, which he did and saw the aircraft pull away, it then went into a vertical dive and with the engines flat out hit the sea a mile or so off the coast. He had saved his observers life but given his own and this traumatized him so much that he refused to step into a plane again.

One airman, who is now 80 years old, enlisted in the RAF as a WOP/AG but was unable to fly because he needed a nasal operation which he had at his own expense. He volunteered again and was accepted, but when he was posted on a radio course but because of Morse stress he was unable to complete this. The officer in charge marked him down as LMF. But when he went into front of reselection board he passed and was sent on an air gunners course to Stormy Down in South Wales. He later served with No. 4 Group and then No. 38 Group at Tarant Rushton, at Earls Colne, on Glider tugging and dropping supplies to the resistance in France, Belgium, Holland and Norway. On one of his last missions to Strasburg, because of an engine catching fire, the mission was aborted and the pilot landed his aircraft on a road near the village of Phalepin. They were looked after by the villagers and then taken to Lisle hospital, France, which by this time was in Allied hands. Most of the crew had burns, some worse than others. He feels that the LMF markings may still be on his records today.

One Sergeant found guilty of LMF lost his badge but retained the rank of Sergeant and was posted to become an Airfield Controller. But another Sergeant was reduced to the rank of AC1, he had lost a leg in a training accident which was no fault of his own.

One air gunner reported to No. 103 Squadron in 1942 and stated he was unfit to fly. The medical officer said he was fit to fly but when detailed to fly on an air firing practice by the squadron gunnery officer he refused to fly saying he was too frightened. He was then given every opportunity to change his mind by his Commanding Officer but when he still said he was too frightened he was advised he had lost the confidence of his CO. He had joined the RAF in 1940 but after his gunnery training he applied for a commission to become a Link Training Instructor but was then posted to 103 Squadron; his AG brevet was removed. The CO said he had been drawing aircrew pay without earning it since enlistment and he was a coward and requested that he be removed from his squadron immediately. He also recommended that he be reduced to the ranks. The air gunner then made a statement in which he said that owing to a complete lack of confidence he asked to be relieved of aircrew duties and revert to ground duties. He ended his statement by saying I would rather be doing ground duties with complete confidence than flying in mortal fear.

The man that all cases of LMF were submitted to was Wg Cdr Jimmy Lawson. In 1945 after the war was over he recorded his impressions of the general working of the LMF system He pointed out that men who were LMF cases were trained in ground jobs and transferred to the Navy or Army and later to the mines. Some were given commissions in the army. He said he never agreed with the term Lack of Moral fibre, it was much too general and conveyed too much of complete cowardice. It was meant to convey a lack of that particular kind of moral fibre required for the strain of flying duties. A man may be prepared to exercise the control required to face up to hazards at sea or on the land, but not flying. He had, in June 1943, tried to get the term LMF eliminated but this was strongly opposed by Bomber Command. He also said that the main fear was not the combat side of flying but flying itself. There were others who were not frightened of flying but were frightened by the enemy opposition, and lastly there were those that were frightened of both.

One bomber aimer was reduced to AC and taken off the station with LMF in red on his records, this was later changed to 'W' for Waverer. Edward Shrimpton was flying as an air gunner with F/Sgt Norrie, a New Zealander, on No. 31 SAAF Squadron, at Foggia, Italy. In October 1944, they were detailed for an operation to Budapest. On testing his guns over the Adriatic the rear gunner Sgt Chas Shearsby found his turret was US. As Edward was a trained armourer he was asked to go and check the problem and Edward found the guns would not fire either manual or electrically. They then saw a German spotter plane in the area which meant fighters were around, their target was a solo effort and between them and their target was a German fighter station at Szekesfervar which had about 200 fighters so they returned. However, this was much to the displeasure of the CO of No. 31, so he ordered both Edward and Chas to go to dispersal and meet the Gunnery Leader. The guns were tested on the ground and found to be working satisfactorily. But Edward then asked the Gunnery Leader to make a flight up to 1,200 ft for a gun test, the height at which they had experienced the problem. At this height the Gunnery Leader tried the guns and found the turret to be US, the armourer on the ground had put ordinary oil in the solenoids instead of anti-freeze oil which caused the guns to freeze up. On landing they were told to go to bed but were again awoke to report to the CO a Lt Col Du Nel. He told them that they had again been detailed to go to Budapest and that the pilot F/Sgt Norrie had refused to fly as the gunners were unfit because of a lack of sleep. All the crew had now been seen and would not fly without their own pilot. They were all placed under open arrest to await charging. The charge was Mutiny, LMF, and Conduct Prejudicial and placed under close arrest. Statements were taken by the same officer who had turned out to the witness for the Prosecutor at their trial, the court martial lasted 3 days. They were found not guilty of the charge of Mutiny, and LMF but guilty of the third charge. They were reduced to the ranks from Sgt and put in prison. After six months they were released and dispersed. Edward was posted to Naples as an armourer and it was there that he found out that F/Sgt Norrie had been reinstated as a F/Sgt and sent back to New Zealand. The base padre was contacted and he organised a petition on his behalf Sqn Ldr Jestice, the senior Group Padre, was familiar with their case. The petition went as far as General Alexander but after nine months he heard nothing and was posted to Greece. It would appear that they were not liked on 31 Squadron, and that Sgt Straker the W/Operator, being a black man, immediately upset the SAAF Warrant Officer. They had also seen this Warrant Officer clearing the belongings of a crew who had failed to return, photographs were thrown on the floor and trodden in without any care and so they reported it to Padre Jestice and from there on things got worse. Today Edward, after a 30 year unblemished record in the police force, and now in his 80s is trying to get the record changed, if the charge against the pilot was changed and he reinstated then this should apply to all the crew whose only crime was to support their pilot's judgement. The charge was not one for LMF yet the sentence was!

Sgt Skin was a pilot who had severe headaches which affected his flying. He also had stomach problems and lost interest in all social and private affairs. When he reported sick thinking he would be cured in a week or so he found himself in hospital for 6 weeks and grounded from flying. His problem was found in his frontal sinus, which from flying had turned into sinusitis and was so bad that they proposed to drill a hole into his nose. But for some reason he was posted to an army hospital which contained all men with nervous disabilities, he was given an army uniform but allowed to keep his stripes. They were all ex-aircrew and had formed a club called The Dodo Club. His sinusitis improved and surgery was not needed.

He had flown Blenheims, Wellingtons, and Mosquitos and on one operation returned with the blood of his second pilot splashed over him. He also said he was the only one when they got hit to come back untouched. At the RAF Central Medicine Board in London he was asked, "If you were sent on another operational trip tomorrow would you do it?" He replied, "Yes, I will go and do whatever I am required to do". The outcome was that, for some reason, he was classed LMF, had his wings and stripes taken away and given no opportunity to fly again. He had flown twenty operations but he had seen one chap who had flown sixty and been awarded the DFM, and two air gunners with the Order of Lenin be classed LMF.

Another air gunner, Cecil Skin, was wounded on his thirty-fifth operation was deprived of his brevet and tapes because he was unfit to fly. He was, despite being branded LMF, allowed to be posted to a flying station. Cecil was then posted to the army and became a signaller in the Royal Signals. Within 8 weeks he was offered a commission but because of his RAF experience turned it down. The army allowed him to wear his pilot's wings on the basis he had earned them. He had a sister in the ATS, a sister in the WRENS, another in the Land Army and later WRENS and his mother a nursing sister; even his brother who was only 13 was in the Home Guard (although only 13 he was issued with a rifle and twelve live rounds).

Today, 60 years on, we should look at these cases with more sympathy. In WWI men were shot for cowardice but many years later in the majority of cases found to be ill not cowards. In WWII these men, in the great majority of cases, had given everything they had but just could not do any more: their body would not let them go any further. Today I hope and feel these cases would have been dealt with in a completely different way and with much more understanding and compassion. In today's wars and conflicts men are given counselling which those men over 60 years ago were not afforded.

CHAPTER SEVENTEEN

The Air Gunners' Association

The Air Gunners Association was formed in March 1949, and was one of the first, if not the first, Associations to be formed after WWII. Its coming into being was after an advert was put in the RAFA Magazine *Air Mail* by an ex-Warrant Officer/air gunner Jack O'Hara who resided in London. This followed much hard work and pounding of leather soles in locating ex-aircrew and in particular air gunners. It was after having no luck at the Nuffield Centre that he placed his advert. In it he asked for any air gunners interested in forming an Association to meet at the public house The Pillar of Hercules in Soho.

It all came about after Gordon (Howie) Wing dropped into the Ship pub in Richmond for a drink. As he went up to the bar wearing his RAF tie he noticed another with a similar tie and engaged him in conversation, it was Jack O'Hara from Wigan but now living in the London area. They soon discovered they had both been air gunners in the RAF, as they talked the idea of an association of air gunners came to the fore. Jack said he knew another air gunner living in Surbiton called Freddie Sutton and that he would be willing to help set up the Association. The first meeting of the AGA was held in Freddie Sutton's flat in Surbiton. To add to the coincidences, Gordon's girlfriend, Mary, was a former WAAF balloon operator and her parents were the licensees of the Pillar of Hercules pub in Soho. And so this became the meeting place for the London Branch. Gordon later married Mary. Soon came thoughts of a badge or in today's terms a logo and it was Gordon's brother who designed the Winged Bullet badge that has been their insignia for all those years. Gordon still has his No. 3 membership card; Jack had No. 1 and Freddie Sutton No. 2.

The response to the advert was good with 100 ex-air gunners and Wireless-Operator/Air gunners responding. A meeting was arranged and G.W. (Howie) Wing was elected Chairman, Freddie Sutton Honorary General Secretary, G. Peake Treasurer and Jack O'Hara and E. D. Brooks as committee members, they were later joined by Bill Dart. The first official meeting of London No. 1 Branch was arranged at the Pillars of Hercules public house in Greek Street, Soho, and it was agreed that this would continue on the last Friday of each month. The Association is exclusive and restricted to airmen trained and qualified as Air Gunners in the three armed services of the Crown. Training for air gunners stopped in 1955.

They met in Soho until Freddie Sutton managed to arrange for them to meet in Kensington Road and the home of 601 Squadron AAF. The motto of the AGA was conceived by Jack O'Hara. In a Richmond, Surrey library he spent an afternoon pouring over Burkes Peerage and other such publications searching for something he thought fitted the bill of the AGA. He eventually came across *Vigilantia et Virtute* which is the motto of a branch of the Porter family. Translated it means Vigilance and Valour. And so in 1949 by the founding committee of the AGA adopted this as the official motto of the Air Gunners Association. Strangely enough having done the spade work Jack disappeared and signed on in the RAF once more and was not heard of again. Many dinners and dances were held at Kensington Park Road and which would have satisfied many air gunners because it had a good bar.

In May 1949 came the first news sheet entitled *The Turret*. In this first issue the objects of the Association were set down:

1. To foster good fellowship.
2. To encourage and promote social gatherings among members.
3. To facilitate service by members to one another.
4. To perpetuate and enjoy the comradeship born and bred in his Majesty's Air Forces in time of war.

By the end of 1949 the membership had increased to 500 and by June 1950 nine branches had been formed in other parts of the country from Bristol

Jack O'Hara founder member of the AGA. *Fred Stead*

in the South to Leeds in the North. In the same year the Association had its first President, Sir Basil E. Embry, KBE, CB, DSO, DFC, AFC, himself having a wonderful war record in the RAF. In 1953 the first Association dinner was held at the Union Jack Club, Waterloo, London and now the regular meeting place of the London Branch.

Each year in May the AGA at the official RAF Remembrance Day at Runnymede for airmen airwomen who have no known grave are present and later after laying wreaths in memory of air gunners lost in the war have a reception at the local British Legion where many a tale is told.

After five years Freddie Sutton handed over to Bill Dart as Hon. Secretary. Sid Cannon became the treasurer, and other stalwarts of the AGA came along: Les Jealous(later a long term treasurer), Pete Smith, Ian Hunter the present treasurer of the London Branch, and Pete Carey, the President of the Association up to 2003 when the AG Association disbanded. Norman Storey also joined at this time, his membership No. 185.

At the Coronation in 1953 Bill Dart and Hugh Clarke represented the AGA and the same year the dedication of the AGA Standard in Croydon with member Eddy Power (now in Australia) the standard bearer. There was a move to the Duke of York's HQ , and then the RAFA Club, Fulham. Bill purchased the seat he sat on at the Coronation but in a move some years later it went missing. The standard was purchased with the generous help of Ian Hunter's mother. It was dedicated at the Parish Church of St Martin, Croydon, on 28 June 1953. The lessons at the service were read by the CO of RAF Kenley and the Mayor of Croydon.

As time went by the Association, through a number of reasons went into the doldrums but somehow kept going. The Nottingham Branch kept it going for about ten years from 1961 to 1971 and the Secretary of the Nottingham Branch Bill Bailey wrote to every member of the Association to announce an 18th Reunion Dinner to be held in Oxford. The outcome was a good one and many members attended the reunion. It also enabled many old members to rekindle their membership. At this dinner Bill Bailey informed Norman Storey that a member, Ted Shaw, wanted to start a London Branch. Ted contacted a few members in the London area and about ten members turned up for a meeting at the Savoy Tavern off the Strand. The outcome was that Ted became the Secretary of the London Branch and Norman the Chairman. After about 6 months Ted had to retire and Freddie Gill, a policeman, contacted Norman and said he wanted to take over as Secretary. In 1974, Norman became the National Chairman and Freddie the National Secretary.

In 1974/75 the membership grew from 278 to 509 members, nearly five new members per week. In 1979 the membership rose to 1,261 and in 1984, when, sadly, Freddie Gill died, this had risen to 1,600. Ron Powers took over as National Secretary and was there until the Association curtain finally came down in March 2003. In October 1982 Norman Storey resigned as Chairman and became Vice President. The President from 1972 to his

On the left W/C Joe Skinner DFC * President AGA. *Alan Cooper*

death in 1996 was Wing Commander Joe Skinner DFC and bar, he was 24 years at the helm and now greatly missed. Joe was born at the Kennington Oval in 1909. He joined the RAF in April 1940 and served with a number of squadrons. He then converted to WOP/AG and joined No. 9 Squadron and went on to complete two tours of operations, the second as Signals Leader. In 1942 he was awarded the DFC and 1943 a bar. In June 1944 he was promoted to Wing Commander.

On one occasion on 24 October 1942, Joe was on an operation to Milan and flying with the commanding officer Wing Commander Southwell. Having dropped their bomb load Joe decided to open up with all turrets and put about 7,000 rounds into two trains travelling on the Milan line. He then carried on and shot up the town of Navaro from very low level with what Joe described as 'Very interesting results'. The next day the Italian press went to print with huge headlines 'These English Gangsters'. He joined the AGA in October 1949.

In 1977, out of the Dorset Branch of the AGA, which had been formed in 1975, came the founding of the Air Crew Association. The first Chairman was John Williams, the Secretary Roland Hammersley DFM and the Treasurer John Nunn, One strange invitation came to the London Branch of the Air Crew Association in 1982 from the German ex-anti-aircraft

Arthur Newman on the left and Al Huberman on the right. *Alan Cooper*

Arthur Newman in 1987 wearing his RAFES Badge. *Alan Cooper*

gunners who had defended one of the notorious areas of the Ruhr Ladbergen around the Dortmund Emms Canal during January 1945. This included a reception in Ladbergen to meet the Mayor and council and a visit to the *Luftwaffe* Museum at Hamburg. The interesting thing was the former gun crew in Germany who contacted the ACA in the UK were 15 and 16 years old in 1945. At the time it met with great amusement but since then such reunions are common place

On its 40th Anniversary in 1989 the Association had 1,700 members in the UK and overseas with twenty-four branches. Also in 1989 the original but small air gunners' memorial room was opened at the Yorkshire Air Museum and Allied Air Forces Memorial at Elvington, York.

In 1996 Norman Storey was elected President and was its last President. During Norman's presidency there were 25 branches and 1,800 members. The London Branch had a number of venues in its 54 years: The Talbot, off the Strand, and another pub in Leicester Square and then The Duke of York's HQ in Chelsea, From there to the Polish Air Force Club, Earls Court, and finally the London Branch's home was the Union Jack Club, Waterloo. The York branch was formed in 1976 after an advertisement ion the Yorkshire Evening Press.

In 1996 part of a building at Elvington was offered to the AGA, it was 40 ft long and 28 ft wide. Plans were drawn up but it was March 1997 before the room was complete. The work had being carried out by members of the York branch.

In July 1997 a new Air Gunners Memorial room as opened at Elvington by the President Norman Storey. The items on show are Flying Suits, Helmets, deactivated weapons, gun sights, uniforms, medals, log books and many personally donated items and photographs. The array of gun turrets is something to behold. They include the Armstrong Whitworth, Boulton Paul MkVIII Nash and Thompson FN5, 120, 121, and 150. It also has a data base of 33,000 names and details of former air gunners. Since those days the memorial room has expanded and it contains what is probably the largest, and possibly the only, collection of memorabilia and artefacts to do with air gunners in any museum. Among the medals on display are those of Jack O'Hara, his widow donated them to be displayed in the Memorial room. Jack's service spanned from 1942 to 1969 when he retired as Station Warrant Officer at RAF Odiham. The memorial has also accumulated a large collection of archive material and individual stories concerning air gunners and this is all dedicated as a memorial to Air Gunners and the Air Gunner Association.

Each July they have an annual Air Gunners' Day when former air gunners come from all parts of the UK and the world for a service of commemoration and a social gathering; friends and other visitors are always welcome to take part.

In 1982 the members subscribed to a statuette modelled in bronze by Pam Taylor. This was handed over to the RAF Museum by Norman Storey;

it depicts an air gunner in typical flying kit. It is said to be on open display in the first floor gallery of the museum.

Also in 1982 to mark the 40th Anniversary of the ATC (1941) a trophy in the form of a Wellington bomber was presented by Joe Skinner, the Chairman, to the Air Officer Commanding Air Cadets at RAF Leeming. It was paid for by the AGA and known as the Air Gunners Association Trophy and is competed for annually by ATC Squadrons throughout the UK.

There is also a Freddie Gill trophy, which is shot for each year at Bisley.

On 29 March 2003, in Nottingham came the last official AGM of the Air Gunners Association although many branches throughout the UK will continue to meet. The former branch in London became Air Gunners' Association London. They met on the second Thursday in the month at the Union Jack Club, Waterloo. Sadly, in 2007 they also decided to call it a day but still meet on an informal basis at the Club.

On Lancaster PA 474 of the Battle of Britain Memorial flight is an Air Gunners Association badge bolted to the Fraser Nash gun turret as a permanent memorial to all air gunners who defended their aircraft against incredible odds. The remarks made on the recommendation for the Distinguished Flying Cross for an Air Gunner by a Station Commander sums up an air gunner perfectly. 'An air gunner enables his crew to operate with the full knowledge that they are well defended from fighter attack. This is the greatest contribution a gunner can make in the success of bombing operations'.

A GUNNER'S VOW

I wish to be a pilot
And you along with me,
But if we all were pilots ,
Where would the Air Force be?
It takes guts to be a gunner;
To sit out in the tail
When the Messerschmitts are coming,
And the slugs begin to wail,
The pilot's just a chauffeur,
It's his job to fly the plane;
But it's we who do the fighting
Though we may not get the fame.
If we all must be gunners,
Then let us make this bet
We'll be the best damned gunners,
Who have left this station yet.

Author Unknown.

AGA Annual Dinner at Eastbourne. The speaker is the Guest of Honour Gp/Capt Leonard Cheshire VC. *Alan Cooper*

AGA London Branch members. *Alan Cooper*

AGA March past on Remembrance Day 1987. *Alan Cooper*

The Queen Mother meets members of the AGA at the Field of Remembrance. *Alan Cooper*

Left: Jack Catford DFC. *Alan Cooper*

CHAPTER EIGHTEEN

Dronten / Vaassen

For some ten centuries the Netherlands had been fighting against the water but in the year 1000 the people began to resist. The first dykes were built and then windmills which made it possible to drain lanes and ponds. The windmills were replaced by steam, diesel and electric pumps and the dyke builders undertook larger projects and at the beginning of the century a dream of the Dutch became a reality: The damming off and partial reclamation of the Zuyder Zee began. A barrier dam was built in 1932 and four of the five planned polders were created. The polders were originally meant for agriculture but it also included recreation areas and areas of natural beauty.

In September 1917 Queen Wilhelmina spoke the following historic words at the opening of the session of the States General:

> I consider that the time has come to undertake the damming off and reclamation of the Zuyder Zee. Its results will be an improvement of the drainage of the surrounding provinces, expansion of the land area and permanent increase of employment.

Between 1920 and 1975 the Dutch population doubled with a great concentration of people in the west of the country. The Eastern and Southern Flevoland were called upon to provide a solution. Work on the dam began in 1920 with a dam construction of 1.5 miles long between the mainland of North Holland and the island of Wieringen. This was completed in 1924. In 1927 the construction of an artificial island and several lengths of dam had been linked together with only two gaps remaining. One was closed ahead of time in 1931. And in May 1932 the final gap, after a five-year struggle with the sea, was closed. This meant that the Zuyder Zee had now been achieved. On the site of this closure a plaque has been placed with an inscription: 'A living nation builds for its future'.

On 29 June 1957 the Eastern Flevoland fell dry. Work on the 60-mile long ring dyke had lasted 7 years. Provision was made for a district centre, Dronten, and a regional centre, Leystad. In addition to these two the plan comprised no less than ten villages spaced five miles apart.

The municipality of Dronten, as well as other settlements, was established on 1 January 1972. It had 16,000 inhabitants by the end of 1975 and has a modern shopping centre and a market once a week. In 1980 the inhabitants had reached 20,000, and in 2000, 32,000. It is about an hour's drive from Amsterdam.

During the Second World War large numbers of aircraft fell into the then Ijsselmeer. Numerous wrecks were found during and after the land had been reclaimed. In the town of Dronten, in the De Rede Square an Airmen's Memorial was erected, this commemorated the many fallen Airforce men.

The Bomber Command offensive mounted by the Royal Air Force during the Second World War has been described as the most gruelling operation of the war ever carried out. It lasted 2,000 days and nights over four long years and served as the only effective means of waging war against Hitler's European fortress. For the British and the occupied peoples alike, the bombers droning across the night skies in ever growing numbers were a symbol of Britain's will as well as its might. While the world waited for the tide to turn, while the Germans stood at the gates of Moscow and at the doors of Egypt, Bomber Command wielded the only weapon capable of reaching the throat of the Third Reich.

On an operation to Dusseldorf on 11/12 June 1943, during the Battle of the Ruhr, Flight Sergeant Daniel Thomson from Victoria, Australia was the pilot of Lancaster ED 357 of No. 12 Squadron. It was his and his crew's third operation. They reached and bombed the target successfully and were on the return trip to base when one engine caught fire. Thomson, and the flight engineer Sgt James Osborne, managed to put the fire out and feather the prop. The main problem was maintaining height so it was decided by Danny Thomson to go down low and crawl home. As they came down all hell let loose when they were attacked by a German fighter. The Lancaster was raked from in front of the mid-upper turret to the front of the Lancaster. The last thing Bill Pingle, the mid-upper gunner from Canada, heard was Danny Thomson shouting, "Bale out". Bill climbed out of the turret and went to the back of the aircraft and opened the exit door by which time fire was coming all along the side of the aircraft. He could not see his fellow rear gunner Sgt 'Sparky' Sparling who also came from Canada. Bill then went to the rear gunner's door and opened it. Sparky was stuck so Bill pushed and pulled and out he came. Then Bill went back and put on his parachute, they shook hands but before they were able to bale out somebody came from the front and jumped out. Afterwards they decided that whoever it was did not have a parachute on. They then jumped out. As Bill floated down he saw what he thought was sand but when he landed he found himself in water over his head and with his parachute wrapped around his legs. He inflated his Mae West and came to the surface but could not get out of his parachute. He had dropped down near a tug towing barge whose crew pulled him aboard. He was taken to a cabin and given a shot of Schnapps. No one on board spoke any English but somehow they managed to communicate. He told them that there were more of his crew in the water. The next day the tug, now free of its barges, made a wide sweep of the area and after an hour they came across Sparky who was being dive bombed by seagulls. As they pulled him aboard he said he was just about to give up. His main problem was not being able to keep the air in his Mae West. They were both taken to Amsterdam and turned over to the Germans and were prisoners for 23 months. The older man on the tug wanted to hand them over to the Resistance movement in Holland but the younger members of the crew were scared and insisted they were handed to the Germans.

Sadly, Sgt Danny Thomson, aged 26 was drowned and is now buried in Amsterdam as was Sgt Osborne, aged 20, and from Daventry, Northampton, and Sgt William Ward, aged 21, from Edinburgh, the bomb aimer. They were all washed up on 21 June. The body of Sgt Douglas Campbell, the wireless/ operator, aged 21, from Glasgow was washed up four days before on 17 June and is also buried in Amsterdam. Sgt Kenneth Bowes, aged 23, from Darlington, was never found and his name is on the Runneymede Memorial for airmen who have no known grave.

It turned out that they were one of twenty-three aircraft shot down in the Netherlands that night, and ED 357 was shot down by Ofw Schorfling of the IV/NJG1 operating from Leeuwarden airbase at about 0203 hours.

It was the Netherlands Air Force under recovery officer Gerry Zwanenburg who located ED 357 on farmland between Dronten and Lelystad. The people of Dronten decided to erect a monument dedicated to the Allied airmen killed during the war and found in that area. In the 1960s one of the propellers from ED 357 was made available and 4 May 1965 it was unveiled in Dronten by Air Commodore J.L.Bosch of the Netherlands Air Force. The propeller is now situated in front of the Town Hall in Dronten.

In 1975 ex-Air Gunner Mick Smith happened to read about the Dronton memorial in a book and after some communication with Dronton he was invited by the Burgermaster of Dronten to visit Dronten in 1975. He paid a second visit in 1976. After this visit he was invited to organise a party of ex-air gunners and their wives to attend the service in 1977. A party of about fifty was suggested and so the annual pilgrimage began on 4 May 1977 and still continues today, although because of age numbers are becoming smaller. The air gunners were accommodated by three villages: Dronten, Swifte Bouk, and Biwdinghoizen, and was such a success that the number increased to 150. A search, initiated by J L Kuiper, was started to find any survivors from the ED 357. Sparky Sparling died in Canada in 1973 but Bill Pingle was still alive and also in Canada. It was Bill's son John who noticed the picture of the propeller in a book on the Lancaster. John contacted the Dutch consulate and a retired reserve Brigadier-General Reg Lewis, Canadian co-ordinator of the Amsterdam Salutes Canada Committee. This went down the line to a Dutch TV correspondent who contacted Bill and the Dronten Burgomaster Eppo P van Veldhuizen was soon on the phone to Bill and sent him aeroplane tickets for his wife and him to come to Dronten. He visited Dronton in 1980 and received a royal welcome. He was also surprised to find eight streets were named after him and his crew: Lancasterdreef, Thomsonstraat, Osbornehof, Campbellhof, Wardhof, Sparlinhof, Boweshof, and Pinglesstraat. During his visit he and his wife were accorded tickets to the Coronation of Princess Beatrix when she succeeded her mother Queen Juliana. In the passing of time Bill has now gone up into the big airfield in the sky but his name will remain for ever in Dronten.

Inside the Town Hall at Dronten there is a special room for the Air Gunners, apply named the Air Gunners Room. It contains photographs and paintings and all kinds of memorabilia appertaining to Aircrew, but especially to the Air Gunners of the Air War of 1940–1945. This was organised by Leo Van De Klis. The Air Gunners room was opened by the then Chairman of the Air Gunners Association Jim Carpenter and admission to this room is free.

In 1984, Prince Bernhard visited Dronten on 2 May at the same time that the Air Gunners were visiting the town and met the Chairman Jim Carpenter and Mick Smith also many other ex-air gunners.

During each visit one day is set for a ceremonial occasion with a visit to the church for a service and then a march to the memorial for wreath laying. All the wives in the party lay wooden crosses with the names of those known to have lost their lives over Holland. Then the children of Dronten lay flowers on the memorial. The parade is led by the Dronten pipe band. A number of Dutch people who helped Allied airmen evade capture are often present. One Dutchman had been tortured and left with crippled hands, another had no less than eighteen times visited Spain and taken thirteen airmen with him.

Harry Bowes originated from Billingham, County Durham and was trained in Canada early in the war. He married a girl Joyce from Darlington in June 1943 and two days after he returned from his honeymoon he was posted missing. His parents never got over his death and always believed he was alive somewhere and had lost his memory.

When Ernie Cummings the then Chairman of the Bomber Command Association visited Dronten in 1984. After he had returned he received a letter from an Eric Leyenauur:

I'm writing this in a free country, without fear thanks to you and your fellow airmen, and all the others, fighting for a free world. I'm only 31 years old, so I am an 'after the war kid', but I and most of the people of my generation do realise the great things you did for us. Thanks.
Dated 4 May 1984.

The Air Gunners have their own Anthem:

There, there they go-o, through the stars they plough,
Aerial gunners, by that name they're known!

Air gunners all, Fighting men so brave-,
Saving their comrades from the vengeful foe-o.
Where are they now? Who were once so young?
Gone to join their comrades, on the way to glory!
On their way to triumph, they so surely earned.
There, there they go-o, through the stars they plough,
Aerial gunners, by that name they're known!
Air gunners all, Fighting men so brave.
Saving their comrades from the vengeful foe-o.

Dedicated to Flt Sergeant Lillicrap

Sergeant Lillicrap was killed in Action 1944 and buried in the Reich Wald War Cemetery, Germany. He was an air gunner with 576 Squadron and died on 7 June 1944. He was 19 and came from Erith in Kent.

Harry Brown, who flew as an air gunner with Nos 50 and 233 Squadrons was moved to write a poem entitled Dronten.

DRONTEN

We did not weep-nor count the cost, As one by one, our friends
    were lost.
Nor did we when the war's great toll took all the best of our
    young men.
We did not weep as we saw them go down to the storm of the
    mighty foe,
we did not weep-not-once, not-then, nor in the years to come,
When on parade to do them honour,
came Kings and Queens and Chiefs of State in pomp and
    splendour
to relate how their cause was just,
and justified by the freedom bought as they fought and died.
We did not weep, not once, until, in a little Dutch town, in a
    silence,
the children came to honour our dead quietly from out of the
    crowd,
With just a few flowers their little heads bowed, in a line they
    came to lay them down
by the Lancaster prop, in Dronten Town,
And then, despite our will,
we felt our watching eyes o'erfill with tears
and yet we smiled.
How great the power of an innocent child.

In 2004 ninety former air gunners visited Dronten again and during their visit they were taken to the Royal Dutch Air Force base at Soesterberg for a helicopter flight. On landing they attended a passing out parade of helicopter air gunners. About fifty Dutch air gunners were presented with their wings. On 4 May there was a fly-past, firstly by a Mustang, followed by the local 'Edambusters' and then by two Tornados from No. 12 Squadron.

On 16 December 1942, came a message to No. 15 Squadron from Bomber Command Headquarters that an operation was on to Germany that night and they were required to supply three aircraft. One of the three Stirlings detailed was R 9168 T-Tommy piloted by P/O Frank Millen RCAF aged 21. Although in the RCAF he was in fact from the USA and was at the time he enlisted, still in University. This Frank's 12th operation since joining 15 Squadron. The target was a German aircraft depot at Diepholz.

The navigator was P/O Harvey Kieswetter, aged 24, also an American in the RCAF, who came from Seattle. The wireless operator/air gunner was P/O Russell Homes a Canadian from a village in the Edmonton area of Canada and also aged 21. The flight engineer was in the RAF as were the majority, if not all, flight engineers. His name was Sgt George Hutton at 19 the youngest member of the crew. He was an important member of the crew because he helped the pilot make all the last minute checks and with the take-off, which, with a full bomb load was the most testing part of the flight. The bomb aimer, who would come into his own in the target area, was Sgt Robert McKillop RNZAF, aged 25. He came from Wellington in New Zealand and this was his 7th operation. His other role was, if necessary, to man the front guns. There were two gunners: P/O Ernest Hill, aged 20, and the mid-upper turret also in the RCAF and, the rear gunner was the oldest man in the crew, 26 year old Sgt Jim Perring from Liverpool. He was to get married in a week's time. He had the coldest and loneliest position in the aircraft; seeing no one after take-off and only keeping in touch with the pilot via the intercom. He had a vital role to cover the aircraft's back at all times. They were the last of the three to take off at 1730 hours. At 16,000 ft, and the air now thin, oxygen masks were put on.

After two hours they approached the target area of Diepholz. The attack was to be carried out at a height of 7,000 ft so they had to start descending. Soon the flak opened up and shells were exploding all around them. But the worst fear was searchlights. The bombs were dropped successfully then a course set for home. Suddenly, they were hit by anti-aircraft fire, but although damaged they were able to continue. Their main problem now was fighters; a damaged bomber limping back home was easy prey. An Me110 soon picked them up on its radar screen and they were recognised as a Stirling. Strikes were made on the Stirling's cockpit, fuel tanks and the wings. The aircraft was soon in flames and the only man to get out was Jim Perring the rear gunner. The aircraft then crashed taking the other members of its crew with it. It was ten minutes past eight. A guard was put on the wreckage which, by now, was not recognisable as an aircraft and a wooden cross had been placed on it scratched:

Here rest the remains of an
unknown English airman.

Jim Perring, despite being given some help by the locals was arrested by the Germans and ended up at *Stalag* 344, near Lamsdorf and did not return to the UK until 1945. He then married the girl he was to have married in 1942 and they had three children. Jim sadly died in 1969.

A memorial was placed near the site of the crash just after the war but in June 1992 a new memorial was placed at the site, its base having been cemented there by pupils from a local Primary School, Christelijke Basissschool in Vaassen. In May 1986 a teacher, Harry Bouwman, at the school saw two elderly gentleman approaching in the main street at Vaassen. This was John Hardeman and Charlie Holderness, both former air gunners who was looking for a public toilet and were en route to Dronten for the annual Memorial Service held in May each year. Harry invited them to use the school toilet and then asked them to talk to the children about their experiences as air gunners in WWII. Two years later they again returned to Vaassen, they were now celebrities and everyone wanted to meet them and shake their hands. They went to Vaassen in 1989 and 1991.

Sadly, 1991 was the last time for John Hardeman who emigrated to New Zealand later that year and died two years later in 1993.

In 1992 Peter Radford, another air gunner visited Vaassen, and plans were laid for a memorial to T-Tommy. He promised to return in 1993 and bring other air gunners with him. In June 1992 the memorial was erected in the woods near Gortel. On 3 May 1993 the promise was kept and a delegation of air gunners visited Vaassen and the school where many questions were asked by children. In May 1994 fifteen air gunners again visited Vaassen, and an air-gunner doll made by one of the parents was presented to them. It now resides in the club room of the Air Gunners Association Branch in Ipswich. In 1995 all the air gunners who were visiting Dronten also went to Vaassen, it was to celebrate the 50th year of peace. It had been the last wish of John Hardeman that all the air gunners would make a visit, his widow Joan and Charlie Holderness and his wife were there with 110 air gunners and ninety ladies. Norman Storey, the then Vice President and later President of the Air Gunners Association spoke a few words to the children for whom I am sure all the air gunners had the greatest admiration for their interest and great kindness. The Air gunners song set to the music of *My Bonny lies over the Ocean* was sung by the children.

The six men killed and buried at Epe General Cemetery Gelderland, The Netherlands, are:

P/O Frank Severne Millen RCAF age 21 from North Providence, Rhode Island, USA: Plot 2, Row 10, Grave 627.

P/O Hugh Ernest Hill RCAF age 20: Plot 2 Row 10 Grave 625

Sgt Grantley Charles George Hutton RAF age 19: Plot 2 Row 10 Grave 626

P/O Russell Neal Holmes RCAF age 21: Plot 2 Row 10 Collective Grave 616–618

P/O Emerson Harvey Kieswetter RCAF Age 24 From Seattle, Washington, USA: Plot Row 10 Collective Grave 616–618

Sgt Robert Hugh McKillop RCAF age 25 From Wanganui, Wellington, NZ: Plot 2 Row 10 Collective Grave 616–618

In 2004 the Vaassen trip was arranged by the Broken Wing Foundation. In 2005, 2006 and 2007 former air gunners again visited Dronten and Vaassen. This will continue, one feels, for many years, perhaps until the last air gunner is alive and despite the AGA having been disbanded.

In the future if you see an elderly man with an RAF tie with the symbol of an air gunner's brevet on it, look at him with the greatest respect as of all aircrew he had in many instances the hardest and loneliest job in the crew. Perhaps we shall never know how many crews returned because of the courage and diligence of their gunners but one thing is certain without them they stood a much greater chance of not returning.

In the last 25 years I have met and befriended many former air gunners and you soon realise that they are a breed of their own, next to ex-RAF prisoners of war I think they have the greatest bond to each other, and I, as a non-air gunner, have been very privileged not only to have known and been their friends but for them to have accepted me in such a way that in many instances over those 25 years I felt they accepted me as one of them. No one could ask for more.

Alan Cooper 2008.

Air Gunners' Association
STANDARD

The Standard of any Regiment, Corps or Squadron has historically been of immense importance.

It was a rallying point in battle, a symbol of past glories, memories of fallen comrades and hope for the future. It also displayed the Honours and Insignia of the group.

This Standard, the National Standard of the Royal Air Force Air Gunners Association, was dedicated at The Union Church, Mill Hill, North London on 6ᵗʰ April 2002. The majority of members of the Air Gunners Association flew during World War II and many fought and died in the skies above Holland in the battle for freedom.

The Standard was handed into the safe keeping of the Municipality of Dronten in perpetuity on 4ᵗʰ May 2002.

It is to be paraded each year on 4ᵗʰ May at the Monument and at an appropriate date at the Memorial in the woods at Gortel near Vaassen.

Signed: ....   Signed: ....

Mayor of Municipality of Dronten
Mr Anton Gresler

National President of
The Air Gunners Association
Mr Norman Storey

Signed: ....   Signed: ....

Air Gunners Pilgrimage Organiser
Mr Jan Rozendal

National Chairman of
The Air Gunners Association
Mr Fred Stead

4ᵗʰ May 2002

The National Standard. *Fred Stead*

Laying a floral tribute at Dronten. *AG Association*

Dronten Memorial. *Alan Cooper*

Lancaster propeller memorial at Dronten. *Alan Cooper*

Norman Storey the last President of the AGA. *Norman Storey*

Air Gunner Casualties

3 SEP 1939 TO 31 MAY 1946

FIGHTER COMMAND

Operations	Accidents	Ground	Sub Totals	Grand Total
RAF				
109	61	4	174	
New Zealand				
2	9	1	12	
Egypt				
1	--	--	1	
Allied				
5	5	--	10	
Canada				
5 (Missing)	6	--	11	
Australia				
2 (Missing)	--	--	2	
				210

BOMBER COMMAND

Operations	Accidents	Ground	Sub Totals	Grand Total
RAF				
7764	908	14	8686	
New Zealand				
199	18	--	217	
Egypt				
1	--	--	1	
Canada				
2539	413	9	2961	
Australia				
810	100	1	911	
South Africa				
3 & 1 Missing	--	--	4	

India				
2	--	--	2	
Allied				
282	54	--	336	
				13,118

COASTAL COMMAND

Operations	Accidents	Ground	Sub Totals	Grand Total
RAF				
334	77	3	414	
New Zealand				
6	6	--	12	
Australia				
39	4	1	44	
Allied				
47	7	--	54	
				524

SEAC

Operations	Accidents	Ground	Sub Totals	Grand Total
RAF				
148	19	2	169	
Canada				
25	6	3	34	
				203

MEDITERRANEAN

Operations	Accidents	Ground	Sub Totals	Grand Total
RAF				
672	109	9	790	
Canada				
70	2	1	73	
New Zealand				
21	1	--	22	

Australia				
52	5	1	58	
South Africa				
136	--	--	136	
Egypt				
1	--	--	1	
Allied				
39	5	3	47	
				1,104

OVERALL TOTAL 15,090

Index